PRAISE FOR *HOW WE WON THE WAR FOR LGBTQ EQUALITY*

"For decades, Kevin Naff has been a trusted leader at the forefront of LGBTQ equality who leads best-in-class journalism and coverage of LGBTQ people and issues. This book reflects his fierce commitment to excellence and integrity in shaping and reporting on LGBTQ issues. With his unique insights and perspectives, Naff has created a comprehensive and necessary record of the recent history and successes of the LGBTQ community."

—**Sarah Kate Ellis**, GLAAD President and CEO

"This book is a comprehensive window into how LGBTQ equality moved rapidly ahead from someone who has had a front row seat and access to all the players. Kevin writes in a personal way that is quickly engaging in a spirited, sometimes appropriately humorous, straightforward manner that touches on all the many aspects that were needed to create the progress that moved so quickly once the fire of equality was ignited. I was particularly pleased that Kevin included the biggest hurdle to LGBTQ equality, religion. True Christian teachings move equality forward for all. Unfortunately, often misguided and outdated religious teachings are at the core of harm for too many people. It is a roadblock that many shy away from discussing. A great resource for current and future generations."

— **Mitchell Gold**, co-founder, chairman emeritus, Mitchell Gold + Bob Williams Home Furnishings and equality activist who led the way on challenging religious bigotry

"Kevin Naff has had a birds-eye view of LGBTQ history. He offers us a sharp, incisive look at the powerful ways activism can change the world, as well as the ways that progress can quickly be rolled back. Read this book and take it as another reminder of how fragile equal rights are — and how victorious we can be when we wake from complacency and organize fiercely."

—**Michelangelo Signorile**, SiriusXM radio host and author of *It's Not Over: Getting Beyond Tolerance, Defeating Homophobia and Winning True Equality*

"The only way we're going to succeed in the future is by understanding our past. Kevin Naff was a bystander and a chronicler of our recent political history, *and How We Won the War for LGBTQ Equality* is a comprehensive and compelling read that is essential for anyone who wants to move forth with wisdom and insights that will make the path easier."

— **Howard Bragman**, founder of LaBrea Media and one of the nation's best-known PR experts

How We Won the War for LGBTQ Equality

How We Won the War for LGBTQ Equality

And How Our Enemies Could Take It All Away

Kevin Naff

20 Years of Collected Essays & New Insights
from the Editor of the *Washington Blade*

Published by Redwood Publishing, LLC
Orange County, CA
www.redwooddigitalpublishing.com

ISBN: 978-1-956470-80-2 (hardcover)
ISBN: 978-1-956470-81-9 (paperback)
ISBN: 978-1-956470-82-6 (e-book)

Library of Congress Control Number: 2023905280

First edition.

CONTENTS

For Mom & Dad
and Brian

INTRODUCTION

The exhilarating days of Obama-era LGBTQ activism have given way to a dangerous complacency that threatens all the unprecedented gains of the past 20 years.

Two decades represents a mere blip in the arc of a civil rights struggle, yet in that span, the LGBTQ community in the United States went from legally second-class status to enjoying near full protection of federal law along with widespread societal acceptance and even full marriage rights.

How did that happen? And could it all be erased? The easy answer to the second question is absolutely yes. The answer to the first is a bit more complex.

In this book, I will take a look back at the last 20 years of LGBTQ advocacy in the United States and how we went from a closeted gay Republican National Committee chair running President George W. Bush's reelection campaign on the backs of our relationships to an out gay military veteran credibly running for president. It's an incredible, unprecedented story of a hated and feared minority rising from the despair of AIDS to conquer our formidable enemies and winning equality under the law. It's also the tale of a determined enemy — the far right — using every legal and political scheme imaginable to keep us down, roll back our progress and relegate us to second-class status once again. Make no mistake: The forces that worked relentlessly for nearly 50 years to overturn Roe v. Wade are the same that have turned their sights on the Obergefell marriage ruling now that abortion rights are undone. At a time when the LGBTQ movement feels adrift amid scandal and lack of leadership, our enemies are working overtime to put us back in the closet.

But the key to fighting back lies in understanding and replicating our recent history: organizing, raising money, funding supportive candidates, filing the right lawsuits and putting pressure on an array of allies in government, media and pop culture to have our backs. It's my hope that this book serves as a history lesson for young people. They must know their own community's history because it's not taught in schools. The contributions of LGBTQ Americans are rendered invisible in U.S. curricula. And it's getting worse, as some states like Florida are now passing laws criminalizing the teaching of LGBTQ topics in schools. So if our youth don't take it upon themselves to read and learn about our struggles, they will never know what led to this precarious moment. It's a moment when one of our two national parties works to rewrite the fatal atrocities of Jan. 6 as "legitimate political discourse." And a moment when former President Donald Trump's three Supreme Court picks are poised to reorder American society in chilling ways, first by rolling back Roe v. Wade, and then by undoing the historic Obergefell marriage ruling.

This book is mostly about the LGBTQ movement of the past 20 years and its stunning success. It's also a little bit about me, a closeted suburban kid who suffered in silence until he couldn't any longer.

From the age of 10, I knew emphatically that I would be a newspaper journalist. The 1981 baseball strike had just ended and I was a pissed off 10-year-old Baltimore Orioles fan. I wrote a letter to the editor of the Washington Post urging Major League Baseball fans to boycott for two weeks in protest of these rich, entitled athletes striking during the season. To my surprise and delight, the Post published the letter and illustrated it with a cartoon image of me. I still remember opening the Post that morning, turning to the editorial section and seeing my ideas in print for the world to read and was hooked.

Thus began a long, winding, unpredictable career in newspapers and digital media: founding my middle school newsletter, editing my high school newspaper, reporting and editing for the Daily Collegian at Penn State, interning at CBS News in Washington, working as a financial journalist at Reuters in New York, helping to create the Baltimore Sun's website in 1996, joining an internet startup in 2000, moving to mobile data at Verizon Wireless and helping to create the first generation of apps, then returning to my first love of journalism at the Washington Blade.

Concurrent with discovering my love of journalism and carving out a career during the most tumultuous time in the industry's history thanks to the digital revolution, I was on another journey, grappling with my sexual orientation and struggling to come out. There are enough indulgent books detailing overwrought coming out stories during the 1980s and 1990s. Every gay man thinks their story is unique and worthy of a book. This is not such a book. Yes, coming out was hard in that time. I'm part of a unique generation of gay men old enough to have lived through the worst of the AIDS epidemic, but young enough to have avoided the deaths. I didn't know the pain of watching entire friend groups disappear to a mystery illness.

Not a week has gone by in my 20 years at the Blade that I didn't think of the generation of gay men before me who didn't live to see all of this progress. They inspire me. I do this work for them. They did not die in vain. Not just the men who died, but the lesbians who cared for them when no one else would. They are not forgotten; this book is intended as a celebration of their lives. There's a well-known expression on Capitol Hill that there isn't a successful Hill office or campaign that doesn't have an out LGBTQ person at the top. And it's true: from Hillary Clinton's gay campaign manager Robby Mook to Sen. Rick Santorum's gay communications director Robert Trayhnam, you'd be hard-pressed to find a Hill or campaign office not led by an out LGBTQ person. That's because AIDS taught us how to get shit done. When the government abandoned and ridiculed us, the community organized and the first dollars raised to fight the plague came from gay bars. When the government failed to act, our activists took to the streets, and fought to get drugs approved. The courage of that generation lives in me, and my 20 years at the Blade are a direct result of my wanting to give back to a movement that gave me so much. To speak bold, harsh truth to power in the name of all those whose voices were snuffed out by AIDS. I may fall short. I may not be worthy of that legacy. But I have tried each day for 20 years to be true to that generation — a generation that inspired me and so many others to fight on. When young people ask me what they should know about the LGBTQ movement, I tell them to learn about AIDS. That's really all you need to know.

AIDS terrified me, coming of age at a time when gays were demonized by politicians and religious leaders as sick, diseased, unnatural, doomed and "other." Raised Catholic, I heard the sermons and grim warnings and wanted nothing to do with being gay. At first. Gradually, I came to terms with the truth and began the slow process of coming out. There were no support groups in school, no out gay public officials and few openly gay or lesbian celebrities. It was a different time, unimaginable to today's youth. (That's a good thing.) Contrary to today's social media-soaked teens and young adults who want the world to know every mundane detail of their lives and expect full understanding and acceptance of every pronouncement, the process in the '90s was slower. Coming out wasn't a one-time Insta post celebrated by parents and friends. It was a prolonged process, starting with finding a sympathetic friend, moving on to broader friend groups, then a sibling, and finally the parents. I was nearly 30 when I reached that last stage and my parents couldn't have been more supportive. I am one of the lucky ones.

Still, all those lost years in the closet stung. I felt a powerful need to make up for the lost time in my personal life and the years lost during my circuitous career path that led me away from my true love of journalism. Landing at the Blade was a full-circle moment that began as a teenager in the '80s. I remember driving into D.C. with friends and parking in the Dupont Circle area. My high school friends were the alternative or punk rock crowd — lots of thrift store clothes and Flock of Seagulls haircuts. But no one was openly gay. We sat down for lunch at Zorba's Greek restaurant in Dupont and I made up an excuse to wander off. I found Lambda Rising, the iconic gay bookstore, and nervously opened the door. Just inside was a newspaper rack holding a towering pile of Washington Blade newspapers. I furtively grabbed one, shoved it into my backpack and fled back to the restaurant. When I got home, I locked my bedroom door and opened the Blade. It was a revelation — an entire world of news, personalities, businesses, bars, nightclubs, shops and personal ads awaited me. The front page byline of Lou Chibbaro Jr. had been there since the '70s and remains there today. I never could have imagined that decades later I'd be editing this important community institution and that I'd be Lou's boss. On my first day at the Blade, I waited nervously for Lou to arrive. It was a long wait, as Lou and many others there started late and worked late into the night. When he finally arrived, I tiptoed into his office and introduced myself as his new editor. He seemed nonplussed; there had been many editors before I arrived and everyone assumed I wouldn't last a month. They were wrong. Lou was a gentleman and a professional then and always. Years later, I was honored to induct him into the Society of Professional Journalists Hall of Fame.

I arrived at the Blade with four opinion articles already written. Themes of anger emerged in my work from that very first letter in the Washington Post. Larry Kramer famously said that anger is the best motivator for activism. That speaks to me. For sure, many of my opinion pieces in the Blade over two decades were motivated by anger — at hypocritical politicians, duplicitous "allies," bigoted religious leaders and closeted traitors. My list of targets is long.

So, why this book? Why now? As I reach 20 years editing the nation's oldest LGBTQ newspaper, the Washington Blade, it's clear the country has traveled at light speed, from George W. Bush's cruel and cynical attacks on marriage equality to the triumphant inauguration of Joe Biden and Kamala Harris. Twenty years in a civil rights struggle is a mere blip, yet the United States has achieved more in that time for LGBTQ equality than I ever imagined I'd live to see. Marriage was never something I envisioned for myself. It's true that sometimes you really do outlive your oppressors and live to see revolutionary change. During those two decades at the Blade, I have been privileged to have a front row seat to some of the most historic moments in the history of the LGBTQ movement. From watching President Obama sign the repeal of "Don't Ask, Don't Tell," to attending the first White House Pride receptions, to interviewing presidential candidates, to meeting a range of leaders, personal heroes and out celebrities (yes, I really did introduce Laverne Cox to Antonin Scalia) it's been quite a ride.

This book is a compilation of opinion pieces from my Blade career that illustrate the impact of those pivotal 20 years in the LGBTQ movement. In addition to the original text, I'm reflecting and adding some new context and previously undisclosed stories that inspired those original editorials. To break up all that anger, I've included some memorable feature stories from that time, from a timely post-Super Bowl interview with Janet Jackson to outing Fox News' Shepard Smith to doing battle with John Travolta and his Scientology cult. After all, progress isn't only measured by legislative wins, but by societal change. From an out gay NFL player to a transgender Golden Globe winner, the Blade chronicles all of our progress, so there are reflections here on pop culture, sports and other areas of American life that have been transformed over two decades.

Knowing that history is critical to understanding what's coming next — the backlash and inevitable setbacks made possible by Donald Trump's court picks and his validation of the worst American impulses. When a president tweets that trans people are banned from serving their country "in any capacity," there are ramifications that extend far beyond military policy. We see the impact of Trump's rhetoric when two sitting Supreme Court justices feel comfortable publicly announcing their desire to revisit the Obergefell ruling.

Our enemies are emboldened and the Obergefell ruling won't deter them now that they have a 6-3 conservative majority on the court. But before we get into the challenges of 2023 and beyond, let's look back at how we got here. The early 2000s was a very different time with President George W. Bush in the White House and almost no one talking seriously about marriage equality.

CHAPTER 1

MARRIAGE

"No union is more profound than marriage ... marriage embodies a love that may endure even past death. It would misunderstand these men and women to say they disrespect the idea of marriage. Their hope is not to be condemned to live in loneliness, excluded from one of civilization's oldest institutions. They ask for equal dignity in the eyes of the law. The Constitution grants them that right."
— Justice Anthony Kennedy

Collected Essays, 2003-2022

"COURT IGNITES MARRIAGE BATTLE," JULY 4, 2003

The date of this piece is striking — Independence Day 2003 — as I commemorated the historic Supreme Court ruling striking down sodomy laws in 13 states. It was one of my first opinion pieces weighing in on the marriage issue. I had no idea when I wrote it that the issue would dominate the next 12 years of Blade coverage as states, and finally the federal government, grappled with the then-controversial question of same-sex nuptials. But before marriage, there was the rather inconvenient issue of sodomy laws to address.

Let's be clear about the origins of this case: Two gay men, John Geddes Lawrence, Jr. and Tyron Garner, were having sex at Lawrence's apartment in Harris County, Texas. Garner's ex-boyfriend called the police, falsely alleging that someone had entered the apartment with a gun. The police showed up and found Lawrence and Garner engaged in sex and arrested them under the Texas anti-sodomy law. That's right: Two gay men were arrested for having consensual sex in a private home in 1998. Think about that for a moment — and the mind-numbing hypocrisy of Republicans who are supposedly anti-government intrusion into our private lives, until gay lives are involved. It took a Supreme Court ruling to validate the right of two consenting gay adults to have sex in a private home.

Justice Kennedy wrote the majority opinion in the landmark case Lawrence v. Texas, which overturned the previous ruling in Bowers v. Hardwick (1986), where the high court failed to find a constitutional right to privacy in sex.

The court in Lawrence v. Texas explicitly held that intimate consensual sexual conduct was part of the liberty protected by the substantive due process under the Fourteenth Amendment.

The decision in this case was a breakthrough for the gay rights movement and helped to set the stage for Obergefell v. Hodges, which recognized same-sex marriage as a fundamental right under the United States Constitution.

Indeed, anti-gay Justice Antonin Scalia wrote a stinging yet prescient dissent in the Lawrence case that predicted the outcome of Obergefell many years later.

June 2003 will surely be remembered as a landmark month for advances in gay rights. From the Supreme Court's historic decision striking down sodomy laws in 13 states to the legalization of gay marriage in Canada, gays and their supporters had much to celebrate at Pride Month festivities around the country, which culminated last weekend with events in San Francisco, New York, Atlanta and elsewhere.

But as revelers were sipping their mimosas and closing out Pride weekend events on Sunday, the next battle for full gay equality was taking shape on the morning news. Bill Frist (R-Tenn.), who recently took over from Trent Lott as Senate Majority Leader, told ABC's "This Week" program that he endorses a constitutional amendment banning gay marriage.

"I feel very much that it is a sacrament, and that sacrament should extend and can extend to that legal entity of a union between, what is traditionally in our Western values has been defined as between a man and a woman," Frist said. "So I would support the amendment."

Once again a prominent Republican leader is confusing religion and state. A sacrament refers to certain Christian rites (baptism, confirmation, receiving of the Eucharist) that have nothing to do with the legal rights and benefits conferred by the state on legally married couples. I have no expectation of ever walking down the aisle of a Catholic church to marry my partner; I do, however, hold out hope that the state will one day recognize my relationship and those of my straight friends equally.

Frist didn't stop there. He added, "I have this fear that this zone of privacy that we all want protected in our own homes is gradually

— or I'm concerned about the potential for it gradually being encroached upon, where criminal activity in the home would in some way be condoned."

It was an ironic moment for Frist, given the expectation that he would represent another new face of "compassionate conservatism" and an antidote to Lott-like bigotry. Frist revealed himself to be just the opposite: another Republican leader determined to infuse fundamentalist Christian beliefs into discriminatory laws. A constitutional amendment banning gay marriage would be a disaster for the gay rights movement and a blow to America's credibility as a freedom-loving nation. In a time when Belgium, the Netherlands and now Canada have legalized gay marriage, certain Republican leaders in the United States are still pining for the gays when gays stayed in the closet.

President Bush responded to the Frist trial balloon on Wednesday. "I don't know if it's necessary yet," Bush said of the amendment. "Let's let the lawyers look at the full ramifications of the recent Supreme Court hearing. What I do support is a notion that marriage is between a man and a woman."

There is no doubt that gay marriage rights represent the next major legal and cultural battle for gays. In fact, Justice Antonin Scalia's stinging dissenting opinion in the Lawrence v. Texas decision predicts it.

"Today's opinion dismantles the structure of constitutional law that has permitted a distinction to be made between heterosexual and homosexual unions, insofar as formal recognition in marriage is concerned," Scalia wrote. "This case 'does not involve' the issue of homosexual marriage only if one entertains the belief that principle and logic have nothing to do with the decisions of this Court."

Scalia's words were likely intended as a wake-up call to gay rights opponents that a constitutional amendment is the only way to ensure perpetual discrimination against gays and lesbians. If so, then Rep. Marilyn Musgrave (R-Colo.) is listening.

Musgrave is the main sponsor of a proposal to ban gay marriage through a constitutional amendment. The measure was referred to the House Judiciary subcommittee on the Constitution last week. According to the proposed amendment, "Marriage in the United States shall consist only of the union of a man and a woman."

"The traditional values Americans hold are being traded in for counterfeit marital unions. It is important to secure this institution and protect it from distortion," Musgrave said in a press release.

She is no stranger to crafting such legislation. Musgrave devoted much time and effort to passing an anti-gay marriage bill while she was a state senator in Colorado. Each year from 1996-2000, she introduced the measure, which was vetoed twice by Democratic Gov. Roy Romer, but was finally passed and signed by Republican Gov. Bill Owens in 2000. With such stellar achievements under her belt, the good people of Colorado sent her to Washington.

Her latest effort to prevent gays from enjoying equality under the law may be a long shot — a constitutional amendment requires approval by two-thirds of the House and Senate and 38 state legislatures — but gay rights advocates shouldn't underestimate the power of prejudice. After all, 37 states already have anti-marriage laws targeting gays on the books.

In some states, including Massachusetts, the gay marriage battle is already underway. The case of Goodridge v. Department of Public Health is pending before the Massachusetts Supreme Judicial Court and a decision is expected this summer, possibly sometime this month. The suit, which was filed by the rights group Gay & Lesbian Advocates & Defenders on behalf of seven same-sex couples who were denied marriage certificates, asserts that the right to choose a spouse is protected by the state Constitution and that there is not an emotional distinction between straight and same-sex couples.

At a Capital Pride event last month, Matt Foreman, the director of the National Gay & Lesbian Task Force, warned in a speech that a constitutional amendment banning gay marriage was "an ember becoming an inferno." His remarks seemed dramatic at the time, but with the Scalia dissent and now Frist's endorsement of a constitutional marriage ban, Foreman's words seem prescient and appropriate. The Supreme Court's ruling last week has likely supplied the spark needed to ignite the inferno.

"WEDGING HIS WAY TO THE WHITE HOUSE," NOV. 12, 2004

This post-election piece candidly addresses the impact of marriage on the 2004 presidential election in which George W. Bush won and 11 states passed bans on same-sex marriage. Bush's win was one of the darkest days of my 20 years at the Blade. His campaign manager, Ken Mehlman, was closeted and helped orchestrate the cynical exploitation of the gay marriage issue to win evangelical voters and ultimately a second Bush term. We tried desperately to out Mehlman during the 2004 campaign but couldn't find anyone who'd ever dated or hooked up with him. He seemed, by all accounts, asexual, with multiple sources telling us that Mehlman was known as a workaholic and never had a dating life. He eventually came out publicly but his extensive damage was done and he owes the community a hell of a lot more penance. Fast forward 15 years and Bush was photographed partying in a private suite at the Super Bowl with queer icon Ellen DeGeneres, for which she received much justifiable backlash. More on Ellen later. But Bush's "evolution" on LGBTQ issues has never included an explanation, apology or queer press interview as of 2022. People are allowed to evolve and we want them to. But forgiveness has to be requested and earned. Bush hasn't earned it as yet.

Any hope that President Bush would moderate his position on gay marriage in his second term quickly evaporated on Sunday when the "architect" of his reelection, Karl Rove, declared on Fox News, "If we want to have a hopeful and decent society, we ought to aim for the ideal, and the ideal is that marriage ought to be, and should be, a union of a man and a woman." Rove then affirmed that Bush would continue his push to ban gay marriage via constitutional amendment. Of course, this should not come as a surprise. Evangelical Christian voters in Ohio, many of whom were motivated to get to the polls by that state's ballot initiative to ban gay marriage, delivered Bush the state and with it the White House. Now it's quid pro quo time. Rove's promise that Bush will again push for a federal constitutional amendment banning gay marriage confirms that gays will bear the brunt of evangelical payback. In all the fawning over Rove and his campaign tactics, one point has been ignored: Pandering to voters' most base instincts and worst prejudices is not brilliant or clever. It's sleazy, hurtful and barely rises to the level of used car salesman. Gay couples are not lacking in hope or decency, as Rove's homily on Fox News implies.

Gay rights advocates have been ducking blame for Rove's wedge strategy since Election Day. Unfortunately, it's impossible to deny that all the hoopla surrounding gay marriage gave Rove the issue he needed to appeal to all those "moral issues" voters, many of whom voted against their own economic self-interests for Bush. San Francisco Mayor Gavin Newsom, and New Paltz, N.Y. Mayor Jason West, as well as officials in New Mexico and Oregon who married gay couples must accept that their actions contributed in a big way to last week's Democratic defeat and the passage of anti-gay marriage amendments in 11 states. Marriage advocates ignored the warnings of Congressman Barney Frank (D-Mass.), who cautioned that Newsom's actions would have undesirable consequences. In a letter to the Blade, Frank wrote, "I feared that an outbreak of marriages held in violation of various statutes in various parts of the country would generate pressure on members of Congress to support the [federal] amendment." Frank told the New York Times last week, "The thing that agitated people were the mass weddings. It was a mistake in San Francisco compounded by people in Oregon, New Mexico and New York. What it did was provoke a lot of fears."

In an editorial one year ago, I wrote, "Chief Justice Margaret Marshall of the Massachusetts Supreme Judicial Court on Tuesday gave us something else to be thankful for this year." Did I ever eat those words last Tuesday. One prominent Republican last week suggested that Bush should send Marshall a bouquet for delivering him the election.

The reality is that most Americans aren't ready for same-sex marriage. With the Employment Non-Discrimination Act and hate crimes legislation still languishing in Congress, our movement got ahead of itself. But all this second-guessing won't change the outcome. We started this fight, and so gay rights advocates must finish it. We can take some solace in President Bush's announcement that he supports allowing states to enact civil unions and that, according to exit polls, a wide majority of voters support either civil marriage or civil unions for same-sex couples.

The United States may be, for the moment, heading backward on the question of gay rights, but marriage equality is becoming reality in Europe and Canada. A Saskatchewan court ruled just last week that existing marriage laws discriminate against gay couples and were unconstitutional. Courts in Quebec, British Columbia, the Yukon, Manitoba, Ontario and Nova Scotia have already come to the same conclusion, and Canada's Supreme Court is reviewing a law that would make same-sex marriage legal across the country. Meanwhile, Spanish Prime Minister Jose Luis Rodriguez Zapatero has made good on promises to push for legalized same-sex marriage; in England, the House of Commons has given preliminary approval to a bill that would give civil partnership rights to gay couples; German lawmakers last month expanded rights for gay couples, allowing domestic partners to adopt each other's children; and even in Roman

Catholic Ireland, lawmakers last month initiated a review of rights for gay couples.

Last week's election outcome is a bitter reminder that a civil rights struggle involves coping with setbacks as well as celebrating advances. We won't win equality because Rosie O'Donnell asked for it at a black-tie dinner. It's too late to put the marriage issue back in the bottle, so over the next four years gays and lesbians must be more visible, not less. Only when gay people come out and force their families, neighbors, friends, colleagues and, yes, politicians to rationalize their anti-gay sentiments will real progress and change happen.

"LEFT AT THE ALTAR," SEPT. 28, 2007

The fight for marriage equality in Maryland represents one of the few times I arguably crossed the line from journalist to activist. As a Maryland resident, the outcome of this fight had a direct impact on my life; namely, whether I could legally marry my longtime partner. I pride myself on maintaining professionalism at all times — I never shed a tear while interviewing Pulse massacre survivors nor got choked up talking to family members of TWA Flight 800 crash victims — but the Maryland marriage fight was different. I engaged in off-the-record calls and meetings with Maryland activists, coordinating efforts and messaging. When Gov. Martin O'Malley reached out and asked to meet with me in Annapolis, those same activists were upset. "Why is he meeting with YOU?!?" they wondered. The answer is that I outed his brother and the governor was angry at me. O'Malley was privately supportive but publicly, as recounted here, he invoked the Catholic sacraments in defending the sanctity of marriage between a man and a woman.

When the Maryland Court of Appeals ruling against marriage rights came down, we were crushed. There was a protest at an affirming church in Mount Vernon, the gayborhood in Baltimore, and I headed there to cover it for the Blade. Most everyone was crying. I remember standing on the corner as cars drove by, motorists shouting "faggots" at us as they passed. I cannot recall a more depressing setback in 20 years — remanded to second-class status by the appeals court in a supposedly "blue" state AND being called a faggot in the same day.

People were pissed. PISSED. They had donated to O'Malley, voted for him; I talked to gay couples who had spent their summer vacations volunteering for him, knocking on doors instead of lounging on a beach somewhere. And O'Malley's response to the court's appalling, offensive decision was to issue a cold statement invoking the Catholic sacraments in asserting his opposition to marriage equality.

When O'Malley's press secretary called, he made no secret about how they all felt about me and what I'd done. I didn't give a shit. Your own brother is gay and you are working against his equality. That sucks. Besides, O'Malley's brother was out to a wide circle of gay friends and a regular patron of gay bars in Baltimore and Washington. He wasn't what I would call "closeted." I reached out to him on social media and he promptly closed his accounts. So, really, I had no choice, and outed him in the Blade. I told O'Malley's press secretary that I would come to Annapolis on two conditions: that the meeting be on the record and that I could record it. He reluctantly agreed. (More on that later.)

The unfortunate thing about it is that I actually like O'Malley. I voted for him for Baltimore mayor and believe he did a good job, despite later criticism of his no-tolerance policing policies. I've been in Baltimore bars with him late at night while he performed with his band, O'Malley's March, downing shots and swearing into the microphone. O'Malley is no saint. And that's a good thing. But it made his (public) opposition to marriage equality all the more galling. I began to get calls from prominent gay Democratic Party activists who told me of O'Malley's private support for gay marriage years before it was acceptable. He should have been a pioneer on the issue. But his religious background and fear of backlash led him to endorse civil unions long after that separate-but-equal ship had sailed.

I walked into his office wielding my tape recorder and refused to address him as "governor," referring to him instead as "Martin." The truth is he's just not that smart. We talked for about 30 minutes and he bobbed and weaved as usual. At the end of our conversation, I asked him about a recent Washington Post column that asserted

O'Malley was uncomfortable with the word "gay" and hadn't uttered it in public in ages. It was a softball question. But O'Malley panicked. His expression reminded me of those cartoons where you can see the wheels turning inside a thought bubble over a character's head. He was trying to figure out how to respond. After a long, awkward pause, I ventured, "Well, can you say it?" He stared at me wide-eyed, wheels turning, and finally uttered, "gay." That's all I was after, I assured him, and laughed nervously.

Years later, during the Hillary Clinton email scandal in 2016, I was stunned to learn that a column I'd written about O'Malley's flip-flopping on marriage was part of the cache of emails that was publicly released by WikiLeaks. Hillary's senior campaign staff had circulated my column on O'Malley's various marriage positions with glee after he took a jab at her. "History celebrates profiles in courage, not profiles in convenience," O'Malley said in a video. "The dignity of every person tells us that the right to marry is not a state right, it is a human right."

The idea of O'Malley criticizing Clinton on marriage was laughable, yet also a sign of our progress. He was no pioneer, but neither was she. The fact that they were fighting over who was a bigger proponent of marriage equality illustrates how they both ultimately evolved.

Last week's Maryland Court of Appeals ruling upholding a ban on same-sex marriage left the state's gay couples standing at the altar, stunned at the unduly harsh language in the lengthy opinion.

The divided court, in a 4-3 ruling, turned to procreation as a "legitimate governmental interest" in its reasoning. Of course, no one is suggesting that straight couples incapable of — or uninterested in — having children be denied marriage rights. That would be a logical extension of this ruling, but this court wasn't concerned about logic.

The majority wrote, "... safeguarding an environment most conducive to the stable propagation and continuance of the human race is a legitimate government interest."

Those callous words ignore the plight of several plaintiffs in the case who are raising children without basic protections granted to their straight counterparts.

The court also appeared to turn to the "ex-gay" movement in justifying its decision. The justices could not conclude that homosexuality is an immutable characteristic, thereby buying into one of the most harmful myths circulated about gays.

"We decline on the record in the present case to recognize sexual orientation as an immutable trait and therefore a suspect or quasi-suspect classification," according to the majority opinion.

In other words, gay Marylanders already have access to marriage rights. They just need to pick a different sexual orientation and all is remedied. There's a lot of offensive language in this ruling, but the passages questioning the very nature of homosexuality are the most disturbing. They suggest that no legal argument or tale of plaintiff woe would have swayed their dim, uneducated view of human sexuality. Given that fact, the only surprise is that it took so long to render this decision.

In another striking passage, the majority opinion addresses the issue of whether gays and lesbians are sufficiently discriminated against to warrant court intervention. The justices conclude that because gays are a "politically powerful" group that we don't need their help.

"We are not persuaded that gay, lesbian and bisexual persons are so politically powerless that they are entitled to 'extraordinary protection from the majoritarian political process.' To the contrary, it appears that, at least in Maryland, advocacy to eliminate discrimination against gay, lesbian and bisexual persons based on their sexual orientation has met with growing successes in the legislative and executive branches of government."

They must have forgotten about former Gov. Robert Ehrlich's veto of the Medical Decision Making Act, which would have granted unmarried gay and straight couples hospital visitation rights, and the Transfer & Recordation Tax Exemption Act, which would have exempted gay couples from the taxes involved in transferring the title of a home. Maryland's gays aren't so powerful that same-sex couples have even basic rights, despite the progress seen in other states across the country.

The justices ruling in the majority sound completely ignorant of the plight of gay couples, despite the stories told by the plaintiffs. Were they asleep during oral arguments? Did they read any of the briefs filed in the case? It does not appear so.

In one of the more galling passages, the majority rejects a New Jersey-like compromise suggested by Justice Irma Raker compelling the state to grant the rights of marriage to gay couples but allowing the legislature to call it civil unions. In its response to Raker's proposal, the majority uses the plaintiffs' own words against them, arguing that to grant civil unions would be second-class citizenship, something rejected by plaintiffs as insufficient.

"[Raker's] dissent attempts to bestow upon Appellees the benefits of marriage, without actually granting them the right to marry, proposing exactly that which Appellees in the present case expressly chose not to seek in this litigation," the justices wrote.

This flip response to a serious proposal from Raker illustrates just how little consideration the court gave to finding a reasonable compromise — one that was good enough for the New Jersey court.

After spending more than 100 pages rejecting our right to equality under the law, the court wraps its opinion with this: "Our opinion should by no means be read to imply that the General Assembly may not grant and recognize for homosexual persons civil unions or the right to marry a person of the same sex."

And with those words, the Maryland fight moved to the legislature, where two lawmakers have already promised to introduce a marriage bill in both houses in January. Meanwhile, the state's most powerful Democrats, Gov. Martin O'Malley and Senate President

Thomas V. "Mike" Miller Jr. reiterated their opposition to marriage rights for gay couples; Miller even told the Washington Post he opposes civil unions.

O'Malley had assured gay rights activists and plaintiffs in the Maryland marriage case that he supported same-sex marriage, only to reverse course after the lower court ruled in the plaintiffs' favor in January 2006. After last week's ruling, he invoked the Catholic sacraments in justifying his opposition to full marriage rights.

It's an all-too-familiar tale of a Democratic candidate promising to stand up for an all-too-loyal gay constituency, then abandoning us when times get tough.

This is what happens when gays blindly hand their support to candidates and demand nothing in return. When will gays learn that subjugating ourselves to any one party is a doomed strategy?

But "respect" for a court's authority isn't the same as agreeing with it. And there was a promising development this week when O'Malley invited the Blade to meet with him to discuss the issue in an on-the-record interview next week. During his four years in office, Ehrlich never agreed to a sit-down interview with the Blade, so O'Malley's invitation is a welcome sign of progress. A pledge to aggressively lobby for a civil unions bill that confers all the rights of marriage to gay couples would be a very positive step. The Blade will report O'Malley's responses to all of the questions surrounding the marriage debate next week.

In the meantime, we can turn to the Republican mayor of San Diego for an example of true political courage. Jerry Sanders, in a tearful news conference last week announced his own flip-flop on gay marriage — in the other direction.

"I have decided to lead with my heart — to do what I think is right — and to take a stand on behalf of equality and social justice," Sanders said. "The right thing for me to do is to sign this resolution.

... The concept of a 'separate but equal' institution is not something that I can support."

Bravo, Mr. Sanders. Let's hope Maryland's Democratic politicians follow the brave lead of a Republican mayor.

"No more Mr. Nice Gay," Nov. 21, 2008, and "A year to remember," Jan. 2, 2009

These pieces serve as another reminder that in the quest for equality, you will encounter setbacks. The passage of Prop 8 in California in 2008 represented a huge setback for marriage equality as voters in the overwhelmingly "blue," progressive state enacted a same-sex marriage ban. It was a crushing blow. Equally frustrating was the mainstream media coverage at the time, with pundits blaming Hispanic voters, a majority of whom supported Prop 8. But, of course, those same MSNBC and CNN talking heads ignored the fact that 81 percent of white women in Orange County voted for Prop 8. They never blame the white women. We saw the same phenomenon in 2016, when Black voters were blamed for not turning out in Obama-level numbers for Hillary Clinton, even though they backed her in overwhelming numbers. When Doug Jones won the Senate race in Alabama over a credibly accused pedophile, Roy Moore, it was Black women who turned out in astonishing numbers to put him over the top. But no one blames the majority of white voters who backed Moore. It's always the underrepresented voters — Black, Hispanic, LGBTQ — who get blamed when turnout dips and Republicans eke out a victory.

Rather than take those votes for granted, the Democratic Party must earn them. We must not go back to the days of this 2008 piece, when senior Democratic leadership (I'm looking at you Nancy Pelosi) was managing expectations, preparing LGBTQ Americans for a federal hate crimes bill instead of ENDA or relationship recognition. Sources told us at the time that conservative "Blue Dog" Democrats were opposed to taking more than one vote on an LGBTQ issue and so Pelosi told them it would be the hate crimes bill, which passed. The problem was, most activists considered that bill low-hanging fruit and we all expected more after working tirelessly for Obama's election. One upside was seeing Frank Kameny, regarded by many as the grandfather of the LGBTQ movement, in the White House at Obama's side as he signed the bill into law. It was a journey that began in the 1950s, when Kameny was fired from his federal government job for being gay. He went on to devote his life to our cause and became an icon of the movement. Kameny could be cantankerous, but I miss his periodic phone calls complaining about a Blade headline or late distribution of papers to his neighborhood box. He died on my birthday, Oct. 11 — also National Coming Out Day — in 2011.

An uproar ensued after Pelosi and other top Democrats secured the hate crimes bill and erroneously thought we would all bow down and thank them for the crumbs. Instead, protests erupted, gay and lesbian service members handcuffed themselves to the White House fence and Obama was heckled at an LGBTQ event in the White House.

This piece also references Wanda Sykes, who came out at a 2008 protest, and criticizes fellow celebs Anderson Cooper and Queen Latifah for remaining closeted. Cooper, of course, eventually came out and his career only flourished. Latifah is another story.

The 2008 year-in-review essay nicely recounts several important firsts, including our newsworthy interviews with multiple presidential candidates in 2008, including Obama, Clinton, Bill Richardson and John McCain. I alluded to the recession of 2008 at the end of my piece but little did I know that 2009 would bring the greatest challenge the Blade has ever faced.

"NO MORE MR. NICE GAY"

As Wanda Sykes put it last weekend in her coming out remarks, "They pissed off the wrong people."

Average citizens, many of them straight, are reacting with disbelief and anger following California's passage of Proposition 8 — and the Arkansas adoption ban and same-sex marriage bans in Florida and Arizona.

In the absence of an identifiable national gay rights leader, everyday people stepped into the leadership vacuum and produced marches in hundreds of places large and small on Saturday. An estimated 5,000 took to the National Mall in D.C. to demonstrate against the anti-gay ballot initiatives that passed on Election Day.

But the demonstrations are about more than a few specific laws. Average Americans are finally beginning to understand that LGBT people lack equality under the law and they're angry about it. Prop 8, in particular, has focused attention on that inequality and galvanized and transformed previously apathetic observers into angry marchers.

What's more remarkable is that last weekend's protests in cities across the country were loosely organized via the web and sites like Jointheimpact.com and Facebook. The largest gay rights groups were mostly on the sidelines, though they helped promote the marches after it became clear people needed an outlet for their anger.

Many gay bloggers and commentators have described these events as the next great chapter in gay rights activism after years of trying to work the system from the inside. But there's room — and need — for both approaches. As too many gay people, perhaps burned out from fighting government apathy over AIDS, took a checkbook approach to activism from the late '90s to today, we forgot about the need for mass visibility. Sorry, but a few token gay characters on TV sitcoms and an out lesbian talk show host don't cut it.

The opening of the film "Milk" next week is a reminder that Harvey Milk's pleas for gay Americans to come out still go unheeded by many. Thirty years later, we're still fighting (and losing) anti-gay initiatives at the ballot box and still suffering from a dearth of openly gay public figures. Wanda Sykes deserves our gratitude for coming out last weekend at a Las Vegas protest, but her voice would have meant more in the weeks before Nov. 4. Few even knew she was married until Saturday. And too many fellow celebrities remain closeted, from

Queen Latifah to Anderson Cooper. Their silence helps reinforce the destructive message that homosexuality is shameful.

The big question, of course, is where do all those marchers and their justifiable anger go from here? For too long, we've been told to be patient. The excitement over Bill Clinton's 1992 victory was followed by crushing disappointments that included "Don't Ask, Don't Tell" and the Defense of Marriage Act. Then came George W. Bush and gay rights advocates were on the defensive; we were told not to expect any progress on our issues. When the Democrats took Congress in 2006, expectations were tamped down because, of course, Bush was still in the White House. Instead of confronting the "compassionate conservative" with a nondiscrimination bill to sign or veto, we waged a divisive fight over trans inclusion in ENDA. And now, even with Barack Obama's historic win and larger Democratic majorities in both houses of Congress, the expectations management has begun.

Sources on the Hill and within the gay rights movement have told us not to expect great strides right away, but smaller wins, like the hate crimes bill and maybe domestic partner benefits for federal employees. Meanwhile, our so-called allies in the Democratic Party continue to disappoint. In the Washington area, we've seen this problem manifest in D.C., Maryland and Virginia. Newly elected Sen. Mark Warner (D-Va.) is happy to make brief appearances at gay fundraisers and barbeques, but he opposes same-sex marriage and civil unions and supports "Don't Ask, Don't Tell,"

In Maryland, Gov. Martin O'Malley threw gay residents under the bus after the high court ruled against marriage last year. Since that betrayal, he has failed to enact DP benefits for state employees, something he could have done via executive order long ago. He has failed to champion any gay rights legislation, despite expressing phony support for civil unions. And he has all but ignored Equality Maryland during his lackluster tenure as a governor who never met a tax hike he didn't like. Maryland will be much better off when he leaves office — bring on Doug Gansler for governor!

And in D.C., Mayor Adrian Fenty, who enjoys strong gay support, lost his voice this fall as local gays marched in response to a rash of hate crimes. He refused to speak out and even told a Blade reporter at a press conference that he "doesn't respond to perceptions." Fenty has refused repeated interview requests since October. The Blade has had better luck getting answers out of John McCain than its own hometown mayor. And Fenty has turned the once relevant job of GLBT liaison into an extension of his press office — someone to read toothless proclamations at gay confabs.

In the face of these and countless other slights, the reaction from gay rights activists is predictably muted because we don't go after Democrats. Now that Democrats are in charge, our advocates must get over their aversion to taking on their supposed allies. If they don't, they will be overshadowed by less easily cowed voices that have finally tired of patience and are demanding accountability and progress.

One way for those who marched last week to stay active is to take the message home for Thanksgiving. No more Mr. Nice Gay, as many have chanted. No more letting relatives off the hook for their silent, passive support. Our parents, grandparents, nieces, nephews, aunts, uncles, cousins and siblings represent untapped allies and we will need all the straight support we can get to reverse the outcome of Election Day.

So take your partner home for the holidays. Talk about marriage and Prop 8 and the Arkansas adoption ban over sweet potatoes and candied yams. Last week's protests are a reminder that going soft, being patient and writing checks isn't enough. No more Mr. Nice Gay.

"A YEAR TO REMEMBER"

Journalism is, by nature, a thankless profession. Its practitioners are supposed to cover the news, not make it. Many work long hours for low pay because they have a passion and calling for a profession that is so much more than a job.

The nation's Founding Fathers deemed the role of journalists so important to a functioning democracy that they protected freedom of the press in the Bill of Rights in 1791.

Today, journalists face daunting challenges, from the current economic recession's toll on advertising to changes brought about by the Internet. The advent of free classified ads on Craigslist is just one blow online media have dealt to the traditional newspaper's bottom line.

But the rewards of this work outweigh the negatives and every so often an event of such significance comes along to reenergize those oft-maligned ink-stained wretches.

One such event occurred with the 2008 general election. Just one year ago, the Blade's front page featured an in-depth interview with presidential candidate Bill Richardson, the Democratic governor of New Mexico. The headline: "Richardson claims best record on gay issues."

It was a remarkable story and something of a landmark, as presidential candidates for the first time were engaging with the nation's gay press. And they didn't take a mere question or two; several candidates submitted to lengthy Q&A's or live interviews and even argued over who was best on gay issues.

"I, by far, have the best record, not just the record of voting right but of pushing for gay and GLBT legislation throughout my career," Richardson boldly asserted in the interview with the Blade's longtime senior news reporter, Lou Chibbaro Jr.

Shortly after Chibbaro's talk with Richardson, Sen. Hillary Rodham Clinton granted the Blade an interview on the eve of the "Potomac Primary," reiterating her support for a range of gay rights initiatives.

"I've been a longtime friend of the gay community — I've been talking about these issues since 1999 when I first ran for Senate and went on record as the first major candidate to say we're going to repeal 'Don't Ask, Don't Tell,'" she said. "I talk about ending discrimination all the time."

Barack Obama answered a lengthy list of questions submitted by the Blade in September.

"Michelle and I have been blessed with many openly gay and lesbian friends and colleagues whom we have been close to for many years," Obama wrote. "While that fact has made the issues facing the LGBT community more personal, the fundamental reasons I have for supporting equality are greater than an individual."

And in a historic first, Republican presidential nominee Sen. John McCain also agreed to answer a broad range of questions submitted by the Blade. His Q&A was hailed by gay Republican activists and raises the bar for the next GOP nominee when it comes to accessibility and articulating views on gay issues.

"I hope gay and lesbian Americans will give full consideration to supporting me," McCain wrote. "The stakes are high in this election. I will have an inclusive administration and I will be a president for all Americans."

What a difference four years makes. During the 2004 election, Democratic nominee John Kerry declined Blade interview requests; his running mate, John Edwards was a no-show at a candidates' forum sponsored by the Human Rights Campaign. Kerry supported state constitutional amendments banning same-sex marriage and incumbent President George W. Bush had backed the Federal Marriage Amendment and even singled out gays in his State of the Union address for an unprecedented attack on our civil rights before a worldwide audience.

Fast-forward to 2008 and the Democratic candidates were accessible to the gay media, granting interviews to the Blade, the Advocate and the Philadelphia Gay News. The Democrats, minus Joe Biden, took gay-related questions at an HRC-Logo forum televised nationally. The Republicans nominated a senator who publicly broke with Bush on the FMA and denounced it in a floor speech.

Although the times are clearly changing, Election Day '08 brought a sobering reminder that the fight for equal rights is far from over when California's Proposition 8 overturned same-sex marriage in the state.

The Blade devoted an entire special issue to Prop 8 back in September, triggering email from local readers who wondered why we were giving so much space to a story unfolding 3,000 miles from our home base. Now, the devastating implications of Prop 8's passage are clear: 18,000 legal marriages in jeopardy; a long setback for marriage equality in the nation's most populous state; and a chilling message to other jurisdictions contemplating marriage equality legislation. In D.C., Prop 8's success has some activists thinking twice about moving ahead with a marriage bill here, which could happen as early as next week when gay Council member David Catania is widely expected to introduce a bill.

The Blade's Prop 8 coverage took an unexpected turn when tens of thousands of demonstrators in cities and towns across the country took to the streets to protest, something that failed to materialize when state after state passed similar amendments in 2004 and 2006. The strong turnout revealed the feelings of shock and deep anger among gay and straight people alike that the rights of a minority group could be subjected to a popular vote and that existing rights could be snatched away.

It was an eventful and memorable year for those of us at the Blade: from the euphoria over the California court ruling on marriage to the crushing disappointment of Prop 8; from the grueling primary battle between Clinton and Obama to his historic win in November; from landing interviews with presidential candidates (Clinton, Obama, Richardson, McCain) to Blade exclusives with pop stars and celebrities (Liza Minnelli, Janet Jackson); from moving personal coming out stories (gospel singer Ray Boltz) to tragedy in Iraq (Maj. Alan Rogers' death); from an awful local murder mystery (Robert Wone) to a rash of crimes in D.C. with gay victims (Tony Randolph Hunter; Durval Martins).

The Blade's staff is the most dedicated and passionate I've had the pleasure to work with in my career and their hard work paid off in 2008, as the paper took home a series of prestigious awards from the Society of Professional Journalists, National Newspaper Association and National Lesbian & Gay Journalists Association. Our sales, classified, production, marketing and administrative teams have excelled and persevered throughout a deepening recession and unprecedented changes within the industry. Our publisher, Lynne Brown, has navigated it all with an unwavering commitment to local LGBT residents, businesses and our allies.

To each of the professionals on the Blade team, thank you for all you do. To our readers and advertisers, thank you for sticking with us. And stay tuned: The Blade turns 40 this year and our best is yet to come.

"One giant leap for gay rights," Feb. 23, 2011

This was another momentous, if not surprising, development as the Obama administration stopped defending the indefensible Defense of Marriage Act, signed by President Clinton and supported by many Democrats, including one or two closeted elected officials.

The Obama administration today delivered a massive victory to the LGBT movement, marking a historic turning point in how gay and lesbian Americans are treated by the government.

The Justice Department announced it would stop defending the Defense of Marriage Act, the 1996 law signed by President Clinton that bars federal recognition of same-sex marriages.

"After careful consideration, including a review of my recommendation, the President has concluded that given a number of factors, including a documented history of discrimination, classifications based on sexual orientation should be subject to a more heightened standard of scrutiny," Attorney General Eric Holder said in a statement. "The President has also concluded that Section 3 of DOMA, as applied to legally married same-sex couples, fails to meet that standard and is therefore unconstitutional. Given that conclusion, the President has instructed the Department not to defend the statute in such cases."

Under that new "heightened scrutiny" test, Obama and his Justice Department view DOMA as unconstitutional. Obama has said this before and the news wasn't entirely unexpected. But it's no less dramatic.

The government's assertion that a state seeking to discriminate on the basis of sexual orientation must present a compelling interest — rather than a plausible reason — for such discrimination represents a major change in how our rights are viewed.

Obama has come under much fire by LGBT activists for his slow-go approach to change, but today's announcement puts him squarely on the side of justice and restores his credentials as a "fierce advocate" of LGBT equality.

"Behind Maryland's marriage debacle," March 15, 2011

As a lifelong Marylander, the fight for marriage equality in the "Free State" was especially personal. There were so many disappointments — bad court rulings, duplicitous politicians like Gov. Martin O'Malley and failed bills — that I began writing regularly about the cause and engaging directly with many of the players. Things came to a head when I outed Gov. O'Malley's gay brother in a column. People were pissed, to say the least. But, fuck it, I'm not in the business of protecting fragile people's dirty little secrets when civil rights are at stake. You don't get to masquerade as a progressive and have a gay brother — who was fully out in his personal life — while simultaneously selling out the community that supported your many political campaigns with votes, money and volunteers.

The problem in Maryland, as these next two pieces outline, was apathy. Too few Marylanders engaged in the fight and too many well-to-do gays sitting on the sidelines expecting a handful of out activists to do all the work. Of course, we eventually won the fight and sustained that victory in a referendum in large part due to the belated support of O'Malley, and the visibility of Black pastors in the state.

The debacle that unfolded in Annapolis last week can be traced to multiple causes with one common root: old-fashioned homophobia.

The Maryland House of Delegates abandoned a bill that would have granted marriage equality to gay and lesbian couples in the so-called Free State.

But an epic train wreck derailed the wedding plans of so many deserving couples that have waited so long for justice. In all their hateful gloating after the bill's defeat, opponents like those at the National Organization for Marriage seem to forget that this isn't about a bunch of gays wanting to throw a fabulous wedding reception. It's about real people — committed couples and families facing discrimination and adversity because of our second-class status.

My heart broke last week for so many of those Marylanders I've come to know and respect during this process. Elderly couples together for 40 years now worried about having to return to the closet as they move to retirement communities. Gay and lesbian parents raising kids without the protections and respect afforded by marriage. The gay schoolteacher whose partner died suddenly and was sued by his ex's parents because they wanted to exhume the body and move their son to the family plot against his directives. A gay man who legally adopted his partner because lawyers determined it was the only way to guarantee hostile family members couldn't sue for half their estate in the event one of them died. Foreign-born partners facing deportation because U.S. laws don't recognize our relationships as legitimate.

And there are more subtle ways this discrimination affects us. After 13 years together, my relationship with my partner isn't viewed as equal to our straight counterparts. It is always something less than, even though we've seen our straight friends and family members marry, divorce and remarry. They immediately enjoy the legal benefits and instant respect afforded by that word, "marriage," while we are referred to by the cold and clinical "partners." It's an empty, meaningless term. And it's insulting. Our society has a term for our relationship — marriage — but lawmakers aren't willing to take a stand and face down their ignorant (and often closeted) pastors. They run in fear of Fox News' blowhards and NOM's $1 million war chest. They are cowards and don't deserve our support for reelection.

This is what gets lost in all the venom spewed by our opponents and all the halfhearted, hollow arguments made on our behalf by well-meaning Democrats afraid to fully embrace us and demand our full equality under the law. It's about love and family and children and being able to properly care for our loved ones when times are tough.

But our allies sold us out. They are weak and afraid and driven by self-preservation. Lawmakers who campaigned on support for marriage equality and cosponsored the bill pulled out and opposed it. The betrayals of Dels. Sam Arora (D-Montgomery County), Jill Carter (D-Baltimore), Tiffany Alston (D-Prince George's) and Melvin Stukes (D-Baltimore) must not be forgotten. No LGBT money, votes or support for those backstabbing traitors.

Maryland has the largest caucus of openly LGBT state legislators in the country, yet they couldn't sway one or two votes to bring the bill across the finish line. Maybe Sen. Rich Madaleno could host a Lobbying 101 seminar in the House. He was able to shepherd the bill, with support from key straight allies, through the more conservative Senate. He helped convert former opponents into supporters. And Madaleno's presence in the chamber seemed to have a calming effect on even the most strident opponents of marriage equality, ensuring a professional and hate-free debate.

But seven openly gay and lesbian members in the more liberal House couldn't replicate that success. The most senior out gay member, Del. Maggie McIntosh, didn't even bother to deliver a floor speech for the bill. With the vote so close — perhaps as close as a single vote — didn't it occur to her that junior members who were undecided might be swayed to support their senior colleague?

Freshmen Dels. Luke Clippinger and Mary Washington deserve our gratitude for their visibility and impassioned floor speeches. They were not intimidated by NOM and Del. Don Dwyer and put their own self-interests aside to do what's right. Perhaps the most gratifying moment of the House debate came when Del. Peter Murphy stood up to correct a colleague who'd said the House had six openly gay members. Murphy bravely came out in an interview with me last week. A grandfather of two, Murphy represents conservative southern Maryland, yet found the courage to take a public stand when it counted the most. He stood on the House floor to correct the record — there are now seven, he said.

As Murphy stood up, McIntosh sat down — because she knew the fix was in. The Human Rights Campaign and Gill Action intervened and urged the LGBT Caucus and Equality Maryland to cancel the vote. They feared that a failure might jeopardize similar efforts in Rhode Island and New York. It's more likely they're worried about the demoralizing effect of a marriage defeat on wealthy gay donors. We wouldn't want to upset them so close to 2012.

The people who actually live in Maryland deserved a vote. They've worked hard for years to get to this unique opportunity and it was snatched away prematurely. Some have speculated that there were 71 votes to pass the bill; now we will never know.

HRC and Gill argue that if lawmakers are forced to vote and then cast a vote against us, that it's unlikely they will change their vote a year later. I would point them to Sen. James Brochin, a Baltimore County Democrat who campaigned against same-sex marriage but who switched his view after hearing the sickening, bigoted testimony in the Senate committee hearing. Or to Sen. Allan Kittleman, the former Senate minority leader who gave up that post over his unexpected support for marriage equality.

The people at HRC and Gill are strategic and well intentioned, but this was a bad call. In a state dominated by Democrats, this vote should never have been in doubt. But it fell apart because support was soft. How will we know who really supports us and is deserving of our money and votes in the next election if we don't take the vote? Canceling the vote only gives cover to cowards. The collective sigh of relief in the House last Friday was deafening. Even the LGBT Caucus didn't speak up to oppose the motion to send the bill back to committee. Whew! Kick the can down the road, avoid a vote and let's call it a day.

No one was more relieved than Gov. Martin O'Malley, who has been celebrated and feted by LGBT activists and donors from around the country, despite his outdated support for civil unions. In a 2007 interview, O'Malley told me he would sign a marriage bill if the legislature could pass it, knowing there was zero chance of that happening anytime soon. He reiterated that pledge this year to the LGBT media but was more circumspect about it when talking to the mainstream press. In the run up to the House vote, O'Malley reportedly helped lobby some delegates. Either he lied or he's just ineffective.

Where was his public advocacy during the session? His wife found time to record a video for the "It Gets Better" campaign but Maryland's first couple lost their voice when it came to marriage equality. We know the O'Malleys are privately supportive and have gay friends and family members, but their unwillingness to speak out undermined the effort to pass the bill.

So what now? One key lesson from this failure: Do not underestimate the influence of Black pastors. Equality Maryland failed to solidify support among Black lawmakers from Baltimore City and Prince George's County. And when the preaching began on Sundays in February, several Black delegates caved under the pressure. Equality Maryland must take a page from their counterparts in D.C., where the visibility of pro-gay Black ministers and the involvement of Black gay and lesbian couples were at the center of their successful strategy.

In addition to cultivating Black support, advocates must grow a backbone and work to oust Dels. Arora, Carter, Alston and Stukes. Arora represents liberal Montgomery County. Surely we can find a marriage equality supporter there. Stukes and Carter are from Baltimore, which suffers from a dearth of LGBT activism. If a politician in D.C. had done what Carter and Stukes did, they'd be hammered and drummed out of office. But Baltimore lacks a vocal and visible activist presence. So it will fall to Equality Maryland to finally get tough with those who take our money and votes and then toss us under the bus.

Sadly, it really does come back to simple homophobia. Democrats who say they support us during their campaigns go soft because they, deep down, don't really think our relationships are equal to their own marriages. Others cave to pressure from pastors because somewhere beneath the surface promises, they're not so sure we're not sinners destined for hell. The governor tells us in private that he supports us, but can't find his voice in public because it might offend conservatives who hate us irrationally — and O'Malley might need some of those votes in a future run for Senate. And some members of the LGBT Caucus, too, lose their voice because they're terrified of being known as the "gay delegate." As if that's a bad thing.

As a lifelong Marylander, I'm hurt, disappointed and disillusioned by what happened. I expect better results in a state with monopolistic Democratic control. Marriage equality isn't some bizarre, threatening or abstract concept. It's a reality in a growing list of countries around the world. It's a reality in five U.S. states. I can hop on the MARC train and get married in neighboring D.C.

As Maryland's Attorney General Douglas Gansler has said, marriage equality is inevitable in all 50 states. We know the work that lies ahead and so we must pick ourselves up and get on with it with a renewed sense of urgency and passion.

"What's wrong with Maryland's gays?," April 7, 2011

Many of us are searching for answers following the Maryland Legislature's breathtaking failure to pass marriage equality and its similar bungling of a bill to bar discrimination based on gender identity in the session that adjourns Monday.

Both initiatives had strong support and seemed destined to pass this year. But both were undermined by a combination of factors — soft Democratic support, anti-gay Black pastors, inadequate lobbying. Unfortunately, this will end in the search for a convenient scapegoat, most likely Morgan Meneses-Sheets, executive director of Equality Maryland.

To be sure, Meneses-Sheets made some mistakes, but the blame for this failure does not fall on her shoulders alone and it would be a mistake to fire her and declare the problem solved.

There is no easy fix for what hampers Maryland's efforts at achieving equal rights for its LGBT residents. The root cause of all the disarray and missed opportunities is the general apathy of Maryland's LGBT community and the lack of activist and donor presence in the state.

Maryland remains the country's wealthiest state, according to Census Bureau data released in December. Maryland's median household income is about $70,000 — much more than the nationwide median of about $51,400 — and the state ranks #2 for the most millionaires in the country, about 150,000. That means more than 6 percent of the state's population boasts liquid assets in excess of $1 million, according to a 2010 report by Phoenix Marketing International.

Yet, despite all that wealth, the state's LGBT advocacy group is chronically underfunded. Equality Maryland is on its third executive director in nearly as many years, its staff is small and board turnover unacceptably high.

When the Senate committee assignments were abruptly shifted in January and suddenly enough votes existed to move the marriage bill to the floor, Equality Maryland faced an impossible task: lobby for passage of a controversial, hot button issue in a matter of weeks with a small staff and insufficient resources. Adding to the challenge was the fact that so many members of the House of Delegates were newly elected and had never before faced the onslaught of media attention, religion-based attacks and constituent response that so often accompany the debate over marriage equality. So Equality Maryland had the resources to count the votes, but it didn't have the staffing required to maintain that support and hold nervous hands throughout the process.

In perhaps the most egregious case of betrayal in the House, Del. Melvin Stukes (D-Baltimore City) withdrew his sponsorship of the bill. Stukes told the Baltimore Sun he thought the bill would have given same-sex couples the right to obtain civil unions rather than marriage rights, an absurd claim for a sponsor to make. When he realized the measure would allow gays to marry he determined he made a mistake, he told the Sun.

"I'm very sorry that I got on the bill," he said.

Stukes represents arguably the "gayest" neighborhood in Baltimore — Bolton Hill, home to many well-to-do gays living in expensive, historic townhomes.

Activists said privately that they were baffled over Stukes' change of heart on the bill because the majority of his constituents would not object to his support for marriage equality. But the silence from those constituents is deafening — no protests, no calls for his resignation.

Imagine a similar scenario unfolding in D.C. If Council member Jack Evans, for example, had flip-flopped during D.C.'s marriage debate and opposed the bill, the outcry would have been earth shaking and his political career wouldn't have survived. But in Maryland, in the gayest neighborhood in Baltimore, such behavior is tolerated and politicians know they can sell us out with impunity.

The general apathy that afflicts Maryland's LGBT residents creates problems large and small. In D.C., for example, the Washington Nationals baseball team has hosted an appreciation night for gay fans for several years. A gay person throws out the first pitch, the Gay Men's Chorus sings the National Anthem, LGBT fans are recognized on the JumboTron and the event draws between 2,000 and 3,000 fans to the ballpark. The Baltimore Orioles have never hosted a similar event. And remember that Baltimore is a larger city by population and geography than D.C. and its baseball team has been around a lot longer than the Nats.

If Maryland is to catch up to other "blue" states and enact marriage equality and bar discrimination based on gender identity, its LGBT residents will need to get visible, donate money, protest, lobby and demand equal rights. As long as residents quietly assume that someone else is doing the heavy lifting, the outcome in Annapolis will remain stubbornly the same.

"Time for Obama to evolve," June 21, 2011

Less than a year after I wrote this column urging President Obama to publicly endorse marriage equality, he did just that in a televised interview. (More on that problematic interview later.) Many LGBTQ advocates thought it best that Obama wait until after the election to make this announcement, but as I argue here, there was no need to wait. And he didn't wait, and then trounced Mitt Romney to win a second term, becoming the first presidential candidate to win while publicly supporting marriage equality.

It's been painful to watch various White House spokespeople over the past week twist themselves into knots trying to explain President Obama's flip-flop on marriage equality.

In 1996, while running for a seat in the Illinois state Senate, Obama stated in a written questionnaire that he supports same-sex marriage. Obama wrote, "I favor legalizing same-sex marriages, and would fight efforts to prohibit such marriages."

That infamous questionnaire has haunted him ever since and re-emerged this week as a series of spokespeople tried to minimize its importance.

First up was White House Communications Director Dan Pfeiffer, who didn't do such a good job of communicating while speaking at Netroots Nation in Minneapolis.

He suggested the questionnaire response was not written by Obama, asserting that the survey, "was actually filled out by someone else, not the president."

Then Shin Inouye, a White House spokesperson, issued a statement clarifying that Pfeiffer "was not familiar with the history of the questionnaire."

Finally, White House Press Secretary Jay Carney was drawn into the dispute under questioning from the Blade's Chris Johnson. Carney said that Pfeiffer was mistaken and was referring to some other, unnamed questionnaire during his Netroots remarks.

Meanwhile, with the president headed to New York this week for a first-of-its-kind 2012 campaign fundraiser with the LGBT community, some are demanding that Obama endorse marriage equality in exchange for all the gay money about to flow his way.

Add to the equation the fact that it's Pride month and the New York Legislature is debating a marriage rights bill this week and we have arrived at the perfect storm of events and timing. Obama should take advantage of the serendipity and finally say publicly what we all know he believes privately: that same-sex couples deserve the same rights as Anthony Weiner, Newt Gingrich, Arnold Schwarzenegger, Bill Clinton and all the other cheaters and hypocritical scumbags out there.

There's no point in waiting for a reelection victory to announce support for marriage equality. The people who would vote against Obama for his views on marriage rights aren't going to support him anyway. A slight majority of the country now supports marriage equality, according to recent polls. And, with the economy continuing its stubborn slide, the 2012 election will not be won or lost on social issues.

In addition, Obama's refusal to evolve on the issue gives cover to our opponents on the right, who routinely cite the president's opposition to marriage equality in state fights from California to New York to Maryland.

The idea that Obama can't quite get there on marriage is absurd, given that his own administration won't defend the Defense of Marriage Act in court. That move has forced the hand of House Republicans, who are scrambling to find the money to pay for a pricey private attorney to continue the fight for discrimination. Make no mistake that the Republicans don't want to carry on that fight too publicly for too long. They know that marriage is a losing issue for them — advocating anti-gay discrimination doesn't play with the independent voters who decide elections. And as more and more prominent Republicans endorse marriage equality, it's only a matter of time before the party will have to abandon its anti-gay platform language.

Unfortunately, the tactics of marriage equality activists don't always help. Last week at Netroots Nation, former Army officer Dan Choi tore up an Obama campaign pamphlet and flung the pieces at a volunteer during a panel discussion. The melodramatic outburst minimizes the myriad accomplishments of Obama's administration, from repealing "Don't Ask, Don't Tell" to declaring DOMA unconstitutional. Sometimes there's a fine line between advocacy and grandstanding. There are more effective ways to push Obama on marriage than to attack and embarrass low-level campaign volunteers.

The upside to all the mainstream media attention now being focused on Obama's marriage views is that by the next presidential election, it will be untenable for a Democratic presidential nominee to oppose marriage equality. Better to be on the right side of history and consistent with that 1996 questionnaire than to continue playing this silly game.

Come on, Mr. President, we know where you stand. Just say it out loud.

"Biden Releases the Marriage Genie," May 8, 2012

We may never know if then-Vice President Biden intended to endorse marriage equality ahead of his boss or whether he unintentionally stumbled into it during an interview on "Meet the Press." I remember watching it live and doing a double take when he made those stunning remarks. Whatever the circumstances, that interview changed everything. Days later, President Obama endorsed marriage rights for same-sex couples in an interview with Robin Roberts. I was angry that Obama gave her the interview, given she was closeted at the time. Roberts did eventually come out publicly, but she did not deserve that Obama interview. It should have gone to an out journalist like Anderson Cooper, Rachel Maddow — or better yet, me.

President Obama and Vice President Biden are an amusing study in contrasts. Obama is deliberate, contemplative and takes his time to evaluate an issue or problem before venturing a solution. Biden, meanwhile, wears his heart on his sleeve and frequently finds himself in trouble for talking out of turn.

So it was on Sunday, when Biden appeared to endorse marriage equality during an interview on "Meet the Press."

"I am absolutely comfortable with the fact that men marrying men, women marrying women and heterosexual men marrying women are entitled to the same exact rights," Biden said. "All the civil rights, all the civil liberties. And quite frankly I don't see much of a distinction beyond that."

But Biden did something that most reluctantly supportive Democrats refuse to do and spoke eloquently about our love and relationships, rather than deliver the usual legalistic "civil rights" argument.

"As more and more Americans come to understand what this is all about, it's a simple proposition: Who do you love? Who do you love and will you be loyal to the person you love?"

It's the sort of basic, root argument that we don't hear nearly enough of from our allies. Sen. Ted Kennedy articulated similar sentiments during the debate over the Federal Marriage Amendment, but very few Democratic supporters get it the way Biden does. It's not just about accessing a laundry list of rights, it's about something much more important: societal respect and equality for our relationships.

The administration's lame attempts at minimizing Biden's statements were laughable.

Immediately after the interview ended, a Biden spokesperson released a statement. "The Vice President was saying what the President has said previously — that committed and loving same-sex couples deserve the same rights and protections enjoyed by all Americans, and that we oppose any effort to rollback those rights," the spokesperson said.

Obama campaign strategist David Axelrod then tweeted, "What VP said — that all married couples should have exactly the same legal rights — is precisely POTUS' position."

Then on Monday came a news conference in which Axelrod said, "I think that they were entirely consistent with the president's position, which is that couples who are married — whether gay or heterosexual couples — are entitled to the very same rights and very same liberties."

Also Monday, White House press secretary Jay Carney found himself in the unenviable position of defending Obama's confounding position. Only this time, it wasn't just members of the LGBT press asking the questions, but a full-court press by the mainstream members of the White House press corps demanding answers.

The problem with all the backpedaling and spinning is that Obama doesn't publicly support the "very same liberties" for all — apparently he only supports rights for couples living in a handful of states where same-sex marriage is legal. That's not equality. It's splitting hairs and after Biden's remarks, Obama's position is exposed as absurd and unsustainable.

Gay rights advocates have been pushing Obama to complete his "evolution" on marriage before the November election. Like Maryland Gov. Martin O'Malley, who recently revealed that he was privately supportive of marriage before finding the courage to say so publicly, Obama's announcement is just a matter of time. His campaign strategists clearly think the timing — just before an election — is risky and wrong. The polls show a contest between Mitt Romney and Obama will be close.

But after Biden's interview and the uncharacteristically sloppy response by the White House, it's time for Obama to stop this embarrassing charade and say what he means. And if Romney attacks him for it, Obama can remind everyone that he's merely catching up with Dick Cheney and Ken Mehlman. This election won't be about marriage and a growing number of Americans support equality anyway.

The dominoes are falling, the genie is released: Obama's own education secretary, Arne Duncan, announced Monday his support for marriage equality. Hillary Clinton and other members of the cabinet can't be far behind. It's too late for Obama to lead on this issue, but how far behind will he follow?

"OBAMA'S MARRIAGE BOMBSHELL," MAY 9, 2012

President Obama shocked the political establishment this week by completing his 19-month "evolution" and publicly endorsing marriage equality.

"I have to tell you that over the course of several years as I have talked to friends and family and neighbors when I think about members of my own staff who are in incredibly committed monogamous relationships, same-sex relationships, who are raising kids together, when I think about those soldiers or airmen or marines or sailors who are out there fighting on my behalf and yet feel constrained, even now that 'Don't Ask Don't Tell' is gone, because they are not able to commit themselves in a marriage, at a certain point I've just concluded that for me personally it is important for me to go ahead and affirm that I think same-sex couples should be able to get married." (Obama made the remarks to ABC News' Robin Roberts, an interesting choice for the interview given she has long battled rumors of being a closeted lesbian.)

It was a bold statement for Obama to make during what will undoubtedly be a close general election contest against Mitt Romney. But bold leadership is what we should expect from our elected officials. Romney can't decide whether to wear jeans or roll up his sleeves during campaign stops without consulting a pollster. Obama's brave decision this week again exposes Romney for the weak, unprincipled flip-flopper that even the most loyal Republican voters know him to be.

Yes, Obama should have done it sooner — preferably before North Carolina voters decided Tuesday to enshrine discrimination in their constitution. He shouldn't have let his own vice president and Cabinet members get in front of him on the issue. And this surely wasn't planned. Vice President Joe Biden's unexpected marriage endorsement on Sunday, followed by all the laughable efforts at damage control by the campaign and the White House press secretary forced Obama's hand.

But none of that matters now. For the first time, we have a sitting president unafraid to say publicly what we all assumed he believed privately — that same-sex couples deserve the rights of marriage. Kudos to Obama for not waiting until after the election — or until after he leaves office — to make this announcement. Too many public officials, including President Clinton and Vice President Dick Cheney, have waited until they left office to announce their support of marriage equality. Not exactly profiles in courage. But Obama is different. He's deliberate and contemplative and, yes, he sometimes takes awhile to make a decision, but once it's made he communicates and leads. That's what a president ought to do.

And now politicians from both parties can point to Obama's precedent-setting leadership and announce their own support. Can Hillary Clinton and other sitting Cabinet members be far behind? Obama's announcement will inspire others who have remained quiet allies to come out in full support of LGBT equality.

Obama's decision certainly means that support for marriage equality will become the default position of Democratic presidential nominees going forward. Who could have foreseen this moment just 20 years ago? President Clinton signed the Defense of Marriage Act and bragged about it in campaign radio ads. John Kerry, John Edwards, Hillary Clinton and other Democratic contenders took gay money and votes while cynically delivering nothing more than lip service to our issues. President Bush used marriage as a wedge issue in 2004 and called for a federal constitutional amendment banning same-sex marriage in his State of the Union address. Then Obama came along and promised change and boy did he deliver this week.

But let's not be lulled into complacency by this historic moment. It's not the end of the road for the LGBT movement, but rather a promising new beginning. This question of will-he-or-won't-he has sucked too much oxygen from the movement and so we must now move on to other pressing issues, like barring discrimination against LGBT workers in both the public and private sectors. Not everyone wants to get married, but everyone has to work. Obama should sign an executive order barring workplace bias against LGBT employees of federal contractors. And Congress needs to revive the Employment Non-Discrimination Act, which has languished since the 1970s.

The road ahead is long, but the LGBT movement took a huge leap forward this week. LGBT voters should line up and fight to ensure President Obama's reelection.

"Defending decision to publish names of Md. marriage opponents," Aug. 21, 2012

In 2012, opponents of marriage equality in Maryland rounded up enough petition signatures to force the law onto the ballot, effectively subjecting our right to marry to a majority vote of the public. We came into possession of a database of all those Maryland residents who signed the petition. My decision to publish the database to the Blade's website created a storm of controversy, with angry criticism from the left and right. The Family Research Council's Tony Perkins denounced us, as did a prominent transgender rights advocate. But privately, many friends and Blade readers confided their gratitude. LGBTQ Marylanders all over the state were frantically searching the database to see if their parents, friends, bosses, neighbors had signed a petition to revoke their right to marry. Many discovered that their loved ones had signed; that database created rifts in many Maryland families. But it was the right decision; it shined a bright light on bigotry and it enabled LGBTQ Marylanders to engage with their loved ones, who could no longer hide their bigotry. Months later, the ballot initiative was defeated and gay couples in Maryland could marry.

The Blade earlier this month posted online a database of more than 100,000 names and addresses of Maryland residents who signed a petition to force the state's marriage equality law onto the November ballot.

Our decision to post the database was immediately criticized by voices on the far right — and far left.

Monica Johnson, an evangelical writer for the Examiner newspaper, accused us of using "intimidation tactics," writing, "will they take responsibility in the event that someone uses this information for evil purposes, or will they defer to their right to publish the information as a good enough reason?"

Right-wing homophobe Matt Barber accused us of "homo terrorism." Family Research Council's Tony Perkins tweeted, "@

WashingtonBlade's decision to publish the names of those who signed MD's marriage amendment petition is nothing short of intimidation."

Meanwhile, on the other side of the political spectrum, transgender rights activist Dana Beyer told gay magazine Metro Weekly that the decision to post the names was unwise. "Given what the coalition has stated, that they don't want to muddy the message, this does not help," she said. "You now have an interested third party, the Blade, releasing those names and potentially muddying the message."

Critics of the decision made for strange bedfellows indeed. The only "intimidation" I've seen has come in the form of threats the Blade has received in phone calls to our office and emails to staff warning "I know where your at!"

Of course, it's not our job to keep the message from being "muddied." The occasional coziness between LGBT activists and journalists sometimes results in confusion about our role, but to be clear, the Blade employs journalists and not activists — or even "journo activists." Our job is to shine a light on the truth; sunshine is the best antiseptic.

As Andrew Sullivan put it in defending our decision: "Some argue that this is a tool for intimidation or a violation of privacy. I'm afraid I cannot see that. Signing a political petition is a public act. If you are ashamed of trying to deny your fellow citizens their civil rights, you probably shouldn't have signed the petition in the first place."

The database of names in question was verified and compiled using public money. Taxpayers have a right to know how their money is being spent and, as Sullivan rightly notes, signing a petition to take away rights from a class of people is a public act. We don't allow our lawmakers to take their votes in secret and similarly we shouldn't tolerate secrecy in the petition process, which is being used more and more in Maryland and elsewhere to circumvent the legislature. In essence, those petition signers are acting as legislators and as such their names must be open to public scrutiny. It's mind-boggling that

LGBT rights supporters would advocate for a shadowy, opaque political process.

Kevin Nix, a spokesperson for Marylanders for Marriage Equality, the coalition fighting to preserve the marriage law, said he doesn't condone our decision to publish the names. If he were more strategic in his thinking, he'd embrace this as an opportunity to engage with some of those 100,000 people to change hearts and minds before the November vote. The database is sorted by neighborhood — among other criteria — enabling the Marylanders for Marriage Equality coalition to see exactly where the highest concentrations of our opponents live. They should be thanking us for this tool rather than publicly criticizing the Blade.

Luckily, there are many average LGBT Marylanders who understand that this database presents us with an opportunity to engage with our loved ones who signed the petition. I have heard from multiple friends and even one openly gay elected official that upon searching the database they discovered family members and neighbors had signed. They are now actively reaching out to them to explain the law and how it helps our families in hopes that those petition signers don't turn into votes against our equality.

Some have asked if the shooting last week at the Family Research Council headquarters allegedly by a man who volunteered at the DC Center for the LGBT Community would have changed our decision to publish. The answer is no. That isolated incident was a tragic aberration and not indicative of the mindset of the LGBT community. We have been the victims of violence long enough to know that violence is not the way to resolve political disagreements.

The best way to counter the hate — and, yes, the Family Research Council is a hate group — of the far right is with truth and an open dialogue. We should all fight to ensure transparency in government, especially when our opponents are counting on secrecy and lack of accountability to hide their dirty deeds from public scrutiny.

"At Long Last, Equality in Maryland," Nov. 7, 2012

Any second-guessing that decision to publish the database of anti-marriage petition signatories disappeared after election night 2012, when Marylanders upheld marriage equality and the nation reelected Barack Obama just six months after he publicly endorsed marriage rights. It was one of the most joyous nights of my Blade tenure.

It was the biggest and busiest night in my 10 years at the Washington Blade: President Obama's reelection, Tammy Baldwin's Senate triumph, openly gay and bi candidates winning seats in Congress and the first-ever wins in state marriage ballot fights.

Amid the avalanche of unprecedented good news, my partner and I took a break to visit an election night party sponsored by Marylanders for Marriage Equality, which fought to uphold the state's marriage equality law. A lifelong Marylander, I scanned the crowd and saw so many familiar faces. Gay couples together for more than 20 years; other couples raising children; openly gay and lesbian members of our state legislature; past leaders of the state's LGBT rights group who toiled in obscurity for so long.

Gov. Martin O'Malley was there, too. Five years ago, when the Maryland Court of Appeals narrowly ruled against marriage rights for gay couples, I launched a tough campaign to hold Democrats like O'Malley accountable for their promises to our community. At the time, O'Malley said no one should be messing with the sacraments anyway and he denied his earlier public support for marriage equality. After the court's 4-3 ruling, I joined a group of demoralized LGBT activists in front of a supportive Baltimore church for a rally. We were called "faggots" and worse by passing motorists. Most people there cried, their hopes dashed and wedding plans canceled. It was a crushing defeat.

After a string of editorials criticizing the governor for his betrayal, he invited me to a meeting in his Annapolis office, which I agreed to attend only if it were on the record. There had been enough secret meetings and abandoned backroom promises. O'Malley was awkward and, like George W. Bush at the time, pointedly refused to even use the word "gay." He said he supported civil unions and cited his Catholic faith.

I left feeling even worse: This was a governor who had attracted a strong LGBT following and previously pledged support for civil marriage in an on-camera TV interview. But he changed his mind and there didn't seem to be much hope for a bill without his backing.

What I didn't fully realize then was that the genie was already out of the bottle. The brave and public stand of the Maryland lawsuit's plaintiffs had illustrated the diversity of our community and just how downright normal our struggles are. They told stories of raising kids without legal protections; losing a partner and the attendant tax burdens of dying single but owning a home and other property jointly; and the fears of entering a nursing home and being forced back into the closet in elder years. Those courageous plaintiffs planted the seed that sprouted this week into full state marriage rights for same-sex couples.

Their bravery emboldened gay and lesbian members of our state legislature to speak out more forcefully and inspired others like Del. Peter Murphy to come out publicly. Maryland boasts the most openly gay and lesbian members of a state legislature in the country and their visibility is what made it possible for the marriage bill ultimately to pass.

There are so many people responsible for the victory in Maryland this week that it's impossible to draft a complete list, but a few key names come to mind deserving of some credit: Lisa Polyak and Gita Deane; Charles Butler, Jon Kaplan, Dan Furmansky and other early leaders of Free State Justice and Equality Maryland; Patrick Wojahn,

Dave Kolesar and the rest of the 2006 lawsuit plaintiffs; Attorney General Doug Gansler for recognizing out-of-state marriages and for becoming the first statewide elected official to embrace the cause; HRC for stepping in this year when many national gay donors and other advocacy groups said Maryland was a lost cause; the openly gay and lesbian members of the state legislature; President Obama, Brendan Ayanbadejo and the NAACP for their support; and, yes, O'Malley for not only signing the bill into law but putting the weight of his administration behind its preservation.

Ultimately, the biggest thanks goes to average Maryland voters who saw through the recycled hate rhetoric from past campaigns against our rights in 32 other states. They were not fooled by fools like Derek McCoy, Emmett Burns, Tony Perkins and Harry Jackson who found out the hard way that appealing to voters' most base instincts no longer constitutes a winning strategy.

And, finally, a thank you to my partner, Brian, and my family, friends and colleagues for enduring years of my own rants, frustration and venting about Maryland. It's been a long road to this sweet destination and I look forward to a 2013 filled with the long-delayed weddings of so many friends. Congratulations Maryland, for living up to your "Free State" moniker.

"VICTORY, VINDICATION AND TEARS," JUNE 27, 2013

We wrote hundreds of stories over the years about the impact of the Defense of Marriage Act on LGBTQ couples. The Supreme Court's ruling that DOMA was unconstitutional marked a tremendous victory and yet another milestone toward equality under the law. I won an award from the Society of Professional Journalists for this piece, celebrating the end of DOMA.

For those of us old enough to remember the passage of the Defense of Marriage Act — and then-President Bill Clinton's craven boasting about it in Christian radio ads during the 1996 campaign — this week brought vindication, a victory unimaginable just a few years ago and more than a few tears of joy.

In a 5-4 ruling, the Supreme Court declared that DOMA "is unconstitutional as a deprivation of the liberty of the person protected by the Fifth Amendment of the Constitution."

Justice Anthony Kennedy added to his considerable pro-gay legacy penning the majority opinion joined by Justices Sonia Sotomayor, Ruth Bader Ginsburg, Elena Kagan and Stephen Breyer.

In it, Kennedy issues a bold, broad ruling and gets at the heart of the matter: the indignity that DOMA visited upon our relationships.

He writes, "DOMA instructs all federal officials, and indeed all persons with whom same-sex couples interact, including their own children, that their marriage is less worthy than the marriages of others. The federal statute is invalid, for no legitimate purpose overcomes the purpose and effect to disparage and to injure those whom the State, by its marriage laws, sought to protect in personhood and dignity. By seeking to displace this protection and treating those persons as living in marriages less respected than others, the federal statute is in violation of the Fifth Amendment."

It's a refreshing and honest take on the impact of DOMA, which has stigmatized gay and lesbian couples for 17 years and done real harm to our families. Kennedy's opinion at long last recognizes this basic fact. The stories of DOMA's impact on our community have formed the basis for literally hundreds of Blade stories over the years. Many of those stories involve serious life-changing consequences as in survivors like the courageous Edith Windsor facing financial ruin after the death of a partner. But those dark days are over. Kennedy touches on the broad reach of the decision in his opinion.

"By its great reach, DOMA touches many aspects of married and family life, from the mundane to the profound. It prevents same-sex married couples from obtaining government healthcare benefits they would otherwise receive. It deprives them of the Bankruptcy Code's special protections for domestic-support obligations. It forces them to follow a complicated procedure to file their state and federal taxes jointly.

"DOMA also brings financial harm to children of same-sex couples. It raises the cost of health care for families by taxing health benefits provided by employers to their workers' same-sex spouses. And it denies or reduces benefits allowed to families upon the loss of a spouse and parent, benefits that are an integral part of family security."

Kennedy rightly points out that the only reason DOMA came about was anti-gay animus.

"The history of DOMA's enactment and its own text demonstrate that interference with the equal dignity of same-sex marriages, a dignity conferred by the States in the exercise of their sovereign power, was more than an incidental effect of the federal statute. It was its essence."

More vindication for the scores of activists, lawyers, politicians, journalists, bloggers and everyday Americans who've been fighting this most odious of laws for nearly two decades.

In Justice Antonin Scalia's overwrought and predictably curmudgeonly dissent, he fears judicial overreach.

"It is an assertion of judicial supremacy over the people's Representatives in Congress and the Executive. It envisions a Supreme Court standing (or rather enthroned) at the apex of government, empowered to decide all constitutional questions, always and everywhere 'primary' in its role."

He goes on to say the question of same-sex marriage "should be resolved primarily at the state level."

That is now an open question, as same-sex couples in California rejoin the growing group of now 13 states and D.C. that have enacted marriage equality. Will a gay couple in Texas sue the government for marriage rights? Has Kennedy set the stage for a Loving v. Virginia-type showdown for the gay community?

Tantalizing questions for the future. For now, it's time to celebrate a victory nearly 20 years in the making.

"AFTER CAR CRASH, RETHINKING LIFE'S PRIORITIES," OCT. 1, 2014

This was a tough one. I have focused my work on news, analysis and solutions-oriented opinion writing, rather than the first-person spleen-venting and bloviating that are so common today. And so it was difficult to write about my car accident. And even more difficult to admit that after so many years of ranting about marriage rights and advance directives and equality under the law, that I didn't have any legal protections in place at the time of this car accident that could easily have killed me. I had one of those "a-ha moments" discussing this piece with a friend and longtime LGBTQ advocate in Maryland, Lisa Polyak, one of the key figures responsible for the state's marriage law. She told me that she, too, had neglected securing these legal protections and realized it was because deep down we didn't really believe we were worthy of them. That we were so conditioned to believe in our own second-class status that even the most outspoken among us were suffering from an internalized homophobia. It was a disturbing revelation that I have since worked hard to overcome. Prior to the accident, Brian and I had been planning a rather extravagant wedding at the Four Seasons in Baltimore, with a ballooning guest list and all the usual trappings of a ceremony. After the accident, we couldn't imagine spending all that money on a ceremony. I received an email advertising an all-gay, 11-day cruise from Singapore to Hong Kong and called Brian at work. I said I'd rather use the money from the wedding for that trip and he agreed. I warned him that I was serious. When we hung up, I booked the trip and we scaled back our extravagant wedding to a simple ceremony on the beach in Rehoboth with three friends as witnesses and a gay justice of the peace presiding. The whole thing cost $75. I can't say all of our family members approved, but it was just the right vibe for us at the time, my face still severely bruised from the accident and surgery. Part of me wishes we could have had the big showy wedding. But looking back, it was a perfect moment on the beach in the town we love. And a reminder that weddings should be about the couple and not the expectations of others.

Here's the thing about being rushed to the hospital on a backboard and neck brace, covered in blood: It'll change your perspective on what's important.

On Aug. 26, I had just hailed a taxicab with a friend headed to gay night at Camden Yards in Baltimore to watch the Orioles close in on the AL East crown, when another driver ran a red light at full speed. We didn't have time to fasten our seatbelts. He T-boned us, sending the sturdy Crown Vic over a curb, through a lamppost and ultimately into a rowhouse where we smashed through ground floor windows before finally coming to a stop.

My friend, the driver and I all walked away from the car. Looking back at photos of the wreckage, it's miraculous that no one was killed. The cab driver had the benefit of airbags and suffered cuts to his face; my friend suffered a broken thumb and bruised ribs. It turns out while I was fine from the neck down, my face took the brunt of the crash. (I hesitate to use the word "accident," because when you drive in a distracted manner at full speed and sail through red lights, what do you expect will happen?)

Shock and adrenaline kicked in immediately after the crash, as my initial thought was: We're gonna need a new cab. Then something dripped into my eye and when I wiped my face, it dawned on me that I was bleeding profusely.

I broke several bones in my face, including the orbital around the left eye, and sustained a slew of deep cuts to my face that required so many stitches the ER doctors "lost count."

Strapped to a stretcher, I was rushed to the ER as hospital officials greeted me with a slew of questions: "Are you married?" "Do you have an advance medical directive?"

I'm embarrassed to say the answer to both was "no," despite a nearly 17-year relationship with my partner. We always seemed to have an excuse for putting off getting those affairs in order. When you're healthy and (relatively) young, it's so easy to procrastinate such things. Over the years, I've written about countless gay couples that found themselves in financially desperate situations after illness or accident because they weren't married or lacked a medical directive. I've editorialized about the importance of marriage and other protections for LGBT people yet never got around to taking care of it for myself.

Lying there immobile and awaiting CT scans and X-rays with hospital staff buzzing frantically around, I felt like a hypocrite and worried about what would happen to my partner and family if I should die.

Two weeks later, doctors determined that I needed surgery to implant a titanium plate in my head to realign the bones. One of the broken bones severed a nerve, leaving me with no feeling on the left side of my face; my doctor gave me a 75 percent chance of regaining feeling there within nine to 12 months. And faced with hours of general anesthesia, more facial trauma and another long period of recovery, those mortality issues came rushing back. Upon check-in at the hospital, those same questions about marriage and advance directives were again asked.

I'm fortunate to have had terrific care at Sinai Hospital, a supportive partner, parents, siblings and friends. After a five-week ordeal, I'm on the mend, though facing much uncertainty about long-term vision problems and the potentially permanent nerve damage, as well as facial scars. But the scars don't bother me. I'm grateful to be alive, to be able to walk and to have my vision. And I'm grateful for a second chance at so many things, including taking a more responsible approach to mortality and long-term financial planning.

Last weekend, my partner and I were married. We'd spent more than a year debating the details of the ceremony, the reception, guest list — all the details that seem so important on that all-important day.

In the end, we realized our wedding risked becoming more about those materialistic considerations and the expectations of others than about what we really wanted. And so, on Sept. 26 — exactly one month after the crash — we met the clerk of the peace on a quiet stretch of Rehoboth Beach under a flawless fall sky and exchanged simple vows, the bit about "in sickness and in health" carrying a special and deeper new meaning. It wasn't the wedding of most couples' dreams — we were barefoot and I wore sunglasses to conceal the extensive bruising around my eye — yet there was perfection in the simplicity of the setting and an overwhelming sense of gratitude to finally join an institution we'd been excluded from for so long. There was no guest list. No fancy reception or band or cake or any of those usual trappings. Just two people on a quiet beach committing to a life together.

"Marriage is a bond between two people who have pledged to love each other, trust each other and face life together," said the Sussex County clerk of the peace, John Brady. "There is no relationship that is stronger, yet more delicate, than the bonds of marriage."

So we're facing life together with a fresh point of view — and working on that advance medical directive. Take it from me: You're not invincible or immune to life's curve balls. There's no guarantee that the hospital staff will recognize your partner as next of kin. Do all you can to protect yourself and loved ones now; it'll save you a lot of added guilt and stress in the ER.

"O'MALLEY'S AMNESIA ON MARRIAGE," APRIL 20, 2015

Imagine my surprise when during the 2016 presidential campaign, this piece wound up in the infamous WikiLeaks dump of Hillary Clinton's emails. Apparently, her senior campaign staff appreciated my takedown of Martin O'Malley (then a candidate for the Democratic presidential nomination) and his inane flip-flopping on marriage equality over the years, and circulated this piece via email to other campaign staff. It was among the emails that Julian Assange's WikiLeaks dumped online in an effort to smear Clinton and other democrats and to assist Donald Trump's campaign.

There he goes again. Former Maryland Gov. Martin O'Malley, who once extolled the virtues of centrism, now wants us to believe — in an unintentionally hilarious rewriting of history — that he's more liberal than Hillary Clinton and a "profile in courage" when it comes to fighting for marriage equality.

In a not-so-subtle jab at Clinton, O'Malley in a February speech said, "History celebrates profiles in courage, not profiles in convenience. The dignity of every person tells us that the right to marry is not a state right, it is a human right."

A Clinton aide last week, responding to a Blade inquiry, affirmed that the 2016 hopeful views same-sex marriage as a constitutional right. That statement marked a change from her earlier position, articulated in an infamous NPR interview last year, that she viewed marriage as a state issue.

Clinton, like President Obama and Martin O'Malley and many others, evolved on the issue.

The problem with O'Malley is that he's had more positions on marriage than all the 2016 hopefuls combined. And after pushing for civil unions right up until 2011, he now wants voters to believe that he's a pioneer on the issue. What nerve!

Let's revisit O'Malley's actual record rather than listen to his calculated amnesia.

In 2004, O'Malley told a Baltimore TV station, "I'm not opposed to civil marriages." Also that year, he emailed a plaintiff in the state marriage lawsuit that read, "I'm just supporting something I strongly believe in," referring to marriage equality. But by 2006, O'Malley's position was shifting and he said, "I was raised to believe that marriage is between a man and a woman. This is a fundamental issue of the state's public policy, and a decision that ultimately should not be made by a single trial court judge." When confronted by gay activists after issuing that statement, O'Malley disavowed any previous support of marriage equality.

After a 2007 Maryland court ruling limiting marriage to opposite-sex couples, O'Malley issued the following statement as heartbroken gay residents were busy cancelling their weddings and mourning the court's misguided decision: "I look forward to reading the court's full opinion, but as we move forward, those of us with the responsibility of passing and enforcing laws have an obligation to protect the rights of all individuals equally, without telling any faith how to define its sacraments. I respect the court's decision."

Privately, O'Malley had assured gay rights activists and plaintiffs in the case that he supported marriage equality, only to reverse course and ultimately invoke his Catholic religious beliefs to justify his support of discrimination.

From 2008-2010, O'Malley publicly backed civil unions as bills to legalize marriage equality were defeated in committee. He was even booed off the stage at a private LGBT donor gathering after advocating for civil unions over full marriage rights.

In 2011, O'Malley finally said he would sign a marriage bill if passed. "I have concluded that discriminating against individuals based on their sexual orientation in the context of civil marital rights is unjust." That bill ultimately failed.

It wasn't until New York Gov. Andrew Cuomo embraced the cause of marriage equality as a civil rights issue — and well after

Maryland Attorney General Doug Gansler did the same — that O'Malley evolved yet again. Whereas Cuomo made it clear even before he was elected that he supported full marriage rights and then lobbied for the needed votes to pass it, O'Malley was — until 2012 —the reluctant advocate, offering meek, private assurances of support but refusing to publicly embrace the cause, even after winning a second term in a landslide.

Though he eventually came around to full support and was instrumental in preserving the law after it went to referendum, O'Malley was late to the marriage party and certainly doesn't deserve credit for its success.

O'Malley has, for years, embodied the poll-driven milquetoast politician who checks the wind before staking out a position. Now he wants us to believe otherwise.

"We have the ability as a party to lead by our principles or are we going to conduct polls every time we try to determine where the middle is on any given day," he told NPR this week.

We should welcome O'Malley's more progressive positions without forgetting his disappointing record of saying one thing in private and the opposite when the cameras are rolling.

"A COUNTRY BATHED IN RAINBOW LIGHT," JULY 1, 2015

This essay followed the earth-shattering ruling by the Supreme Court that established marriage equality in all 50 states, something I never dreamed I'd see. I cried when the ruling was announced and was brought to tears again when President Obama had the White House illuminated in rainbow colors. A truly surreal, mind-boggling and beautiful sight. As Oprah says, some dreams are so big that you never even imagined them for yourself. That's why I always tell younger generations never to be limited by even your imagination. Our country may be imperfect and slow to change, but when it comes, look out, because truly anything is possible.

Words seemed inadequate at the news that the U.S. Supreme Court legalized same-sex marriage in all 50 states last week. The images of that day were overwhelming — couples celebrating, James Obergefell standing on the steps of the court and the ultimate: the White House lit up in rainbow colors.

Who could have imagined such a scene 10 years ago when President Bush was cruelly and cynically running his reelection campaign on our backs?

But that feels like an eternity ago, a time when Democrats supported us privately but almost never in public. When a closeted Ken Mehlman pushed constitutional amendments in key battleground states to ban same-sex marriage and drive out conservative voters. When brave soldiers served from the closet.

And then came President Obama. No matter what you think of him or his policies on other issues, Obama's push for LGBT equality will likely rank as his second biggest achievement and key part of his legacy, right after healthcare reform.

Obama has eloquently stood up to the hypocrites in his own party, to our opponents in the Republican Party and to the critics in the Black church to push for equality. He publicly endorsed marriage equality before the 2012 election, when even LGBT advocates were privately hoping he'd wait until after Election Day to do so.

Of course, he didn't do it alone. Last week's victory was the culmination of a decades-long struggle pioneered by many brave and patient souls, including Evan Wolfson and Andrew Sullivan, among many others. But the real credit goes to everyday LGBT people who waged their own private and often thankless and difficult battles to come out and live honest lives. Forcing the world to see us as we are and not as hateful stereotypes is what ultimately enabled a sitting president to support us so openly. We must never forget the sacrifice of a generation of gay men who did not live to celebrate last week, who suffered and died while an indifferent government looked the other way. The AIDS epidemic forced many of us out of the closet and taught the survivors how to organize and fight effectively. The impact of the epidemic on last week's victory can't be overstated.

And now we must continue the fight and capitalize on the momentum of the moment. In too many states, you can still be fired for being gay or transgender. You can be denied housing or credit. Our youth are bullied and suffer disproportionately from homelessness. The transgender community suffers disproportionately from violence and unemployment. Too many young gay men, particularly men of color, are contracting HIV. Our LGBT elders are too often forced back into the closet.

We should continue pushing for comprehensive civil rights protections so that LGBT employees can be judged on their competence and not their sexual orientation or gender identity at work. And we must fight back against so-called religious freedom bills. The fact remains that 40 percent of Americans in recent polls remain opposed to our right to wed. That number will continue to fall, but judging from reactions on the right, we have much more work ahead in convincing fellow Americans that we deserve equality of opportunity.

And we shouldn't be shy about it. The right is wrong when it comes to LGBT issues and we should tell them so. In a recent Fox News piece, Howard Kurtz claims the media owe anti-gay voices "tolerance." Bollocks. The hate mongers of the right had their day and it's mercifully over. A new generation and era have arrived and there's no need to apologize for it. LGBT people have suffered long enough and have earned the right to celebrate and to see the country we love bathed in rainbow light.

"Marriage bill ceremony a full-circle moment after 20 years at the Blade," Dec. 23, 2022

The headline says it all — the very week I was commemorating 20 years at the Blade, I attended the White House signing ceremony for the Respect for Marriage Act. It was held outside on the South Lawn on a chilly but sunny, beautiful December afternoon. Sam Smith performed along with Cyndi Lauper. What a thrill it was to be back on White House grounds after four years in the cold during the Trump administration.

The one cloud over the day, as I reported in this piece, was the homophobia spewed by several mainstream still photographers who were stationed on risers overlooking the crowd on the White House lawn. They mocked and ridiculed guests and performers throughout the day, using anti-gay slurs and it was all overheard by two of my staffers. Unfortunately, my employees didn't record the comments or get the names of those involved but I filed a complaint with the White House Correspondents' Association and the White House upon hearing about it. We'll see if anything comes of it. Two steps forward and two steps back, I guess. Just further proof that increased rights and protections under the law don't necessarily come with increased acceptance. It's yet another reminder that we must remain vigilant because our enemies are all around us — even on the White House grounds as the president is signing the marriage bill into law.

Last week's White House ceremony in which President Biden signed the Respect for Marriage Act in front of hundreds of LGBTQ activists from around the country was a historic, surreal, full-circle moment for me after 20 years at the Washington Blade.

It was a moving walk down memory lane making my way across the White House lawn, greeting longtime activists and politicos, many of whom have retired or moved on from LGBTQ activism. It reminded me of my first White House event — President Obama's 2009 Pride reception and all the unfinished business at that time. What a thrill to be around to witness history as President Biden, who famously leapfrogged his old boss Obama in endorsing marriage equality, signed the bill codifying federal recognition of interracial and same-sex marriages.

When I joined the Blade in December of 2002, marriage equality didn't exist and almost no one was talking about the possibility. George W. Bush was president and busy trying to ban recognition of our relationships in the Constitution. Fast-forward 20 years and the progress is truly breathtaking — inclusion of sexual orientation and gender identity in the federal hate crimes law, repeal of "Don't Ask, Don't Tell," the Bostock ruling boosting employment protections, marriage equality in all 50 states, electing the first Black president and first woman vice president, and so much more.

Amid the celebrations last week were reminders of the work ahead.

"When a person can be married in the morning and thrown out of a restaurant in the afternoon, this is still wrong," said Biden. "We must stop the hate and violence."

To address the ongoing issue of workplace and other discrimination, we still need Congress to pass the Equality Act, which ended up stranded in the Senate. The measure is surely DOA with Republicans taking control of the House next month.

There are other problems that surfaced last week, ironically on the White House South Lawn just feet away from where Biden was making history. Several mainstream media photographers were overheard using anti-gay slurs at the ceremony. Two Washington Blade contributors who were on — and adjacent to — the risers where video and still photographers were stationed on the White House lawn overheard a stream of slurs and invective directed at guests and performers.

The brazen nerve of these photographers to traffic in anti-gay slurs while covering President Biden's historic signing of the marriage bill is shocking and repulsive. Their behavior disrespects not just the LGBTQ community and the president, but the hard work by countless advocates over 20 years to arrive at this moment. It should have been a moment of celebration and joy but it was marred by the blatant, overt homophobia of a few bad apples.

Editors at mainstream outlets should investigate and compel their staffs to take sensitivity training or be fired.

That incident notwithstanding, the ceremony marked an important milestone that so many of us fought for over 20 years, enduring disappointing court rulings and election results and other setbacks to arrive at this moment and witness the president validate our unions joined by Vice President Kamala Harris, House Speaker Nancy Pelosi and Senate Majority Leader Chuck Schumer.

Harris delivered a powerful speech emphasizing the interconnectivity of the moment. She said the Supreme Court's Dobbs decision is a reminder that "fundamental rights are interconnected, including the right to marry who you love, the right to access contraception, and the right to make decisions about your own body."

Biden noted Congress passed the Respect for Marriage Act "because an extreme Supreme Court has stripped away the right important to millions of Americans that existed for half a century."

Indeed the Dobbs decision brought a renewed sense of urgency to passing the Respect for Marriage Act after Justice Clarence Thomas expressed a desire to revisit the Obergefell ruling in his concurring opinion in Dobbs.

It was a beautiful, sunny day featuring uplifting performances, insightful speeches and emotional tributes. We should enjoy this moment as we prepare to gather for the holidays. Then we should return in 2023 ready for the battles ahead to protect and expand on our many victories.

CHAPTER 2

POP CULTURE

"Everybody comes to Hollywood ... how could it hurt you when it looks so good?"
— Madonna

"Janet Jackson talks new album, same-sex marriage — and Madonna," Sept. 29, 2006

My love of Janet is well known and goes back to the '80s. I have interviewed her three times for the Blade over the years. I became friendly with her former publicist, Patti Webster, after writing very nice things about Janet in the Blade. Patti once called me and excitedly said, "Hey Kevin, it's Patti, I have a surprise for you — Madison Square Garden, 14th row on the floor!" I responded, "Thanks, Patti, but I already have seventh row." She called me a week before Janet's ninth album "20 Y.O." was being released and offered me the first interview with Janet on the morning of the album's launch. "Let me check my schedule," I joked. When I talked to Janet the following week, I got up at 5 a.m. to download the album and listen to each track before the interview. Janet was right on time, as always, and professional as ever. I wasn't supposed to ask questions about the Super Bowl, but couldn't resist after hearing the album and realizing she hadn't addressed the nipplegate controversy. She told me that she'd written about the Super Bowl incident, but decided not to include those songs on the new album because she wanted to move on. Fair enough. At the Madison Square Garden show, my husband met a handsome guy in line at the bar. When he pointed him out to me, I said, "That's Cheyenne Jackson!" We ended up hanging out and talked about our shared love of Janet. A week later, Cheyenne sent me his latest CD with a handwritten note, "Thanks so much for your consideration. From one Janet fan to another." Sadly, Patti Webster died of brain cancer in 2013 at age 49. She was a total pro. During that interview, I asked Janet about her chart rival Madonna. One of my coworkers, Greg Marzullo, happened to walk by my office at just that moment. Later, he said to me, "Did you ask Janet about Madonna?" I said, of course I did. He replied, "You just conducted the gayest interview ever." Here it is.

Without Janet Jackson, no one would be one-two stepping to Ciara or celebrating Beyonce's B'Day. And Mouseketeer Justin Timberlake — who has shamelessly appropriated the Jackson family's moves for years — would be dancing in theme park musical productions instead of bringing sexy back.

After inspiring a league of imitators during 20 years in the music business, Jackson releases her ninth studio album this week, "20 Y.O.," a wonderfully self-referential return to the top of her game and a nod to the 20th anniversary of her groundbreaking 1986 album "Control."

In the midst of a whirlwind media tour to promote the album, which has included a stop on Oprah's couch and a "Today" show appearance, Jackson granted the Blade an exclusive interview this week in which she talked about the album, the MTV boycott of her videos, her gay fans and even Madonna.

Although Jackson has always said she writes songs about what's happening in her life, there is no mention on "20 Y.O." of the Super Bowl controversy or her brother Michael's acquittal on child molestation charges.

"I got all of that out of my system," she says in explaining the decision not to reflect on those events. "That's not what I'm feeling right now. I wrote about [those controversies] but I didn't choose to put it out there on the album."

In 2004, for the first time since the 1980s, a Janet Jackson album failed to hit No. 1 on the Billboard charts. The commercially disappointing "Damita Jo" opened at No. 2 and went on to sell about one million copies. Despite the lackluster response to that album, Jackson says she's not feeling pressure to hit No. 1 with "20 Y.O."

"It's more important for the record company than for me," she says. "I just want to bring happiness to people. Of course you want it to be successful, but I really just want to bring a smile to people's faces."

One factor that will impact sales of the new album is video exposure. Although BET and VH1 have been playing the first two singles, "Call on Me" and "So Excited," MTV appears to be boycotting all things Janet.

MTV, which named Jackson its inaugural "Icon" award winner in 2001, produced the infamous half-time show in which Jackson's breast was exposed. But MTV's anger over the incident apparently doesn't extend to Timberlake, whose new single is in heavy rotation. Jackson says she's heard that MTV has disrespected her fans, but she brushes off the snub.

"The fans get upset and talk about boycotting [MTV]," she says. "It is what it is, but I'm not losing sleep over it. I appreciate the love and support the fans have shown me."

To reach those fans in the absence of MTV support, Jackson and her promotions team have waged an aggressive web promotion campaign that includes a revamped official website, janet-jackson.com, and a new MySpace site that includes an exclusive video diary. She teased fans earlier this year with the online-only release of a cover of Debbie Deb's 1980s song "Lookout Weekend."

Janet clearly recognizes that many of those fans she's reaching out to are gay. She clarified that she has never been involved in a gay relationship herself, but that she has many gay friends, several of whom are dancers in her upcoming tour.

She says she doesn't understand why so many people oppose same-sex marriage, "We're all human and we all fall in love, so why should our sexual preference matter?"

There are no wild innovations or dramatic departures on "20 Y.O.," but the album is chock-full of hits. There is no dead weight on this record, as on "Damita Jo."

This time out, with help from longtime beau and hit maker Jermaine Dupri and producers and cowriters Jimmy Jam and Terry Lewis, Jackson delivers a string of well-crafted tunes. "There's something to be said for not saying anything," she says in the introduction to the album. "I want to keep it light. I want to have fun."

And fun is what she delivers, especially for dance music fans. The album opens with a series of five sure-fire club-banging hits, starting with the current single, "So Excited." Despite lyrics like, "I'll open my spot for you, anytime you want me to," Jackson has ratcheted down the vulgarity this time out. She's still freaky, but the 40-year-old Janet sounds more mature and confident than she has in the recent past.

Dirty Southern rapper Khia (of "My Neck, My Back" infamy) guests on "So Excited," which is followed by four more fast-paced songs: "Show Me," "Get It Out Me," "Do It 2 Me" and "This Body," featuring a rollicking guitar riff that recalls "Rhythm Nation" hit "Black Cat."

In fact, the album is full of sly samples from Jackson's extensive back catalogue. Listen carefully, and you'll hear snippets from "Rhythm Nation," "I Get Lonely" and other previous Jackson hits as she looks back on 20 years in music.

After the opening barrage of infectious beats, Jackson slows things to a mid-tempo groove with songs like "With U" and "Call on Me," a duet with Nelly that hit No. 1 on Billboard's R&B/hip-hop chart.

The interludes that Jackson is known for interspersing on her albums are spare this time, with just three short breaks plus an intro and outro. The interludes succeed in preparing the listener for what's to come and transitioning between the faster, mid-tempo and slower ballad tracks.

Jackson's persona has always included the over-the-top diva as well as the vulnerable and shy side, which she successfully mines on "Take Care," a whispering, smooth ballad.

Among the standouts — and there are many — "Do It 2 Me" and "Daybreak" really shine.

"Enjoy" is classic, upbeat Janet, reminiscent of "Runaway" and "Escapade." She coos, "Livin' every day like it's my last/ I refuse to be stuck in the past/People acting like machines/cause they're scared to live their dreams, no not me."

Jackson says her gay fans have another treat yet to come. She promises a song called "Clap Your Hands" will be a big hit with the gay club crowd. The song isn't on the version of "20 Y.O." released this week, but is coming on a future re-release of the album, along with a possible duet with Mariah Carey, which Jackson says is still in the works.

Asked if she would ever consider a duet with longtime chart rival and fellow gay-favorite Madonna, Jackson says she hasn't thought about it.

"No one's ever asked me that," she says, adding that she and Madonna have never actually met. "Isn't that surprising?"

She declined to speculate about how many singles to expect from the album, saying, "it's up to the market," but did confirm that she will launch a world tour in March.

"I'm sure we'll stop in Washington," she says, adding that the show will include a mixture of new and old hits. "I don't like going to a show where all they perform is the new album."

After the tour, Jackson says she has no idea what's next for her professionally, but she would like to pursue film roles.

"I'd like to have a family and I'm getting older," she says. "I don't know what's next, I'm as much in the dark as you are."

"HOLLYWOOD'S ETERNAL CLOSET," AUG. 24, 2007

Merv Griffin was a powerful, wealthy figure in Hollywood when he died at 82 in 2007. As was common then, mainstream media reporters tripped over themselves to keep Griffin in the closet in death, just as they did when Susan Sontag, Luther Vandross, Ismail Merchant, and many others passed away.

Why does this matter in 2022? For one, it still happens. For another, there's still something that can be done to rectify the problem. Mainstream outlets like the New York Times and Washington Post should hire someone to go back and update the obituaries of prominent LGBTQ people. No straight person's obituary would be considered complete or accurate without the mention of their spouse, children and personal life. Each obituary traditionally ends with "Merv Griffin is survived by …". It's maddening that respected outlets like the Times and Post — whose writers and editors turn up their noses at those of us in the alternative press who write honestly about such topics — had a standard practice of dooming celebrities to an eternity in the closet. It's a shameful practice and legacy that reinforces the offensive, dated notion that being LGBTQ is something to hide. Hey, Jeff Bezos: You can afford to hire a talented obituary writer (yes, there is a particular, unique skill to obit writing) to update the Post's work in this area. Fix those obituaries so our LGBTQ pioneers can finally get the respect and recognition they deserve and finally rest in peace.

The obituaries for entrepreneur and TV legend Merv Griffin in the mainstream media are predictably lacking certain details.

Gay readers have learned from the recent deaths of Susan Sontag, Luther Vandross, Ismail Merchant and others not to expect too much in the way of honest reporting in the obit pages. Celebrities are doomed to an eternity in the closet when it comes to how the mainstream media cover gays, even in death.

In all the fawning tributes to Griffin, praised by everyone from Nancy Reagan to Vanna White, the issue of his sexual orientation is addressed only via mentions of his 1970s-era wife and his "long-time companion" Eva Gabor, a rather unconvincing beard. Some obituaries include a reference to two lawsuits filed against Griffin — one for palimony by a former employee, Brent Plott, in 1991 and another by "Dance Fever" host Denny Terrio for sexual harassment the same year. Both were later dismissed.

But Ray Richmond, a Hollywood Reporter writer, crashed the straight-washing party with a surprising and welcome article published Aug. 17.

"Merv Griffin was gay," Richmond began his piece. "Why should that be so uncomfortable to read? Why is it so difficult to write? Why are we still so jittery even about raising the issue in purportedly liberal-minded Hollywood in 2007? We can refer to it casually in conversation, but the mainstream media somehow remains trapped in the Dark Ages when it comes to labeling a person as gay."

Some of us have been asking these questions for a long time. It's gratifying to see others on board, even if someone should have written the story before Griffin died. And despite the common perception in some circles that being gay is no longer a big deal, the roster of out gay celebrities and public figures remains startlingly short.

As Richmond put it, "While it would seem everything has changed today, little actually has. You can count on the fingers of one hand, or at most two, the number of high-powered stars, executives and public figures who have come out. Those who don't can't really be faulted, as rarely do honesty and full disclosure prove a boon to one's showbiz livelihood."

The problem with that rationale is that there are plenty of wealthy gay closeted stars, executives and public figures who could afford to never work again. Some of those folks need to find the courage to stand up to the Hollywood system that employs countless gays, while hypocritically insisting on their silence.

Griffin died at 82 and so perhaps we ought to cut him some slack. After all, he came of age in an era when coming out in Hollywood meant career suicide. Of course, there are plenty of octogenarians who are proudly out — and who don't have the benefit of hundreds of millions of dollars in the bank — so that slack should be short.

But the extreme secrecy that Griffin lived by concerning his personal life is unfortunately not limited to stars born in the early 20th century. The unwritten rule that says all personal details of straight stars' lives shall be fodder for People, Us Weekly, TMZ.com, etc., while those same sorts of details about gay stars shall remain hidden, persists today. That double standard is wrong and can be seen at work in the obituaries published this month about Griffin's remarkable life.

We can rest assured that as Jodie Foster promotes her upcoming film, "The Brave One," due out next month, she will dodge any questions about her personal life and interviewers will be made to agree in advance not to ask about such topics.

The Griffin obit saga took a predictable turn when The Hollywood Reporter yanked Richmond's piece from the web, presumably after advertiser complaints. After protests from bloggers and satellite radio host Michelangelo Signorile, the article reappeared, though in a less prominent spot. Meanwhile, Reuters, which syndicates content from the Hollywood Reporter also pulled the story.

Support for those cowardly moves came from unlikely places. Respected Washington Post TV critic Tom Shales denounced those who would out Griffin in death, citing anonymous angry web postings as evidence that only "fringe" people were disappointed by Griffin's lack of honesty.

"The Internet is rife with rantings from what sometimes sound like members of a lynch mob," Shales wrote. "In this case, one might think that victims of persecution would feel a tad more reluctant to persecute someone else, especially a recently deceased man."

Shale's assertion that writing honestly about a public figure's sexual orientation amounts to "persecution" is wrong and insulting. He, and so many of his colleagues in the mainstream media, still don't get it. Sexual orientation should be no more a private fact than your eye color. It's not a private fact for straight folks, who wear wedding rings and walk hand in hand down the street. It's even less private for straight celebrities, whose sexual antics, including videotaped bedroom romps, routinely make the news.

Shales and other journalists should be concerned with reporting the truth, however uncomfortable it may be for some to accept. Keeping Griffin's — and Foster's — dirty little secret only reinforces the notion that homosexuality is something to hide. Those who would report the facts honestly, like Signorile, Richmond and even controversial blogger Perez Hilton, should be applauded for their efforts at breaking down Hollywood's closet doors once and for all.

"Don't believe the pro-gay hype," May 15, 2013

Jason Collins came out in 2013 on the cover of Sports Illustrated and many of us expected that it would trigger others in professional sports to follow his brave lead. Ten years later, that didn't pan out. There have been a few prominent male athletes who've come out in the decade since, notably Michael Sam and Carl Nassib, who remains the only out NFL player. I spoke to Nassib in 2022 shortly after he came out and invited him to join me at the White House Correspondents' Dinner. He accepted the invitation, then a few weeks later, called back to say he'd changed his mind. He's not one for media attention and has resisted most efforts at making him the gay face of the NFL. After leaving the Raiders, he was picked up by the Tampa Bay Buccaneers for the 2022 season.

We still have not seen an active openly gay Major League Baseball player, although a handful have come out after retirement, most notably Billy Bean, who serves as MLB's Senior Vice President and Special Assistant to the Commissioner after years working for the league as its first ambassador for inclusion. I've met Bean several times over the years; he's been instrumental in encouraging Pride Nights at ballparks around the country. The Washington Nationals and Los Angeles Dodgers have had the most robust Pride Night events over the years and I was excited to help the Baltimore Orioles start a Pride tradition a few years back, after meeting the O's senior vice president, Greg Bader, who's gay.

Despite all that gay visibility in baseball, we still don't have an active out player. I've had retired professional athletes tell me that Major League Baseball would be the last major male sport to have an out player, mostly because many players are recruited from conservative and religious areas in the Deep South and in the Caribbean. Those predictions are proving true.

When the NBA's Jason Collins came out last month in a Sports Illustrated column, he found cheery public support from nearly all quarters. Everyone from Bill Clinton to Steve Nash tripped over themselves to congratulate Collins on becoming the first openly gay active (male) player in one of the big four American team sports.

But the happy, politically correct mainstream reaction to the momentous news barely concealed what was happening just beneath the surface of George Stephanopoulos' and Oprah's giddy coverage. Anyone who tuned into talk radio — or Twitter — that day heard a very different take on Collins' brave announcement.

Miami Dolphins wide receiver Mike Wallace Tweeted, "All these beautiful women in the world and guys wanna mess with other guys SMH."

Mark Jackson, head coach of the Golden State Warriors, said: "As a Christian man I have beliefs of what's right and what's wrong, that being said, I know Jason Collins, I know his family ... And certainly praying for them at this time." Sportscaster Chris Broussard denounced Collins as a sinner.

CBS' Mike Francesa said, "It means less than nothing to me that there is a gay player now out in the NBA. SI going to reveal this this week in — I don't know why — I guess a dramatic attempt to sell a magazine, I guess. I have the story here and I'm not compelled to run and talk about it or read it. I really don't care. I can't be any more honest. I don't care."

This was the most typical sports talk radio take on the news. While most callers wanted only to talk about Collins and the specter of gays sharing the shower and locker room with straight jocks, the talk radio hosts wanted to change the subject. Monitoring sports radio in the Baltimore and D.C. markets that day, I was amused as the hosts desperately tried to change the subject away from the biggest sports story of the week, no doubt fearing for their jobs if they publicly agreed with their callers' homophobic fears. We've arrived at a strange new place in the movement for LGBT equality where homophobia lives on but those who express it out loud are bullied into apologizing, their very careers dependent upon pretending they really like us.

No one typifies this strange new world better than Kobe Bryant, who chimed in with a supportive Tweet, "Proud of @jasoncollins34. Don't suffocate who u r because of the ignorance of others." Just two years ago, Bryant was fined $100,000 by the NBA for calling a referee a "faggot" during a game. His team, the Los Angeles Lakers, promptly announced a partnership with the Gay & Lesbian Alliance Against Defamation to combat bullying. GLAAD said at the time it would advocate for "zero tolerance policies for anti-gay slurs at home games." It's not clear what that means but it sounds like a dubious mission for a national LGBT advocacy group.

Pretending that homophobia died because a dozen states enacted marriage equality ignores the facts and the reality of a nation still deeply divided over LGBT issues. Remember that there are no laws prohibiting workplace discrimination on the basis of sexual orientation in 29 states (and in 34 states based on gender identity); we account for only about 4-5 percent of the population but 20 percent of hate crimes target LGBT people; 40 percent of homeless youth identify as LGBT; 63 percent of all new HIV infections are among men who have sex with men, up 22 percent since 2008; sodomy laws remain on the books in 17 states, including Maryland and Massachusetts; the FDA still bans gay men from donating blood; immigration law ignores our relationships; DOMA and Prop 8 remain on the books; an estimated 28 percent of Black trans people are unemployed. And on and on.

The support for marriage equality and the public embrace of gay celebrities masks the reality of a nation in which too many LGBT people continue to suffer because of old-fashioned bigotry and prejudice. Don't believe the pro-gay hype.

"That time Laverne Cox met Justice Scalia," April 27, 2015

My favorite celebrity dates for the annual White House Correspondents Association dinner have so far been Judith Light and Laverne Cox. This piece recalls my memorable night on the town with Cox, just one day after Caitlyn Jenner's big coming out as trans interview.

Laverne arrived at the Washington Hilton with full glam squad in tow — hair, makeup, stylist. She looked stunning and the squad handed her off to me at the start of the red carpet. I carried her purse while she walked the carpet. My Mom was watching on C-SPAN and texted me, "I see you! Are you carrying a purse?" The night before the dinner, Caitlyn Jenner's interview with Diane Sawyer aired during which she came out as transgender. So Laverne became the hottest ticket at the dinner, with everyone wanting her opinion on Jenner. She graciously moved from CNN to MSNBC to Fox News down the gauntlet of TV cameras, then she finally turned to me and whispered, "If I have to answer one more question about fucking Caitlyn Jenner, I'm going to lose it." So I escorted her away from the cameras and we headed for security. As we walked in, Laverne stopped to talk to Katie Couric, who brought Antonin Scalia as her date as recounted below. But what I didn't write about then was what happened once Laverne and I got to our table. The lights dimmed and the program was starting. Laverne was wearing a spectacular loaned bracelet worth tens of thousands of dollars. As the lights went down, she turned to me and said, "Kevin, the fucking bracelet is gone!" We both panicked. I got down on the floor and crawled under the table using my cell phone as a flashlight hoping the bracelet had fallen off. No luck. So I went and found the head of security and told him what had happened. "Well, if the staff finds it, it's gone," he said. "Maybe Jane Fonda will find it and turn it in," I replied. I returned to the table and Laverne was frantically texting her stylist, trying to find out the value of the bracelet. She feared they would accuse her of stealing it. At the end of the dinner, I returned to security but no one had turned it in. Laverne and I bid each other good night and I felt terrible about the lost bauble. Then, a few hours later at 4 a.m., my phone rang. It was Laverne. She found the bracelet in the bottom of

her purse. It must have fallen off while she was grabbing something inside. Crisis averted.

The 101ST annual White House Correspondents' Association dinner was held at the Washington Hilton on Saturday night and featured the usual send-ups of the D.C. political class along with celebrities dripping in diamonds and swathed in couture. But there were some surreal, unscripted moments amid the circus better known as "Nerd Prom."

One of the most popular guests proved to be actress and Emmy Award-winning producer Laverne Cox. She attended for the first time as a guest of the Washington Blade and the event was held one night after Bruce Jenner's coming out interview on ABC. Cox was in demand, with reporters swamping her with questions about Jenner. Cox told the Blade that she spoke to Jenner by phone after his interview aired and praised Dianne Sawyer's handling of the questioning. "I think ABC handled it beautifully," Cox said.

As she made her way through the rain and into the jam-packed Hilton, a stylist scurried to arrange her fabulous Ines Di Santo gown, as photographers shouted and jockeyed for position. I was happy to help the "Orange Is the New Black" star by carrying her purse and finally escorting her through the gauntlet. As chaotic as the red carpet paparazzi scene was, things were about to get surreal.

We walked through security and Cox was stopped by Katie Couric. We were introduced and then Couric said she wanted to introduce us to her "date." Cox and I were stunned to see Supreme Court Justice Antonin Scalia standing there with his hand outstretched to greet us. This was just three days before Scalia — a harsh critic of LGBT rights — was to consider arguments in the marriage cases pending before the court. He smiled and shook our hands and there was some brief and awkward chitchat before he shuffled off with Katie.

I thought we should have been ready with a quip or pointed remark about marriage. Then again, perhaps it was best to leave it alone.

As we made our way to the ballroom, there were celebrities galore: Jane Fonda, Martha Stewart, Bradley Cooper, Gabourey Sidibe. Martin O'Malley, the butt of two stinging jokes that night, wandered around like he was waiting to be recognized. Fonda, 77, turned heads in a fitted black dress that one tabloid likened to her Barbarella look from 50 years ago. There were models, actors, CEOs, athletes and, oh yeah, White House correspondents, including the Blade's own Chris Johnson. Among the friendlier famous faces: Tracee Ellis Ross from ABC's "Blackish"; Julie Bowen and Jesse Tyler Ferguson from "Modern Family"; and NBC's Tamron Hall, who, at age 44, appears to be drinking from the Fountain of Youth.

President Obama stole the show as always. He made two gay jokes. Referencing Rick Santorum's comment that he would not attend a same-sex wedding, Obama said, "Gays and lesbians across the country responded, 'That's not going to be a problem.'"

And speaking about his close relationship with Vice President Biden, Obama quipped, "I tease Joe sometimes, but he has been at my side for seven years, I love that man. He's not just a great vice president, he is a great friend. We've gotten so close in some places in Indiana, they won't serve us pizza anymore."

Amid the silliness, there were toasts to journalists who were killed while covering stories and a pledge from Obama to bring home Washington Post reporter Jason Rezaian, wrongfully jailed in Iran on unspecified charges. Many of those in attendance wore "Free Jason" pins. And despite all the criticism of the dinner as out-of-touch and an inappropriate conflict of interest, there is something moving about taking a night to celebrate the profession of journalism and its critical role in America's democracy. While some surely attend to party and snap selfies with celebs, those of us at the Blade do not take it for granted. It wasn't long ago that we were summarily tossed out of the White House briefing room and our credentials canceled. Access to the highest levers of power is critical to informing the public about what our government is doing in our name. So we were grateful and honored to be there, even if we took selfies with Laverne.

"Thank you, David Bowie," Jan. 11, 2016

The Blade doesn't just cover politics; we endeavor to report on broader cultural trends and issues that speak to the LGBTQ experience. And thus we frequently cover issues in popular culture, which holds a unique power to shape public opinion in the United States and around the world. When David Bowie died, I sat in stunned silence staring at my computer, replaying old clips of his TV performances and groundbreaking videos that experimented with and challenged traditional gender roles dating back to the 1970s. I wrote this piece in tribute to his influence on me and so many other "rebels."

I hadn't gotten around to downloading David Bowie's last album, "Blackstar," released just last week on his 69th birthday, when word came Monday that he died following an undisclosed fight with cancer.

It was a final, classic Bowie move — releasing an album without fanfare and letting the art stand on its own. No maudlin pandering for validation or rave reviews. But the raves came anyway, before we knew about the cancer.

Make no mistake that without Bowie there'd be no Madonna or Lady Gaga or any number of acts that have cited him as a primary influence. Even Kanye West tweeted his appreciation. For gay fans, like me, Bowie was a beacon and a revelation. Though married for 24 years to the equally stylish Iman, Bowie flirted openly with gay and bisexual themes in the early 1970s, only a few years after the U.K. lifted its ban on homosexual acts. He once told an interviewer that he was gay, but in later years played down that claim. His biographers describe a hedonistic, cocaine-fueled sex life in the '70s and early '80s that reportedly included romps with men and women.

Recalling Bowie's iconic 1972 appearance on Britain's "Top of the Pops," in which he performed "Starman" dressed in full Ziggy Stardust regalia, British GQ editor Dylan Jones told the BBC that was the moment his life changed.

"He was a dangerous figure on British TV at a point when television didn't do danger," Jones said. "Forty-one years ago, it was an extraordinary experience. It didn't immediately fill me with gay longings — though with some people it did. But nothing was quite the same afterwards."

Indeed, the worlds of pop music and fashion would never be the same after Bowie exploded into public consciousness after that TV appearance.

I was lucky to see Bowie perform live twice, first on the stunning "Sound + Vision" tour in July of 1990 and later at D.C.'s Capitol Ballroom on the 1997 "Earthling" tour. Whether surrounded by props and pyro and supporting players or standing alone at center stage in a simple T-shirt, Bowie was a showman and you couldn't take your eyes off him.

His boldness in subverting gender norms and declining to identify publicly as heterosexual (despite his many dalliances with famous women) gave cover and hope to many closeted gay fans the world over. Bowie showed us it was OK to be weird and different and to not fit in with our conventional teenage contemporaries.

As Tilda Swinton so brilliantly put it in her tribute to Bowie featured in his recent exhibition at the Victoria & Albert Museum, "the freak becomes the great unifier."

His vast influence wasn't limited to the world of music. Bowie was a prolific visual artist and acclaimed actor ("The Hunger," "Merry Christmas, Mr. Lawrence," "The Man Who Fell to Earth"). He always embraced technology, launching an internet service provider, Bowie.net, in the late '90s and giving a startlingly prescient interview in 2000 in which he said, "Rock and roll is now a career opportunity, and the internet carries the flag for the subversive and rebellious, chaotic and nihilistic ... the monopolies do not have a monopoly [anymore]. I think the potential of what the internet is going to do to society, both good and bad, is unimaginable. I think we're on the cusp of something exhilarating and terrifying."

Bowie's music is an indelible part of the soundtrack of many lives. He was an oddity, a hero and, yes, a rebel.

"NFL's embrace of Timberlake a racist, sexist joke," Sept. 29, 2017

There are two reasons to include this essay on Justin Timberlake in a book about LGBTQ equality: First, he attacked and threw under the bus one of our community's most famous and longstanding allies, Janet Jackson. Second, the queer press can say things that mainstream commentators won't about Justin. About three years after this was published in the Blade, Timberlake issued a too-little-too-late apology to Jackson and Britney Spears for his mistreatment of them. Here then is the harsh truth about Timberlake.

Reports that Justin Timberlake will headline the 2018 Super Bowl offer further evidence of the NFL's racism, sexism and ageism. It's craven lunacy that NFL executives would consider asking Timberlake back while continuing to boycott all things Janet Jackson in the wake of the duo's infamous 2004 nipple-baring performance.

The Black woman took the fall for the accident, while the white boy was celebrated and saw his career take off in the aftermath. Yes, I said "accident." Amid the endless speculation about whether it was planned or not, one fact is always forgotten: the FCC under then-Chair Michael Powell launched a thorough investigation into the incident, prodded by angry members of Congress. The senior MTV executive in charge of the show was forced to turn over her laptop to investigators, who concluded: "The FCC found nothing to suggest they had planned the moment," as ESPN reported. That finding is consistent with Jackson's denials that it was planned.

Ten years after Powell pretended to be offended by the split-second nipple flash in a series of TV interviews, he finally admitted the truth to ESPN. "I think we've been removed from this long enough for me to tell you that I had to put my best version of outrage on that I could put on," he said, while rolling his eyes.

Nevertheless, Jackson was immediately blacklisted by CBS, MTV Networks and mainstream corporate radio. She was disinvited from the Grammy Awards that year, despite being a 26-time nominee and five-time winner. Timberlake was welcomed at the ceremony, accompanied by his mommy. He used the opportunity to apologize, dutifully carrying water for a network — and a conservative Republican administration — at the expense of his one-time friend Jackson.

It was a cruel stab in the back for Jackson, who did so much to advance Timberlake's career. Before letting him share her Super Bowl stage, Jackson hired Timberlake and his cheesy boyband mates from N*Sync to open for her on 1997's acclaimed "Velvet Rope" world tour. Many had never heard of Timberlake before that tour.

Timberlake would go on to appropriate Janet and Michael Jackson's style and moves. Jimmy Fallon once dubbed him the "president of pop." Luckily, presidents can be impeached. Timberlake is really the "appropriator-in-chief," stealing liberally from the Jackson playbook and from other Black artists over the years. He once even wore his hair in cornrows, an unintentionally hilarious and cringeworthy choice.

When Timberlake was the target of the MTV prank show "Punk'd," his true personality was revealed. The gag involved IRS agents and a moving truck showing up at Timberlake's mansion as he's told he owes $900,000 in unpaid taxes and his belongings are being repossessed. He bursts into tears and again calls mommy for help.

When he realizes it's a gag and that cameras are rolling, he reverts to his phony "bad boy" persona, complete with "yo yo yos."

Timberlake is a copycat, a cheap imitation of talent. He's an average-looking Mickey Mouse Club alumnus who rode a wave of '90s teeny-bop cheese to undeserved fame and fortune. He is the embodiment of mediocrity. A saccharine, nonthreatening, milquetoast pop star for the white bread Orlando suburbs.

And yet, the NFL is reportedly ready to give him the headliner slot at the Super Bowl at a time when the country is finally beginning to engage in a dialogue about systemic racism thanks to athletes taking a knee during the National Anthem. Two steps forward and two steps back.

Virtually no one seems to think Jackson stands a chance of being invited back to the Super Bowl, even though she's the much bigger star by any measure. Timberlake's four solo studio albums have sold about 27 million copies worldwide, compared to Jackson's roughly 160 million records sold. She's won every music industry award there is — a total of 370, including five Grammys, 33 Billboard Music Awards and 11 AMAs. She even holds nine Guinness World Records, has an Oscar nomination and was named MTV's inaugural "Icon" award recipient.

The next generation of pop stars have unanimously cited Jackson as a primary influence, including: Britney Spears, Christina Aguilera, Beyonce, Usher, Mya, Lady Gaga, Pink, Tinashe, Aaliyah, Ciara, among many others. Jackson has collaborated with a diverse array of music's biggest stars, including Elton John, Luther Vandross, Missy Elliott, Carly Simon, Q-Tip, Chuck D, Kathleen Battle, P. Diddy, Kanye West, Nelly, Herb Alpert and Michael Jackson. And her music has been covered by everyone from Whitney Houston and Prince to Buckcherry and most recently Katy Perry.

Outside of music, Jackson starred in three successful sitcoms as a child actor; she's a New York Times best-selling author and four of her five feature films debuted at No.1 at the box office.

And though Timberlake is much younger, Jackson is proving her modern relevance and staying power. While Timberlake's last album was released in 2013, Jackson's last outing was 2015's "Unbreakable," which debuted at No.1 on Billboard's albums chart, her seventh compared to three solo No. 1 albums for Timberlake. Jackson is currently on a 56-date "State of the World" tour selling out arenas across the country at age 51 without a new single to plug and without doing any media appearances to promote the tour.

She is inexplicably absent from the Rock and Roll Hall of Fame, despite two nominations. Here's hoping the Rock Hall finally gives Jackson her due next year.

But back to Timberlake. The NFL's embrace of this cad, who so blithely tossed Jackson under the bus, reinforces all the racist, sexist and ageist stereotypes about American popular culture. We can only hope the NFL will do the right thing and reconsider giving such a platform to someone so undeserving. Jackson certainly deserves another shot at that stage, but she doesn't like to repeat herself and has nothing left to prove. Jackson gracefully endured years of ridicule and boycotts. She's proved herself the better person and the bigger star, no matter what the NFL decides.

"Behind the Scenes with Kathy Griffin," April 29, 2018

As relatively new members of the White House Correspondents' Association, the Blade has the opportunity to purchase coveted tickets to the annual dinner, known as the "nerd prom." Each year brings the usual criticism that the dinner is a too-cozy, inappropriate schmooze fest for journalists and the government sources they cover. What most don't see is that behind the scenes, celebrity publicists start scrambling in January (the dinner is normally held in April) to convince news outlets to give their clients tickets. Only Association members may purchase tickets and, prior to Trump, the event was on par with the Oscars for the attention and coverage it drew. I have attended several times and brought as my dates numerous celebrities, including Laverne Cox, NeNe Leakes, Melissa Harris-Perry, and Kathy Griffin, among others. One year I received a call from a publicist asking for tickets for her client, Nyle DiMarco. I'd never heard of him and declined. Turns out, he's an actor and activist and went on to win "America's Next Top Model." That was one decision I regretted.

The first year I attended the dinner, I was seated next to the actor Casey Affleck — this was long before the revelations about his alleged sexual harassment came to light and before he'd won his Oscar. He asked about the Blade, so I explained we were the nation's oldest LGBTQ newspaper. I had a tip from the White House that President Obama might mention the Blade in his remarks that night. It was the White House Correspondents' Association's 100th anniversary and Obama was planning to make a speech addressing how the association had diversified over the years and the Blade would be a big part of it. Knowing that, I initiated a bet with Affleck — if Obama mentioned the Blade in his speech, then Affleck and his girlfriend had to jump up and cheer for the Blade. He accepted the terms of the bet and minutes later, Obama mentioned the Blade in his remarks. I looked knowingly at Affleck and he and his girlfriend jumped to their feet and cheered wildly.

NeNe Leakes proved a memorable guest in 2016 and she surprised me with her vulnerability. The day before the dinner, NeNe called me and said she was nervous about her security after attending an event where she was mobbed by fans and felt unsafe. I assured her that with the president of the United States in the room, there would be plenty of security. When we got to the red carpet, I did what I always do — offer to take my guest's purse and let her walk the carpet alone for photographs. But NeNe wouldn't hear of it. She insisted that I not leave her side. So we walked into the Washington Hilton and no one on the red carpet elicited more applause than NeNe, the star of "Real Housewives of Atlanta" who had parlayed that notoriety into high-profile acting gigs on Broadway and on the hit show

"Glee." Once inside, she said she didn't want to do any interviews and wanted to go directly to our table. So I escorted her past the throngs of cameras and into the venue where we sat alone at our table. We dished about all the famous faces walking past us, including Gayle King and Aretha Franklin. So many people wanted to meet NeNe; they kept approaching our table and asking me for an introduction. Thomas Roberts, who later became a neighbor and friend, was anchoring a show on MSNBC at the time and approached me asking for an introduction. We had a hilarious exchange with NeNe in which she told him he was on the "come up" and I remarked that Thomas spent too much time "in women business." NeNe was delightful and kind to all the selfie-seekers, even if she spent an inordinate amount of time searching for photos of herself on social media. Years later, her husband Gregg passed away. Gregg and I had worked together on making NeNe's appearance happen. He was such a gentleman and I regretted not being able to procure him a ticket to join us.

That same year, I also invited Melissa Harris-Perry, the former MSNBC host, to join my table. She taught me an important lesson. I invited her because her show had just been canceled, which I thought was a terrible mistake and loss. Melissa is a brilliant commentator. She's a professor and teaches a course in Black Lives Matter. And she's a natural on TV. When I told her in the car ride to the dinner that I invited her to thank her for being an LGBTQ ally, she put me in my place. "I'm not your ally," she said. "An ally is someone who cheers you on from the sidelines. I am in this fight, I am part of this." I was stunned. I'd never heard that view before but it makes perfect sense. It was another of those "a-ha" moments. I heard a similar view espoused by DeRay Mckesson, the early Black Lives Matter supporter from Baltimore who's gay. He also rejects the term "ally" in favor of the term "accomplice," which I love. That night at the dinner, Melissa was the subject of a joke from the host, Larry Wilmore, who said MSNBC now stands for "Missing A Significant Number of Black Correspondents" after her dismissal.

My favorite guest was probably Judith Light, whom I invited in 2022 after the COVID years ended. Judith is an icon but especially for the LGBTQ community. From her breakout role in "Who's the Boss?" in the '80s, to her many more recent successes — "American Horror

Story," "Dallas," "Transparent," and so many others — Judith has always had our backs. She accepted the Blade's invitation to the 2022 dinner and I was thrilled, and a bit nervous, as there were strict COVID protocols to observe and Judith's publicist warned me that she would have trouble with them. On the afternoon of the dinner, all guests were supposed to upload a negative COVID test result via an app. Judith's publicist reached out to inform me that Judith wouldn't be able to manage the test and upload to an app, so I suggested meeting her in advance to assist. We met in the Hilton's lobby and she was unrecognizable in an oversized hat and no makeup. She said, "I thought they were sending someone to administer the COVID test," and I replied, "Yeah, that's me." I asked if she wanted to go somewhere private, but she said no, and we sat down in the hotel's lobby with scores of people walking by. I was game to administer her COVID test, but not OK with jamming the test strip up her nose, so she managed that bit, and I finished the test. We chatted while waiting the 15 minutes for the result and I was immediately charmed. She's so down to earth and kind; she asked about me, my husband, the Blade. When the result came back negative, we parted ways and she suggested I just come to her room to pick her up for the party. Normally, celebrities have glam squads and publicists who manage all that, but not Judith — she just wanted me to come to her door. So, I did and she complimented me on looking "chic" but it was she who looked amazing. Judith was the best dressed person in the room that night and gave much thought to her designer — Jason Wu, who had dressed Michelle Obama on numerous occasions. Judith wanted to pay homage to that and to dress up for the occasion. I knocked on her hotel room door and she opened it — no handlers or publicists, just Judith in her room. We headed downstairs and she was, of course, a hit on the red carpet. There was no one more popular or in demand for selfies — I have a good knack for picking my guests. And Judith accommodated everyone, no matter how annoying the requests. She also has a wicked sense of humor and deployed some biting commentary on the event. When two women were walking in our direction decked out in what looked like early '80s satin prom dresses, Judith leaned in and whispered, "Stop. I can hear the commentary in your head." I laughed. She said, "D.C. is the worst dressed city in the world." Again, I laughed and agreed that the city has that reputation and its residents truly are sartorially challenged. We sat next to each other and had a blast. She was so kind to ask about my husband. When she found out that we owned a house in Rehoboth, she told me to call my husband and tell him that we were running away together and she's taking the Rehoboth house — he can keep the Baltimore place. At the end of the night, I walked her to the elevator in the crowded lobby. I was about to say goodnight, when she asked if I could take off her necklace, which I did. What she said next shocked me: "While you're back there, can you unhook my skirt?" We were in the Hilton lobby with people all around us. Reluctantly, I said sure, and proceeded to reach into her skirt and try to unhook it. I said to her, "This shouldn't come as a surprise, but I have no idea how to do this." She laughed and I kept at it, eventually unlatching the clasp. Two weeks later, Judith was honored at the GLAAD Media Awards. I texted her and said I'd be there cheering her on with my husband and she insisted on meeting him. We met her after the show and, again, she was her generous, gracious self. Judith is truly the kindest, most generous celebrity I've ever met. Our community is well served with her as an ambassador and accomplice.

The choice to invite Kathy Griffin to the dinner as a Blade guest in 2018 created a lot of attention in the media, mostly negative, after she posed with a mock severed head of Trump. She quickly accepted my invitation, then initiated a series of demands, like providing a second ticket for her boyfriend at the last minute. The day before the dinner, I received an email from her boyfriend (who was acting as Griffin's agent after her publicist abruptly quit, telling me "good luck with her!"). The boyfriend promised the Washington Post an "exclusive" story about Griffin's experiences at the dinner and informed me the Post's reporter would be walking the red carpet with her. My head exploded. I called the Post reporter, Dan Zak, and told him Griffin was now his guest and the Blade would revoke Griffin's tickets. He panicked and said he didn't control the Post's tickets and wouldn't be able to accommodate Griffin at the Post table. In the end, everyone backed down, Griffin attended with me, and the Post and the Blade each wrote stories about the night. Wrangling celebrities is truly the most dreaded part of my job.

After all that, Griffin didn't even thank the Blade during her media appearances in the days that followed, including on "The View" and

"The Late Show." She's not the only ungrateful guest we've invited to the Correspondents' Dinner. Jeopardy champion Amy Schneider was my guest in 2022. She quietly left the table while my back was turned, never saying thank you or goodbye. I guess she didn't have a good time.

Many people have asked why the Blade chose to invite comedian Kathy Griffin to its table at Saturday's White House Correspondents' Dinner.

The event is a celebration of the First Amendment. As a longtime LGBT rights advocate, a comedian and provocateur, Griffin has made a long and successful career out of exercising her First Amendment right to free speech. The stunt last year in which she posed with a mock severed head of Donald Trump — which needlessly led CNN to fire her from a longstanding New Year's Eve hosting gig with Anderson Cooper — was a textbook case of satire, which is constitutionally protected speech.

Thus, the decision to invite Griffin proved an easy and obvious one. (We also invited Stormy Daniels, but her attorney, Michael Avenatti, told me without irony that it would be too much of a "sideshow" for her to attend.)

Griffin didn't disappoint, bringing her quick wit and fearless, LGBT-centric sense of humor to the dinner table. I met her and her boyfriend, Randy Bick, on the red carpet and held her purse as she posed for photographers and granted a series of TV interviews. Inside the heavy purse was a stapler; it turns out she suffered a last-minute wardrobe malfunction leaving the hotel, breaking a strap on her gown. After it was repaired, she feared a repeat and asked to borrow the stapler, just in case.

She proved a good sport throughout the night, posing for an endless stream of selfies with (mostly gay) fans who congratulated her on surviving the Trump machine's attacks in the aftermath of the photo scandal. When asked how her famous mom Maggie is at age 96, Griffin replied, "drunk."

The only awkward moment came when Deputy White House Press Secretary Hogan Gidley tried to squeeze past our table. Griffin stopped him and said, "How do you sleep at night?" Gidley replied, "Very well, thank you." When Griffin expressed doubt about that, Gidley asked, "Are we really going to do this?"

That's when things got interesting. Griffin, in her trademark style, retorted, "Yes we are, suck my dick! No, really, suck my dick!"

There was some back-and-forth, then Gidley, who was holding a Tecate, announced he was off to enjoy his Mexican beer "before we build the wall and you can't get these anymore." That prompted a farewell "fuck you" from Griffin, triggering nervous laughter around our table.

Later, when Politico's Josh Dawsey was announced winner of the Merriman Smith Award for his story about the resignation of White House Press Secretary Sean Spicer — who was seated at the table next to us — Griffin stood up and applauded loudly in his direction, eliciting guffaws from our neighbors.

One personal highlight of the night: the Blade's Chris Johnson was honored as the honorable mention for the Merriman Smith award for a story he broke in December about Trump firing all members of his AIDS advisory committee. Chris' name was called and he stood to a round of applause from the room. That would have been unthinkable 40, 30, 20, 10 or even five years ago, when much of the journalism and political elite of D.C. wouldn't deign to acknowledge the gay press, much less honor one of its journalists. Congratulations to Chris for his dogged work in the White House, pressing officials to address our community's issues.

Another noteworthy moment came when gay country singer Ty Herndon took to the podium to perform "America the Beautiful" and "God Bless America." Unlike last year, the party drew current and former members of the administration, including Sarah Huckabee Sanders, Kellyanne Conway, Spicer, Reince Priebus and Omarosa Manigault-Newman. Deputy Attorney General Rod Rosenstein attended, too, drawing curious stares from many.

But the highlight of the evening's entertainment came when Michelle Wolf delivered a riotous keynote, roasting everyone from Trump and Sanders to Sean Hannity and the Democratic Party. Afterward, Griffin raved, saying she "loved" the performance, despite some audience discomfort with an abortion joke. I was surprised by the mainstream media's depiction of Wolf having bombed and offended the room. She did what any fearless comedian should do in that moment — skewer everyone and make us all laugh at ourselves.

Which brings us back to Griffin. Comedians occupy a unique and important role in our popular culture. We've long turned to them for incisive social commentary delivered with a sting; they say out loud what most of us are thinking. Attacking a comedian for doing her job as Trump and his cronies did to Griffin is petty and betrays deep insecurities. So, thank you, Kathy Griffin, for making us laugh and for holding your own in the face of scorching attacks by those humorless GOP bores.

"HAPPY 60TH BIRTHDAY, MADONNA!" AUG. 16, 2018

Who could write an LGBTQ-themed book and not mention Madonna? Not I. So here's the tribute I wrote to her on the occasion of her 60th birthday.

Madonna turns 60 today and respect must be paid.

To the young and uninitiated, she's an aging pop star desperately clinging to her youth by stripping during concerts and dueting with rappers half her age.

The rest of us know better. Believe it or not, there was a time when publicly embracing the LGBT community wasn't a safe career move — long before Katy Perry, Lady Gaga, Britney and a horde of others cloned from the Madonna-Janet Jackson cloth penned pop anthems for the young gays.

In the '80s and early '90s, you could count on one hand the celebrities who reached out to their LGBT fans and advocated on our behalf at the height of the AIDS epidemic amid all the hatred and fear. There was Princess Diana, Liz Taylor, Elton John, Whoopi Goldberg and, yes, Madonna, among the handful of supportive celebs. Madonna once donated the proceeds from a 1987 Madison Square Garden concert to AIDS research.

Her gay moments are too numerous to recap but they include the pioneering 1991 film "Truth or Dare," which brought gay men of color into the nation's multiplexes in an open way most filmgoers had never seen before. And who could forget the dance floor at Tracks when "Vogue" debuted? You could get trampled if you didn't run fast enough to the dance floor. She's been criticized for appropriating vogueing from the NYC ball scene but it looks like all's forgiven because Madonna was invited to join season two of "Pose" by one of its stars.

She always advocated for compassion while combating the AIDS epidemic and for equality while endorsing LGBT rights and marriage. She's stood up to everyone from the pope to the Boy Scouts and denounced anti-LGBT discrimination all over the world during tour stops in Russia, Romania and beyond. She drew much inspiration from the gay community and its nightclubs but also our embrace of the subversive and avant garde.

I could go on. Madonna changed the face of pop culture and helped foster a more accepting world for LGBT people and people with HIV/AIDS. At a time when role models for young gays were hard to find, Madonna inspired many to come out, stand up and fight back. Now at 60, she's challenging another form of discrimination — ageism — and I'm guessing she has a lot to say. Happy birthday,

Madonna, and thanks for sticking your neck out for us when almost no one else would.

"AMERICA THE HUMORLESS," APRIL 11, 2022

I have zero patience for cancel culture. Sure, some people deserve to be canceled, like overt racists, insurrectionists and criminals. But as applied to everyday Americans who misspeak, or to celebrities who tell an offensive joke, the notion of "cancel culture" runs contrary to our country's long history of freedom of speech and expression.

Our community spends an inordinate amount of time canceling our own. Ellen DeGeneres was criticized after telling a supposedly offensive joke about Liza Minnelli at the Oscars one year. Martina Navratilova was canceled after speaking out on the issue of trans inclusion in sports. They are both true pioneers of LGBTQ equality — does anyone really think DeGeneres and Navratilova are our enemies? Ridiculous. Navratilova is one of my personal heroes after coming out in the 1980s and suffering the consequences — audiences booed and threw batteries at her; she lost endorsement deals. That's what a true pioneer looks like. She didn't wait to come out until safely retired as so many male athletes have done. I interviewed Navratilova once and later met her at an awards show. When I asked why she came out so early instead of waiting for retirement, she told me that it never occurred to her to lie, that she hadn't intended to make a big statement about being gay but a reporter asked her and she answered truthfully. She said she was raised to always tell the truth. It was that simple for her. Rooting for Martina in the '80s was my subversive way of being gay long before I found the courage to come out. Her unapologetic fearlessness inspired me tremendously. It's not often you get to meet a personal hero and so when I saw her at an awards show in New York, I approached nervously. She seemed guarded at first, probably assuming I was a star-struck fan looking for a selfie. When I told her she was a hero to me, she melted. She hugged me and we chatted for a while before taking that selfie. It was a moment I'll never forget.

I hesitated to write this next piece, which includes a defense of Dave Chappelle, out of fear I'd be canceled too. My staff begged me not to defend Chappelle, fearing for their paychecks if the Blade were canceled. But I couldn't resist. Chappelle is a brilliant comedian — and a trans rights supporter. His commentary on the current state of the LGBTQ movement is spot on (he prefers the "Stonewall gays"). Hilarious.

Two weeks ago, the Blade's print edition cover date fell on April 1, known to most of us as April Fools' Day.

In the spirit of the holiday, which History.com says originated in 1582 when France moved from the Julian calendar to the Gregorian calendar and confused some gullible residents, I decided the Blade should join the fun.

The paper has a long history of participating in April Fools' jokes, once publishing a cover photo of the office shot upside down to make it appear the Blade offices had been ransacked by anti-gay activists.

For this year's cover, we published an image of Sen. Lindsey Graham, fresh off his melodramatic temper tantrum at Ketanji Brown Jackson's confirmation hearings, with a headline that read, "Yep, I'm gay," an obvious parody of Ellen DeGeneres' infamous Time magazine coming out cover.

I thought it was funny. Predictably, many on social media did not.

"There are kids dying and you're making fun of coming out!" "I demand an apology from the editor!" And "Don't pick on Sen. Graham, you're punching down!" were among the reactions.

Not sure how an alternative news outlet "punches down" at a senior U.S. senator.

I should have known better than to attempt a little fun, but such is the state of our thin-skinned society offended by jokes and bent on punishing comedians.

We saw this sad trend play out at the Oscars, when Will Smith — on the precipice of the biggest moment in his career — marched on stage and slapped Chris Rock for a lame joke about his wife. It was stunning for its stupidity, and for its patronizing, patriarchal treatment of Jada Pinkett Smith, hardly a shrinking violet in need of a man's protection.

Other comedians have since fretted publicly that they will be next — confronted and assaulted by an audience member offended by a joke.

But what's more concerning than the safety of comics is the state of America's waning sense of humor. When did we become so easily offended and frightened? Watching the horrors unfolding in Ukraine, it's difficult to imagine Americans standing up en masse to an invading dictator's army when we can't even take a joke without demanding apologies and even protection from such minor offenses.

When Kathy Griffin posed with a fake severed head of Donald Trump — an obvious parody of ISIS videos — she was fired, canceled and even abandoned by longtime friend and colleague Anderson Cooper. In 2018, the Blade invited Griffin to our table at the White House Correspondents' Association dinner, triggering protests and hate mail that we were rewarding a "terrorist." At that dinner, comedian Michelle Wolf delivered a genius keynote, skewering everyone from Trump to the Democratic Party. But it was a joke about abortion that made headlines and offended the masses.

Here's what she said: "Mike Pence is very anti-choice. He thinks abortion is murder, which, first of all, don't knock it till you try it. And when you do try it, really knock it. You know, you've got to get that baby out of there."

For that joke, the New York Times pondered in a headline whether Wolf had "killed the Correspondents' Dinner." Well no, she did her job and told some jokes, just like Dave Chappelle did in his recent Netflix special that resulted in protests and calls for his cancellation.

If you watch that special in its entirety — rather than read select quotes out of context — you learn that Chappelle had a friend who was transgender. He championed her career and even hired her to open his show. At the end of the special, he delivers a touching tribute to his trans friend, who died by suicide. I don't know how one could watch that show and come away thinking Chappelle is transphobic.

It wasn't the first time Chappelle found himself on the wrong side of the LGBTQ community. In 2017, he told some trans jokes that offended activists. When the Blade reached out to him for an interview, he said he would talk to us only if the reporter sat through his entire show and then interviewed him immediately after back stage. We accepted his invitation. During that interview, he denied being transphobic and assailed North Carolina's HB2, which banned trans people from using the restroom consistent with their gender identity.

"You could say whatever you want about someone's lifestyle, but denying them access to a restroom is a denial of their humanity," Chappelle told the Blade.

There is plenty to be offended about in our modern world, from the Ukraine crisis to the legislative attacks on trans people across the United States, that we should learn to take a joke, laugh at ourselves and focus on what's important. If you go through life looking to be offended, you'll never be disappointed.

CHAPTER 3

POLITICS, LEGISLATION, & COURTS

"The whole aim of practical politics is to keep the populace alarmed (and hence clamorous to be led to safety) by menacing it with an endless series of hobgoblins, all of them imaginary."
— H.L. Mencken

"Don't forget about ENDA," July 30, 2004

Poor ENDA. While wealthy gay donors were spending aggressively to advance marriage rights, everyone forgot about workplace rights. Not everyone wants to get married, but everyone needs a job. So why did marriage leapfrog employment nondiscrimination rights in the national LGBTQ movement? The answer to that is somewhat complicated. It turns out that many Americans assumed it was already illegal to fire someone for being gay or lesbian. They were wrong. It remains legal to fire LGBTQ workers in a majority of states in 2022.

For some reason, employment nondiscrimination never took hold as a No. 1 movement priority. A federal hate crimes law was passed (yet is rarely invoked); the "Don't Ask, Don't Tell" law was repealed; and marriage became a right in all 50 states. And still, no workplace protections. Progressive Rep. Bella Abzug (D-N.Y.) introduced the first employment nondiscrimination bill that included gays and lesbians in 1974. Nearly 50 years later, it remains a dream.

In this piece, I reference my experience at a "Fortune 100 company" where I was discriminated against for being gay. I don't recall why I didn't identify the company; it seems pretty lame looking back now. For the record, the company was Verizon Wireless and I worked in Laurel, Md., for its mobile data group back in 2001. Worst job ever. My boss kept a Bible on his desk and openly blamed "the gays" for 9/11, as recounted in this piece.

After I walked out and abandoned my job at Verizon Wireless, I began digital consulting, which is how I came across the Blade. The paper had a rudimentary website in 2001, complete with a cheesy Dorothy red slipper icon you clicked to return to the homepage. I reached out to the publisher about a consulting gig to update the site and they ended up offering me the job of managing editor.

ENDA, the Employment Non-Discrimination Act, would become one of the hottest issues we wrote about. A contentious battle over the bill raged for years in Congress, culminating in a terribly divisive 2007 showdown when the "T" in LGBT was removed from the legislation. That created a schism between the practical voices in the movement that believed in incremental progress and that we should take what we could get vs. those who thought it anathema that we would leave a segment of the community behind. The latter voices ultimately won out, thankfully, but it wasn't easy getting there. I remember attending the Human Rights Campaign National Dinner in 2007 and having to cross a picket line of mostly transgender protesters to enter the black tie event. I regret attending that event. It felt like a betrayal, turning our backs on members of our community protesting in the streets while the rest of us donned tuxes and proceeded inside to enjoy the open bar. The good news is that the result of that reckoning is that it's now untenable to even consider leaving a segment of our community behind. The "T" is an intractable part of our movement for equality, in part because of the dialogue sparked by ENDA in 2007 and the removal of transgender protections from the bill. In the end, it didn't matter; ENDA failed in the Senate in 2007 after passing the Democratic-controlled House. It remains a pipe dream in 2022, despite candidate Joe Biden promising the Equality Act would be his "No. 1 legislative priority." That measure passed the House but hasn't budged in the Senate, where not even all 50 Democrats are on board with barring employment discrimination against us.

With the nation's attention focused on the same-sex marriage debate, the long-suffering Employment Non-Discrimination Act remains all but forgotten as lawmakers adjourn for the sumner and the Democrats wrap their national convention in Boston. The Democrats, for all the support they receive from gay men and lesbians, claim in their platform that their commitment to civil rights is "ironclad." But a closer look reveals mixed messages.

The official position on the question of gay marriage reads as follows: "We support full inclusion of gay and lesbian families in the life of our nation and seek equal responsibilities, benefits, and protections for these families. In our country, marriage has been defined at the state level for 200 years, and we believe it should continue to be defined there. We repudiate President Bush's divisive effort to politicize the Constitution by pursuing a 'Federal Marriage Amendment.' Our goal is to bring Americans together, not drive them apart."

Not exactly a ringing endorsement of gay equality. Remember, while the Democrats assert here that marriage should be defined by the states, John Kerry supports the constitutional amendment in Massachusetts that would ban same-sex marriage in his home state. A number of groups, including the National Gay & Lesbian Task Force, have called these state constitutional amendments the gravest threat facing marriage equality, and obviously an amendment in Massachusetts would be especially damaging, since it is the only state currently marrying gay couples.

The Democrats' position on ending workplace discrimination against gays is stronger. According to the platform statement, "We will enact bipartisan legislation barring workplace discrimination based on sexual orientation."

There are 44 cosponsors of ENDA in the Senate, including 39 Democrats, and 180 cosponsors in the House, 164 of whom are Democrats, according to the Human Rights Campaign. Sen. Ted Kennedy (D-Mass.) deserves much credit for his support of gay rights, including sponsoring ENDA and speaking out forcefully on behalf of gay equality on the Senate floor two weeks ago during the Federal Marriage Amendment debate. While the gay marriage issue deserves the attention and focus of gay rights advocates, it should not come at the expense of ENDA, which promises to impact the lives of gays and lesbians in workplaces everywhere. In this era of "Will & Grace" and "Queer Eye," it's important to remember that gay workers are not viewed as fabulous, fun and entertaining by most employers. While gays are slowly winning marriage rights, our right to keep our jobs remains an elusive victory.

Gay workers are routinely targeted by anti-gay bosses for discrimination and harassment. I know because it happened to me while working for a Fortune 100 company in a D.C. suburb just three years ago.

After the terrorist attacks of Sept. 11, my boss repeated to me Jerry Falwell's sick assertion that gays and women who had had an abortion were somehow to blame. When I protested, he figured out I'm gay and the subject of my sexual orientation quickly became fodder for office gossip and discussion in open meetings. I began receiving literature from the group "Parents & Friends of Ex-Gays" in my office mailbox. It didn't take long for my work assignments to dry up, even though I had just received a glowing performance review and was working on one of the most high-profile projects in the department. The office secretary was instructed to track my whereabouts, including making a note of how many times I went to the bathroom and for how long.

Anti-gay jokes were told — and tolerated — by senior management in meetings and just outside my office where I wouldn't miss a punch line. The vice president of the department would avert his eyes if we passed each other in the hallway. In just a few short weeks, I went from busy standout worker to a pariah with absolutely no work assignments.

I fought the overt discrimination as aggressively as possible, confronting bosses, filing complaints with human resources and finally retaining an attorney. The breaking point came when a senior director told an anti-gay joke in my presence.

I informed HR that the work environment had become overtly hostile and the situation untenable. I was sent home for two weeks pending an investigation of my allegations.

Two weeks later, I received a call from corporate HR. They had concluded their investigation and could only confirm two of my accusations. The guilty parties had been "disciplined" and I was to return to work the following day.

No one was fired, demoted or transferred. No apology was offered. I refused to return to the office and forfeited my job.

My attorney was not confident about pursuing a case. In the absence of federal workplace protections, no gay person is safe from overt, even sanctioned, discrimination and harassment on the job.

I never considered myself an activist, never opined on gay issues to coworkers, did not even display a picture of my partner on my desk. Standing up to a boss who blames gays for 9/11 was my transgression, and I paid for it with my job.

And all of this transpired at a large, national company just outside of Washington, D.C., where gays feel safe in their urban bubbles. If it's this bad here, imagine what gay workers are enduring in Kansas, Alabama, and Nebraska.

Full marriage rights are important, but gay rights supporters in Congress and elsewhere should remember that ENDA represents a chance to extend existing nondiscrimination protections based on race, gender, religion, national origin, and disability to include a segment of workers facing hostile work environments every day.

ENDA exempts small businesses, the military and religious groups and will not create "special rights" or quotas for employers. The House and Senate versions boast bipartisan support and the time has come for Congress to pass ENDA. Lawmakers should bring it to a vote when Congress gets back to work in the fall.

"Good riddance Rick Santorum," Nov. 10, 2006

The 2006 election was notable in that attacks on LGBTQ rights seemed to finally lose their resonance. The leading homophobes in Congress — Sen. Rick Santorum and Rep. Marilyn Musgrave — were reprimanded by voters, the former losing his seat. Santorum's race was personal for me. I interned for Sen. Harris Wofford's press office in 1993 and lost my prospects for permanent employment when he fell to the odious Santorum. Wofford was appointed to fill out the term of Sen. John Heinz, who was killed in a plane crash in 1991. It was reported that Bill Clinton considered Wofford for his vice presidential running mate in 1992. That would have been something — a gay vice president! I had no idea Wofford was into guys when I joined his press office as a 22-year-old novice. (I should note that he never said he identified as gay, even though he married his male partner later in life.) It never struck me as odd that I had such easy, regular access to the senator, even though my boss, the press secretary, seemed perplexed, even frustrated by it. I interviewed Wofford for his weekly radio actuality service and have a framed photo of me strolling with him behind the Hart Senate Building in my office. He was a gentleman, an intellectual and the kindest official I ever encountered in Washington. I once accompanied him on a book signing event. His book, "Of Kennedys and Kings" recounted his experience marching with Martin Luther King, Jr., and his work as a special assistant to President John F. Kennedy. Wofford was one of the founders of the Peace Corps. I was in awe of him and his myriad accomplishments.

I remember one Friday when the office was quiet and much of the senior staff was back in Pennsylvania campaigning and we were allowed to dress casually (a rare thing in the early 1990s). I was wearing jeans. The senator showed up unexpectedly and called a staff meeting. I was mortified to be seen by him in my jeans and so took a seat at the back of the room. Sen. Wofford spotted me in the back, then walked around the room behind me, put his hands on my shoulders, and conducted the meeting from there, the entire staff staring at me and the senator. In my jeans. I was so naive — it never registered that he was gay or bi; I assumed he treated all the interns like that. Again, he never did or said anything remotely inappropriate, just paid attention to me and engaged in meaningful conversations with me.

Many years later, in 2016, after Wofford's wife had died, he wrote an op-ed in the New York Times announcing his engagement to Matthew Charlton. He was coming out at age 90.

As the Times reported, "In the article, Mr. Wofford did not define himself as gay, writing: 'Too often, our society seeks to label people by pinning them on the wall — straight, gay or in between. I don't categorize myself based on the gender of those I love. I had a half-century of marriage with a wonderful woman, and now am lucky for a second time to have found happiness.'"

Shortly after that, I was attending a Pride reception at the Obama White House when I spotted Wofford and Charlton across the room. I couldn't resist ribbing him about coming out in the Times instead of the Blade. I reminded him of my time in his office and, as usual, he was funny, smart, and kind. Congress could use many more like him.

If ever there was a polar opposite of Wofford, it was Santorum, the crass, bigoted homophobe who defeated him and served two terms in the Senate. Incredibly, Santorum had a gay communications director, Robert Traynham. One of my favorite Blade stories ever was about a meeting Santorum's staff arranged between him and a group of PFLAG moms. They confronted him about his attacks on their sons and daughters and described to the Blade how Santorum tripped over a chair trying to leave the meeting in a hurry.

It was a happy day when he lost his reelection bid and I wrote the following column.

Gay rights supporters cheered this week's election results, hailing the end of a Republican-dominated era that has seen zero progress on gay rights legislation and the introduction of a federal constitutional amendment to ban gay marriage.

But the news wasn't all good. Although Arizona became the first state ever to defeat an anti-gay marriage amendment on the ballot, similar measures passed overwhelmingly in seven other states, including Virginia.

Despite those setbacks, we should celebrate the reelection of Rep. Barney Frank, who is now in line to chair the powerful Financial Services Committee after the Democrats took control of the House.

But of all the positive developments this week, none is sweeter than the defeat of rabidly anti-gay U.S. Sen. Rick Santorum (R-Pa.).

It's not nice to gloat, but Santorum's defeat has plenty of us dancing in the streets.

Santorum, a second-term Republican and chair of the GOP conference in the Senate, was the third-ranking member of his party's leadership. In 2003, discussing the U.S. Supreme Court case Lawrence

v. Texas, which eventually overturned the nation's remaining sodomy laws, Santorum made his most infamous anti-gay remark.

He told the Associated Press, "If the Supreme Court says that you have the right to consensual [gay] sex within your home, then you have the right to bigamy, you have the right to polygamy, you have the right to incest, you have the right to adultery. You have the right to anything."

The remarks sparked an outcry among gay activists, but the GOP leadership did nothing in response to Santorum's hateful comments. When former majority leader Trent Lott (R-Miss.) appeared to make racist remarks at a birthday celebration for Strom Thurmond, he was relieved of his leadership role. No such penalty for Santorum. In fact, national Republican leaders quickly lined up to support him.

"It's solid, it's absolutely solid," Senate majority leader Bill Frist (R-Tenn.) said of Santorum's leadership position. "Absolutely he will remain in the leadership. He has the full 100 percent confidence" of Senate Republicans.

Santorum's remarks were not the first time he targeted gays. In 2001, he sent a controversial letter to the conservative group Alliance for Marriage, affirming his support for a constitutional amendment banning same-sex marriage. The mailing sought money so the non-profit could flood Congress with petitions to "protect marriage between a man and a woman against the attacks of the homosexual activists."

"I know it may sound like a huge exaggeration, particularly in light of the attack on America, but this may truly be the most important letter I ever write you," Santorum wrote.

In the wake of 9/11, Santorum was more concerned with codifying anti-gay discrimination in the U.S. Constitution than protecting the country from further terrorist attacks. That kind of sick pandering to conservative Christian activists is what cost Santorum his job.

To be fair, Santorum's Senate record included commendable work on poverty and AIDS issues and he did reach out to the Log Cabin Republicans on more than one occasion, including to discuss HIV initiatives.

But his focus on hot-button social issues, including banning same-sex marriage and late-term abortions, and his support for other controversial measures, like tax exemptions for religious charities, proved too much for Pennsylvania voters. Santorum's views are better suited to Alabama than Pennsylvania and the state's voters delivered a richly deserved pink slip to their senator.

And so the Senate's leading homophobe is gone and his counterpart in the House, Marilyn Musgrave (R-Colo.), barely survived a surprisingly strong challenge from Angie Paccione. Musgrave, lead sponsor of the anti-gay marriage amendment, failed to win a majority of votes. She took about 46 percent to Paccione's 43 percent; a third-party candidate won 11 percent.

Musgrave made gay marriage a centerpiece of her campaign, despite the fact that the U.S. is currently fighting two wars. She was no doubt helped by the introduction of two gay-related measures on the Colorado ballot, one to ban same-sex marriage and another to grant gay couples domestic partnership rights. The marriage ban passed and the DP measure was trailing badly as of this writing.

Ironically, the Senate lost a marriage equality ally in Sen. Lincoln Chafee of Rhode Island, a Republican who should have switched party affiliations.

In Virginia, the marriage amendment also passed, by a margin of about 57-43 percent. The final tally wasn't as close as activists had hoped, but certainly far less decisive than in other states, notably South Carolina, where the marriage amendment was approved by nearly 80 percent of voters. Clearly, we have a long way to go in convincing rural voters that our relationships and families deserve equal protection of the law.

With Musgrave's reprimand and Santorum's ouster, there is hope that the tone in Washington will change. Karl Rove's broken-record strategy of attacking gays is finally played out. Yes, we have incurred huge setbacks in the road to marriage equality, but the profound changes coming to the Hill present new opportunities for advances on other fronts.

Leading gay rights activists meeting to make post-election plans have rightly chosen a trans-inclusive Employment Non-Discrimination Act as their top legislative priority.

ENDA has languished for far too long and polls have consistently shown that Americans are much further down the path of opposing employment discrimination than marriage discrimination. Barney Frank told the Blade last month that in a Democrat-controlled House, ENDA and a repeal of "Don't Ask, Don't Tell" would get renewed attention.

Neither is a sure thing, of course, but at least gay rights supporters now have a chance to play offense instead of devoting time and political capital to fighting discriminatory measures.

It's tempting to pop the Champagne corks, but the real work lies ahead. Many Democrats coming to Washington ran on conservative platforms and won't vote in lockstep with the liberal wing of the party.

Democrat Brad Ellsworth, for example, unseated Rep. John Hostetler (R-Ind.), but he opposes abortion rights and supports constitutional amendments to ban gay marriage and flag desecration. Democrats in many other races, including Tennessee, Virginia and Pennsylvania, spoke out against gay marriage during the campaign and some support constitutional bans on same-sex marriage.

Gay voters have earned a few days of celebration, after enduring the last few years of attacks on our rights and families. But then we must get to the real work of changing laws. ENDA is the place to start.

"Cruising the High Seas," June 8, 2007

Looking back on this essay, I can't believe my husband and I were such nervous prudes about taking our first all-gay cruise. What a blast we had and, as I predicted back then, we did form lasting friendships with a handful of the guys we met on board the QM2. The topic of friendship came up a lot over the years writing for the Blade and it's clear that friendship means something extra to the LGBTQ community. So many of us have been shunned by family that we create something akin to a chosen family in our friend groups, from the now-famous houses of the 1980s New York ballroom scene to modern "friendsgivings." We do seem to invest a lot of time and emotion in our friends, more so than our straight counterparts, who have closer relationships with extended family and are more likely to have their own children.

This passage from that column I wrote 14 years ago remains urgently relevant today: "A quick look at the current effort to ban gay marriage in Massachusetts offers unsettling proof that even after a victory is won, it's not necessarily secure." That's the point of this book — we can't afford to become complacent. As my old friend David Mixner recalls when his former partner, near death with AIDS, insisted on walking to the voting booth under his own power, we must stay vigilant and participate in our democracy. We've now seen the consequences when we don't stay engaged with the overturning of Roe v. Wade and the impending attacks on the Obergefell marriage ruling.

To say I was apprehensive about my first cruise and first-ever all-gay vacation would be an understatement.

Working at the Blade, my life is gay enough without taking an all-gay vacation, I reasoned. And who wants to spend their vacation seasick, anyway? Besides, a combination of the two would surely mean a week trapped aboard a floating bathhouse, right?

Wrong. Way wrong.

I just returned from the first all-gay trans-Atlantic crossing aboard the Queen Mary 2, organized by RSVP Vacations. The experience proved empowering and taught me some unexpected lessons about the importance of friendship in our community. It also reminded me of the need to avoid engaging in stereotyping. All good lessons as Pride season arrives.

As much as we fight the unfair and cruel stereotypes directed at us by our opponents, I found myself engaging in the very same behavior. With events like a singles party, leather party and uniform party, I assumed the worst of my fellow gay (and a few lesbian) shipmates. I was expecting tawdry, drunken, drug-fueled parties and was already at work composing a prudish screed in my mind as the awe-inspiring ship sailed out of New York.

Sure there was partying, but there were also intimate formal dinners and panel discussions on the gay rights movement. Instead of empty conference rooms, those panels attracted hundreds of attendees. We laughed, learned and even cried together. I can't imagine a straight cruise drawing 300 vacationers for a history lesson on civil rights.

And one of those meetings proved the highlight of the voyage. Four gay pioneers took the stage for an afternoon discussion on how far the gay rights movement has progressed: political strategist and AIDS activist David Mixner; activist and philanthropist Herb Hamsher; European Union parliament member Michael Cashman; and former clerk of the U.S. House of Representatives Jeff Trandahl.

What ensued took everyone by surprise. Instead of a wonky 90-minute lesson in politicking, each gay man spoke about his personal path to activism. Cashman's remarks served as a poignant reminder that the goal of equality under the law isn't a dream in some parts of the world. In Cashman's U.K. it's a reality, where gays serve openly in the military and same-sex relationships enjoy national recognition. It's a vision of what the United States can become with better leaders on both sides of the aisle.

Hamsher was a dignified presence throughout the trip, offering insightful commentary on a range of issues and cautioning us against demonizing our opponents in the religious right. (Of course, that didn't stop us from laughing uproariously later in the trip when Margaret Cho fantasized about Jerry Falwell's reincarnation as a power bottom on an eternal tour of Eagle bars.)

Mixner's reminiscences of the early fight against AIDS and the loss of his partner left the crowd in quiet sobs. Choking with emotion, he recalled the day his hospitalized partner demanded to be taken to a polling place to vote, walking under his own power to the booth. Mixner's warnings about apathy serve as an important reminder that our fight is not just to win equal rights, but to guard against backsliding. A quick look at the current effort to ban gay marriage in Massachusetts offers unsettling proof that even after a victory is won, it's not necessarily secure.

I will never forget Mixner's words. Every gay man and lesbian in their teens and 20s should have been in that room. Those of us who survived the '80s carry a tremendous burden to never forget and to teach the next generation so that the heartless cruelty of an uncaring government that watched passively as an entire generation of gay men died is never repeated.

This is my fifth year writing about Pride for the Blade and each year it's the same thing; we all wring our hands about the purpose of the celebration. Here's an idea: turn Pride into an event that honors those lost to AIDS and encourages us to rediscover the courage embodied by those who fought back.

In this era of protease inhibitors and crystal meth, it's easy for some to forget about that lost generation. Shame on us for perpetuating the reckless impression that HIV is some inconvenient, "manageable" problem.

When it came Trandahl's turn to speak, I expected scripted, guarded remarks from the Republican who became the reluctant behind-the-scenes star witness in the Mark Foley scandal. Instead, Trandahl spoke with a disarming warmth and honesty about working hard to prove to the most powerful people in Congress that a gay man could run their show. His quiet resolve should inspire each of us to work a little harder. After all, Trandahl survived the efforts of former Rep. Tom "The Hammer" DeLay to oust him from the clerk's post.

Here again I found a cautionary tale about the dangers of stereotyping. Trandahl found himself in the media spotlight last year connected with the Foley story and many assumed he was somehow involved in the GOP leadership's cover up of Foley's wrongdoing. Nothing could be further from the truth, but Trandahl didn't hold angry new conferences or denounce his critics on Fox News. Instead, he kept quiet and let his record speak for itself. In the end, Foley resigned in disgrace and Trandahl emerged as an out figure of unimpeachable integrity. It's gratifying to know that if Foley ever resurfaces to write a book or otherwise try to cash in on his misdeeds, that Trandahl will be there to remind us of the truth.

The week aboard the Queen Mary 2 included many touching moments like those from that panel discussion. After a screening of the new film "Save Me," several men stood before a packed auditorium to tell their stories of growing up gay in evangelical households and the emotional toll it took on them, including struggles with addiction. The film is a remarkably restrained look at the "ex-gay" movement featuring a subdued and stellar performance by Judith Light.

And the surprises kept coming. During the decadent dinners, I was lucky to meet a host of diverse (and fun) travelers, several of whom I am confident will become lasting friends.

Perhaps we're so quick to bond because no matter our differences we are all the same. The poor rural southern gay kid, the Manhattan hipster and the Texas lesbian have all been bullied, discriminated against, demonized, called "faggot" or "dyke" and rejected by family and friends.

Maybe that's why we need a Pride — to bring us all together, even if it's just for a day — to remind our neighbors that we're part of the local community. We should follow the examples of the Mixners, Trandahls, Cashmans and Hamshers among us. The visibility of out people is the weapon that will eventually win the war for equal rights under the law.

"Too little, too late?", Oct. 12, 2007 and "Bella's bill," Nov. 9, 2007

The 2007 fight over the Employment Non-Discrimination Act was one of the most divisive issues I've seen in 20 years at the Blade. When trans protections were dropped from the bill, the Human Rights Campaign was put in the impossible position of either supporting the gay-only ENDA or opposing the only gay rights legislation in Congress. In 2022, we still don't have federal legislation barring anti-LGBTQ workplace discrimination. The Equality Act passed the House and Joe Biden campaigned on making it his No. 1 legislative priority. Despite that, it has languished in the Senate, where just four Republicans are reportedly in favor of the bill. As noted here, the original nondiscrimination bill was introduced in 1974 by Rep. Bella Abzug of New York. Her bill was expansive and died. The 2007 measure was more limited and ultimately killed in the Senate after Rep. Barney Frank shepherded it through the House. Matters were complicated in 2007, when I endorsed the gay-only bill. It was doomed anyway with President Bush in the White House, but Senate passage would have made it easier to come back in 2009 with a trans-inclusive bill and Barack Obama in the Oval Office. Of course, that didn't happen either as Democrats focused on a federal hate crimes bill and then repeal of "Don't Ask, Don't Tell" before losing control of the House in the disastrous 2010 midterms.

All those efforts in 2007 proved futile as ENDA died in the Senate and conservative Democrats refused to take up the issue of employment nondiscrimination in the first two years of the Obama administration, then lost the House, dooming any chance of passage for years to come. Fast-forward to 2022 and LGBTQ workers still lack federal workplace protections. Although the 2020 Supreme Court ruling in Bostock v. Clayton County said Title VII of the Civil Rights Act of 1964 bans employment discrimination based on sexual orientation and gender identity, legal experts agree that federal legislation is needed to fill gaps and ensure full protection under the law.

"TOO LITTLE, TOO LATE?"

The disappointing news regarding ENDA has triggered a tidal wave of indignation and, unfortunately, attacks on our most powerful ally in Congress, Rep. Barney Frank (D-Mass.) Last week, as the Victory Fund honored Frank for serving openly in Congress for 20 years, others were denouncing him for his "betrayal" of trans people.

Meanwhile, others were gunning for the Human Rights Campaign, accusing its leaders of abandoning the "T" in GLBT. The snarky press releases have been flying, online message boards are filled with anti-HRC invective and trans protesters picketed the HRC National Dinner Saturday night in D.C.

We all love a protest!

The problem with this overheated reaction is it's self-destructive, counterproductive, oversimplified and, in some cases, strikingly hypocritical. Some of the most vocal opponents of Frank's amended ENDA bill supported state nondiscrimination measures that also omitted trans people not so long ago.

The Blade broke the story that congressional Democrats didn't have the votes to pass a trans-inclusive ENDA. Some of those Democrats have been telling the Blade and gay supporters on the Hill that they don't understand ENDA and have no idea what "gender identity" means. So where were all the organizations now attacking Frank and HRC when they could have made a difference?

Some have criticized HRC for not releasing the names of the House Democrats going soft on trans inclusion. But it doesn't take an insider to figure out who they are — think Heath Shuler, a Democrat elected last year from North Carolina's 11th District, and other more conservative politicians like him. Equality North Carolina signed on to the coalition opposing Frank's ENDA bill that does not include protections based on gender identity, but how much time did that group and others spend educating Shuler in advance of last week?

Others are angry that HRC does not support a sexual orientation-only ENDA, but also won't actively oppose it. Whatever you think of HRC, it's important to remember that its staffers are the ones at the table on the Hill. It is inconceivable that HRC would slap Frank on the wrist and work to oppose a gay rights bill pending in Congress. Frank's seniority and role as chair of the Financial Services Committee make him the most powerful gay rights advocate in the country. The nation's largest gay group engaged in federal lobbying can't afford to alienate him — it would be self-defeating and short sighted.

House Speaker Nancy Pelosi (D-Calf.) advocated for a trans-inclusive ENDA in her keynote speech at the HRC dinner: But she chose her words carefully, promising to "fight for the most inclusive ENDA possible." She deliberately did not rule out supporting an ENDA without trans protections and many view a vote on that bill as inevitable.

In some ways it's been gratifying to see all the gay rights groups come out of the proverbial woodwork (who knew there were more than 200 of them?). It shows that we are still capable of rallying the troops and uniting around an important cause. And keeping trans people part of ENDA is a worthy and important cause. It's just too bad that this outpouring came so late in the game. Many supportive members of Congress are complaining that they didn't hear a peep from gay rights supporters or any of the 200 plus groups in the coalition until last week. That's disappointing, but not surprising.

Attacking one another over ENDA is playing into the hands of those Christian conservatives who would like nothing more than to further divide us. "Over the years, homosexual activists including Rep. Barney Frank (D-Mass.) have chafed at their alliance with a transsexual movement — knowing that it only makes their cause look even more radical to the general public," according to a statement on the Americans For Truth About Homosexuality website that gleefully reports the division within the GLBT movement.

Sara Whitman, a lesbian blogger at Huffington Post, wrote to Frank, "I cannot believe you are supporting a gutted version of the Employment Non-Discrimination Act (ENDA) ... Maybe you've been in office too long. Maybe you're too jaded to remember how people stood by you when it wasn't necessarily a popular thing to do. ... Shame on you."

That sort of reaction has been common and unfortunate. Passing a federal law of this magnitude requires years of work; in fact ENDA has been around in one form or another since the '70s. It's not as simple as is being portrayed.

There is a real danger to proceeding with a trans-inclusive ENDA that we know to be doomed. It would trigger an ugly debate over, among other things, exemptions for schools. Opponents would invoke unfair and offensive anti-transgender stereotypes to torpedo the bill, moderate Democrats and Republicans would start abandoning ship and ENDA would be killed off in a landslide vote. That would be the worst possible outcome.

Two years from now, when lawmakers try again with an inclusive ENDA, the memories of a fight over trans stereotypes would likely scare off potential supporters. Alternatively, passage of a sexual orientation-only bill by the House, which would either die in the Senate or by President Bush's veto pen anyway, might just set the stage for a happier, trans-inclusive outcome in 2009, when allies are betting the House has 20 more Democrats and Hillary Clinton in the White House.

To be sure, no one is blameless in this mess. HRC must accept its share of responsibility for failing to adequately educate and lobby new conservative Democrats on trans issues. That responsibility isn't HRC's alone, though, and all those energized by this debate should stay active, visible and aggressive in meeting with and educating House members in their districts.

No one is arguing that the law should leave trans people behind. In fact, transgender people are most in need of protection from employment discrimination. But achieving these goals requires strategy and patience, not emotion and personal attacks. Instead of petitions and angry blogs, gay rights advocates should be focused on using the reprieve granted by House Speaker Nancy Pelosi to educate members and strategize for the best outcome.

The answer may be to pull both of Frank's bills and come back in 2009. If that happens, gay activists need to be more careful about the Democrats they choose to support. As we've seen in this debate and elsewhere in recent weeks, it's not a given that Democrats will stand with us. They have taken gay support for granted for too long and gays have let them get away with it.

"BELLA'S BILL"

Former Rep. Bella Abzug (D-N.Y.) probably had no idea that 33 years after she introduced the original Employment Non-Discrimination Act in 1974, that the nation would still be debating whether or not gays should be protected from legal job discrimination.

To get an idea of how slowly things change, take a look at the Blade's coverage of the late Abzug's bill from the July 1974 edition:

"For the first time in American legislative history, proposed gay rights legislation has reached the federal level. On May 14, Bella

Abzug, Democratic representative from New York's 20th congressional district, introduced a bill which seeks to include gays among the classes protected from arbitrary discrimination.

"The bill, H.R. 14752, proposes that the new categories of sex, sexual orientation, and marital status be added to the 1964 civil rights act. If it were adopted, the new legislation would thus prohibit discrimination on the basis of these new categories in housing, public accommodations, and federal programs, including federal employment.

"The bill was forwarded to the civil rights subcommittee, which is chaired by Don Edwards (D-Calif.) and part of the Judiciary Committee. Because the Judiciary Committee is presently in the throes of impeachment hearings, chances for any hearings being held on Abzug's bill during this congressional session appear nil. If and when hearings are held, opposition is expected to be stiff. 'I imagine the administration will oppose the bill,' was the wry but understated comment of Ms. Marilyn Mavcoson, Abzug's press secretary, in a phone conversation with the Gay Blade. She encouraged gay groups and individuals to write to Rep. Edwards and urge him to hold hearings on the bill."

It took 33 years, but ENDA is finally getting some serious attention on the Hill, where it passed the House this week in a 235-184 vote. Gay Reps. Barney Frank and Tammy Baldwin, along with the Human Rights Campaign, deserve much credit for the bruising work it took to pass this bill.

Now that the House vote is (finally) over, the fight moves to the Senate, where hopes are high for a similar outcome. That chamber nearly passed ENDA in 1996; it lost by just one vote. Among the 45 current senators who were in office in 1996, 26 voted for the bill and 19 voted against it. That bill, like the one that passed the House this week, had no language regarding gender identity.

What a refreshing change to hear lawmakers this week step up to defend the right of gays and lesbians to be free from legal workplace discrimination. It seems like an eternity ago that we were made to endure President Bush's cynical and demoralizing anti-gay attacks during his State of the Union address.

Unfortunately, ENDA's supporters are divided too sharply along partisan lines and the House debate included the usual scare tactics about infringing on the right of Christian workers to post anti-gay Scripture at the office.

Galling as it was to listen to some of the misguided opposition to ENDA during the debate, Republican complaints about Baldwin's move to introduce and almost immediately withdraw her transgender amendment were valid. That was a cynical ploy to placate trans rights advocates, while simultaneously ensuring that the Democrats wouldn't have to go on record and vote on a transgender issue.

As in Abzug's day, the current administration also opposes the bill. And it's a much-watered down version of what Abzug, who died in 1998, envisioned. Her original bill would have barred anti-gay discrimination in public accommodations and housing, something not addressed in the current legislation.

Then, as now, proponents of the bill were urged to contact their lawmakers to express support. Unfortunately, that's a critical step in passing legislation that gays haven't yet learned in adequate numbers. We are far too apathetic to expect easy passage of anything related to gay rights. It's a criticism we've heard from supportive members of Congress and activists on the state level. Social conservative activists are skilled in the art of bombarding lawmakers with emails and phone calls, while gay rights backers seem to have trouble picking up a phone when it comes to interacting with their representatives.

As a former Hill staffer on the Senate side, I know from experience just how carefully lawmakers listen to constituent sentiment on hot-button issues. Each call and email is logged and members of Congress are regularly briefed on feedback from back home. If gay rights supporters continue to assume that someone else is doing the heavy lifting, then it will be another 33 years before we see real progress on federal gay rights legislation.

In the 2007 ENDA fight, members of Congress might be confused about the messages that have come from their gay constituents — some advocating for any version of ENDA and others urging a "no" vote on any bill not trans-inclusive. Contrary to the claims of United ENDA, gays and lesbians are not of one mind on the question of whether or not lawmakers should support gay-only ENDA.

Now the focus turns to the Senate and it's more crucial than ever that gay rights advocates speak clearly. This Congress is on the verge of making history by passing a freestanding gay civil rights bill in both houses and sending it to the president's desk and no one should be working to undermine ENDA's changes in the Senate.

Sure, Bush will veto it. But the memory of a supportive Congress passing ENDA in both houses will outlast Bush's efforts at killing it.

Sen. Ted Kennedy (D-Mass.) is expected to introduce ENDA in the Senate at any time. His office has not revealed whether it will contain a transgender provision. Let's hope it does not. This is not the time for grandstanding; nor is it the time for well intentioned members of the United ENDA coalition to actively oppose ENDA in the Senate. The debate over trans inclusion was had and it's finished. Supporters of that approach didn't have the votes so we must all go back to local districts and do the hard work of educating lawmakers on gender identity issues.

But in the meantime there is pressing work to be done in the Senate. Gay rights supporters must overcome their apathy and place calls to their senators' office demanding passage of ENDA. If President Bush wants to be remembered for vetoing an anti-discrimination bill, so be it. But passage of ENDA by both houses this year will make it far easier to pass again when Bush is mercifully gone in 2009.

"HILLARY FOR PRESIDENT," DEC. 21, 2007

The Obama campaign certainly didn't appreciate this one. I heard quickly from Obama's communications team after endorsing his primary opponent, Hillary Clinton, and they registered their displeasure. During eight years in office, Obama never granted the Blade a sit-down interview, though he did call on the Blade's Chris Johnson for the third-to-last question of his presidency in December 2016. Our relationship with the Obama White House was definitely strained at the beginning, largely thanks to this endorsement. As the primary contests ground on in the spring of 2008, Hillary granted me an interview in advance of the "Potomac Primary," the Maryland, D.C., and Virginia contests that come so late in the calendar that they almost never matter. But 2008 was different and Hillary stayed in until the bitter end. I interviewed her by phone for 30 minutes. She's definitely a tough interview; her strategy became immediately clear — Hillary can talk for 30 minutes about anything, so she aimed to simply run out the clock on the first question. It takes a lot of interrupting and talking over her to get a word in but we had a good conversation, even if her answers on marriage left me somewhat disappointed. Some of the gay bloggers objected to my interviewing Hillary after endorsing her, but seemed to be placated when they read the final piece in which it was clear I did not go soft on her. I'd hoped that Obama would give me an interview after Hillary sat down with me, but it never happened. His staff was too pissed about the endorsement to consider it. Obama did grant the Blade an interview in September in advance of his contest against John McCain, but it was a written Q&A rather than in-person interview, which amounted to a lame cop-out by the Democratic nominee.

Looking back, my observation about the importance of foreign policy experience proved prescient — I just hadn't thought about Obama as president and Hillary as Secretary of State. A brilliant solution! Four years later, I endorsed Obama; four years after that I again endorsed Hillary.

Many gay voters, this one included, are reluctant to trust Bill and Hillary Clinton's promises on our issues after the euphoria of

1993 turned into the crushing disappointments of "Don't Ask, Don't Tell" and the Defense of Marriage Act.

After courting the gay vote back then, Bill Clinton embraced a disastrous policy that has led to the expulsion of 12,000 service members at a time when the military needs all the help it can get. The U.S. military is kicking out brave, competent service members, including dozens of desperately needed Arabic-speaking linguists, solely because they are gay. The military's gay ban amounts to un-American overt discrimination — a fact apparent to any rational, fair-minded person.

Bill's transgressions didn't end there. He signed DOMA and cynically bragged about it in ads that aired on Christian radio stations during his 1996 reelection campaign. More recently, he reportedly urged Sen. John Kerry to support state constitutional amendments banning same-sex marriage during the 2004 race.

Publicly, we are told that this is not Bill's campaign for a third term; rather it's Hillary's opportunity to shine on her own. But no one is that naïve. Make no mistake that voters will again get a twofer if Hillary wins.

Despite this complicated history, Hillary Clinton, and most of her Democratic rivals, deserve much credit for evolving quickly on gay rights issues. Just four years ago, Kerry endorsed same-sex marriage bans. Today, all the Democratic candidates have backed some form of relationship recognition for gay couples. Former Sen. John Edwards, Sen. Barack Obama and Gov. Bill Richardson favor repealing all of DOMA, while Clinton has taken the more cautious approach of advocating a repeal only of Section 3, which defines marriage under federal law as a union only between a man and woman. That section prevents same-sex couples who are married or have entered into civil unions from accessing the many federal benefits of marriage. Advocating for its repeal marks major progress for a leading presidential candidate.

On many other high-profile gay issues, there's not much to distinguish the Democratic contenders. They all support the Employment Non-Discrimination Act, a gay-inclusive hate crimes law and repeal of "Don't Ask, Don't Tell."

So, then, why Hillary? Her chief rival, Obama, has disappointed in the debates, appearing to lack confidence and talking mostly in generalities. George W. Bush has certainly lowered the bar when it comes to expecting experience in our presidential candidates, but Obama was an Illinois state senator just three years ago. Obama's speeches are often inspirational and he has bravely stood up to homophobic Black ministers and advocated for equal treatment of gays. He's certainly earned his considerable gay support. But the world is a complicated mess: warring religious factions in the Middle East, rising anti-American sentiment around the globe, the dollar in a free-fall. Electing a president with virtually zero experience on the world stage would be a mistake.

By contrast, Clinton has demonstrated a mastery of detail during the campaign. Whatever you think of her, there's no denying her intellect and willingness to work hard. She knows the issues, the history and players and has repeatedly pledged to work to restore the country's reputation around the world. That's a much-needed commonsense perspective on where to start in 2009. And with an eight-year record of extensive globetrotting as first lady, she's well positioned to serve as the diplomat the country needs.

For those who doubt her ability to win over moderate and conservative voters, look at what she accomplished in upstate New York, where she carried "red" counties in a landslide Senate reelection victory. I've interviewed elected officials, including conservative Republicans, from those areas and they agree that Clinton is a hard-working and accessible leader with a focus on constituent service. In addition, she worked from day one in the Senate to cultivate relationships with even her most conservative Republican colleagues.

She has promised that gay Americans will have an "open door" to her White House, a welcome change from the nonstop demonizing of gays under Bush.

The Democrats rightly won praise for including a forum on gay issues in the primary campaign season. The leading Republican candidates wouldn't even attend a debate on Black issues, let alone gay ones. The GOP, by continuing to align itself with evangelical Christian extremists, has clearly not learned anything from the failed Bush era. Its standard bearers appear increasingly out of touch — from Mike Huckabee's shockingly ignorant remarks about "isolating" AIDS patients to Rudy Giuliani's suddenly nuanced positions on gay rights.

Gay Americans cannot afford another four years of a Republican administration in the White House. Attacking gays and opposing even the most benign forms of incremental rights advances is now part of the GOP playbook, no matter the nominee. Bush has helped block ENDA and the hate crimes bill via veto threats. He has attacked our relationships in his State of the Union address, cruelly pushing for a federal ban on same-sex marriage. He — along with all the Republican candidates for president — supports the antiquated and reckless "Don't Ask, Don't Tell" policy.

Many supporters of independent candidates argue that there is no longer a difference between the Democratic and Republican parties. But on gay issues, that is simply not the case.

As gay Rep. Barney Frank told the Blade last summer, "all the Democrats are very good and all the Republicans are very terrible." For sure, gay Americans will be vastly better served by any of the Democrats now in the running than any of the Republicans.

But in the end, Hillary Rodham Clinton stands the best chance of sending the Republicans into eight years of a well-deserved political wilderness. She's smart, tenacious, hard working and willing to cede the spotlight in the interest of bipartisan cooperation. She has marched in our Pride parades, promised unprecedented access to her administration and backed nearly all of our issues.

Clinton has earned the support of gay voters in 2008.

"Hillary, the time has come," May 9, 2008

Less than five months after endorsing her, I was urging Hillary to drop out. The collapse of Hillary Clinton's 2008 presidential campaign was a stunning thing to behold. The woman many of us praised as intelligent and strategic presided over a campaign crippled by incompetence and ill-advised photo ops. By May, it was clear that Obama would be the party's nominee. Simultaneously, GOP nominee Sen. John McCain was sending ominous signals to the Republican base about his intent to nominate conservatives to the Supreme Court in the mold of Samuel Alito. To McCain's credit, he granted the Blade an interview that year, the first and only time a Republican presidential nominee has given an interview to the gay press. Donald Trump turned us down several times; but McCain, true to his maverick image, agreed to talk. And his interview was refreshingly candid as he spoke about having gay friends and staffers and even identifying Mark Bingham — the gay rugby player who helped lead a revolt on Flight 93 during the 9/11 attacks — as a personal hero. Despite such overtures, McCain's record on LGBTQ rights was dismal and the choice was clear — Hillary needed to get out, endorse Obama and work for his election. Despite my advice in this piece, Log Cabin Republicans President Patrick Sammon endorsed McCain. He noted that his organization has "honest disagreements with Sen. McCain on a number of gay rights issues," and said that they will "continue our conversation with him and other Republican leaders about issues affecting gay and lesbian Americans." Sammon left Log Cabin shortly after and went on to a successful, award-winning career in filmmaking. I consider him a friend and he was one of several Log Cabin leaders that I was close to over the past 20 years. Despite my obvious political differences with Log Cabin, I have always recognized the importance of working for change from within. As Sammon has noted, no civil rights struggle is won with the support of a single party. And so I always sought connections to Log Cabin's leaders over the years and there have been several principled, effective presidents who achieved a lot for LGBTQ visibility and acceptance within the GOP. Leaders like Sammon and Patrick Guerriero before him, as well as R. Clarke Cooper and Gregory Angelo, took heat from fellow gays and fellow Republicans alike. It's a tough job, but an important one. I broke with Log Cabin in 2020 when the organization not only endorsed Trump but held events in his D.C. hotel. Imagine the whining and outcry from Log Cabin if the Human Rights Campaign held a fundraiser in a hotel owned by Barack Obama. Log Cabin has lost its way, like so many other Republicans entranced by the '80s relic and washed-up reality show host Trump.

This week's results in the North Carolina and Indiana primaries have left Sen. Hillary Rodham Clinton out of options. She ran a tough and spirited campaign that will be talked about for a generation. But it's over.

The time has come for Clinton to adopt a gracious and conciliatory tone, end her campaign and endorse Sen. Barack Obama for president.

Tuesday night was, indeed, a game changer: Clinton suffered a drubbing in North Carolina — a "big" state, in her terminology — and barely squeaked out a win in Indiana. She needed a convincing win there and a strong finish in the Tar Heel state to convince voters and, more importantly, donors that she still had a chance to win over the dwindling number of uncommitted superdelegates.

As someone who endorsed Clinton early in the campaign (well before the mainstream media went ga-ga over Obama after his Iowa victory), I saw her as the party's best chance to beat the GOP nominee and as the candidate with the most relevant international experience to tackle the myriad crises inflicted on us by George Bush.

Unfortunately, all the talk of experience and competence was belied by a campaign rife with incompetence. From Bill Clinton's ruinous (and arguably racist) campaign swing through South Carolina, to an obvious failure to craft a strategy past Super Tuesday, her campaign staff made so many miscalculations that Hillary went from a coronation to a shocking defeat.

And her behavior during the recent and infamous ABC News debate was over the line. During that debate, Charles Gibson and George Stephanopoulos grilled Obama over the Rev. Wright controversy and, incredibly, his thoughts on wearing flag pins. Obama was overdue for some more aggressive questioning from the mainstream media, but not on those topics.

Rather than insist on taking the questioning to a higher level, Clinton gleefully joined the Obama bashing that night. The Obama campaign should never have agreed to a debate in which Stephanopoulos was asking the questions. As a veteran of the first Clinton administration, he could hardly be expected to approach the event with any modicum of objectivity. He's a celebrity talking head, not a journalist.

In sharp contrast to Clinton's transparent, over-the-top pandering (downing shots with the locals and touting a phony love of guns), Obama has managed to stay above the fray, even during the darkest moments of the Wright saga. He could have gone sharply negative in the run-up to North Carolina and Indiana, as some advised him to do. Instead, he stuck to his own metaphorical guns and rose above the faux controversies and petty attacks. Even in victory Tuesday night, Obama praised Clinton and promised that his supporters would back her if she emerged as the party nominee.

But she didn't emerge victorious and the time has come for her supporters, gay and straight, to embrace Obama's campaign for the White House. The stakes are too high to allow primary race disappointments to demoralize Democratic voters. And the stakes for gay voters are higher.

Just yesterday, Sen. John McCain reiterated his intention to appoint conservative justices in the mold of Samuel Alito and John Roberts to the Supreme Court.

In addition, McCain this week announced creation of his "Justice Advisory Committee," which will offer advice on Supreme Court picks. Among the members of that group is Sen. Sam Brownback (R-Kan.), a staunch conservative and notorious opponent of gay rights.

A McCain presidency would set back the cause of gay rights by a generation. A 50-year-old justice could serve 30 years or more on the high court. With same-sex marriage continuing to roil legislatures and courts across the country, it's only a matter of time before the Supreme Court will be asked to weigh in on recognition of same-sex relationships.

Last week, I moderated a panel discussion on national politics at the annual Equality Form in Philadelphia. The most heated exchange of the night came when I asked Patrick Sammon of the Log Cabin Republicans whether his group would endorse McCain. He replied that a decision on an endorsement had not yet been made but that Log Cabin was in talks with McCain's campaign. Sammon offered praise for McCain's opposition to a federal marriage amendment.

Indeed, McCain's opposition to the odious amendment was important and appreciated. But that's where his support for gay rights begins and ends. McCain opposes the federal Employment Non-Discrimination Act, repealing "Don't Ask, Don't Tell" and extending the federal hate crimes law to cover gays. Most disturbingly, he supported his home state of Arizona's ballot initiative that would have banned not only marriage, but civil unions and even domestic partnerships.

It is unconscionable for Log Cabin to entertain a McCain endorsement. Yes, it can be argued that McCain is better on gay issues than Bush, but that's not saying much. Let's not be fooled twice by a supposedly moderate Republican candidate. Bush won in 2000 after a pledge of "compassionate conservatism," which proved an empty slogan. In its place we saw cruel attacks on gay rights, an effort to pervert the U.S. Constitution to discriminate against gays and even public ridicule of our committed, loving relationships during the State of the Union Address.

Log Cabin's work is important and, as Sammon pointed out, no civil rights struggle has been won with the support of a single political party. Republican allies are critical to passage of gay rights legislation, especially when Democrats are so prone to going wishy-washy on us after they win elections with near unanimous gay support.

But with the Supreme Court in the balance, no gay voter should pull the lever for McCain in November. Sammon's predecessor, Patrick Guerriero, took a principled stand — for which he was unfairly criticized by some gay Republicans — and declined to endorse President Bush in 2004. Sammon should follow that example and Log Cabin should resist going to bat for someone who has publicly pledged to appoint justices hostile to gay rights advances.

Meanwhile, Hillary Clinton's gay supporters should take a day to mourn her defeat and then join Obama's cause. She's resilient and will bounce back, probably as Senate majority leader, a job much more in line with her skills than that of president.

And Obama should continue to reach out to Hillary's disaffected supporters and work to unite the party. It's time for Hillary's gay donors and volunteers to look past short-term disappointments and consider the long-term impact of a McCain administration. It's a scary thought that renders all other considerations moot.

"SECOND IN COMMAND," SEPT. 5, 2008

This was published long before Sarah Palin committed her many gaffes on the national stage and my quibbles with her mostly centered on her thin resume. It's not worth rehashing Palin's record on LGBTQ issues here as she quickly faded from laughingstock to has-been, even losing a 2022 race for the U.S. House from Alaska to a Democrat. A Democrat!

But Obama's vice presidential pick, Joe Biden, didn't emerge unscathed as I noted his vote for DOMA and a lackluster score on HRC's Congressional Scorecard. Biden, of course, has since redeemed himself and emerged as a strong LGBTQ ally, even describing transgender rights as the "civil rights issue of our time."

Now that the two parties have finally selected their candidates and wrapped their conventions, we can at last get down to the business of the relatively short general election campaign. Too bad the primary season can't be run as quickly and efficiently.

The conventional wisdom about quadrennial party conventions is that they are scripted and choreographed and fail to break any real news. Perhaps. But given Americans' ever shrinking attention span, there is a lot of value in staging conventions to showcase the party platforms — and the speaking skills of those who would lead the nation.

Over the past couple of weeks, Barack Obama and John McCain made their first big decision since being anointed to lead their respective parties: the choice of running mate. Obama went with experience, selecting Sen. Joe Biden of Delaware as his No. 2. No one will confuse Biden for a gay rights activist — he voted for the Defense of Marriage Act and has failed to cosponsor various pro-gay bills over the years, including the Uniting American Families Act. His HRC scorecard in the 2001-2002 Congress was a 78. (To be fair, he lost points for failing to sponsor UAFA, but Delaware activists told the Blade last week they're confident he would vote for the bill if it made it to the Senate floor.)

Obama's own mention of gay issues during his historic and captivating acceptance speech was disappointing. He said gays deserve the right to visit their partners in the hospital. Gee, thanks, Barack. But gay Democrats are by now accustomed to breadcrumbs. Am I the only one who thinks it appalling that politicians continue to ask us for money and votes while relegating the important subject of our right to equality under the law to a footnote in a speech? They dole out basic rights — like hospital visitation — piecemeal each year in the hopes of keeping us on the hook.

Despite the disappointments and shortcomings on the Democratic ticket, Biden's record is generally supportive when it comes to important gay issues and he backs a trans-inclusive Employment Non-Discrimination Act and extending full rights to same-sex couples joined in civil unions.

Certainly, on the question of experience and readiness to assume the top spot, there's no question that Biden is a solid choice. His background in foreign affairs is of particular importance given the range of foreign policy challenges that await the next president.

And on the campaign trail, Biden should be an asset, his down-to-earth accessibility the perfect antidote to the GOP's elitist "arugula" attacks against Obama. As a fellow train commuter, I've run into Biden a few times on the Amtrak out of Union Station and can attest to his approachability. He's smart, likable and easy to talk to.

By contrast, McCain's selection of Gov. Sarah Palin to be his running mate lowers the bar to frightening new levels on the question of experience. Sure, she's a governor — but of a state with a population about the size of Baltimore. Her last job? Mayor of a town with just 9,000 residents. My college football stadium held 10 times that many people.

McCain is a 72-year-old cancer survivor, making the issue of his running mate's competence and readiness for the presidency a major concern for voters. As for gay voters, Palin's thin record leaves little to analyze. According to the Log Cabin Republicans, Palin's record is not anti-gay. In 2006, the Anchorage Daily News quoted Palin as saying she's "not out to judge anyone and has good friends who are gay."

Well, we've heard that before. Remember George W. Bush's Austin 12? They assured us that Bush knew and liked gay people and that he was committed to "compassionate conservatism."

Log Cabin commended Palin as someone who "isn't a bigot." Talk about lowering the bar on expectations. If that's the best they can say about her, we're in real trouble. The organization's decision this week to endorse the McCain/Palin ticket was clearly not an easy one. Officials waited until the very last minute to make an announcement, suggesting board members were not enthusiastic in their support. It's a disappointing decision, considering McCain's position in favor of state constitutional amendments banning same-sex marriage and Palin's nonexistent resume. (Incredibly, GOP pundits have resorted to trumpeting her work as commander of the Alaska National Guard as a qualification for serving as commander in chief. Jon Stewart couldn't have come up with a more humorous defense.)

The decision to vote for Obama should be a no-brainer for gay Americans. From his support on a range of gay rights measures to his call for federal recognition of our relationships to his judgment in making Supreme Court appointments, Obama is far and away the superior candidate. Gay Republicans will tout McCain's opposition to the Federal Marriage Amendment in 2004 as reason enough to support him. But a McCain administration will not support ENDA or repeals of DOMA and "Don't Ask, Don't Tell," and, judging by the Palin choice, McCain must not be allowed to name a Supreme Court justice.

Palin has not taken public positions on most gay rights issues, including the need for nondiscrimination protections for gay workers and the repeal of "Don't Ask, Don't Tell" and DOMA. She opposes same-sex marriage and supported the 1998 state constitutional amendment banning same-sex marriage. She vetoed legislation that would have denied same-sex partners of state employees' health and retirement benefits, but that's a complicated story and she actually opposes offering the benefits to gay partners.

McCain's choice of Palin only solidifies the inescapable conclusion that Barack Obama has superior judgment and temperament and deserves the support of gay voters in November.

"Inside the White House," July 10, 2009

I will never forget attending the first White House Pride reception in 2009. Roughly 250 of us stood in the sunshine waiting in line at the gates — the same gates to which some in attendance had handcuffed themselves in earlier protests. Once inside, there were cosmos and a DJ spinning Madonna. It was, in a word, surreal. And I will never forget President Obama's words as he opened his remarks: "Welcome to your house." Nearly everyone was in tears. There were old school activists like Frank Kameny, celebrities, media personalities and out government officials. At the White House. Drinking cosmos and listening to Madonna. Surreal.

After a hectic Pride season came to a close, I took last week off to spend at the beach in Rehoboth. As I logged off my computer to head home, I breathed a sigh of relief that vacation had finally arrived. I didn't even make it out of the door before the cell phone started ringing.

The White House was calling to invite me to the LGBT reception held last Monday. As part of the Blade team that covered the Bush administration, I am unaccustomed to calls from the White House, so the invitation came as a pleasant surprise. Bush's White House revoked the Blade's press credentials and our calls went mostly unreturned during his second term. It was the black hole of news as secrecy reigned and stonewalling reporters was commonplace.

Just six months after taking office, President Obama hosted about 250 LGBT rights leaders in the East Room for a surprisingly lengthy and wide-ranging 20-minute speech on gay rights. And Obama, accompanied by first lady Michelle, didn't bolt after the speech. He left the stage and greeted us in the adjacent hallway, shaking hands and chatting with dozens of us, while Michelle graciously posed for photos nearby. Just as she turned to shake my hand, the president appeared next to me, flashed his trademark grin, and apologized for having to rescue his wife; they were late for another event. But he implored all of us to stay and enjoy "your White House."

Those were unexpected words. For many LGBT Americans, the White House has never felt like it belonged to us; we've always been in the margins. As one attendee pointed out to me, the last time a major announcement on gay rights was made at the White House came when Bush publicly called for the Federal Marriage Amendment. But on that day last week, President Obama, who still seems as surprised to be inside the White House as many of us were, made the outcasts feel welcome. The DJ spinning Madonna remixes outside the East Room might have been a gesture too far for some, but it was a powerful, symbolic show of support nonetheless.

Some bloggers are angry at those of us who attended. But this was not a DNC fundraiser; it was the president of the United States extending an invitation to the people's house. Several longtime activists, including Frank Kameny, spoke incredulously about the day's events, telling me that they never could have envisioned a day when instead of picketing in front of the White House they would be invited guests inside.

Dismissing the event as an empty gesture is cynical and misguided. Of course we won't settle for words without action. And most of those inside the White House last week have fought long, lonely battles for decades and deserved to be recognized by their president on the 40th anniversary of Stonewall. I'm confident that the next time LGBT leaders are invited to the White House it will be to attend a bill signing.

"Our First Victory," Oct. 30, 2009

This essay commemorates the passage of our nation's first federal LGBTQ legislation: the Matthew Shepard & James Byrd Jr. Hate Crimes Prevention Act. It wasn't anyone's top priority, but it represented a

start and an early victory in the new Obama administration. There were more significant victories to come.

President Obama this week signed into law the Matthew Shepard & James Byrd Jr. Hate Crimes Prevention Act, which becomes the nation's first federal LGBT rights law after decades of trying.

Wednesday's signing ceremony at the White House proved an emotional event for many who worked so hard since the brutal 1998 killings of Shepard and Byrd.

Hate crimes laws don't have universal support, even among gay rights advocates. Indeed, you can make a compelling libertarian argument against such laws. But it's unconscionable to exclude from an existing law a group so disproportionately impacted by hate crimes as LGBT people.

Current federal law covers attacks motivated by race, religion, national origin or color. The new law adds crimes committed based on sexual orientation, gender identity, sex or disability and includes a provision that makes it a federal crime to attack military service members.

Attacks on LGBT people remain far too common and perpetrators often invoke the "gay panic" defense to seek reduced sentences. In recent months, just here in D.C., we've seen the senseless killing of Tyli'a "NaNa Boo" Mack, a transgender woman stabbed to death in the middle of the afternoon while walking to a trans services center; and the gross miscarriage of justice in the case of Tony Randolph Hunter; who was beaten and died while walking to a local gay bar. His killer, Robert Lee Hanna, was sentenced to just six months in jail.

Those cases didn't receive the national attention paid to Shepard's gruesome murder, a fact that leads some critics to decry the disparity in media coverage between incidents when white gay men are killed and Black gays or transgender women are victims. Indeed, the Blade's pages have seen endless accounts of Black gay and trans people killed over the years. Far too often those stories never find their way into the mainstream media. And when the national media pick up on such a story, reports will sometimes omit any reference to the victims' sexual orientation.

In just one such case, three Black college students were shot to death on a New Jersey playground in 2007. The incident grabbed national headlines when the story broke, but quickly faded from view after the Blade reported that at least one of the victims was gay and the group of friends had been en route to a Black Pride event in New York when they were shot.

There's no question that attacks on Black and trans victims are not widely reported. Despite that unfortunate fact, Shepard's parents, Judy and Dennis, deserve much credit and praise for bringing such visibility to the scourge of anti-gay violence. They could have disappeared into their grief and no one would have blamed them. Instead, they got angry and organized and worked tirelessly through the bleak Bush years, when White House officials signaled the president would veto a hate crimes bill, to add LGBT people to the existing law.

It's false to suggest this law will "protect" anyone from a crime. No law can accomplish that feat. LGB — and especially T — people will continue to face violence. But now we are recognized at the federal level as equal to other groups under the law. It's a small step, one made smaller by the fact that the bill didn't pass on its own merit but had to be attached to a Pentagon spending bill to squeak through Congress.

With LGBT people now treated equally under the federal hate crimes law, our advocates can move on to new challenges, like passage of the Employment Non-Discrimination Act and the repeal of "Don't Ask, Don't Tell" and the Defense of Marriage Act.

"Back to reality for LGBT movement," Jan. 25, 2011

President Obama was a game-changer for LGBTQ equality, but even he had limitations. Like a hostile, GOP-controlled House, for example. This piece sought to quell some of the frustration in the community over the pace of change under Obama's leadership. He always urged us to call him out when he let us down, but sometimes activists' expectations ignored the practical realities of passing legislation in a divided government. Also, I correctly predicted that Obama would endorse marriage equality before the 2012 election in this piece.

(Apologies to Dan Savage for the shade here. Dan's an important figure in the movement and certainly knows his way around a political argument. No hard feelings?)

The thrill of "Don't Ask, Don't Tell" repeal has left some LGBT rights advocates whipped into a froth about continued advances, despite the outcome of the mid-term elections.

Suddenly, we're expecting the president to endorse marriage equality in the State of the Union address.

"Why not save everyone on both sides of the debate a lot of time, trouble and money by approving the entire gay rights agenda," wrote Dan Savage in a Sunday New York Times piece.

Savage should stick to sex advice. As Rep. Barney Frank told the Blade in November, there's zero chance of any pro-LGBT advances so long as Rep. John Boehner holds the gavel.

The Obama administration has certainly raised the bar and boosted expectations after "Don't Ask" repeal and a string of pro-LGBT administrative policy changes, but it's time to come back down to earth. As those of us who covered the eight painful years of the Bush administration know, change comes incrementally in Washington. And with a GOP-controlled House and a looming 2012 presidential election, we'll be looking to the states and to the courts for progress in the next two years.

That said, I'm confident that President Obama will endorse marriage equality — maybe even before the 2012 election — but it wasn't going to happen in the State of the Union address. How quickly we forget that in President George W. Bush's 2004 State of the Union address (just seven years ago), he said, "Our nation must defend the sanctity of marriage." Bush added that a constitutional ban on same-sex marriage would be necessary if "activist judges" legalized marriage for gay and lesbian couples. I remember watching that speech in disbelief, stunned that a U.S. president would use his most prominent speech of the year, which is watched around the world, to denounce our relationships and call for our second-class status in the Constitution.

No matter what you think of Obama's record on LGBT rights, there can be no doubt that he views us as part of his America and his agenda. Yes, we should press him to do better, but let's not lose perspective in our post-"Don't Ask, Don't Tell" exuberance.

His support for same-sex marriage is well known from that infamous 1996 questionnaire in which state Senate candidate Obama wrote, "I favor legalizing same-sex marriages, and would fight efforts to prohibit such marriages."

With a few exceptions, Obama has been a remarkably supportive president and no one believes he opposes marriage equality; he just doesn't deem it politically smart to announce it right now. But it's coming.

In the meantime, we should be working to advance marriage rights in Maryland and Rhode Island; to prevail in a number of court cases on marriage, adoption and trans rights; and to fight GOP efforts to repeal marriage equality in New Hampshire. There's plenty of work to do and there will be victories in the next two years. Just don't look to Congress to deliver them.

"Solmonese era comes to an end," Sept. 2, 2011

Joe Solmonese ran the Human Rights Campaign for seven years and proved a competent leader. We had a good rapport, though plenty of ups and downs. Solmonese wears his emotions on his sleeve — you always know where you stand. So, when HRC disapproved of a Blade story, I heard about it. My most memorable interaction with him occurred during the debate over the Employment Non-Discrimination Act. A transgender provision was removed from the bill, putting HRC in the position of having to withdraw support from a pro-gay piece of federal legislation. There were debates over incrementalism: Wasn't something better than nothing? "We'll go back for the trans community later." Besides, the United States has a long history of incremental progress — after all, Black men won the right to vote before women did. On the other side, the trans community rightly felt betrayed and thrown under the bus of political expediency. I remember attending the HRC National Dinner that year in Washington. It's a black tie affair of mostly well-to-do white men. I stopped attending in part because it's impossible to find someone in the crowd of white faces and black tuxes. That year, transgender activists protested outside the hotel. Many of us felt like we were crossing a picket line. It was such an ugly time in the movement. At some point during the debate over the bill, Solmonese called me and asked if he could stop by my office to talk. We ended up talking for nearly two hours about how to handle the issue. I didn't envy Joe's position. On one hand, the trans community was understandably and justifiably irate that HRC would even entertain a bill that stripped them out. On the other hand were congressional supporters like Rep. Barney Frank who didn't want to be left holding the bag of a bill no one wanted. Solmonese was clearly stressed out and needed some off-the-record venting. My take was that a gay-only bill would be a mistake. It was a strategy that had been used in state fights, as in New York, where gays won protections and promised to add trans people later, then disappeared and left the trans community unprotected and abandoned. In the end, HRC took no position on the bill, either for or against, and it died. ENDA never became law and its successor, the Equality Act, remains stalled in Congress as of 2022, despite President Biden's promise to sign it in his first 100 days. The

silver lining: Never again would the movement entertain a rights bill that failed to include the transgender community.

The Human Rights Campaign announced this week that Joe Solmonese would step down in March as president after nearly seven years at the helm of the nation's largest LGBT advocacy organization.

Running HRC is a relatively thankless job: legislative victories can't come fast enough to satisfy critics — and God help you if you throw a cocktail party for inside-the-Beltway "elitists."

Solmonese will be most remembered for presiding over HRC during a period when we saw repeal of "Don't Ask, Don't Tell" and passage of an expanded federal hate crimes law that includes sexual orientation and gender identity. But his tenure was also marked by controversy, when in 2007, a bruising fight over the Employment Non-Discrimination Act threatened to tear HRC apart. Solmonese — and many others in the movement — agonized over the question of whether to support an ENDA that was stripped of its gender identity provision. Ultimately, HRC punted and neither supported nor opposed the bill, which died after a painfully divisive debate in Congress. The lasting impact of that episode: any version of ENDA that omits gender identity/expression is dead in the water. Four years after that bruising debate, ENDA remains a dream — perhaps permanently.

The next HRC leader should work to further repair and strengthen relations with the transgender community, which is most impacted by employment discrimination. Many grassroots activists remain deeply suspicious of HRC, though some of their criticisms are unfair. The organization has been attacked for its spending, salaries, new headquarters building and coziness with the administration. But the truth is that our opponents on the right are far better funded than the so-called LGBT movement. The vast majority of LGBT people don't donate to HRC — or any other rights group fighting on their behalf. HRC claims 1,000,000 members under Solmonese's tenure, but that number is ludicrous and laughably inflated. If only there were a million people paying annual dues to a national LGBT rights group.

If we are ever to pass ENDA, repeal DOMA, protect the rights of bi-national same-sex couples and convince the Republican Party to cease its attacks on us, we will need to pay competitive salaries to our lobbyists and leaders. The HRC headquarters was expensive, but a smart, long-term investment. As for being cozy with the administration, I prefer the White House gates remain open to LGBT voices. Some of us too easily forget the Bush years, when even our gay journalists were thrown out of the White House. The Obama era has delivered on the promise of change to our community and while we still need grassroots activists pushing for more progress, so too we need lobbyists on the inside.

One problem that continues to hamper our visibility is that we lack a stable of slick and confident TV-ready commentators to take on the endless voices of bigotry on the right. Sure, Solmonese made a few appearances on "Hardball" during the "Don't Ask" debate, but the next HRC president should be more aggressive in defending our community in public forums and on TV. The void created by that reluctance leads to the LGBT community being represented by gay actors, musicians and sex advice columnists — surely we can do better.

The next HRC president should also work to combat the impression of tone deafness. At a time of national recession when so many Americans, including LGBT people who are disproportionately impacted by job discrimination, are out of work, Solmonese was profiled by Washington Life magazine, which dubbed him the "elegant activist," who favors designers Ann Demeulemeester, Billy Reid and Dolce and Gabbana. While actual activists like Dan Choi were being arrested at the White House, Solmonese was staging cheesy photo ops nearby with Kathy Griffin for her reality TV show. Enough with the star fuckery already. HRC shouldn't be a reality TV platform or a fashion house.

Also as we look to HRC's future, the next president must make it a priority to forge inroads with Republicans. As we've seen under House Speaker John Boehner, our legislative fights cannot advance as an occasional Democratic Party pet cause. The Democrats have proven again and again the fickleness of their support, nearly squandering majorities in both houses of Congress during Obama's first two years in office. The Republicans are worse, but we haven't really tried to win them over. Writing off Republicans all these years has stymied the movement and delayed our progress. The GOP reads the same polls we do — its future leaders understand that anti-LGBT prejudice doesn't resonate with younger voters and it already turns off independents. So let's get out of the DNC's back pocket and engage with the rest of the political universe.

In all, Solmonese was a vast improvement over his predecessor, Cheryl Jacques. HRC under his leadership is stable, more respected in Washington and has had a place at the table during Obama's term.

His departure enables HRC to chart a new course as we head into 2012, but Solmonese righted the ship and HRC is better poised to play a serious role in the national debate today than when he took over.

"CLINTON FOR PRESIDENT," MAY 10, 2016

I will cover the rest of Obama's administration and his successes, such as repealing "Don't Ask, Don't Tell," in other chapters. Fast-forwarding a bit here, this was my second endorsement of Hillary. The first came in 2007 in her primary race against Barack Obama, something that Obama's communications team never let me forget. This time, the choice was much easier. I rightly warned about the stakes for the Supreme Court, noting Justice Antonin Scalia's vacant seat and three more justices aged 77 or older.

Sen. Bernie Sanders has done the country a great service by shining a bright (if shrill) light on the entrenched problem of income inequality but his message failed to produce the revolution he sought and now it's time for practicality to prevail.

While the Republicans have burned through 16 losing candidates and turned their party over to a racist, sexist bully with zero experience in elected office, the Democrats are still slugging it out — in May. This should be a time for Hillary Clinton's victory lap, not a time for enduring more misguided attacks on her fitness for office from fellow Democrats.

Sanders deserves credit for running an effective campaign that caught the imagination of a younger generation tired of the status quo. His presence in the primaries has forced Clinton to up her game and sharpen her economic message. We owe him a big "thank you" for that.

But he has been mathematically eliminated from winning the nomination with pledged delegates. There simply is no credible path to victory. And the specter of what comes next should scare all voters into realizing the responsible thing for Sanders to do is to withdraw, endorse Clinton and start planning a national tour of college campuses to rally young voters to her side.

With Trump waiting in the wings, there is too much at stake to risk further damaging Clinton in the eyes of Sanders' supporters, 25 percent of whom in a recent poll foolishly and naively said they would not vote for Clinton. Sanders must disabuse his followers of such self-destructive nonsense. Ralph Nader's causes didn't fare so well under George W. Bush. We mustn't repeat the mistakes of third-party folly or pouty stay-at-home stubbornness.

The notion that Clinton is unqualified for the presidency, as Sanders has intimated, is absurd; Trump's claims that she'd be soft on terrorism is at odds with her sometimes hawkish record.

On LGBT rights, Clinton was late to the marriage party but she has arrived — and there's no turning back now. The time has come to forgive the many Democratic Party leaders who paid lip service to our issues for so long and move forward in this radically changed political environment in which anything but full-throated support for LGBT rights will not fly for any Democrat seeking the presidency. Clinton has pledged her full support for a range of LGBT causes. She even hired a gay campaign manager. Our progress is not only safe in her hands, it will continue.

Clinton has pledged to support the Equality Act, to allow transgender people to serve openly in the U.S. military and to end widely discredited "ex-gay" conversion therapy for minors. In addition, she has said she would expand access to HIV prevention and treatment; confront disproportionate violence facing transgender people, especially trans women of color; and continue her work as former secretary of state on international LGBT rights. She has consistently raised LGBT issues during the primary season, making them a centerpiece of her campaign.

At risk of playing the "woman's card," we should also seize this historic opportunity to elect the nation's first female president. I want my 11 nieces and nephews to grow up in a country where electing an African American or female president is no big deal. We're halfway there.

Perhaps most importantly, we can trust her judgment in making at least one — and possibly multiple — Supreme Court picks. With Justice Antonin Scalia's seat vacant amid unprecedented, reckless GOP obstructionism, and three more justices aged 77 or older, it is imperative that Trump not be allowed to put his stamp of ignorance and bigotry on the high court.

We've made stunning progress thanks to President Obama, but make no mistake that Trump can and would turn back the clock on our equality in myriad ways. First, Trump has pledged to immediately revoke President Obama's executive orders, which would certainly include the order that bars discrimination against LGBT employees of federal contractors. That order covers about 20 percent of the entire American workforce and our advocates fought hard to get it implemented. The thrice-married Trump has also promised to nominate Supreme Court justices who would overturn the Obergefell ruling and end marriage equality.

He has endorsed the First Amendment Defense Act, a federal version of the so-called "religious freedom" bills that have emerged in North Carolina and elsewhere that would legalize discrimination against LGBT Americans from coast to coast.

The LGBT community cannot risk a Trump presidency.

Hillary Clinton has promised to continue President Obama's fierce advocacy on LGBT issues. And she's backed up those words with specific, detailed policy proposals. Further, she has a record now of advocating for LGBT people around the world as secretary of state. The Blade has interviewed scores of overseas activists and they routinely cite her Geneva speech in which she famously said, "gay rights are human rights" as a game changer. Make no mistake that her public stand in defense of gay rights abroad has saved lives.

The time has come to move past divisive fights of the past and rally around an ally who has pledged to put the full weight of her administration and bully pulpit into maintaining and advancing LGBT equality. Hillary Clinton is that ally and has earned LGBT support in November.

"Melania for First Stripper!," Sept. 13, 2016

Just two months before the 2016 election, Hillary seemed inevitable. The pollsters, led by the chronically wrong Nate Smith, declared her the overwhelming favorite. But I had an uneasy feeling that fall looking around my liberal Baltimore neighborhood, where nearly every lawn had displayed an Obama sign in 2008 and 2012. There were almost no Hillary signs in 2016. And on the drive from Baltimore to Rehoboth Beach, endless Trump signs on display with nary a Hillary sign for 90 miles. It was an anecdotal observation, but one that troubled me nonetheless. Could the "short-fingered vulgarian" outsider defeat the Hillary juggernaut? After the "Access Hollywood" video was leaked, I assumed like many that Trump was toast. But then came James Comey and his disastrous, game-changing press conference announcing the FBI's investigation into her email scandal that proved the ultimate October surprise. It was game over for Hillary. But in September, things seemed to be going her way. She won the debates without delivering the knockout blow that many of us were expecting, while Trump was busy courting the votes of conservative Christians, an unlikely constituency for a philandering, gambling racist.

Donald Trump's appearance at Friday's Values Voter Summit included more of his usual hypocrisies and Bizzaro-world remarks. There have been so many that we've lost count and Trump's supporters clearly aren't going to let facts and logic get in the way of their vote regardless.

The very sight of Trump addressing a roomful of conservative Christians is right out of a "Saturday Night Live" skit. In other words, utterly absurd and comical. This is a man who owned casinos. As in where gambling occurs. And prostitution prospers. A man who has been married three times. Who demonstrates no familiarity with the Bible and can't correctly quote a passage, even when reading off a script. A man who mocks the disabled and curses during rallies and who won't release his tax returns because presumably he doesn't donate to charitable causes other than his own faux foundation.

Trump is not a pious man, to put it mildly. Yet, there he was preaching to an audience of supportive Christians who vote their values, raising the question: Do they now value gambling, prostitution, misogyny, racism and ignorance?

More troubling than the theater of the absurd setting was the substance of his speech. He praised Tony Perkins, head of the Family

Research Council, an anti-LGBT group so extreme that the Southern Poverty Law Center labels it a hate group. He promised that Christian heritage will be "protected like you've never seen before," a vow that should send chills throughout the LGBT community for Trump's repeated calls for a federal "religious freedom" law. He referenced "religious liberty" in the speech amid his criticism of Supreme Court justices who "rewrite the Constitution to impose their own personal views on 300 million-plus Americans." We know that means appointing justices who would overturn the marriage equality ruling. Trump went on to praise Antonin Scalia as the "ultimate example of what we're looking for" in a justice. He promised to fight for "family values" and then praised Phyllis Schlafly, a right-wing homophobe who spoke out against women's rights, gay rights and trans rights right up until she died two weeks ago.

Most improbably, Trump also attacked the media for demeaning people of faith, bemoaning how hard it is to raise children "in today's media environment."

You mean the same media environment that published nude photos of your third wife??? The hypocrisy is so blatant and shameless that your head could explode listening to it all. Melania Trump was paid to appear naked in magazines published by big media companies; she is complicit in creating the very tawdry media culture inappropriate for children that her husband now criticizes.

And, no, this is not about "slut shaming," though I'd submit that we don't want our country represented on the world stage by a first lady best known for entertaining the masses by taking off her clothes. Melania for first stripper! I'd also submit that if Michelle Obama had been photographed naked, the right-wing racist hypocrites wouldn't have allowed her husband within 100 yards of the White House.

But, again, none of this matters because, as Hillary Clinton intimated, many of his supporters aren't thinking people. That's putting it diplomatically. As the Atlantic reported this week, "When Hillary

Clinton claims that half of Trump's supporters qualify as 'racist, sexist, homophobic, xenophobic, Islamophobic,' data is on her side." Indeed, two-thirds of voters with a favorable opinion of Trump believe President Obama is a Muslim, and a quarter believe that Scalia was murdered, according to a poll from Public Policy Polling.

When facts don't matter, there's no limit to the demagoguery you'll fall for. When conservative — and even fundamentalist — Christians are cheering for Trump, you know we've reached a new and frightening time when emotions rule, logic and intellect are deemed "elitist" and thus bad, and loony, narcissistic demagogues come to power.

"Here's how President Trump could undermine LGBT rights," Nov. 9, 2016

I wrote this in the immediate aftermath of Trump's stunning win over Hillary Clinton. The LGBTQ movement was in shock and terrified of what would come. Not many imagined just how bad it would get: Charlottesville, three right-wing Supreme Court picks, a botched response to a pandemic, the insurrection.

The stunning result of Tuesday's presidential election stands as a chilling reminder of the work ahead. After eight years of President Obama's fierce advocacy, we grew complacent. We assumed that since a bare majority of straight Supreme Court justices voted our way on marriage that the fight was over. We were wrong.

The United States remains a deeply sexist, racist, homophobic culture and undoing and overcoming those prejudices will take more than filing a few well-timed lawsuits. Realizing those cultural changes takes generations and most of us won't see the end of that road in our lifetimes. For those of us who remember when gay people were hated and persecuted during the onset of the AIDS epidemic — or those older still who remember the height of the Civil Rights

Movement — Tuesday's result hurts but also serves as a reminder that social change movements take time and are marked by setbacks.

It was only a few years ago that marriage equality was a dream; George W. Bush was president and cynically used our rights as a wedge issue to win swing states; and "Don't Ask, Don't Tell" was the law of the land. Obama brought change to the bully pulpit, but one person alone can't change the culture.

Now the LGBT community is back on defense; the campaign is over and it's time to dust ourselves off and prepare for the myriad fights ahead. They will include preserving President Obama's executive actions related to LGBT rights, especially his 2014 executive order prohibiting federal contractors from engaging in anti-LGBT workplace discrimination. Also at risk is a rule prohibiting anti-LGBT discrimination in health care and insurance and a Department of Housing & Urban Development regulation prohibiting anti-LGBT bias in government-sponsored housing. Trump has said he'd appoint Supreme Court justices in the mold of the anti-LGBT Antonin Scalia, potentially putting the marriage equality ruling in jeopardy. Trump has said he would sign the First Amendment Defense Act, a "religious freedom" bill that would enable anti-LGBT discrimination across the country. In an interview in May, he said he would rescind the joint guidance from the Departments of Justice and Education prohibiting schools from discriminating against transgender students and guaranteeing them access to the restroom consistent with their gender identity.

There's more. Advocates have said they fear Trump could roll back administrative changes, such as those benefiting LGBT veterans or status of forces agreements allowing service members to bring a same-sex spouse with them overseas, or halting movement on lifting the ban on openly transgender service.

As painful as this result is for LGBT Americans, it's worse for our allies among people of color, immigrants, Muslims and others so cruelly demonized and attacked by Trump during the campaign. There is real anxiety among immigrants who fear Trump's oft-repeated threats of deportation forces and walls. The hopes of Syrian and other refugees fleeing civil war and ISIS attacks for a chance at freedom in America are dashed today. It's my hope that LGBT movement leaders will stand in solidarity with other underrepresented groups in Trump's crosshairs.

And as we mourn this outcome from the comfort of our homes and offices, the Blade is reporting on yet another murder of a transgender woman of color, this time in Richmond, Va. Noony Norwood was shot and killed on Sunday, marking the 23rd reported killing of a transgender or gender nonconforming person in the United States that the National Coalition of Anti-Violence Programs has responded to in 2016. Yes, Trump is awful, but some in our community are fighting more urgent battles just to live and work free from violence.

So, yes, we are shocked and disheartened. But the road to equality is long. This is a detour, not a dead end. Take a day to mourn, then take comfort in how far the LGBT movement has come in eight quick years and get back to work.

"THANK YOU, MR. PRESIDENT," JAN. 12, 2017

The Blade's Jan. 12, 2017 issue was the last of Obama's presidency and came just days before Trump's inauguration. It felt like the calm before the storm.

"Welcome to your house." With those simple words, President Barack Obama and first lady Michelle Obama received an audience of LGBT advocates at the 2009 White House Pride reception. Those of us lucky enough to be in the room were standing on the shoulders of generations of LGBT people who protested and picketed outside the White House and were never welcomed inside.

And we weren't just welcomed; there were bartenders serving Cosmos and Madonna dance music blared in the East Wing. We were promised change, but this was more than any of us had bargained for.

Fast forward eight years and Obama indeed proved to be our fierce advocate, upending decades of Democratic Party lip service to our issues and finally delivering real change. From the "Don't Ask, Don't Tell" repeal to a full embrace of marriage equality, Obama went further on LGBT rights than even some activists expected. Who could have imagined the White House lit up in rainbow colors after the Supreme Court's marriage ruling? Even now, that image remains gasp inducing.

This special issue of the Blade is a sendoff and thank you to President Obama, first lady Michelle Obama and all those tireless staffers who made this change possible. The cover image sums up the way the Obamas made many of us feel over the past eight years — downright giddy at times. Journalists aren't supposed to thank the subjects of their coverage, but once in a rare while there's room for an exception and this is it. Make no mistake: the credit for much of what's changed on LGBT acceptance goes to Obama. Not to the DNC or to previous Democratic presidents. Not to the media or to gay-friendly celebrities. The bully pulpit is powerful and when Obama used it to endorse marriage equality prior to the 2012 election, the dam burst and suddenly it was OK — cool even — to support the cause that terrified so many other Democrats.

For a glimpse at what was achieved these past eight years, check out the timeline of LGBT progress in this issue compiled by our White House reporter Chris Johnson. It's not just about marriage, but a host of policy statements, federal guidance, Justice Department briefs and more that helped shift the culture and bring us to where we are today.

No one is perfect and Obama has his flaws. His administration proved opaque and Obama himself insular, in stark contrast to his campaign promises of transparency. In eight years, Obama never made time for an interview with the Blade, even though our reporters are in the White House and State Department each day and part of the pool rotation. Whistleblowers were targeted for retribution. Obama's Syria policy will likely go down as the biggest stain on his presidency.

But on so much else — the economic recovery, job creation, restoring America's reputation around the world, LGBT equality — Obama surpassed expectations. Top adviser Valerie Jarrett told the Blade in an exclusive interview this week that she's confident the culture has come far enough on LGBT rights that President-elect Trump's administration won't be able to roll back the advances we've seen. I wish I shared her assessment. Given the myriad bigots about to populate the White House, led by Steve Bannon, the LGBT community is in for a rough ride and setbacks await.

But we know how to fight and we'll take our places back outside the White House fence. Thanks to President Obama, we have an impressive string of victories to protect. Thank you, Mr. President.

"Remembering Harris Wofford," Jan. 28, 2019

I interned in Sen. Harris Wofford's press office and had no idea he was gay or bi. Looking back, there were some awkward moments with my immediate boss, the director of communications, who was flummoxed that I had so much face time with the senator. Wofford was friendly, unlike my boss, and would occasionally invite me into his office to chat. He was an old-school gentleman and academic. I thought the world of him.

The death of former U.S. Sen. Harris Wofford (D-Pa.) barely registered on the mainstream media's radar last week, lost amid the never-ending obsession with covering the latest Tweet storm from the Oval Office.

What a contrast in style and character — the selfless, honorable career of Wofford, who traveled extensively in India, studying non-violent protest from followers of Gandhi and who later marched in Selma — versus the crude, grammatically challenged and racist demagoguery of the current president.

Wofford, who came out late in life, died at a Washington, D.C. hospital last week after suffering a fall. He was 92.

Wofford had a long career in civil rights activism before joining the Senate. He graduated from Howard University Law School and marched with Rev. Martin Luther King Jr. He served in the Kennedy administration as special assistant for civil rights and was instrumental in creating the Peace Corps before moving to academia where he served as a university president.

Wofford was married to his wife Clare for 48 years before she died in 1996. They had three children. He recalled their romance in a 2016 New York Times essay, writing, "Our romance and adventure continued for five decades. When I was running for election to the Senate in 1991, Clare gave up her job to become an all-out campaigner, helping us win in a landslide. In my narrow losing reelection campaign of 1994, astute Pennsylvanians observed that if Clare had been the candidate, she would have won."

In that same essay, Wofford shared his coming out story. At age 75, he met Matthew Charlton, 50 years his junior, on a Fort Lauderdale beach. The two became close friends, eventually lovers, and married in 2016.

"Too often, our society seeks to label people by pinning them on the wall — straight, gay or in between," Wofford wrote. "I don't categorize myself based on the gender of those I love. I had a half-century of marriage with a wonderful woman, and now am lucky for a second time to have found happiness."

Wofford was appointed to fill the Senate seat of John Heinz, who was killed in a 1991 plane crash. He later held the seat in a special election upset, defeating the popular Richard Thornburgh, in part because of his focus on health care reform. Three years later, Wofford was defeated in his reelection bid by Rick Santorum, who would go on to become one of the Senate's most notorious homophobes.

I worked for Wofford in 1993 in his Senate press office and reconnected with him years later after he came out in the Times essay, teasing him that he should have come out in the Blade. I used to interview him for his office's weekly radio service and we had many meaningful conversations. In February 1993, I accompanied him to a book signing for his inspirational work, "Of Kennedys & Kings: Making Sense of the Sixties."

In it, Wofford quotes everyone from Tocqueville to Lincoln, lamenting "the cynicism about all government that has paralyzed our politics." And that was 1993. Things have only gotten worse in that regard, something that clearly upset Wofford who believed strongly in the importance of public service and academic rigor, noting presciently in his book that energy is no substitute for wisdom.

After reconnecting at an Obama White House event, I had the pleasure of meeting Matthew. They were a loving, dashing couple. Our country could use more smart, thoughtful, selfless people like Harris Wofford in public service.

"SCOTUS DELIVERS WIN FOR LGBTQ WORKERS," JUNE 23, 2020

This ruling arrived just in time for Pride month and was secured by the most unlikely of justices: Neil Gorsuch. The Supreme Court ruled in 2020 that Title VII of the Civil Rights Act of 1964 bars discrimination against LGBTQ workers, a momentous decision that caught many of us off guard. In the wake of the ruling, some have suggested that our work here is done, but that's not accurate, as the ruling has holes that are addressed by the stalled Equality Act. Still, this ruling ranks

up there with Lawrence and Obergefell as the most consequential for LGBTQ equality.

Earlier this month, the U.S. Supreme Court ruled 6-3 that Title VII of the Civil Rights Act of 1964 bars discrimination against LGBTQ workers. It was a sweeping and unexpected ruling from a conservative-majority court.

The seeds for that milestone victory were planted nearly 50 years ago in 1974, when Rep. Bella Abzug (D-N.Y.) introduced the original Equality Act, an expansive measure that sought to amend Title VII to ban discrimination "on the basis of sex, marital status, or sexual orientation in public accommodations, public facilities, public education, federally assisted programs, housing, and financial services."

That bill failed, of course, as did several others in the intervening decades, leaving millions of LGBTQ workers vulnerable to harassment and discrimination on the job.

I experienced that discrimination firsthand while working for a large telecommunications firm in 2001, when my boss, who displayed a Bible on his desk, openly blamed gays for the 9/11 terrorist attacks. When he realized I was gay, the retaliation began; I was disinvited from meetings, work assignments dried up and eventually I was made to report my whereabouts to the office secretary anytime I left my desk, even for a trip to the bathroom.

Despite filing complaints with HR and hiring a lawyer, there was nothing I could do as no federal law prevented employers from harassing and firing their gay workers and fewer than half of the states had such laws on the books. It's a problem that affects untold numbers of workers around the country.

Then along came three plaintiffs: Aimee Stephens, a transgender funeral home director; Donald Zarda, a gay skydiving instructor; and Gerald Bostock, a Clayton County, Ga. official. All three were fired for being gay or trans. Bostock was fired after his supervisor learned he had joined a gay recreational softball league. Their combined cases led to the historic court ruling that determines anti-LGBTQ bias is a form of sex discrimination, thus prohibited under Title VII.

"An employer who fires an individual for being homosexual or transgender fires that person for traits or actions it would not have questioned in members of a different sex," Associate Justice Neil Gorsuch wrote. "Sex plays a necessary and undisguisable role in the decision, exactly what Title VII forbids."

At a time of increasing attacks and rolling back of LGBTQ rights at the federal level, the decision — notably penned by Trump-appointee Gorsuch — is a well-timed Pride month reminder of how far we've come and how far we still have to go.

The ruling should apply to laws other than Title VII, including the Fair Housing Act, the Affordable Care Act and Title IX of the Education Amendments of 1964. That would mean LGBTQ people now have federal protections not only in employment, but also in housing, health care and in school systems.

As the Blade reported, because no federal law prohibits discrimination on the basis of sex in public accommodations or federal programs, the ruling does nothing for LGBTQ protections in those areas. For example, Colorado baker Jack Phillips of Masterpiece Cakeshop, who refused to make a custom wedding cake for a same-sex couple and narrowly won a previous case before the Supreme Court, would still be able to refuse service to LGBTQ customers under this ruling.

No federal law prohibits discrimination on the basis of sex in the U.S. military, so President Trump's ban on transgender military service will remain in effect.

So the road ahead for the LGBTQ movement will include efforts to finally pass the Equality Act, which remains bottled up in the Senate. It will likely take a Democratic Senate and president to finally realize Rep. Abzug's dream of nearly 50 years ago.

In the meantime, LGBTQ Americans can finally report to work as first-class citizens, confident they will be judged by their performance and not based on whom they love.

"Vote for Biden (duh)," Sept. 10, 2020

The 2020 election arrived amid the pandemic, economic upheaval and Trump's increasingly unhinged rhetoric. Joe Biden wasn't my first choice, but I did predict he would win the nomination and choose Kamala Harris as his running mate. After so much sadness and darkness, Biden promised a return to common sense and compassionate governance and, most of all, a return to normalcy. He won more votes for president than anyone in history. And in second place for all-time vote getters is Trump, illustrating just how divided our country has become.

The list of Donald Trump's affronts is long. The unlikely evangelical darling operated casinos, paid off porn stars, bragged of grabbing women by the "pussy," mocked a disabled reporter, praised white supremacists, insulted a Gold Star family, attacked a revered POW, flirted with his own daughter, tweeted support for a murderer, and bullied foreign leaders into helping him steal the election.

And those are just some of the most infamous of Trump's transgressions.

There's no reason for any informed American voter to grant Trump another four years. There's even less reason for LGBTQ voters to support him, no matter what the hypocrites at Log Cabin tell you.

His botched COVID response has needlessly cost tens of thousands of lives. Rather than model commonsense mask use, Trump mocked those like Joe Biden for wearing them. Rather than level with the American people back in February and March about the severity of what was coming our way, he downplayed coronavirus, called it a "hoax" and ridiculously said it would "go away like a miracle." Even as we watched heartbreaking and frightening YouTube clips of Italians suffering in quarantine as bodies piled up in morgues, Trump held firm that it was not a threat to us. He was dead wrong. When we sought answers and comfort from leading infectious disease expert Dr. Anthony Fauci — well known to the gay community from his days fighting AIDS in the 1980s — Trump turned on him too, unleashing opposition research to undermine his credibility.

The resulting chaos has left nearly 200,000 Americans dead and the economy in shambles. When everyday Americans and small business owners needed another relief package, Speaker Nancy Pelosi's House responded swiftly with a bill and passed it, while Senate Majority Leader and Trump loyalist Mitch McConnell let his colleagues go home for an August vacation. I don't know any small business owners who took a vacation this summer; we are all struggling to stay afloat without any communication or direction from the federal government.

This sad performance alone on coronavirus should be enough reason to vote Trump out in November, but, of course, there is more.

The parallel crisis of police brutality against Black Americans has reminded us yet again of the stubborn entrenchment of systemic racism. George Floyd, Breonna Taylor and Jacob Blake joined the unending list of Black victims of police abuse. As protests flared around the country, Trump gassed peaceful demonstrators at the White House so he could stage a clumsy photo op with an upside-down Bible, a book he has never read and cares nothing about. When 17-year-old Kyle Rittenhouse, armed with an AR-15, shot and killed two protesters in Kenosha, Wis., Trump defended him. Trump adviser Kellyanne Conway later admitted what the rest of us already knew: that Trump believes violence in American cities benefits his campaign. He's encouraging his armed supporters to show up at Black Lives Matter protests to intimidate and taunt peaceful demonstrators. It's unconscionable and people are dead as a result. More blood on Trump's hands and his Republican enablers in Congress, on state propaganda

Fox News, and on online inane conspiracy theorists who justify his reckless assault on our democracy.

Make no mistake that this election will determine whether the great American experiment continues or it unravels. Trump's admiration for dictators like the murderers Vladimir Putin and Kim Jong-un; his attacks on our allies like Germany, France and the Kurds; and his backing out of the Paris climate accord and rolling back myriad environmental protections in deference to his corporate golfing buddies further illustrate just how unfit Trump is for office. Make no mistake that all of this chaos is by design — the plan all along was to gut and cripple the federal government. We've seen it agency by agency, from the Education Department's efforts to promote the privatization of public schools through vouchers, to the Interior Department being co-opted to host Trump campaign events on federal lands, to even the Postal Service being undermined to thwart mail-in voting, no agency has been unaffected. Let's not forget Trump was impeached for his efforts to undermine our democracy and he presided over the longest U.S. government shutdown in our history.

What about Trump's record on LGBTQ issues? It's the disaster many of us predicted it would be. In a 2016 endorsement of Hillary Clinton for president, I wrote: "the Republicans have turned their party over to a racist, sexist bully with zero experience in elected office. ... The LGBT community cannot risk a Trump presidency." I was right. From Trump's very first day in office, when LGBTQ issues were deleted from the White House website, right up to today, when his State Department is denying citizenship to children of same-sex couples born via surrogacy overseas, the attacks have been constant and sometimes cruel.

Trump's tweet banning transgender patriots from serving their country in the military "in any capacity" is perhaps the most egregious and blatant of those attacks, but there are countless others. The blame for a nationwide dramatic rise in hate crimes, which disproportionately impact the LGBTQ community, lies at Trump's feet. Previously, Americans who held bigoted views felt at least some pressure to keep those opinions to themselves. But under Trump, those views are validated and encouraged, motivating scores of "deplorables" to come out and express their hatred openly, as we saw in Charlottesville, and sometimes violently as seen in the FBI's report noting that attacks motivated by bias or prejudice reached a 16-year high in 2018. The Trump administration has allowed discrimination under the guise of "religious freedom" across the board, from adoption agencies to faith-based schools. This administration has worked overtime to render us invisible, removing "sexual orientation" and "gender identity" from the list of categories the Education Department tracks in compiling data on bullying and canceling plans to include us in the Census. The administration has filed a long series of court briefs attacking LGBTQ rights, from seeking to block workplace protections for trans workers to allowing discrimination against same-sex couples seeking to foster children.

Attacks on the trans community are particularly acute and nasty, including allowing homeless shelters to discriminate against transgender people and rescinding Obama-era guidance that allowed trans students to use facilities that correspond to their gender identity.

He opposes the Equality Act, despite originally supporting it. He named notorious homophobe Mike Pence as his vice president, who famously signed a bill as Indiana governor allowing businesses to discriminate against LGBTQ customers. He has named scores of judges hostile to LGBTQ equality to the federal bench, jeopardizing our community's gains for years to come. He surrounds himself with bigots and homophobes, like Tony Perkins, Gini Thomas, Brent Bozell, Franklin Graham and Jerry Falwell, Jr.

I could go on for pages, but you get the point. The Blade's archives over the last four years are filled with reasons for queer voters to reject Trump.

So, why vote *for* Joe Biden and not just *against* Trump? Again, the list is long.

Biden has vowed to make the Equality Act his top legislative priority in his first 100 days. This is an important step, as the historic Bostock ruling can be undermined by other lawsuits seeking "religious freedom" carveouts to legalize discrimination and by interpreting the ruling narrowly to allow discrimination in other areas outside of the workplace.

Back in March, Biden unveiled a comprehensive plan to advance LGBTQ rights. In addition to the Equality Act, he pledges to support international LGBTQ human rights and to ban harmful, discredited conversion therapy nationwide. He vows to reappoint a special envoy to advance international LGBTQ rights, form a coalition of countries to advance international LGBTQ rights and guide the GLOBE Act into passage, as the Blade reported. Further, Biden will work to end the HIV/AIDS epidemic by 2025 and expand PEPFAR.

"As president, Biden will stand with the LGBTQ+ community to ensure America finally lives up to the promise on which it was founded: equality for all," the plan says. "He will provide the moral leadership to champion equal rights for all LGBTQ+ people, fight to ensure our laws and institutions protect and enforce their rights, and advance LGBTQ+ equality globally."

The 17-page plan is detailed and thoughtful and offers a clear vision of how he will work for LGBTQ equality.

Biden praised the historic June Supreme Court ruling in Bostock that the U.S. Civil Rights Act of 1964 includes LGBT people in its prohibition on employment discrimination based on gender or sex.

"Today, by affirming that sexual orientation and gender identity discrimination are prohibited under Title VII of the Civil Rights Act, the Supreme Court has confirmed the simple but profoundly American idea that every human being should be treated with respect and dignity." Biden said. "That everyone should be able to live openly, proudly, as their true selves without fear."

In other words, Biden will use the bully pulpit for good and to inspire others, rather than to foment division and hurl juvenile insults.

Biden endorsed marriage equality in 2012, beating his boss President Obama to the punch. Make no mistake that the bully pulpit is powerful; when the president of the United States speaks, the world listens. When Biden and days later Obama endorsed marriage equality, the floodgates were opened and a slew of celebrities, politicians and everyday Americans followed, eventually aiding the Supreme Court's 2015 marriage equality ruling. Imagine a president using that awesome power again for good rather than for exacting petty revenge on real and imagined enemies.

Trump and his toadies like Ric Grenell — who likes to boast of being the first gay Cabinet member, even though he was not Senate confirmed and lacked qualifications for the job — have foolishly tried to paint Biden as anti-gay, citing 1970s era comments about gay federal workers. If Trump wants to talk about the 70s, let's do that. At that time, Trump's mentor was Roy Cohn, the notorious closet case who died alone of AIDS after devoting his career to ridding the federal government of gay employees in the Lavender Scare era. Also in the 1970s, Trump was investigated for discriminating against Black renters seeking to live in his apartment buildings. The Justice Department filed a civil rights case against the Trump firm, accusing the company of violating the Fair Housing Act of 1968. The case was eventually settled after a protracted court battle. Trump should be careful about re-litigating the 1970s with Biden.

And if you needed more reason to vote for Biden, think of the Supreme Court. Trump has already had two conservative picks, but in a second term he could get at least two more. Ruth Bader Ginsberg is 87 years old with recent health scares, and Justice Stephen Breyer is 82. That's two of the court's remaining four liberal justices in their

80s. A second Trump term could mean a solid 7-2 conservative majority for years to come. In that case, Roe v. Wade, Obergefell and Bostock would all be in jeopardy. That's not hyperbole. Challenges to those rulings continue and will only intensify under a second Trump term. Last year, nine states passed bills restricting abortion rights. Undermining and overturning Roe remains the #1 goal of the right, and marriage equality is next on their target list.

Whatever you think of Biden's policies, there's no disputing he is a decent man, an honorable father and husband who has dedicated his life to public service. His first big decision as the presumptive nominee was to pick Sen. Kamala Harris as his running mate, a historic and stellar choice. The California senator is a longtime LGBTQ ally who will work with Biden to reverse Trump's attacks on our community and to advance an equality agenda.

Joe Biden will work to advance LGBTQ equality. He will restore America's reputation around the world as an ally in the struggle to protect and expand human rights. His administration will look like America and we could finally see an openly LGBTQ Cabinet member and a roster of senior government officials that showcases our great diversity. Once again, it will take a Democratic president and Congress to fix the economic mess created by the outgoing Republican administration. Biden will ensure that science wins the day and procure and distribute a coronavirus vaccine that is proven safe and effective. He will embrace an overdue dialogue on race and enact new policies to address systemic racism. He will stand up to our enemies like Putin and aid our allies. And he will use the bully pulpit to inspire all Americans to achieve their full potential.

There is only one rational choice for president this year. Joe Biden has the experience, the wisdom and the compassion to restore sanity to government and stability to the world.

"Quieter Pride season offers chance to reassess priorities," June 9, 2021

I wrote this piece after cancellation of D.C. Pride for the second consecutive year due to COVID.

For the second consecutive year, most large-scale Pride celebrations have been canceled or postponed due to the pandemic.

Rather than mourn our lost parades, festivals and income streams, we should embrace the pause to reflect on the work that lies ahead. Just as many Pride organizations took advantage of Pride cancellations last year to pivot and focus on supporting Black Lives Matter, 2021 provides another opportunity to reassess our priorities in a post-Trump Washington.

Predictably, the Equality Act appears to be lost again, as the Blade reported recently. As we watch transformative pieces of legislation like the Equality Act, the For the People Act to combat GOP voter suppression, the George Floyd Act to reform police, and a badly needed infrastructure bill die slow deaths at the hands of Sen. Joe Manchin's naivety, it appears the Democrats are once again poised to snatch defeat from the jaws of victory.

Manchin's galling announcement this week that he would vote against Democratic efforts to combat voter suppression by undoing Republican state bills to limit mail-in voting and increase the authority of poll watchers, among other components of the sweeping bill, is just the latest in a string of disappointing and irresponsible moves from the West Virginia senator.

Manchin is the only Democrat not to cosponsor the Equality Act in the Senate and the only Democratic "no" vote on combating voter suppression, which could cost Democrats their majorities next year and Manchin his Energy Committee chairmanship.

Manchin has stoked unfounded fears about trans people accessing the bathroom consistent with their gender identity. He was the lone Democrat to vote in favor of a Title II amendment that would essentially bar transgender kids from participating in school sports. Incredibly, when asked by the Blade about the Equality Act earlier this year, Manchin professed to know nothing about the measure.

And in yet another blow this week, Manchin announced he opposes ditching the filibuster, all but dooming Democratic chances of passing the aforementioned bills. Perhaps Manchin's push for bipartisanship would be sensible and achievable if we didn't have a Senate minority run by Mitch McConnell, who announced his top priority is not helping the country recover from the pandemic, but rather to oppose everything Biden wants to accomplish, just as he did to President Obama. Wake up, Manchin, the Republicans are playing you.

With the LGBTQ movement's top legislative priority DOA, despite Biden's pledge to sign it within his first 100 days, there are other areas where we should focus. From helping Democrats preserve and expand their slim House and Senate majorities, to combating the stunning avalanche of cruel anti-trans laws around the country in the courts, to supporting the administration's efforts at immigration reform and aid to Central American countries, there's no shortage of work ahead.

Just as the LGBTQ movement joined the nationwide protests following George Floyd's murder, we should support Vice President Kamala Harris in her role leading the effort for immigration reform. Too many LGBTQ migrants are suffering in inhumane conditions in ICE custody; too many queer people fleeing poverty, violence and discrimination are marginalized or ignored by mainstream immigration reform efforts. There is an important role for LGBTQ and HIV/AIDS advocacy groups to play as the administration gets serious about improving life for migrants.

By fighting for police reform, immigration reform and having the backs of our trans brothers and sisters in the fight against state legislative attacks, perhaps we'll have more to celebrate at Pride 2022. In the meantime, get vaccinated, stay safe and call Joe Manchin's office once a day to protest his reckless intransigence.

"First They Came for Roe; Obergefell is Next," May 3, 2022

The leak of the Dobbs abortion ruling arrived like a political earthquake and proved accurate weeks later when the final decision was released. Never mind nearly 50 years of precedent. Never mind the new Trump justices who testified under oath that Roe was "settled law." Never mind the closed-door assurances those same justices made to Sen. Susan Collins and the one or two remaining moderate Republicans that they wouldn't undo Roe. And never mind the millions of American women — most of them working class and people of color — who would now be denied a crucial health care procedure that is sometimes life-saving. The Trump court, a 6-3 super majority, is an activist court bent on rolling back LGBTQ equality. It starts with Roe. Obergefell, Lawrence and Griswold are on deck. To the young people reading this: get in the game because it's your future on the line. It's your access to healthcare; your privacy rights and marriage rights. The Boomers and Xers had our turn and we've managed to really screw it up. We are now officially moving backwards and the LGBTQ movement must adapt.

The unprecedented leak of a draft Supreme Court opinion overturning 50 years of precedent in Roe v. Wade shocked the country Monday night.

In it, Justice Samuel Alito writes the apparent 5-4 majority opinion that will lead to roughly half the states outlawing abortion, returning poor women to the back alleys for dangerous makeshift procedures.

But Alito doesn't stop with abortion. He has his sights on two other landmark cases, Lawrence v. Texas and Obergefell v. Hodges. In Lawrence, the court recognized a right to private, consensual sex, and Obergefell legalized same-sex marriage in all 50 states.

Alito's draft opinion ominously cites Lawrence and Obergefell several times. And although Alito writes, "Nothing in this opinion should be understood to cast doubt on precedents that do not concern abortion," he adds, "None of these rights has any claim to being deeply rooted in history."

Alito and fellow arch-conservative Justice Clarence Thomas have publicly called for the court to revisit Obergefell. Make no mistake that the far right conservative legal movement has made overturning Roe its No. 1 priority for 50 years. Obergefell and Lawrence are next.

And let's be clear about the origins of the Lawrence case: Two gay men, John Geddes Lawrence, Jr. and Tyron Garner, were having sex at Lawrence's apartment in Harris County, Texas. Garner's ex-boyfriend called the police, falsely alleging that someone had entered the apartment with a gun. The police showed up and found Lawrence and Garner engaged in sex and arrested them under the Texas anti-sodomy law. That's right: Two gay men were arrested for having consensual sex in a private home in 1998. Think about that for a moment — and the mind-numbing hypocrisy of Republicans who are supposedly anti-government intrusion into our private lives, until gay lives are involved. It took a Supreme Court ruling to validate the right of two consenting gay adults to have sex in a private home.

Justice Kennedy wrote the majority opinion in the landmark case Lawrence v. Texas, which overturned the previous ruling in Bowers v. Hardwick (1986), where the high court failed to find a constitutional right to privacy in sex.

The court in Lawrence v. Texas explicitly held that intimate consensual sexual conduct was part of the liberty protected by the substantive due process under the Fourteenth Amendment.

The decision in this case was a breakthrough for the gay rights movement and helped to set the stage for Obergefell v. Hodges, which recognized same-sex marriage as a fundamental right under the United States Constitution.

All of that precedent is now in question with a 6-3 conservative majority court that lays bare the risk involved in relying on court cases to cement our equality. The LGBTQ movement will need to shift into overdrive to combat the attacks on our rights already playing out with "Don't Say Gay" bills and the relentless assault on trans rights in state legislatures.

The timing for the LGBTQ movement couldn't be worse, with many advocacy groups struggling from pandemic related funding shortfalls and some philanthropic groups suspending donations to LGBTQ causes. Earlier this year, the Evelyn & Walter Haas, Jr. Fund, a leading supporter of state-based LGBTQ equality work, ended its LGBT Equality program, which has given more than $105 million to such causes. As noted by Inside Philanthropy, "LGBTQ+ people make up at least 4.5% of the U.S. population, yet from 2014 to 2018, nonprofits focused on this community received only about 0.18% of grant dollars from U.S.-based foundations."

There is plenty of blame to go around for the stunning revelation of this court's impending ruling, starting with Senate Minority Leader Mitch McConnell, who thwarted President Obama's nomination of Merrick Garland to the court. That blame game ends with our lazy American electorate. In 2016, after a campaign that highlighted what was at stake — namely the Supreme Court and Roe — only about 60 percent of eligible voters turned out to the polls. So you didn't like Hillary? Well, now come the consequences.

This is truly a frightening time in our deeply divided country that will now become more so, as blue states pass laws and constitutional amendments enshrining abortion laws and establishing "safe havens," while the shithole states impose cruel, draconian restrictions on women's rights, even forcing them to give birth after a rape.

With Roe gone, LGBTQ rights are next on the chopping block. Time to organize, raise funds and refocus the movement on state legislatures as our far right opponents have effectively done. Let's hope it's not too late.

"Gay and Tired," June 7, 2022

The prospect of fighting for abortion rights and marriage equality all over again inspired this piece. After 20 years of constant fighting over hate crimes, "Don't Ask, Don't Tell," the Defense of Marriage Act, marriage equality, presidential campaigns, racial justice, reproductive rights, transgender equality and so much more, many of us are simply tired. My hope is that this essay and this book serve to inspire the next generation of LGBTQ leaders. Your community needs you.

This should be a celebratory moment. We are gathering again for Pride and partying like it's 2019. Mask mandates are gone and the educated are vaccinated. The Democrats control the White House and both houses of Congress. Ketanji Brown Jackson is poised to join the Supreme Court.

So why all the long faces among Democrats and LGBTQ rights advocates? From mass shootings and out-of-control inflation to the baby formula shortage and war in Ukraine, President Biden finds himself buffeted by one crisis after another. His poll numbers, though ticking up slightly last week, remain stuck in the low 40s with a majority of voters disapproving of his performance. Some of the blame goes to Biden, with economists citing his 2021 $1.9 trillion COVID relief bill as a leading driver of inflation that has sent the prices of everything skyrocketing and gas headed toward an unthinkable $5 per gallon national average.

And Biden's communications problems continue with new reporting this week that younger advisers are frustrated at being ignored or mocked by older officials consumed with 20th century ways of handling the media.

But the dreary landscape is not all Biden's making, with Republicans remaining recklessly opposed to gun safety measures, even after the murders of 19 children in Texas. And Donald Trump's Supreme Court could overturn Roe v. Wade this month, turning our

Pride celebrations into a nightmare of backsliding not just on women's rights, but on LGBTQ equality as well.

In Justice Samuel Alito's leaked draft opinion overturning Roe, he cites the landmark Lawrence and Obergefell cases several times, noting, "None of these rights has any claim to being deeply rooted in history."

Alito and the ethically compromised Justice Clarence Thomas have publicly called for the high court to reexamine the Obergefell marriage ruling. Thanks to Trump and Mitch McConnell, they have the votes to do it. I have spoken to a range of advocates about the likelihood of Obergefell being overturned. Many view it as unlikely, given the confusion and avalanche of lawsuits it would trigger from already-married couples seeking to exercise the rights and benefits of state and federal law. But is any same-sex married couple feeling comforted by such assurances? The same sorts of state trigger laws awaiting abortion clinics when Roe goes down exist in some states for same-sex marriage. We are headed backward to a time when America was governed by an unfair and dangerous patchwork of laws governing abortion — and marriage.

Could a backlash over Roe boost Democrats in the November midterms? That's the long-shot narrative being pushed by some who foresee a massive outcry from progressives when abortion is outlawed in 26 states as soon as this month. How many of those protesters voted in 2016 when every politico and commentator warned the Trump vs. Hillary election was really about the Supreme Court and Roe? The answer is only about 60 percent of the electorate voted that year.

It will take an unprecedented midterm turnout of young voters to keep Congress in Democratic hands. And with spineless sellouts like Joe Manchin and, even worse, Kyrsten Sinema, it won't be enough for Democrats to merely hold the Senate; they need more votes to get anything done on voting rights, gun reform, abortion and the long-suffering Equality Act. That measure — once described by Biden as his No. 1 legislative priority — remains stalled in the Senate with rumors of a looming compromise that would add a broad religious exemption to attract GOP support before Democratic losses in the midterms kill any hope of progress.

So here we are, on the precipice of returning to back alley abortions and to another national battle over marriage equality. There's a new T-shirt being marketed this Pride season; it reads simply "Gay and Tired." That about sums it up.

"VOTE AS IF DEMOCRACY DEPENDS ON IT," NOV. 1, 2022

With this essay, I close out this chapter on politics. It seems a fitting place to end, as it previews the midterm elections. Days after the election, we still didn't know the balance of power in Congress. But Dr. Oz lost, so that's good. The results weren't nearly as bad as the pollsters had predicted, with Democrats fending off a feared "red wave," as many voters cited abortion as their No. 1 issue. There is something fundamentally wrong with polling these days; the pollsters aren't capturing enough youth representation, perhaps. Or maybe respondents aren't honest in their answers. Whatever the problem, the flawed polls in the last three elections are stunning and they have the potential to depress turnout. With divided government, the final two years of Biden's first term will be filled with House investigations into the Afghanistan withdrawal and Hunter's laptop. The Jan. 6 committee will be dissolved. And the country will move on to 2024 and the inevitable fight between Trump and DeSantis. The good news? Trump is probably the only Republican that Biden can beat so bring him on.

It was a perfect fall afternoon at Beaver Stadium in State College, Pa., last weekend and I was enjoying a homecoming tailgate party at my alma mater when I noticed something strange.

Amid the peak fall foliage and tens of thousands of students and alumni playing corn hole or watching TVs perched in the back of pickup trucks broadcasting the game via portable satellite dishes, a handsome man in a suit and tie was making his way through the crowd. He had two camera men and a sound guy in tow. We watched with interest as he made his way toward our circle of camping chairs. Then he approached me.

"I'm Robert Costa with CBS News, can I interview you," he said to me.

I told him I recognized him and asked what he wanted to talk about. He replied, "politics and the upcoming election."

At a tailgate? My husband intervened and suggested that I decline as I'd already had a beer. But I couldn't resist. Costa asked what I thought was at stake in next week's elections.

"Our very democracy is at stake in this election and soon it could be taken from us," I replied. "And that's what this election, I think, is about. Because when these election deniers come into office as secretaries of state and in roles where they control the process, and somebody wins an election that they don't like, they'll overturn it. And will we care then? It'll be too late."

That may sound hyperbolic, but consider that CBS News has identified more than 300 Republican candidates for state and national office who are on the record as election deniers, falsely claiming that President Biden is illegitimate due to fraud in the 2020 election. It's all demonstrably false and at least 60 lawsuits filed on behalf of Donald Trump and his enablers challenging the 2020 results were dismissed by judges across the country, including judges appointed by Trump himself.

But the lunatics of MAGA never let facts get in the way of a good conspiracy theory. The results of a former president endorsing Q-Anon conspiracy theories can be seen in last week's horrific and brutal attack on Paul Pelosi. When presidents talk, people listen and act. When Trump denies the results of the 2020 election and spreads dangerous, reckless conspiracies, his followers act and one of them nearly killed Nancy Pelosi's husband.

The antidote to all this madness infecting our politics? Well, until the MAGA nuts can be deprogrammed — that's what must happen to cult followers, after all — the rest of thinking people must vote like our democracy depends on it, because it does. Don't let the talk of inflation and crime distract you from the key issue in this race: upholding our Constitution and our democratic principles of free and fair elections.

Nothing else will matter if we lose the integrity of our elections and make no mistake that GOP candidates on the ballot next week, if elected, will refuse to certify elections of Democrats and will undermine the process and continue to erect barriers to voting by people of color.

Stopping the MAGA lunatics won't be easy and won't happen in a single election. After all, they now have a super majority on the Supreme Court and have already overturned Roe; affirmative action is next and marriage equality not far behind.

But voters can blunt the progress and influence of these Trump cultists by sending a message on Nov. 8 that we won't embrace authoritarianism and we will defend our democratic institutions from the MAGA crowd. They've already defiled and invaded our Capitol, threatened the lives of scores of Democratic and Republican lawmakers and attacked the husband of the House Speaker. What's next could be worse if they come into political power.

CBS aired Costa's report on Sunday featuring my remarks from the Penn State tailgate as well as comments from Margaret Sullivan, the former public editor of the New York Times. She and I share concerns about Republican election deniers.

"I think we need to stop being asleep at the switch and sound the alarm more about what could happen if election denialists are, you know, in power and decide, 'Oh, well, we only like the results of this election, but not that one,'" Sullivan said. "I mean, we no longer have a country anymore."

"Overcoming the Enemy Within," May 14, 2004

This piece included the first reference to my eventual outing of Fox News anchor Shepard Smith, who hit on me at a New York City gay piano bar (shout-out to Brandy's!). I waited a bit longer to finally out him but this piece again reminds us how shaky our allies could be in their "support." It also addresses the phenomenon of the "DL," which got a lot of attention in the early 2000s, including from Oprah. Looking back, it's worth noting that the term "MSM" (men who have sex with men) was an important designation for health professionals tracking the spread of HIV and AIDS. I was a bit cynical in 2004 in describing the "DL" craze. It seemed unfair to me — someone who was publicly out — having to excuse the behavior of closeted men hooking up in grocery stores and bathrooms. But, of course, the reality in communities of color is that many men do not identify with the monikers "gay" or "bi" and whatever associated behaviors they may imply and so MSM is an important designation, particularly in health care.

We and our allies bemoan attacks on gay rights from Lou Sheldon, Marilyn Musgrave, Antonin Scalia and others on the far right, but a more frustrating enemy lurks among us. Closeted gays — from gay Republicans working for virulently anti-gay public officials, to Black men on the "down low," to gay TV anchors at Fox News — are doing more damage to the interests of their fellow gays than any right-wing bogeyman. Gay rights activists have rightly said that the greatest untapped resource in the fight for full equality lies in the millions of us who remain closeted. Imagine if all those closeted gays came rushing out — professional athletes, corporate executives, politicians, movie stars, parents, siblings and children. Not only should gay people come out; those of us who are already living an honest, open existence should let our presence be known to family, friends and colleagues. In this election year, it is not enough to merely be out. We must remind our loved ones that President Bush seeks to enshrine anti-gay discrimination in the nation's founding document.

Bush would like to amend the Constitution to deprive rights to a large segment of society. No attack could be more personal, repugnant or lacking in compassion.

In the midst of this grave fight against the Federal Marriage Amendment, too many gays are checking their identity at the door. Christopher Barron, political director of the Log Cabin Republicans, recently told the New York Times, "The perception outside the Beltway would be that if there are gay staff members, they must work on Barney Frank's or Teddy Kennedy's staff. The reality is there are gay men and women working in tons of Republican offices, in the White House and in the president's reelection campaign."

If there are closeted gay men and lesbians working at the highest levels of Bush's reelection campaign, they should come out and face the music or else face the likelihood that someone else will make that decision for them. We are not a homogenous lot and there will certainly be those of us who will vote for Bush, despite the FMA issue. But let them make that case in person. Face those of us who made the difficult but affirming decision to live openly and honestly and explain why we should vote for George W. Bush.

But closeted gay Republicans aren't the only ones guilty of selling out their own community. Take the much-publicized plight of Black men living on the "down low": men involved in relationships with women who like to have sex with other men but don't "identify" as gay. These Black men are much en vogue these days, commanding ink from the New York Times, and even air time with Oprah Winfrey, who isn't known for devoting much attention to gay rights issues on her popular, self-obsessed show. She recently featured author J.L. King, who said, "You're not going to find me in a gay club because I have nothing to do with that culture. That's them."

King, who is Black, wrote a book titled, "On the Down Low." Instead of going to gay bars, he prefers to meet closeted men in grocery stores and churches, much to the shock of Oprah's enraptured audience of naive, pampered, upper middle class women. I met my partner of nearly seven years at the Hippo nightclub in Baltimore. We didn't cruise the produce aisle or sneak off to a public toilet. We met, chatted and exchanged phone numbers, then scheduled a date. King, and others like him living such blatantly dishonest lives, should try "that culture." They might be surprised.

Black men on the "DL" aren't carving out some cool new subculture to which anyone should aspire. They are lying to themselves, and more tragically, to the African-American women they're infecting with HIV at alarming rates. And African Americans as a whole, particularly Black ministers, need to accept some responsibility for pushing these men into a dangerous existence in the closet.

There are plenty of white men living their own version of the DL. On a recent trip to New York, I visited a gay bar on the Upper East Side, where I met a familiar-looking man wearing an expensive suit and excessive makeup. After a drink or two, I realized that he was one of the star anchors at Fox News, that tool of the conservative right masquerading as a "fair and balanced" news operation. He wouldn't admit his identity, only that he "worked for News Corporation," the parent company of Fox, so I played dumb and let him buy another round of martinis.

At 3 a.m. and after more than a few drinks, the closeted Fox star could barely balance on his bar stool. His solicitations for a date became more intense and desperate. So I told him I was not single and, "not interested dating anyone in the closet," and left him wobbling on his stool. The stakes are too great this year for any of us — Democrat, Republican, Black, white, famous or infamous — to hide in the closet and grant Bush another four years to pander to his fundamentalist Christian, anti-gay base.

Payback for a Bush victory in 2004 will come from our collective hides: more anti-gay legislation and rhetoric, more bigoted judicial nominees, and undoubtedly one or two (or more) Supreme Court picks. Anyone living in the closet will deserve a small piece of the blame if Bush is reelected.

"Out, out damn celebs!," Oct. 21, 2005

Well, this was a big one. In this column, I outed Fox News anchor Shepard Smith, who had hit on me at a New York bar. The bar in question was Brandy's piano bar on the Upper East Side, a longtime favorite for my husband and me. On that night, I went to Brandy's with two friends, one of whom coincidentally worked at News Corp., Fox News' parent company. I sat down and noticed the well-dressed man next to me looked familiar. It was late, after midnight, and he was still wearing his heavy TV makeup and suit and tie. He started chatting me up and we had a nice conversation about movies and books. He was engaging, handsome in a nontraditional way and smart. I quickly realized who it was but didn't let on I knew. When I asked what he did for a living, he replied, "I work at News Corp." I said, "Oh, are you like the janitor or something?" He chuckled, changed the subject, then bought a round of martinis for me and my friends. It was getting late and he was clearly intoxicated, belting out the lyrics to the Broadway tunes being performed nearby by longtime Brandy's star Bobby Belfry and others. Finally, he worked up the nerve to ask me out. First, by clumsily inviting me back to his place, which I politely declined, then by persistently asking me to dinner the following night. Again, I declined, telling Smith I had a partner. The night ended at 3 a.m. when we all went our separate ways and stumbled home.

Contrary to perceptions of my many critics at the time, I did not rush home to out Smith. In fact, it was a full year later that this column was published. The reason I waited: Even though Smith worked for Fox News, an enemy of LGBTQ equality and mouthpiece for Bush's homophobia, Smith himself kept a low profile and hadn't been asked about his sexual orientation. It wasn't until Hurricane Katrina struck New Orleans in August of 2005 that Smith rose to national prominence. His on-the-ground coverage undercut the Bush administration's absurd assertions that they'd done a "heck of a job," as Bush famously said of FEMA chief Michael Brown while more than 1,800 people died. Smith did excellent reporting, contradicting Bush live on Fox News. He stood in flooded French Quarter streets, illuminating for Fox viewers that they were being lied to by the administration. It was a bold move for Smith that some speculated would cost him his job. He began to attract widespread media attention, sitting for profiles in magazines, all the while playing coy about his dating life when asked. That's when I decided to out him. Here's the thing about privacy — it's surprisingly easy to achieve. Go home after work, pull the curtains and voila, privacy. But when you hire publicists, grant interviews to reporters and sit for photo shoots, you are not seeking privacy. And if you seek that media attention, you have an obligation to answer truthfully. When he didn't, I wrote the column outing him.

For the most part, mainstream media didn't report this news; those outlets were terrified of "outing" and clueless about covering the community. I used to field calls and attend meetings with Washington Post reporters and editors looking for sources inside the community. They would routinely ask, "But how do you know they're gay?!?" Well, because we ask them. To this day, most news about the LGBTQ community in the Post lands in the Style section. Because we're so stylish!

Back to Shep. Although the mainstream media mostly ignored my outing him, the queer press and the tabloids reported it widely. I was sitting at my desk in the Blade office when the phone rang and the voice on the other end said, "I'm with the Globe and had a few questions about your piece on Shepard Smith." I obliged, surprised that a mainstream paper like the Boston Globe would participate in outing Smith. It wasn't until the reporter asked me for my height and weight that I realized my mistake — he was with the tabloid Globe, not the Boston newspaper of the same name. I promptly hung up and sheepishly went to my boss's office to warn him I accidentally gave an interview to a supermarket tabloid. They published a splashy story teased on the cover complete with my pallid driver's license photo and a description of me as "athletic" (my friends have never let me live that down).

After that, Smith was asked about his sexual orientation when he attended events for the National Lesbian & Gay Journalists Association. He always dodged them. In 2009, I was approached by acclaimed documentary filmmakers Kirby Dick and Amy Ziering about a new film they were working on called "Outrage," a "shocking and passionate indictment of the clandestine hypocrisy of many closeted homosexuals in Washington, D.C." I gleefully accepted and was interviewed extensively for the film along with many D.C. politicos and media figures including Andrew Sullivan, Elizabeth Birch, Kirk Fordham, Jim McGreevey and others. In the film, I am quoted telling the story of outing Smith.

But the highlight of that film for me comes at the very end, where I implore closeted people to come out, declaring it the "sleeping giant of the movement." To my great surprise, the filmmakers segued from my quote to footage of Harvey Milk saying almost the exact words decades earlier. I assumed it would be an obscure documentary screened in a handful of LGBT film festivals. After the film debuted at the 2009 Tribeca Film Festival, HBO picked it up and for a month, you couldn't turn on one of HBO's channels without seeing it.

Not much changed for Smith after the column was published; he continued in his role as primetime star of Fox News. Finally, 11 years later, in 2016, Smith came out in an interview with the Huffington Post.

Shortly after, he told the Advocate, "If you live your truth, there are no limits. I'm so proud and happy to be part of this loving gay community. It's fantastic." Indeed. I have never met Smith, but as I wrote upon his coming out in 2016, "He's a good guy, a skilled journalist and I'm relieved he's finally out. It's unfortunate it took so long, but welcome to the sunshine."

National Coming Out Day came and went last week without any public declarations from celebrities or other public figures long rumored to be gay, but who simply refuse to acknowledge their sexual orientation. It's a long and varied list, from A-list Hollywood celebrities to popular television anchors to prominent politicians. These closet cases choose to hide and deceive — and to protect their incomes and images — at the expense of contributing important weight and star power to the gay civil rights movement. When rich, famous, wildly successful Americans refuse to acknowledge their sexual orientation, they contribute to keeping us at the margins of society and send a message that homosexuality is somehow shameful. There is nothing more ridiculous than a public figure refusing to reveal whether he or she is straight — no heterosexual person would deny being straight.

Anderson Cooper may be the most ubiquitous personality on cable television these days. Popping up on a best-dressed or most-beautiful-people list, profiled in magazines or penning a column for Details magazine, Cooper gets a lot of ink. But in all the fawning stories about his good looks, sartorial smarts, family wealth and status as one of TV's biggest rising stars, one key detail is always missing. Cooper, the popular CNN anchor, coyly refused to answer "the question" in a recent lengthy profile in New York magazine. Though long rumored to be gay — he once suggested he is gay in comments made at a GLAAD Media Awards event — Cooper chooses the closet over honesty.

"The whole thing about being a reporter is that you're supposed to be an observer and to be able to adapt with any group you're in," Cooper told New York magazine, "and I don't want to do anything that threatens that." Does he believe that female and African-American reporters lack credibility to cover stories since their minority status is showing? Should any heterosexuals who let it slip that they're married to someone of the opposite sex be kept off the air, or does his rule apply only to gay journalists? (Note to Cooper: I have been a journalist for as long as you have and being open about my sexual orientation has never cost me a job, a story, a source or a promotion.)

Cooper isn't the only well-known TV personality hiding his sexual orientation. Shepard Smith, who hosts a popular program on Fox News and received widespread praise for his work covering Hurricane Katrina's aftermath, also dodges questions about his sexual orientation. Smith once chatted me up in a New York City gay piano bar, bought me drinks and invited me back to his place. When I declined, he asked me to dinner the next night, another invitation I politely refused. We sat at the bar chatting and drinking martinis until 3 a.m., our conversation interrupted only when he paused to belt out the lyrics to whatever showtune was being performed.

There are, of course, much bigger stars that remain in the closet. Jodie Foster's recent film "Flightplan" spent two weeks atop the box office charts. She, too, continues to refuse any discussion of her private life. Incredibly, even Sean Hayes, who plays the flamboyantly gay character Jack on NBC's "Will & Grace," won't say whether he's gay. Maybe when his hit show ends its run this year and the acting roles dry up, Hayes will muster the "courage" to appear on the cover of the Advocate. Ironically, Hollywood and New York are regarded as two of the most liberal places on earth. And yet those who inhabit some of the highest positions of visibility and power in those communities remain in the closet. It's the same story in Washington, D.C., where with a few rare exceptions — Reps. Barney Frank (D-Mass.), Tammy Baldwin (D-Wisc.) and Jim Kolbe (R-Ariz.) — lawmakers and their most senior advisers dodge and weave when asked about their sexual orientation.

Congressman Mark Foley (R-Fla.) became the poster child for closet cases when he refused to answer questions about whether he is gay. In 2003, the Express Gay News, a Fort Lauderdale paper affiliated with the Blade, and an alternative weekly in West Palm Beach published stories saying Foley is gay. Foley refused to confirm or deny the paper's report. He later ended his bid for the U.S. Senate, citing family reasons.

When Rep. David Dreier's (R-Calif.) name was floated as a replacement for indicted House Majority Leader Tom DeLay, then promptly withdrawn, speculation swirled that anti-gay conservatives had quashed his promotion because of rumors Dreier is gay. Dreier has similarly refused to answer "the question."

Thankfully, there are a handful of out public figures giving us visibility. Rupert Everett, Rosie O'Donnell, Ellen DeGeneres and Melissa Etheridge come to mind, proving that living an honest life doesn't mean the death knell for a career in the public eye. The biggest sleeping asset in the fight for full gay equality lies in the shadows of the closet. When we live openly, we force those around us to reconsider their negative views of homosexuality. That's when the stereotypes give way to understanding and real change occurs. No Human Rights Campaign ad campaign in the "red states" can produce the impact of gays who live in those states actually coming out. How can we expect the construction worker making $20,000 a year to come out when the rich and pampered are still hiding in the closet? How will gays living in Peoria find the fortitude to live honest lives, when the gay denizens of New York and Hollywood won't? No one is asking Anderson Cooper to wear a pink triangle on the air or Jodie Foster to ride with the "Dykes on Bikes" contingent. Simply acknowledging the truth — whatever it is — would be enough.

We need role models and spokespeople to boost visibility, increase understanding and, most importantly, to inspire those living less privileged lives to come out and stand up to those who would deny us the right to marry, to adopt children and to go to work free from the prospect of legal discrimination. Shame on the rich and famous closet cases who have let us down.

"DON'T CRY FOR LANCE BASS," AUG. 4, 2006

Back in 2006, Lance Bass was closeted and dating Reichen Lehmkuhl from "Amazing Race" fame. The couple partied in Provincetown gay bars over July Fourth weekend and several media outlets and bloggers, including the New York Post, Towleroad, Cyd Zeigler and

I received tips from witnesses and published stories, allegedly "outing" Bass. My assertion then as now is that we did no such thing; Bass was not behaving as someone concerned about being found out. I may have been a tad harsh on Bass back then, but as someone who was professionally out and enduring the resulting hate mail and even death threats, I resented the closeted rich and famous.

Today, Bass is an out-and-proud business owner in West Hollywood and married to his longtime partner. He co-owns the popular Rocco's (the Los Angeles Blade has hosted parties there) and the new Heart nightclub nearby. My favorite thing about Rocco's is the timeline of West Coast LGBTQ history that adorns the wall of a hallway. Bass has championed LGBTQ artists and musicians at Rocco's and the venue has quickly become one of the most popular in WeHo. Kudos to Bass for successfully transitioning from teen star to well-adjusted adult giving back to his community.

Poor Lance Bass. You really have to feel for those downtrodden millionaire celebrities who crave publicity and attention and then cry foul when people talk about anything other than the latest pet project they're hawking.

After much blog-fueled speculation about his relationship with "Amazing Race" winner Reichen Lehmkuhl, Bass did the coming out deed on the cover of the current issue of People magazine, declaring in bold headlines, "I'm more liberated and happy than I've ever been."

If that's the case, then the former 'N Sync-er ought to be thanking the bloggers who reported on his recent carousing at a popular Provincetown gay bar accompanied by his boyfriend Lehmkuhl.

But the snoops at the New York Post, Andy Towle of Towleroad.com, Cyd Zeigler of thedooryard.typepad.com and I probably shouldn't expect a thank you note from Bass, despite all that newly discovered liberation.

The Post, Towle, Zeigler and the Blade all reported that Bass and Lehmkuhl were spotted over the July Fourth weekend partying in

P-town. Some of us wrongly assumed that Bass had come out, what with all public bar hopping and all.

Bass told People that his mother got wind of all the online chatter and decided to Google her son. That's when she discovered the gay rumors, triggering the coming out conversation.

My own report on Bass, posted to the Blade's website on July 13 after reading the Post and Zeigler stories, triggered an avalanche of email assailing the Blade for engaging in "outing." The activists at the Gay & Lesbian Alliance Against Defamation weighed in, telling ABC News, "Media speculation about people's sexual orientation is not something we support."

The same ABC News reporter called me for a comment and confessed that he wasn't happy about having to write a story about the outing of a celebrity.

Some of those who wrote in to protest the supposed outing of Bass were more reasonable than others. One reader writes, "Even if these celebrities are staying closeted because of how it would affect their star status, that should be their choice."

Others were decidedly more colorful in their criticism. "First of all you don't even know Lance Bass. What crime did he commit? He actually went to a gay event or a gay bar without making a pronouncement to the world detailing his sexual status. How shocking. Let's crucify him! No wonder people are afraid to associate with anything with gay with vultures like you waiting to pounce."

Still others were looking for revenge. "Let's all chip in and give Kevin Naff a ticket for Jerusalem so he can participate in the World Pride Day to discover why gay people don't announce themselves to the world!"

To be fair, not all Blade readers are so vitriolic. One closeted gay teen wrote, "I know it would give me confidence if a prominent male celebrity came out of the closet."

The key point that many readers — and mainstream media reporters covering the Bass story — missed is that Bass outed himself. Gays and lesbians are under no obligation to keep each other's dirty little secrets and partying in P-town's gay bars on a holiday weekend with a celebrity boyfriend in tow is not the behavior of someone living a closeted life.

Here's the thing about privacy: it's an easy thing to attain. Go home, lock your door and draw the curtains and you have privacy. Bass' days as a teen heartthrob are long over: There are no paparazzi camped at his doorstep anxious to chronicle his every move. He is fully capable of living a quiet, private, closeted life. He made another choice.

Outing involves investigating and reporting on the private behavior of a public figure who denies being gay. Hanging out in gay bars doesn't constitute private behavior. It didn't take any sneaky detective work to uncover Bass' sexual orientation. No one peered through his windows or sorted through his trash. He walked into a gay bar with his boyfriend and witnesses connected the dots. Sorry, but there's no outing in this case.

Gay blogger Perez Hilton, who has been writing about the Bass gay rumors since 2005, understands what mainstream reporters do not.

"It upsets me that people think what I'm doing is a bad thing," Hilton told Access Hollywood. "I don't think it's a bad thing. If you know something to be a fact, why not report it? Why is that still taboo?"

The simple fact of sexual orientation is not an inherently private thing. Openly closeted celebrities like Bass and an army of others (CNN's Anderson Cooper; Fox News' Shepard Smith, actress Jodie Foster, singer Ricky Martin, GOP Congressman David Dreier and actor Sean Hayes come to mind) do a disservice to fellow gays by perpetuating the damaging and false notion that being gay is something to hide and to be ashamed of. And the reporters who omit any reference to sexual orientation when it comes to writing about gay public figures are only enforcing outdated double standards and enabling cowardly behavior.

In his People interview, Bass said, "I don't think the gay community is going to hop on my back because I'm not going to lead the parades and be this crazy activist. I don't want to be a poster child."

So the activists working for the equality and acceptance of gays that Bass now enjoys are "crazy?" Don't worry, Lance, no one will mistake you for a poster child for gay causes. There are far more worthy poster gays out there who are actually taking risks and leading lives of honest courage.

At least all of his attention is coming at a convenient time. Bass told People that he and former 'N Sync member Joey Fatone are shopping a new "Odd Couple" rip-off sitcom in which Bass' character will be gay. Also, Lehmkuhl is peddling his book "Here's What We'll Say: A Memoir of Growing Up, Coming Out and the U.S. Air Force," which comes out this month.

I'm sure the timing of all this outing drama is coincidental.

Bass should take some of his own advice.

"You know, once you get in the business you know what you're getting into," Bass told Access Hollywood in an earlier interview. "Unfortunately, if you don't want to be in the spotlight get out of it."

"Gay celebs just don't get it," April 27, 2007

Happily, the three subjects of this column — Neil Patrick Harris, Anderson Cooper, and Jodie Foster — are all now out and proud figures and role models to many. I feel vindicated whenever these once-closeted figures we've written about finally acknowledges the simple truth of their sexual orientation and goes on to success and happiness, marriage and families. Harris, in particular, has thrived since coming out — starring in hit shows, hosting the Oscars, getting married and raising children. His latest show "Uncoupled," is a guilty-pleasure treat exploring the plight of a newly single 40-something gay man in New York. Cooper remains a fixture at CNN and it's quite something to watch an openly gay journalist moderating a presidential debate — unthinkable even 20 years ago. Foster has made a string of unforgettable hit films and won two Oscars in the process. Her coming out was clumsy and confusing but she's always been something of a recluse.

The underlying point of this piece from 2007 is that the basic fact of a public figure's sexual orientation is not private. It's certainly not private for straight celebrities or public officials and the same should be true for their LGBTQ counterparts. What you do behind closed doors in the bedroom is private; the simple fact of being gay is not.

The importance of living an honest life is still lost on some gays. Take actor Neil Patrick Harris, who finally came out because he feared the media were targeting him for an outing. Harris told Ellen DeGeneres in a recent interview, "I just feel like as an actor part of your occupation is retaining a bit of mystery so you can be believable in many different types of roles, so I never felt it was an obligation for me to hold pinkies down the red carpet or anything."

The obligation is not to hold pinkies, it's merely to be honest about who you are. And what straight celebrity feels the need to keep their sexual orientation a "mystery"? From Paris Hilton and Pamela Anderson, whose videotaped sexual romps were released for mass consumption, to Brad Pitt and Jennifer Aniston, whose divorce generated headlines for months, the personal lives of straight celebrities are on full view. You can debate whether or not that's a good thing, but it's reality. And the standards should be the same for gays.

Harris continued, "For me that is the greatest ending to the story so far — that nothing really has changed at all. I'm doing nothing different and people aren't behaving differently towards me. ... People heard and they're like, 'Yeah and?' That attitude, I think was great."

Lucky for Harris he's financially independent and lives and works in a gay-friendly world. But that is not the case for most gay people and the importance of visibility and the need for gay role models appears lost on Harris. And even if Harris has no interest in being a role model, he doesn't deserve to have his secrets protected by a 1950s-esque double standard that says the details of straight celebrities' lives are fair game but gay celebrities' lives are off limits.

If Alec Baldwin's private voicemails to his daughter are fodder for mainstream news coverage, then Harris and other gay celebrities should at least be able to answer truthfully whether or not they are gay.

The issue received renewed attention thanks to Out magazine's deliciously brilliant May cover that features the faces of CNN anchor Anderson Cooper and actress Jodie Foster to illustrate a story about the "glass closet." The magazine also named the ambiguous due on its list of the 50 most powerful gays.

The article, by Michael Musto, broke no new ground; the stories about Cooper and Foster and a legion of others have been reported for years in the Blade's pages. But that provocative cover helped bring renewed attention to the issue.

My colleague, Chris Ciompi, editor of Genre magazine, which is affiliated with the Blade, denounced the Out cover in an interview with the New York Daily News.

"Your right to privacy is a constitutional right," Ciompi said. "Maybe Jodie and Anderson would prefer to be known for their work, not their sexuality. The climate of the United States today still would not allow that to occur. With Anderson, many people would perceive his credibility to be undermined."

The problem with Ciompi's reasoning is that straight celebrities don't have the option to be "known for their work," and the rules should be the same for their gay counterparts. And how does being gay undermine your credibility as a journalist? Cooper has cited that offensive canard in refusing to answer questions about his sexual orientation and the gay media ought not give him cover. As for privacy rights, there are far different legal standards of privacy for public figures. Just ask Alec Baldwin.

Ciompi continued, "I think [Out editor] Aaron Hicklin wants to use [Cooper and Foster] to sell magazines. It's politically reprehensible, when he has a list of 50 gay people, to choose two people who are not out."

Using celebrities to sell magazines shouldn't come as a surprise to anyone. But Out's cover was more than a cheap stunt to stoke sales. It sends a long overdue and unmistakable message that the days of powerful gays and lesbians hiding behind double standards governing sexual orientation are finally coming to an end. I wish I'd thought of the idea for that cover.

Another happy byproduct of this debate in the gay media is that it is spilling over to the mainstream media, which so often run and hide from these questions. At least one mainstream media commentator finally spoke out. MSNBC's Keith Olbermann denounced Cooper's coy answers to "the question" in a withering attack on his hypocrisy.

"Don't tell me you don't want to talk about personal life when you wrote a book about your father's death and your brother's death," Olbermann told New York magazine. "You can't move this big mass of personal stuff out for public display, then people ask questions and you say, 'Oh, no, I didn't say there was going to be any questions.' ... Don't tell me you can't talk about your personal life and then, when they send you overseas and you do a report that consists of your voice-over and pictures of you in a custom-made, blue-to-match-your-eyes bulletproof vest, looking somberly at these scenes of human devastation — like a tourist — and that's your report. Your shtick is your personal life."

Amen. As gays win victories for equality, particularly in the area of legal recognition for our relationships, it will become increasingly difficult to hide in the "glass closet." We can't have it both ways — and we shouldn't want to.

"A PREDICTABLE FALL," AUG. 31, 2007, AND "GOTCHA!," SEPT. 7, 2007

It was late summer 2007 and I was on vacation in California when news broke that Idaho Sen. Larry Craig had been arrested for soliciting sex in an airport men's room in Minneapolis. That restroom has since become something of a tourist attraction, with gay men stopping there for a selfie during a layover. August is normally slow with Congress in recess and the Supreme Court between terms. But inevitably something dramatic happens to disrupt my August break as when this news hit about Craig.

I wrote a lot about this tawdry episode and the ham-handed efforts of the mainstream media to cover it, particularly the Idaho Statesman newspaper, which dispatched a reporter to stalk the Union Station men's room to ask patrons if they'd seen Craig cruising there for sex. One tidbit from that time that I didn't write about was the lengthy meeting I had with Statesman reporter Dan Popkey, a nice guy who drew the short straw with this assignment. Popkey sat in my office, visibly uncomfortable with the subject at hand (gay sex in public toilets), and then asked me if I had a copy of "The Book." When I asked which book, he said he'd heard there was a book of names of closeted gay political and media figures and assumed I would have a copy. I assured him that was an urban legend and no such book existed but that if he wanted a good compendium of closeted politicos (mostly Republicans), he could check out the blogging of Michael Rogers, whom I consider a kindred spirit in many ways. Rogers worked doggedly to expose the homophobic hypocrisy of closeted politicians and took a few down. Many people have denounced his tactics, but I say that if you're working against the interests of the LGBTQ community then all is fair. Expose them all. Rogers went further than most in outing, sometimes targeting closeted staff members of conservative Republican lawmakers. I have spoken to a couple of those targets and each is living a happy, out life today. They would dispute that Rogers did them a favor but I think he did.

Back to Craig. He served 18 long years in the Senate and voted against LGBTQ interests whenever he had the chance. Ultimately, he decided not to run for reelection in 2008 and disappeared from public life. Today, he's in his late 70s and presumably living out his life in the closet. It's a sad existence and I hope one that becomes less common as younger generations adopt more accepting attitudes.

"A PREDICTABLE FALL"

The news that U.S. Sen. Larry Craig (R-Idaho) pleaded guilty to disorderly conduct charges stemming from an investigation into sexual activity at a men's restroom in the Minneapolis airport will not come as a surprise to those of us who have heard the gay rumors about him for years.

His office must have been working overtime to suppress the news of the arrest, because it happened in June and only leaked this week in a Roll Call report. Craig paid $500 in fines and fees, had a 10-day jail sentence stayed and received one year of probation in the case.

Craig is a conservative Republican with an abysmal record on gay issues and a 100 percent favorable rating from the Christian Coalition. And, of course, he's married.

Last year, I was visited by a reporter from the Idaho Statesman who was investigating rumors that Craig sought gay sex in D.C.-area restrooms, specifically in Union Station. He went so far as to stake out the bathroom, armed with glossy photos of Craig to show those using the facilities on the chance that someone had seen him there engaged in sexual activities. Not much came of his prolonged investigation, but now it appears he was staking out the wrong toilets.

The tactics seemed dramatic and heavy-handed; the reporter was assigned to investigate the gay "accusations" for months. If only the mainstream media had devoted so much energy to scrutinizing the buildup to war in Iraq. But sex sells, and so the big Idaho newspaper was on the case, desperately trying to confirm the reports by blogger Mike Rogers that Craig had a penchant for bathroom sex.

Now that those rumors appear to be confirmed following Craig's guilty plea, which he now says he regrets, gays find themselves back in the mainstream headlines. The past few days of coverage on CNN and the "Today" show, among other mainstream outlets, have been dispiriting, if occasionally entertaining. CNN's Jeffrey Toobin has had a particularly difficult time discussing Craig's foot-tapping under the bathroom stall without breaking into giggles.

It's unfortunate that gay issues keep landing on the front pages thanks to sleazy sex stories like this one. Craig's bathroom exploits will have Americans groaning and snickering, but the superficial coverage of what happened fails to explore the issue of just how damaging the closet is for those hiding inside.

Commentators this week are baffled over why someone of Craig's stature would plead guilty to a crime like this. But his actions make perfect sense to anyone who has ever been in the closet. Living a double life causes people to do strange things. Craig thought he could get away with it, sweep it under the proverbial rug and no one would know. He couldn't bear the thought of calling his lawyer because that would amount to sticking a toe outside the closet. Of course, if he'd called his lawyer he might have a slightly easier time issuing denials now. It's hard for folks to take those denials seriously when you've pleaded guilty.

When will these closeted officials learn that there is no honor in deceiving constituents — not to mention spouses — in this way? Craig isn't the first and he won't be the last. (David Dreier and Barbara Mikulski, are you paying attention?) It's gratifying to see sanctimonious hypocrites like Craig, Sen. David Vitter and former Reps. Mark Foley and Duke Cunningham fall from grace, but these scandals are not limited to the Republican ranks. Former New Jersey Gov. Jim McGreevey proves that such scandals know no partisan boundaries.

McGreevey brought us tales of sex in highway restrooms. Foley ensured that crude instant message chats and stories of lawmakers masturbating under the desk would make the front page. And now the tactics of those seeking sex in the stalls are parsed for a mainstream audience. Sadly, these crass tales only reinforce the perception among some people that gays are sex-obsessed.

So now Craig's office is once again in full damage control mode, denying the senator did anything wrong. Craig reportedly told police he didn't intend to tap his foot or invade the space of the neighboring stall. He just has a "wide stance" in the bathroom and reached down to pick up a piece of paper from the floor. The undercover cop in the adjacent stall says there was no piece of paper.

The hypocrisy of a closeted conservative politician voting against the interests of the gay community while engaging in some of the most stereotypically harmful behavior attributed to gays is maddening. But despite the unwanted attention to down-low sex, these stories and the wide coverage they draw can ultimately prove helpful. They reinforce just how wrong and dangerous it is to engage in deceit and maybe an aspiring politician somewhere will decide it's better to be honest about being gay than to try to hide it.

It's time for Craig to come clean with himself, his family and constituents and stop issuing laughable denials. Then he could begin to redeem himself by signing on as a cosponsor to ENDA and the hate crimes bill.

"Gotcha!"

The past couple of weeks proved sad and frustrating. First, the compulsively hypocritical Sen. Larry Craig (R-Idaho) was exposed as trolling for gay sex in a men's room. Then, the mainstream media did their usual sloppy best at covering the story.

Almost immediately, CNN began airing grainy and ominous footage of two men sitting in stalls, their feet tapping away. In one particularly galling segment, CNN included scenes of children playing in the foreground with a men's public restroom visible in the background.

Such images miss the point of Craig's preferred sort of sexual encounter. The men who engage in that behavior are so afraid of being exposed as gay that their techniques are painstakingly subtle. The average men's room patron would have absolutely no idea what's going on in the adjacent stall, because that's exactly the point. And bathroom sex certainly has nothing to do with children, no matter what that pansy homophobe Tucker Carlson thinks.

Linking gay men to pedophilia and illicit sex are the most enduring slurs directed at us and this story feeds both. At a dinner party last weekend, a straight friend worried aloud about the safety of his children in public bathrooms. This is the worst story at the worst time. And the cable news networks aren't the only guilty party.

Idaho Statesman reporter Dan Popkey was all over the news last week, following publication of his long-awaited outing piece on Craig. Roll Call beat the Idaho paper to the punch with its report on Craig's arrest and guilty plea stemming from the now infamous restroom incident. But Popkey had spent months investigating the rumors of Craig's homosexuality, which date back to at least 1982. In December, Popkey visited me at my office to ask whether I knew anything about Craig's sexual orientation.

We spent about an hour talking about his assignment, which clearly made him uncomfortable. Here is an account I wrote about our encounter that was published in the Blade in December 2006:

"Just last week, I was witness to yet another example of the media's pathetic squeamishness on the topic [of sexual orientation]. A reporter from the Idaho Statesman, now part of the large McClatchy chain of newspapers, emailed me to ask for a few minutes of my time. He sat down in my office, visibly nervous, and explained that his editor had sent him to Washington to investigate rumors that U.S. Sen. Larry Craig (R-Idaho) is gay.

"Those rumors have been widely circulated both online — thanks to the blogging of Michael Rogers — and in print. Craig's office even issued an official denial of the gay rumors, which the Blade reported last month.

"But even an official statement from Craig's office wasn't enough for the Statesman to report the story. And so it sent a reporter to investigate in the big city.

"His approach? To troll D.C. gay bars, hand out glossy color photos of Craig and ask if patrons had seen him around, as if he were a missing person or a criminal.

"Incredibly, when I asked where the reporter was headed after leaving my office, he said he was off to cruise the Union Station men's room, where unidentified 'sources' claim they had picked up Craig. He had more glossy photos at the ready. Imagine relieving yourself in a public restroom and being confronted by a reporter waving a photo, demanding to know if you'd ever seen this man peeing next to you.

"The reporter said he didn't have a story because no one would go on the record, but I told him he was wrong. The real story is the lengths to which mainstream media will go to tiptoe around the subject of sexual orientation. I advised him to write a column about his week spent in D.C.'s gay bars and public toilets."

My take on the Popkey meeting didn't sit well with Idaho Statesman managing editor Bill Manny, who responded to my comments shortly after they were published. "The Blade's trivializing account of that trip does not represent our significant effort to be thorough and comprehensive and determine the truth before we report," he said.

The Statesman was right to take a cautious approach to the story, but the paper's tactics are troubling, especially the trolling of public restrooms. The investigation had an unfortunate "Gotcha!" feel about it and the resulting story added little new information, except that a source said Craig "cruised" him at a retail store in 1994. Is this what passes for journalism in Idaho?

The paper's efforts illustrate how difficult it is for mainstream media to report on issues of sexual orientation. One happy day we'll arrive at a place where the fact of someone's sexual orientation isn't viewed as a private bit of information.

As the mainstream media struggled to tell the Craig story, some gay Democrats were celebrating the downfall of another Republican official who was guilty of demonizing gays and voting against our interests. But there's no silver lining in this tawdry story. It comes as lawmakers are returning to Washington with two high-profile gay rights bills on the agenda: the Employment Non-Discrimination Act and the hate crimes bill. The long-suffering bills finally have a chance at passage and the Craig scandal certainly won't help the cause.

It is tempting to sympathize with Craig, a man so afraid of being called gay that he chose to live his entire life in the closet. Indeed, that is a sad way to live. But the damage he's done through his congressional votes and the intense media attention he brought to the salacious details of his secret life counteract any sympathetic impulses.

As the scandal unfolded last week, I was amazed at the shock with which political commentators (and even some Blade readers) reacted.

The most common question I've heard is: Who's next? It's fair to assume that Craig isn't the only closeted gay member of Congress, but there are officials that the Blade has described over the years as "openly closeted," meaning they decline to answer "the question."

At least two active members of Congress fall into that category: Rep. David Dreier (R-Calif.) and Sen. Barbara Mikulski (D-Md.). There was much speculation that Dreier failed in his bid to take the

House majority leader post after Tom DeLay resigned because of the rumors about his sexual orientation, which have dogged him for years.

Mikulski has similarly dodged questions about her sexual orientation over the years. She voted for the Defense of Marriage Act, but has an otherwise supportive record and spoke at last year's Equality Maryland brunch fundraiser.

What people need to understand is that living a double life in the closet makes you do strange and self-destructive things, like pleading guilty to crimes you later deny or refusing to answer a simple question about your sexual orientation.

Until the acceptance of gays improves, we'll continue to see sad dramas like the Larry Craig scandal play out.

"The Return of Outing," April 24, 2009

This piece goes into more detail about the documentary "Outrage" that featured my outing of Shepard Smith. Attending the premiere at the Tribeca Film Festival was a treat and seeing my face on a movie screen an intimidating first. To this day, I have a page on IMDB thanks to the film. I'm a huge fan of Kirby Dick and Amy Ziering and fully expect them to win an Oscar at some point. They were sadly not nominated for "Outrage" (I lost my chance to say I was featured in an Oscar-nominated film), but they did nab a nomination for their superb 2012 documentary "The Invisible War," about rape in the military.

A new documentary on outing from Oscar-nominated filmmaker Kirby Dick, premieres tonight at the Tribeca Film Festival in New York and promises to reignite debate about the practice of exposing the sexual orientation of closeted public figures.

It's far and away the most controversial and popular topic the Blade has covered in my six years here. From Anderson Cooper and Shepard Smith to Mark Foley and Larry Craig to Queen Latifah and

Lance Bass, we've reported on a wide array of closeted politicians and celebrities.

"Outrage," the new documentary, focuses on closeted politicians and the mainstream media outlets that so often protect their dirty little secrets. Kirby Dick and his crew spent time in D.C. last year interviewing politicians, activists and media types (the Blade's Lou Chibbaro and me included) about the practice of outing, a dated term that I no longer use.

The film also features interviews with former New Jersey Gov. Jim McGreevey, radio host Michelangelo Signorile, blogger Mike Rogers, gay Rep. Barney Frank and others.

The documentary's resourceful team of researchers and filmmakers reportedly investigated the gay rumors surrounding some of the Republican Party's most prominent leaders. Rumors about one such official, Condoleezza Rice, were probed last year after two reliable sources agreed to speak to the Blade about their social interactions with the former Secretary of State. In the end, they got cold feet and our resulting story was less smoking gun and more speculation.

That experience, which unfolded over the course of several months, revealed just how heated this topic remains and the trepidation many still feel when discussing the basic fact of someone's sexual orientation.

I've long argued that the fact of being gay (or straight) is not private and that the true tipping point in the fight for equal rights under the law will come when we get over our squeamishness and come out to everyone in our lives.

The timing of the film's release will disappoint some who had hoped for an October surprise — a splashy premiere and a good ole' fashioned outing of a prominent Republican politician just weeks before the election. But it turns out Barack Obama didn't need yet another gay GOP hypocrisy scandal to get elected and now "Outrage" serves as a timely reminder that gay Americans have not reached the finish line in our fight, despite the news out of Vermont and Iowa this month.

Make no mistake that the self-imposed closet — not Christian right-wingers or George W. Bush or Pope Benedict — remains the biggest obstacle to equality. Films like this one help to illuminate that fact and, I hope, will inspire more closeted people to come out. Living a lie destroys lives, from loved ones feeling betrayed about the deception to the hoodwinked spouses and children caught in the middle.

Before we declare victory, pop the Champagne corks and celebrate the end of the culture wars, it's sobering to remember that 29 states have banned same-sex marriage via constitutional amendment and that firing an employee for being gay remains legal in a majority of states. In just the last two weeks, two grade school-age boys died by suicide after anti-gay bullying at school. Meanwhile, the window of opportunity for passing gay rights legislation is narrowing; we've learned not to expect anything in election years and 2010 is just eight months away. Although a federal hate crimes bill appears poised to pass, the future for the much more important Employment Non-Discrimination Act is less certain. And a repeal of "Don't Ask, Don't Tell" and the Defense of Marriage Act? Don't expect serious talk of either until 2011.

James Kirchick, an assistant editor for the New Republic and a former Blade contributor, overlooked those facts and got ahead of himself in a Washington Post op-ed piece this month, suggesting that gay rights groups should be closing up shop in the very near future. He argues that because younger Americans (like himself, he's 25) are polling better on gay issues than their elders (like me, I'm 38), that "Victories are not far off, and gay rights organizations should start facing the prospect that in the near future, their missions will be superfluous."

Kirchick writes, "For people who grew up in a time when being open about one's homosexuality could result in being fired or thrown into prison, it's harder to move out of a mindset that sees the plight of gay people as one of perpetual struggle. This attitude is all the more pronounced in those who hold leadership positions in the gay rights movement, as their life's work depends upon the notion that we are always and everywhere oppressed."

Although 2003's Lawrence v. Texas ruling ended the prospect of jail time for sexually active gays, anti-gay discrimination in the workplace remains a very real problem for those living outside liberal urban enclaves on the coasts (unlike Kirchick). As someone who has experienced such discrimination firsthand, I can assure skeptics that it's not an isolated problem trumped up by aging gay activists longing to be victimized. I hope Kirchick is right about impending victories — and I would happily resign as Blade editor if the nation's discriminatory laws were changed to afford gays equality. But, unlike in Canada or the United Kingdom, it's premature to call for closing activist organizations (or the gay press outlets that keep them honest) here.

In fact, activists should be busier than ever now. The need for visibility has never been more important as we open this new chapter in American history that holds so much promise. We should all resist complacency. Equal rights haven't magically arrived simply because the Democrats are in charge — we know how disappointment the party's track record has been on our issues.

Just as Congress begins considering long-suffering LGBT legislation, "Outrage" arrives, reminding us that hypocrisy thrives in Washington's political circles, where too many lawmakers, their Hill staff and members of the compliant mainstream media remain in the closet.

Projects like "Outrage" that challenge viewers' notions of sexual orientation as a private fact or something to be kept secret can only help. Here's hoping it reaches a wider audience than the gay activist choir.

"MEHLMAN'S SECRET FINALLY REVEALED," AUG. 26, 2010

I tried my damnedest to out Ken Mehlman, the former Bush-Cheney campaign chair and head of the RNC, who ran George W. Bush's reelection campaign on the backs of gay relationships. Our Blade editorial team was even followed by documentary cameras for the film "Outrage," as we tried to out him, as well as then-Secretary of State Condoleezza Rice. In the end, we never quite got the confirmations we needed to out either of them. But finally in late 2010, Mehlman came out in an interview seeking "understanding." Let's just say that didn't land well with me.

Ken Mehlman, former Republican National Committee chair and campaign manager for Bush-Cheney in 2004, came out as gay in a stupefying interview with the Atlantic on Wednesday.

In it, Mehlman says he only recently realized he's gay — an absurd claim — and insists that he worked behind the scenes to beat back efforts to attack same-sex marriage during the Bush years. That's a staggering claim from someone who presided over a campaign that exploited homophobia to advance constitutional amendments in 11 states banning same-sex marriage.

Now, long after leaving the public eye and public service, Mehlman wants our collective "understanding" because "everybody has their own path to travel, their own journey."

True, but for most of us, the journey didn't involve working side-by-side with those who fought to enshrine our second-class status in the U.S. Constitution, not to mention what Bush-Cheney did to advance the cause of torture.

Mehlman is the Roy Cohn of his generation, quietly enabling some of the most damaging attacks on LGBT people and our families. But some of the most prominent voices in the movement seem to have amnesia about that past. Chad Griffin and Dustin Lance Black of the American Foundation for Equal Rights are singing Mehlman's praises. Griffin told the Atlantic, "when we achieve equal equality, he will be one of the people to thank for it." Really? Mehlman will need to devote the rest of his life to undoing the damage he helped foster before he earns any thanks. It turns out that Mehlman is helping to raise money for AFER, so the praise is predictable and hollow.

Mehlman's sexual orientation was the subject of rumors for years and the Blade looked into the story numerous times. He dodged the question and flat out denied it on several occasions. We were alternately accused of covering up to protect his secret or propagating salacious gossip. Neither was true; Mehlman remained deeply closeted during his reign of terror and former classmates and associates of his routinely described him as "asexual."

The silver lining to this sickening hypocrisy is that the dominoes continue to fall, as more and more prominent Republicans take up the cause of gay rights and marriage equality. The party is headed for a reckoning in which it will need to address the hateful rhetoric about our families that has been a part of its national platform. How can party stalwarts like Mehlman, Cheney and Ted Olson advocate for marriage equality while their party stubbornly clings to its prejudice?

Indeed, it appears the country has reached a tipping point on the issue of gay rights. Too bad Mehlman arrived so late to the party.

"Shep Smith comes out — 11 years after I outed him," Oct. 17, 2016

Fox News anchor Shepard Smith came out as gay Monday in an interview with the Huffington Post — almost 11 years to the day that I outed him in 2005.

Smith hit on me in a New York City gay bar a year earlier. I didn't immediately out him because he wasn't actively courting media attention at the time. But a year later, after Smith won praise for his coverage of Hurricane Katrina, he began attracting media attention and answering questions about his personal life in a coy way, always dodging the truth. Hence, the outing in the Blade.

After 14 years at the Blade, it remains one of the most popular stories I've written, which is unfortunate. I'd much prefer that privileged celebrities come out on their own and help inspire the next generation. As I wrote in 2005: "The biggest sleeping asset in the fight for full gay equality lies in the shadows of the closet. When we live openly, we force those around us to reconsider their negative views of homosexuality. That's when the stereotypes give way to understanding and real change occurs.

"No Human Rights Campaign ad campaign in the 'red states' can produce the impact of gays who live in those states actually coming out.

"How can we expect the construction worker making $20,000 a year to come out when the rich and pampered are still hiding in the closet? How will gays living in Peoria find the fortitude to live honest lives, when the gay denizens of New York and Hollywood won't?"

Smith hasn't exactly been closeted in recent years, appearing in 2014 at a National Lesbian & Gay Journalists Association event in New York and posing for a selfie with CNN's Don Lemon, who's out. Blade reporter Michael Lavers confronted Smith at that event and asked about his sexual orientation; he quickly disappeared.

The reaction to my outing of Smith ranged from cheers to angry condemnation. It all seems a tad quaint in 2016 — and ridiculous that coming out today in Manhattan attracts any attention at all. But still, thanks to Fox News' role in promoting the Republican agenda for 20 years that has often included vicious attacks on LGBT equality, it's noteworthy that one of the network's top stars is gay.

My outing of Smith was chronicled in the 2009 documentary film "Outrage." When I sat for an interview with director Kirby Dick, I assumed it would be an obscure documentary screened in a handful of LGBT film festivals. After the film debuted at the 2009 Tribeca

Film Festival, HBO picked it up and for a month, you couldn't turn on one of HBO's channels without seeing it.

Throughout the controversy, I felt bad for Smith and how lonely it must be as a closeted gay man at Fox News. He's a good guy, a skilled journalist and I'm relieved he's finally out. It's unfortunate it took so long, but welcome to the sunshine.

"End the ban," Feb. 20, 2009

The fight to overturn "Don't Ask, Don't Tell" was one of the biggest stories the Blade covered over the years. Despite controlling Congress and President Obama's campaign pledge to overturn the law, the Democrats did nothing at first, opting instead to pass the federal hate crimes law and wrongly assuming the gays would accept that victory and be quietly grateful. They were wrong. One of the most emotional sights I've witnessed in 20 years at the Blade came on Dec. 27, 2010, when President Obama signed into law the repeal of the military's discriminatory gay ban that led to more than 14,000 service members being expelled. Among the attendees at the Interior Department ceremony that day were Vice President Joe Biden, House Speaker Nancy Pelosi and Senate Majority Leader Harry Reid, as well as Joint Chiefs Chairman Adm. Mike Mullen.

"I believe this is the right thing to do for our military," Obama said. "It's the right thing to do, period."

In the latest insult and indignity to be heaped upon gay and lesbian service members, the military announced it will begin recruiting immigrants with temporary visas, giving them the chance to become full U.S. citizens in just six months.

The New York Times reported the news on its front page Sunday, noting the program's small initial scope of about 1,000 mostly Army enlistees with a goal of expanding the program to all branches.

The rationale for the change: The military is stretched thin, given our commitment in Iraq and a brand new "surge" of 17,000 troops in Afghanistan (because taking over that country worked out so well for the Soviet Union in the 1980s and the United Kingdom in the 1920s).

And so the answer to the problem of the military's staffing shortfall is not to reduce our troop levels in Iraq or institute a draft, but to hit the streets in poor, immigrant communities and recruit young men with the promise of fast and easy citizenship.

There's no mention in the Times piece about the folly and irony of continuing the military's discriminatory "Don't Ask, Don't Tell" policy in the face of service member shortages. The military has expelled nearly 13,000 gay and lesbian service members since 1993, many of them highly skilled linguists and other badly needed personnel.

The military has already lowered its standards for recruiting to enable convicted criminals — felons in some cases — to enlist. It has issued stop-loss orders and even slowed the expulsion rate of gay service members because of the Iraq debacle.

The Army provided waivers to a whopping 18 percent of active-duty recruits in the last four months of 2008, allowing them to enlist despite criminal records, medical conditions and obesity, according to the Times report. So an overweight convicted bank robber with ADD is deemed eligible to serve his country, while a fit, educated gay Arabic linguist is kicked out.

And now non-U.S. citizens are being welcomed to the party and granted rights that are unavailable to natural-born, educated and highly skilled U.S. citizens who happen to be gay.

What happened to the military's obsession with the "war on terror"? Do our military leaders not see the potential here for terrorists to infiltrate its ranks when standards for enlisting are dropped to such low levels?

Of course, the presence of immigrants in the military is not new and many thousands have served with distinction for years. But embarking on an aggressive new recruitment strategy like this is cynical, reckless and insulting to the thousands of gays and lesbians whose careers have been destroyed by "Don't Ask, Don't Tell."

The high-profile placement of the story above the fold in Sunday's Times failed to generate much public reaction, let alone any outrage or prominent calls for President Obama to make good on his campaign promise of ending the military's gay ban. It's true he can't wave a wand and make it go away by executive order and, in his defense, he's been busy cleaning up the disaster the Republicans made of the economy. But as Obama said many times during the campaign: We can do more than one thing at a time. And if the military is so desperate for recruits that it's turning to immigrants and criminals to fill its ranks, then no reasonable person should object to letting brave and patriotic gays serve openly.

Instead of pushing for a repeal of the gay ban in Congress, Obama has called for yet more study of the issue. It's hard to imagine what's left to study, though retired Gen. Colin Powell and former Sen. Sam Nunn (D-Ga.) have finally seen the error of their discriminatory ways and called for a "review" of the policy.

The previous attempt to lift the ban in 1993 failed after Nunn and Powell led a homophobic effort that included touring cramped submarine quarters with TV cameras in tow to remind the American public — most of whom will never see the inside of a submarine unless it's part of a ride at Disney World — that straights would be forced to bunk just inches away from out gays. Their argument ignored important facts, like the military's history of leading on matters of integration and its very undemocratic, hierarchical structure mandating that soldiers obey orders — even those that make them uncomfortable in the shower.

As Owen West, a Marine who served two tours in Iraq, put it in a New York Times op-ed last week: "The military is a dictatorship, not a republic. It is built to win in combat. Its strict codes of conduct ensure good order and discipline. If 'Don't Ask, Don't Tell' is rescinded, the military leaders will ensure smooth compliance, as the chairman of the Joint Chiefs of Staff, Adm. Mike Mullen, has said. Cohesion depends on leadership. Our troops will follow the lead of our combat-tested professionals who base their opinions on what a soldier brings to the fight, and little else."

Indeed, leadership is required to end the senseless ban on gays serving openly. The vast majority of Americans support the repeal of "Don't Ask, Don't Tell." Our closest allies ended their similar policies years ago. And the country needs more qualified personnel as Iraq and Afghanistan continue to drain the military's resources. The time for study is over. It's time for President Obama to lead on this issue and push Congress to finally end the military's gay ban.

"Will We Remember in November?" May 6, 2010

In the spring of 2010, things were getting heated around the issue of whether and how to repeal "Don't Ask, Don't Tell." Many of us were feeling betrayed by President Obama and some congressional Democrats, who were calling for studies and surveys instead of immediate repeal of the discriminatory law. This felt like yet another example of Democratic betrayal of a key constituency and more double standards directed at its LGBTQ supporters. Obama ultimately proved our "fiercest ally," but it took some pushing and cajoling to get him there. It's important that we not forget our recent history and revisit and understand how these horrible laws were ultimately repealed. They didn't fall because one party bravely stepped into the breach and did the right thing. They fell because a coordinated effort among activists, lawyers, journalists, veterans and politicians from both parties targeted them with the right pressure at the right time. It didn't happen overnight; there were myriad setbacks that sometimes lasted for years. But it all speaks to the importance of resilience, patience and strategic thinking. As our enemies roll back LGBTQ progress in 2023 and beyond, a younger generation of queer thinkers and advocates must remember how we got here because they will have to employ those same tactics to fight back.

Forget about the back of the bus — that whooshing sound you hear is the sound of the administration tossing us under the bus. Again.

Make no mistake that the events of last Friday, in which Defense Secretary Robert Gates sent a letter to House Armed Services Committee Chair Ike Skelton (D-Mo.) demanding a halt to congressional action on repealing "Don't Ask, Don't Tell" amounts to a cowardly and transparent effort to give cover to moderate Democrats in the November elections.

Those midterms are looking ominous for Democrats and so, per usual, LGBT initiatives are the first sacrificial lamb. Not only does this all but ensure "Don't Ask, Don't Tell" won't be repealed this year, some experts predict it's now off the table until 2013 — after the 2012 presidential elections, when the Democrats will be back with their hands outstretched for more mighty gay dollars while offering more empty promises and excuses in return.

White House chief of staff Rahm Emanuel told Servicemembers United that the odds of repealing the military's gay ban this year stand at about 30-40 percent. Someone should tell him that nearly 80 percent of American voters support repeal now, according to several recent polls. Meanwhile, the Palm Center, another of the expert groups working for repeal, says LGBT service members may now have to wait until 2013 for relief from the injustice of this cruel and stupid law.

Gates' letter warned that legislative repeal prior to the completion of the Pentagon working group study (scheduled for Dec. 1) "would send a very damaging message to our men and women in uniform that in essence their views, concerns, and perspectives do not matter." That statement raises the obvious question: When was the last time rank-and-file service members were polled about an impending policy change?

Shortly after Gates' letter leaked, the White House responded: "The President's commitment to repealing don't ask, don't tell is unequivocal. This is not a question of if, but how. That's why we've said that the implementation of any congressional repeal will be delayed until the DOD study of how best to implement that repeal is completed. The President is committed to getting this done both soon and right."

What's left unclear by the White House statement is whether Obama supports a vote in Congress now that delays implementation until 2011.When asked by the Blade to clarify the statement Saturday at Philadelphia's Equality Forum, Brian Bond, deputy director of the White House Office of Public Engagement, said, "I think that's an ongoing discussion right now. ... at the end of the day, it is Congress that will repeal 'Don't Ask, Don't Tell,' not us."

The refusal to endorse a vote for repeal is a striking departure from what we've been told since the 2008 campaign. The Blade has reported for weeks that the House has the votes to pass repeal legislation, thanks in large part to the fierce advocacy not of President Obama, but of Rep. Patrick Murphy (D-Pa.). House Speaker Nancy Pelosi (D-Calif.) told the Blade just last week that she wants a vote on repeal this year. She's not known for scheduling votes on bills that won't pass, so it's a safe assumption that repeal would pass the House.

The situation in the Senate is less clear. Supporters of repeal say they are within a few votes on the Senate Armed Services Committee of securing approval. The full Senate would likely support repeal, though it's doubtful the Democrats have 60 votes to block an expected filibuster. Of course, what's needed to put repeal over the top is hands-on lobbying from Obama. Instead of pressing the handful of fence-sitting Democrats, Obama is telling them not to act this year, a recipe for a much longer repeal delay when Republicans close the gap or even retake the House in November.

Gates — a George W. Bush appointee — reports to the commander in chief and he didn't draft that letter without Obama's knowledge and support. If the Democrats think they have problems now, let's see what happens to their fortunes after they alienate a key part of their base.

If my email inbox is any indication, LGBT Americans have finally arrived at the breaking point, outraged at the endless broken promises and delayed advances. Treating our full equality as an expendable bargaining chip is no longer acceptable. When will the Democrats stop running from their own shadow, ever fearful of what Fox News or

Sarah Palin or the Tea Baggers might say about them? Fox News can't attract two million viewers on a good night. We're a nation of more than 300 million people, the vast majority of whom oppose "Don't Ask, Don't Tell," including many prominent Republicans. Supporting repeal of this odious law that compromises our national security and wastes billions of taxpayer dollars will not cost any Democrat his or her seat.

LGBT lobbyists, activists and everyday supporters of equality must now redouble their efforts. Call your members of Congress and the White House demanding an end to "Don't Ask, Don't Tell" this year. If Obama is unwilling to include repeal in his Defense authorization bill, then Congress must press forward and vote now, before the Republicans have a chance to win back the House in November.

The Human Rights Campaign, Servicemembers Legal Defense Network and all other LGBT groups that are engaged in lobbying the administration and the Hill must make it clear that failure to repeal "Don't Ask, Don't Tell" this year will amount to a betrayal of the LGBT community and that there will be consequences. As Sunday's White House protesters chanted, we must "remember in November."

"A MOMENTOUS ACHIEVEMENT," DEC. 23, 2010

I was honored to receive an invitation to the ceremony during which President Obama signed the repeal of "Don't Ask, Don't Tell," an insidious law that destroyed the careers of thousands of service members. For those tens of thousands more closeted service members who weren't outed and discharged, many of them suffered in other ways, including PTSD. One service member I interviewed at length spoke of his PTSD diagnosis, not from serving in combat operations, but from living in constant fear that his shipmates would discover his sexual orientation, beat him to death and dump his body in the Indian Ocean in the middle of the night. He lived with that fear each day until he left the military and it haunts him years later. Make no mistake that "Don't Ask, Don't Tell," signed by President Bill Clinton, was a cruel law that destroyed not just livelihoods, but lives.

The euphoria in the auditorium where Obama signed the repeal bill was uplifting and historic — the first time that U.S. service members were able to attend a gay-identified event in their uniforms without fear of reprisal. It seemed everyone in the room was crying.

I remember going home afterwards and doing a radio interview with NPR out of San Francisco, ostensibly about the historic moment I'd just witnessed. Imagine my surprise when one of the interviewers demanded to know why we were celebrating. She thought it was horrible that gay people would now fight for their country openly because the United States military was guilty of various atrocities around the world. I was stunned. Even in victory, there's always an LGBTQ constituency that won't be satisfied. Indeed, if you spend your life looking for victimhood, you will not be disappointed.

It still boggles the mind that repealing "Don't Ask, Don't Tell" was so difficult and controversial even with a supportive president, a Democratic Congress and 80 percent public approval. Sound familiar? In 2022, we also had a supportive president, a Democratic Congress, and overwhelming public support for LGBTQ nondiscrimination protections. Yet, despite the House passing the Equality Act, the measure ended up stalled yet again in the Senate. The fight over "Don't Ask" offers an instructive reminder about the entrenched interests in Washington opposed to our basic equality and the perils of putting our eggs in the basket of a single political party.

Dec. 18, 2010 will be remembered as the day the U.S. Congress passed its first stand-alone pro-LGBT piece of legislation, repealing the discriminatory "Don't Ask, Don't Tell" law that has ruined thousands of lives and careers during nearly 20 years on the books.

The progress on gay acceptance in those 17 years is truly remarkable. In 1993, the images in the mainstream media around gays in the military were dominated by a homophobic Sen. Sam Nunn, touring a cramped submarine to dramatize just how closely straight sailors would be forced to bunk with their gay colleagues.

Fast forward to 2010 and Nunn supports repeal and the chief opponent of lifting the ban — an increasingly irrelevant Sen. John McCain — is widely demonized in the media as out-of-touch and bigoted. The dominant images in the debate this time around consist of brave men and women cruelly kicked out of the military who are merely asking for their jobs back. What a difference 17 years makes.

So many brave individuals and hard-working organizations deserve credit for this momentous victory — from all the discharged service members who spoke out, to President Obama, Sen. Harry Reid, SLDN, HRC, GETEqual, Servicemembers United, Palm Center and more.

This win took too long and the 11th hour desperation of it all raises serious doubts about the viability of future pro-LGBT legislation. If an issue backed by nearly 80 percent of Americans is this difficult, imagine the fight over trans-inclusive ENDA or relationship recognition.

For many LGBT Americans, the past two years represented a period of hope and optimism after the dark days of President George W. Bush's administration, which sought to enshrine anti-gay discrimination in the U.S. Constitution. After playing defense for eight long years, President Obama promised to be our "fierce advocate." He has now delivered on two key legislative promises — repeal of "Don't Ask, Don't Tell" and inclusion of sexual orientation and gender identity in the federal hate crimes law. It's not a perfect record and Obama and the Democrats have been rightly criticized for not moving faster and earlier on LGBT priorities, given the short window of opportunity to act.

As gay Rep. Barney Frank told the Blade last month about the prospects for pro-LGBT legislation: "Next year there's no chance of anything happening, there's zero chance." He added, "It will be a status quo. They don't have the votes to hurt us but we don't have the votes to advance anything in the cause."

It was humbling and an honor to attend the "Don't Ask, Don't Tell" bill signing this week. After more than eight years editing this newspaper, I've met far too many brave service members whose careers and livelihoods and dreams were dashed because of the discriminatory law. We've written about many gay and lesbian service members who died in the closet because of "Don't Ask, Don't Tell."

So although we're disappointed that ENDA, UAFA, domestic partner benefits for federal workers' partners and other priorities weren't achieved in this Congress, we celebrate this week's victory. And we remember all those brave service members — like Maj. Alan Rogers — who can't be here to share in this historic moment.

"Lock up the 'ex-gays,'" June 24, 2005

Thankfully, we don't write much about the so-called "ex-gay" movement anymore at the Blade. Most of its leaders have come out as gay — or been outed — and admitted the whole thing was a fraud. But back in the early 2000s, the "ex-gay" movement commanded a lot of attention, not just in the Blade, but in the mainstream media. The evil practice of conversion therapy undoubtedly led to the suicides of untold numbers of teens, whose ignorant and misguided parents subjected them to the cruel, discredited practice. Today, 28 states and D.C. ban the practice for minors either totally or partially, though the bans don't apply to religious providers. Still, the trend is strongly on the side of science and protecting minors. Lawmakers in the other states should get on board and protect youth from phony mental health practitioners who peddle the lie that people can change their sexual orientation or gender identity.

Gay adults learn from an early age to develop a thick skin. From playground taunts to inappropriate jokes in the boardroom, many of us have endured the hurtful anti-gay prejudice of our peers for a long time and, as a result, acquired the armor and perspective necessary to protect ourselves.

I can endure hours of evangelical Christian diatribes about the evils of the "gay agenda." Or quietly suffer the barbs of pandering politicians looking to win elections on our backs. Or turn the other cheek when a gaggle of ministers calls a news conference to announce their support for a ban on gay marriage.

Even the Washington Times' practice of putting the words gay marriage in quotation marks has ceased to send my blood pressure soaring.

There remains just one assault on the dignity of gay men and lesbians that still drives me into fits of rage: the "ex-gay" movement. The quotation marks are deliberate — and appropriate, because there is no such thing as "ex-gay." There is "repress-my-inate-immutable-characteristics-and-deny-their-existence," but no such condition as "ex-gay."

The "ex-gays" usually make headlines only when their leaders are caught emerging from a gay bar at 2 a.m. But they are everywhere these days.

Last week, the tale of Zach, a 16-year-old gay Tennessee high school student who was sent to a reparative therapy camp by his impossibly naïve parents, made its way into the blogosphere. Zach's story serves as a reminder that the zany, funny film "But I'm a Cheerleader" was not entirely a work of fiction.

Last month, the "ex-gay" crowd made headlines in Maryland, where they joined a lawsuit to block implementation of an updated sex education curriculum that included discussion of homosexuality and a condom demonstration. The "ex-gays" are actually demanding that their views be included in health classes, which are ordinarily based on that quaint concept known as science.

The "ex-gays" also caused a stir in Florida this month, after commissioning billboards in Orlando that read, "Gay? Unhappy?" and included a website address www.exodus.to. The site for Exodus International offers various services to those seeking escape from the "homosexual lifestyle" and testimonials from self-described "ex-gays."

In his testimonial, someone identified as Alan Chambers writes, "Disillusioned and desperate, I remember going into my parents' room nightly to see if they had been raptured, taken to heaven, without me." He recounts his addiction to anonymous gay sex and how he turned to the Bible to be saved.

The Exodus site even offers a prayer request page, complete with a drop-down box of prayer options: "for me to overcome homosexuality," "for my child," "for my spouse," "for a family member."

The "ex-gays" got some ink in last Sunday's New York Times Magazine. The cover story, about a group of Christian activists in Maryland desperate to protect the sacred institution of marriage from gays, references the "ex-gay" movement as the antidote to gay marriage.

And the "ex-gay" debate comes to the Seattle area this weekend, with two competing conferences. The first conference, sponsored by Focus on the Family, is titled "Love Won Out," and bills itself as "promoting the truth that homosexuality is preventable and treatable."

The second conference, "Love Welcomes All," is intended to counter the "ex-gay" confab and is sponsored by PFLAG and other pro-gay groups.

At a time when conservative Christians are resurrecting the debate over evolution, pesky details like science matter little to the "ex-gays."

Every reputable medical institution including the American Psychiatric Association, the American Psychological Association and the American Medical Association, has repudiated reparative therapies as dangerous. As the Times story points out, the American Psychiatric Association actually endorsed gay marriage in the interest of promoting mental health.

In light of all the evidence that these reparative techniques are ineffective and, in fact, dangerous to the mental health of young gays, it's time for these camps to be shut down.

An enterprising gay lawyer ought to step forward and, as at least one blogger following Zach's story put it, find grounds to sue these bastards out of existence.

In an ironic twist, the ex-gay ministry at the center of Zach's story is now asking for "tolerance." The request from Love in Action, which sponsors the camp called Refuge, came during a June 16 news conference.

"This program is operated on the will of the guardian or parent. We will work with the minor children as long as they are not overtly distracting to their own program or the program of others," said John Smid, the "ex-gay" executive director of Love in Action. "If it is shown that the client is overtly treatment resistant, we will work with the parent towards alternative options for their care and overall relational health."

What "alternative options" does Smid have in mind? Electroshock therapy? Solitary confinement?

The damage caused to young gays by the views of "ex-gays" should not be underestimated. The two greatest weapons that opponents of gay rights wield against us are charges that gay men are pedophiles and that homosexuality is a choice. Overcoming those two obstacles would mean instant victory for the movement.

And the "ex-gays" are doing their best to reinforce the refuted canard that being gay is a choice; that I could just as easily choose a different pair of shoes as I could choose a different sexual orientation.

Right-handed people can't choose to be lefties, those with brown skin can't choose white and gays can't choose to be straight. Yes, it really is that simple.

Someday, science will discover the biological or genetic root of homosexuality and finally put to rest the absurd notion that sexual orientation is a choice. Until then, we must counter the damaging rhetoric of the "ex-gays" and ensure that young gays like Zach understand that they are perfectly normal as they are.

It's the "ex-gays" that belong in a reparative camp.

"FAREWELL TO AN ICON OF HATE," JULY 11, 2008

I celebrated the death of Jesse Helms just as I celebrated when Jerry Falwell died. Maybe that's unseemly, but it pales compared to the misery those two icons of hate inflicted on our community. The mainstream media have an unconscionable habit of glorifying even the worst racists and homophobes in death, ignoring their hateful records and engaging in revisionist history. The Blade doesn't engage in such irresponsible fake journalism. For teens of the '80s like me, Helms and Falwell were a terrifying twosome, attacking gay men and demonizing AIDS patients. They were to the '80s what Ron

DeSantis and Greg Abbott are to 2022 — right-wing bigots who care nothing about the lives ruined by their dangerous anti-LGBTQ rhetoric. At least Helms and Falwell never made it to the White House; we can't be so sure of the same for DeSantis and Abbott. History repeats.

The collective amnesia and revisionist history that happens when hateful public figures die can be galling to digest.

In the case of former Sen. Jesse Helms, who died July 4, the mainstream media were too often up to the usual tap-dancing around the hard facts. Helms has variously been remembered as a "conservative icon," "tender-hearted" and a "brave and bold man."

For gays, like me, who came of age during the 1980s, Helms will be remembered as a racist homophobe who hastened the deaths of untold thousands through his unrepentant opposition to federal AIDS legislation and hateful anti-gay rhetoric.

Late in life, Helms experienced a much-publicized epiphany on AIDS, thanks to the influence of U2's Bono. In 2001, the Irish rocker-turned-activist praised Helms.

"I told him that 2,103 verses of Scripture pertain to the poor, and Jesus speaks of judgment only once — it's not about being gay or sexual morality," Bono said. "He was really moved. He was in tears. Later he told me he was ashamed about what he used to think about AIDS."

But in those awful early years of the disease, it was about being gay (and still is when you look at recent statistics on infection rates). And Helms wasn't ashamed about his views of gay men who were suffering. He embraced the fight against AIDS in Africa and developing countries after years of opposing any federal action on the disease. His sympathy never extended to gay men, only to "innocent" victims in poor countries, a view reflected by President Bush's policies to this day.

As Republican AIDS activist Carl Schmid told the Blade just last week, the Bush administration "has ignored the gay population as it is related to HIV/AIDS. ... I think if it were another population, they would be all over it."

People with HIV and AIDS are still suffering at the hands of Helms' legacy. He was a pioneer of the shameful ban on immigration and travel by HIV-positive people, a national embarrassment that remains in effect. In the coming weeks, Congress is expected to vote on the PEPFAR bill, which contains a provision repealing the travel ban. It's long overdue and another step in ridding the country of the kind of naked bigotry so often espoused by Helms.

But Helms had a long record of being on the wrong side of history, from his overt racism (he proudly described himself as a "redneck" and once reportedly sang "Dixie" to Sen. Carol Moseley Braun in an elevator) to his homophobia (in 1994, he described gays as "weak, morally sick wretches") to his opposition to funding for the arts and AIDS research.

He frequently blamed gay men for the disease, demonizing us as sick.

"There is not one single case of AIDS in this country that cannot be traced in origin to sodomy," he said in 1988, ignoring all other means of HIV transmission. He once famously refused to speak to the mother of Ryan White, who had just died. But he probably couldn't look her in the eye, given his outspoken opposition to the massive federal aid bill named for her son.

Helms never wasted an opportunity to attack gay and lesbian Americans. He opposed the nomination of Roberta Achtenberg to a HUD position, calling her a "damn lesbian." It's gratifying that Helms himself had a damn lesbian for a granddaughter.

He once sought to strip funding for two National Institutes of Health sex surveys and transfer the funds to a program advocating abstinence before marriage.

"The homosexuals hate it, the 'free sex' crowd hates it," Helms said in 1991 of his amendment. "I'm sick and tired of pandering to the homosexual community in this country."

And Helms was as racist as he was homophobic, resorting to racial stereotyping and fear mongering during various campaigns for public office over the years.

Maybe the prospect of Barack Obama as president was too much for him to bear and so he shuffled off this mortal coil. His death — and Obama's candidacy — mark a historic turning point in race relations for the country. National public figures like sitting senators can no longer get away with open expressions of racism. We are on the verge of electing a Black man president. Gay couples are marrying legally on both coasts. It must have been too scary a world for Helms.

With his death, and the recent death of fellow hate monger Jerry Falwell, the United States moves closer to a more perfect union.

"A Gay Alumnus Reflects on Penn State Tragedy," Nov. 11, 2011

This was another tough, emotional column to write, given my connections to Penn State and role at the time as board chair of the campus LGBTA Student Resource Center. In fact, my tenure as board chair literally began on the Monday after the Sandusky scandal broke. I had already submitted a fundraising letter that the university was scheduled to send out that week and had to rescind it in a panic on my first day as chair.

When news broke this week about the heartbreaking tragedy unfolding at Penn State, a few easy predictions came to mind: iconic coach Joe Paterno wouldn't survive; the university president would have to go too; and anti-gay hate groups would try to exploit Jerry Sandusky's sick crimes for financial gain.

On Wednesday, my first two predictions came to pass, as the university's board of trustees fired both Paterno and Graham Spanier. Then Thursday, Americans for Truth About Homosexuality launched its inevitable broadside against gays and the Westboro Baptist Church announced plans for one of its protests at the Penn State-Nebraska game on Saturday.

Sandusky faces 40 charges related to the alleged abuse of eight boys over 15 years, including allegations he raped at least one young boy in a shower on the Penn State campus. He used his charity, the Second Mile, which ostensibly helped at-risk children in Pennsylvania, to meet his alleged victims.

I am reluctant to address the canard that gay men are disproportionately predisposed to molesting children, as it has been debunked and disproven by dozens of studies. But in anticipation of the right-wing extremists trotting out that old lie, here goes.

AFTAH's leader, Peter LaBarbera, is a man oddly obsessed with gay people and has devoted his life to demonizing us. You know what they say about those who doth protest too much. In his recent commentary on the Penn State scandal, LaBarbera labels Sandusky as "homosexual," and contends, "There IS a long history connecting homosexuality to pederasty, and a disproportionate link between homosexuality and pedophilia."

AFTAH was labeled a hate group by the Southern Poverty Law Center and has a long record of attacking gays using junk science to bolster its false claims. So consider the source.

Simply put, "homosexual men are not more likely to sexually abuse children than heterosexual men are." That's from the American Psychological Association.

LaBarbera cites pedophilia, but that term refers to an "adult psychological disorder characterized by a preference for prepubescent children as sexual partners," according to medical experts. A preference for children has nothing to do with sexual orientation.

"Many child molesters don't really have an adult sexual orientation. They have never developed the capacity for mature sexual relationships with other adults, either men or women. Instead, their sexual attractions focus on children — boys, girls, or children of both sexes," according to experts at University of California-Davis.

And Sandusky was married with two grown children, an inconvenient fact that further undermines LaBarbera's labels. Surveying the faces of the Penn State scandal — Sandusky, Paterno, Spanier, coach Mike McQueary, athletic director Tim Curley, vice president Gary Schultz — all are straight men. This scandal isn't about gay men; it's about greed and a culture that prized money over doing the right thing.

I'm a Penn State alumnus and have served on the board of the campus LGBTA Student Resource Center for several years. The Center is an important and even life-saving resource for students there. Many Penn Staters come from rural parts of the state where acceptance and understanding can be tough to find. Some are disowned by parents after coming out. The Center is there to help and support them, offering a safe space on campus to meet and socialize, educational programming and scholarships and other resources. Only about 7 percent of the nation's colleges and universities operate such LGBT centers on campus and I'm proud that Penn State has emerged as a national leader in this area.

I've watched the incredible changes on campus since my graduation in 1992 with a sense of excitement, optimism and relief. There's so much good in Happy Valley — from the pioneering work of those at the LGBTA Center, to the student athletes whose graduation rates rank No. 1 among the NCAA's top 25 teams. Paterno wasn't a stereotypical college football meathead. He emphasized education; the school's library bears his name. In four years there, I met him just once. On the morning of my graduation, I stepped outside my apartment at 6 a.m. for a cup of coffee. And there, standing on the street corner alone, was JoePa. The street was deserted at that early hour and I introduced myself. He asked about my graduation, what I'd studied and my future plans. He was a grandfather figure to everyone on campus.

All of that makes what's happening now so unimaginable to those of us who know the university. How could this happen on our campus? How could so many turn a blind eye? I fear the answers lie in details of an extensive cover-up yet to be revealed. The fact that Mike McQueary — the witness to rape who failed to intervene — remains on the coaching staff while Paterno is gone strongly suggests that we don't have the full story yet. Did McQueary call university police only to have senior officials bury the report? Nothing would surprise me now. Regardless, Paterno, Spanier and the rest got what they deserved.

But the scandal raises deeper questions about our society. There's been much indignation expressed about then-graduate assistant McQueary's actions. He witnessed Sandusky raping a 10-year-old boy in the showers yet reportedly did nothing. Commentators and bloggers have insisted they would have intervened. Maybe. Or maybe not.

Last month, a two-year-old toddler was struck by two vans on a busy street in China. Eighteen pedestrians and cyclists passed by the child, who later died, before someone finally stopped to help.

That incident — and the Sandusky scandal — reminds me of a lecture I attended while at Penn State. My political science professor was talking about nationalism and the rise of the Nazi party in Germany. It was a frigid February morning and just before class started, she walked to the back of the room and opened a window. As she spoke, the classroom grew colder and colder and students began donning coats and hats. As the professor talked about the circumstances under which societies turn to nationalism and xenophobia, student after student expressed their doubt and indignation — "That could never happen in the United States." Finally, when the cold became too much even for the professor, she said, "How can you be sure you would stand up to the government and its weapons and tanks, when none of you even had the nerve to ask me to close the window?"

It's a lesson that rings tragically relevant today. Were senior officials afraid to call police because they wanted to protect the lucrative revenue stream provided by the football team? Were custodial staff who reportedly witnessed Sandusky's crimes deterred from reporting him out of fear for their jobs? It's comforting to think we'd all have helped that 10-year-old boy, but an entire network of adults failed him. And so many others.

To the students at Penn State: The eyes of the nation are upon you this weekend, so demonstrate the grace and compassion and leadership that was so lacking in your coaches and administrators. The anti-gay protesters headed your way are clowns who picket the funerals of fallen soldiers and AIDS patients. Ignore them and cheer on your team to victory.

To Penn State alumni who are disillusioned and angry: There are good people and institutions at the university and in State College who still need our support and involvement. Don't walk away. Give your time, money and talents to those who are making a positive difference.

And to everyone else shaking your heads on the sidelines: Let this sad spectacle remind us of the need to be better people, to look out for one another and, especially, the most vulnerable among us.

"Reflecting on 10 Years at the Blade," Dec. 26, 2012

The next two pieces were published at the time of my 10-year anniversary at the Blade. It's always interesting and instructive to look back and see how far we've come.

It was December 2002. Sodomy laws remained on the books in 14 states. No state or jurisdiction in the country had yet legalized same-sex marriage ("marriage equality" was not a term in popular use). Congress had yet to pass a single piece of pro-gay legislation. The Democratic Party took gay money and votes but mostly paid lip service to our concerns. Barack Obama was a member of the Illinois state Senate. President George W. Bush was in his first term and the country was still reeling from the terrorist attacks of 9/11. Bush would later make opposition to gay rights a cornerstone of his reelection campaign, pushing for ballot measures on marriage in key battleground states and even using his State of the Union address to call for a federal constitutional amendment banning recognition of our relationships.

What a difference a decade makes.

Ten years after joining the Blade, I have been privileged to occupy a front-row seat to some of the most significant and historic events the movement has seen. Make no mistake that the election of Barack Obama marked the turning point in this quest for equality. Without his (fierce) advocacy, many of the landmark achievements of the past four years would not have been possible. But the tide began to turn before Obama's arrival on the national political scene. And it began in 2003 with the Supreme Court decision in Lawrence v. Texas, which overturned sodomy laws in that state and 13 others, reversing a devastating 1986 ruling in Bowers v. Hardwick that upheld a similar law in Georgia.

Justice Anthony Kennedy, still considered the court's swing vote, wrote the unforgettable majority opinion: "The petitioners [Lawrence and Garner] are entitled to respect for their private lives. The State cannot demean their existence or control their destiny by making their private sexual conduct a crime."

Finally, after decades of struggle, the mere fact of being gay could no longer be considered criminal.

Kennedy noted that the Lawrence case "does not involve whether the government must give formal recognition to any relationship that homosexual persons seek to enter." That, however, has finally changed as the high court this year agreed to hear two such cases on the Defense of Marriage Act and California's Prop 8. In 10 short years, we've gone from fighting over private sex acts to impending Supreme Court rulings on marriage equality.

That ruling helped to trigger a wave of fast-moving change. Just a year later, in 2004, Massachusetts became the first state to legalize same-sex marriage. And the good news keeps coming from Obama's victory in 2008 to Congress passing its first LGBT rights bill — an expansion of the federal hate crimes law — to repeal of "Don't Ask, Don't Tell."

There have been so many highlights during my 10 years at the Blade, but one moment that has always stayed with me occurred in June 2009 at President Obama's first Pride Month reception in the White House. Obama, flanked by first lady Michelle Obama, said, "Welcome to your house." It was such a simple gesture, yet they were words that none of us had ever heard before. And the president and first lady stayed to mingle, chat and pose for photos as a DJ spun Madonna tunes in the East Wing. A joyous and surreal moment after so many bleak years under Bush.

It hasn't been all cocktails and dance divas, though.

I've edited and written countless stories over the past decade and two have haunted me. We profiled a Baltimore gay couple in their 30s, both public school teachers. One was diagnosed with cancer and died within months. He'd been estranged from his family over his sexual orientation and had a will and other legal documents in place at his death. The family sued to have their son's body exhumed and moved to the family plot in Tennessee — and they won. The surviving partner finally prevailed on appeal but lost everything in the process of an expensive legal battle to simply keep his partner in the ground.

In another case, the Blade exposed the fact that four teens shot on a Newark, N.J., playground were gay. Three of them died. The mainstream media refused to report the basic fact that this was a hate crime motivated by the victims' sexual orientation.

It's been a whirlwind and unforgettable decade, from interviewing newsmakers and celebrities to chronicling historic civil rights advances to mourning crime victims to fighting with Bill O'Reilly over the evils of Scientology and outing closet cases like Shepard Smith.

As we celebrate our 2012 Election Day victories, we look forward to a time when true equality comes to all 50 states and to countries around the world. We're not there yet and, so, keep reading.

"Revisiting Sinners of the Past," Feb. 13, 2013

Over the past 10 years, I've often used this space to target and critique a series of anti-LGBT figures — from politicians to criminals to closeted celebrities. My attacks have ranged from stinging to the occasional angry full-on takedown. It's remarkable how much things have changed for the LGBT movement in those 10 years. So a quick look back at some of my favorite targets of the last decade and how they have evolved during that time.

1. The Democratic National Committee. This might seem an unexpected target, but the reality is that the party's support for LGBT rights and legislation is an Obama phenomenon. From Bill Clinton's support for DOMA to Howard Dean's firing of a gay liaison and other shenanigans (pitting Black delegates against gay ones, denigrating the gay press and threatening to sue the Blade), the Democratic Party has a complicated history with our community. Obama deserves the credit for turning around that sorry record. Today, the Democratic Party includes marriage equality in its platform. Ten years ago, there had been no movement on pro-LGBT federal legislation. Today, we have an expanded hate crimes law and have repealed "Don't Ask, Don't Tell." DOMA is next to go.

2. The Bush administration. George W. Bush became the gay community's public enemy No. 1 after his cynical assault on marriage equality in 2004, a crusade masterminded in part by former RNC Chair and Bush-Cheney campaign manager Ken Mehlman. The Bush years were ugly, from his calls for a federal marriage amendment to an odd and stubborn refusal to even utter the word "gay" in public. Ten years later, Mehlman is out of the closet and raising money to support marriage equality. Dick Cheney supports marriage equality, as does Laura Bush. And George has paid a steep price for his horrendous, reckless presidency — relegated to the dustbin of history and rendered persona non grata at last year's Republican National Convention. He is rightly blamed for the country's economic mess and will be remembered as among the worst presidents in American history.

3. Martin O'Malley. Another unlikely target, considering O'Malley was popular with LGBT residents of Baltimore from his days as a City Council member and mayor. He even endorsed marriage equality in a TV interview years before running for governor. He later disavowed that interview and was booed off the stage at a private LGBT donor gathering after advocating for civil unions over full marriage rights. After a 2007 court ruling limiting marriage to opposite-sex couples, O'Malley issued a cruel, stinging statement invoking the Catholic sacraments and reiterating a call for civil unions. But after New York Gov. Andrew Cuomo successfully shepherded marriage through a Republican Senate there, O'Malley had an epiphany and adopted full-throated support for the cause. He was a latecomer, but ultimately played a key role in passage of the bill and of the subsequent ballot measure last year. He's now a rumored 2016 presidential aspirant (along with Cuomo).

4. Religion. Perhaps the greatest force opposed to our full equality, organized religion gets a lot of ink. From the attacks of Pope Benedict to the reparative therapy efforts of Scientology, religions (and cults in the case of Scientology) remain a key threat to LGBT people. But even

that's changing. If you visit a local Catholic church, you'll find openly LGBT people in the pews and gay support groups operating. And they have something to celebrate with the news this week that Benedict is stepping down after nearly eight years of anti-gay pronouncements. More and more religions are moderating their views on our full inclusion in church life, including in marriage. Evangelical Lutherans now recognize the same-sex relationships of church leaders; the U.S. Episcopal Church allows same-sex marriages in states where it's legal. There's a long way to go to full acceptance, of course, but progress is undeniable and change is happening at a brisk pace.

5. Anderson Cooper & Jodie Foster. Closeted rich and famous people have come in for a healthy dose of criticism on this page over the years. After all, if the wealthiest and most successful among us won't come out, how can we expect the schoolteacher in Alabama or the construction worker in Iowa to do the same? Cooper and Foster became the poster children for the closet but in the last year, both publicly came out. Better late than never, right? Maybe Shepard Smith and Queen Latifah will follow their lead.

6. Mark Foley & Larry Craig. The Blade wrote about Foley's sexual orientation for years before he was forced to publicly acknowledge the truth after his page scandal. Craig's story is more twisted but both ultimately got what they deserved. Their names haven't appeared in the Blade for years — two relics of a closeted past. Good riddance. Now if only Lindsay Graham would come out.

Even after all that progress, there's still no shortage of organizations and public figures to take to task — think Sam Arora, Rick Santorum, Tony Perkins and the National Organization for Marriage. And our work is far from complete. We need a federal law outlawing anti-LGBT employment discrimination; a stop to religion-based bigotry; and an openly gay professional athlete would be nice, too. But the list of our enemies is a lot shorter than it was 10 years ago. Here's to the next 10 years of progress.

"Bill Clinton's desperate bid to rewrite history," March 8, 2013

I never voted for Bill Clinton. He embodies the worst stereotypes in politicians: blind ambition, unethical behavior, cringe-worthy pandering and a loyalty to polls over principles. Clinton, like Donald Trump, is incapable of issuing a sincere apology. In a Washington Post op-ed, Clinton tried to distance himself from the Defense of Marriage Act, which he signed, just as the Supreme Court was poised to strike it down. That odious law destroyed lives. It didn't take great political courage to oppose it, as 81 lawmakers did back in 1996. Even in backing away from his support for DOMA, Clinton was incapable of an honest reassessment and simple apology. The next essay addresses Clinton's duplicity as well as the historic Supreme Court ruling that overturned the Defense of Marriage Act, which Clinton cynically bragged about signing in campaign ads that aired on Christian radio stations.

Former President Bill Clinton today penned an op-ed for the Washington Post, disavowing the discriminatory and unconstitutional Defense of Marriage Act that he signed into law 17 years ago.

It's a typically cynical, desperate bid to rewrite history.

Clinton now suggests that his support for DOMA was really intended to thwart a constitutional amendment that would have banned marriage equality for a generation or more.

The truth is that Clinton said at the time that he "had long agreed with the principles in the bill but hoped it would not be used to justify discrimination against homosexuals," according to the New York Times. Of course, the point of DOMA was to discriminate. What's worse, Clinton bragged about his support for DOMA in radio ads during his 1996 reelection campaign against former Sen. Bob Dole, after criticizing Republicans for "gay-baiting." In the same ads currying support among Christian conservatives, Clinton announced his newfound support for abortion restrictions.

Nearly a year after President Obama's courageous endorsement of marriage equality, Clinton chimes in from the safe confines of retirement. Meanwhile, Hillary, still adored by legions of gay fans waiting breathlessly for 2016, has yet to utter a word about marriage.

Clinton's op-ed is a naked attempt to get on the right side of history before the Supreme Court strikes down DOMA. He sounds desperate, highlighting the fact that "DOMA came to my desk, opposed by only 81 of the 535 members of Congress." That only makes his support worse — at least 81 other politicians at the time had the sense and foresight to oppose the discriminatory measure. The op-ed, of course, contains no apology from Clinton for enacting the most hideous piece of anti-gay legislation ever conceived in this country. DOMA has literally destroyed the lives of countless couples — from the financial ruin triggered when a surviving partner is faced with crippling tax bills to the separation of thousands of bi-national couples forced to choose between love and country.

But never mind all those ruined lives. Clinton was just trying to spare us a constitutional amendment. Cue the parade of gay rights advocates, who will commence tripping over themselves to praise Clinton's bold stance for equality. HRC's Chad Griffin has already called Clinton's op-ed "eloquent."

If we're going to so easily forgive and forget Clinton's anti-gay sins, then our advocates should be consistent and shower former RNC Chair Ken Mehlman with similar praise and awards. As horrible as Mehlman's record is, at least no one ever elected him president; and he's been working hard to raise money for marriage equality since coming out of the closet and repudiating his own dirty deeds.

This warm-and-fuzzy new era of gay love is gratifying for those of us who've been working for change for years and decades. And although we should welcome converts to the cause, we must not forget the past or rewrite the ugly history that relegated LGBT people to second-class status. Clinton represents cynicism and politics at its most self-aggrandizing. Obama is the real deal — the president who is leading Americans to a true revolution in thinking on LGBT equality.

"Relieved that Scalia can no longer judge us," Feb. 17, 2016

This was another in a series of essays I wrote for the Blade reminding readers of the problematic, bigoted records of a string of deceased public officials. I had to interrupt the mainstream media's one-sided coverage and praise for these flawed figures. And Scalia was among the worst.

Although it's true that you shouldn't speak ill of the dead, it's difficult to assess the record of Supreme Court Justice Antonin Scalia without getting angry. Especially if you're gay.

The social media spectacle over the weekend of some liberal gays celebrating Scalia's death, while being shamed by their more conservative (and tasteful) friends highlighted this problem.

We can find sympathy for Scalia's family and friends — a group that included Ruth Bader Ginsburg — while feeling relieved that Scalia is no longer in a position to sit in harsh judgment of our lives and love. It's hard to blame those who found some relief in Scalia's death, given his glee in disparaging gays. There has been a lot of misguided praise for Scalia since his death.

Let's be clear: If Scalia had his way, not only would gay couples not be legally marrying, we'd also lack basic anti-discrimination protections. In 1996, in his dissent in Romer v. Evans, Scalia described Colorado's law that sought to kill anti-discrimination protections as a, "modest attempt by seemingly tolerant Coloradans to preserve traditional sexual mores against the efforts of a politically powerful minority."

His dissent in Lawrence v. Texas, which overturned sodomy laws, likened gay sex to incest and bestiality, among other ills the public could justifiably exert its "moral disapproval" to ban.

And in his dissent in the Obergefell case that ended bans on same-sex marriage, Scalia saw a threat to democracy itself. "I write separately to call attention to this Court's threat to American democracy," Scalia began his screed.

He continued, "This practice of constitutional revision by an unelected committee of nine, always accompanied (as it is today) by extravagant praise of liberty, robs the People of the most important liberty they asserted in the Declaration of Independence and won in the Revolution of 1776: the freedom to govern themselves."

So much for protecting the minority from the tyranny of the majority.

Scalia is closely identified with the concept of "originalism," or the view that the Constitution's meaning is locked as of the time it was adopted. This notion, of course, ignores the amendment process and the Ninth Amendment entirely, which states, "The enumeration in the Constitution, of certain rights, shall not be construed to deny or disparage others retained by the people." This concept also constrains justices who might adapt to new times, technologies and concepts that would have been totally foreign to the Founding Fathers. It's a restrictive view that put Scalia at odds with liberals and some conservatives alike during his 29 years on the high court.

What's even more distasteful than the social media celebrations of Scalia's death are the assertions by Republicans like Sens. Mitch McConnell and Ted Cruz that the GOP will oppose ANY replacement put forth by President Obama, per his constitutional duty. Let's hope the Republicans have miscalculated on this craven plan and in blocking a moderate Obama appointee are faced with the prospect of President Hillary Clinton getting the pick — with a Democratic Senate to advise and consent.

There can be no doubt that the GOP has lost its way. There must be a reckoning — the mindless lunatics of the Tea Party must be cut loose so the remaining sensible voices can reshape a GOP for a modern era. The anti-intellectualism endorsed by George W. Bush, Sarah Palin and others has predictably led the party to where it is today: The brink of nominating a racist, washed-up reality TV star as its candidate for president.

Obama should teach them one final lesson and cram the most liberal nominee he can find down the throats of these treasonous Republicans.

"Making America Homophobic Again," Feb. 22, 2016

Trump's landslide victory in the South Carolina primary in 2016 was when things really changed — he went from entertaining joke to frightening inevitability as the GOP nominee. Again, here, I implore LGBTQ voters not to be fooled and to think of the attacks on the trans community and others if Trump were to be elected.

What began as an entertaining summer watching the Republican Party eat its own turned scary last weekend as Donald Trump won a landslide victory in South Carolina. It would take an unprecedented break with electoral history for Trump to lose the nomination, having also won in New Hampshire.

Trump embarrasses himself, the Republican Party and our country each time he opens his mouth. The mainstream media deserve considerable blame for his dominating the polls, granting endless softball interviews since last summer at the expense of airtime for other candidates who, unlike Trump, are required to put on a suit and actually show up in a studio to be interviewed. He lies about everything and is rarely challenged. It took Fox News' Megyn Kelly to stand up to the bully and his misogyny. Otherwise, the softies of morning news allow Trump to say any outrageous thing out of fear he won't come back to their shows and goose ratings again.

Trump's rise is the predictable and unavoidable consequence of glorifying stupidity and anti-intellectualism. In a beautiful display of karma, Sen. John McCain was attacked by Trump for being captured during the Vietnam War. It was McCain who gave us Sarah Palin in a cynical ploy to appeal to uneducated, racist Tea Partiers. You reap what you sow.

The only positive contribution Trump has made: repeatedly assailing presumed front-runner Jeb Bush as "low-energy," a fatal and apt description that Bush couldn't shake, no matter how hard he tried to reanimate. Thank you, Donald, for sparing us another Bush in the White House.

As bad as Trump is, the alternatives could be worse for LGBT Americans, with Sens. Ted Cruz and Marco Rubio already spelling out plans for how to undo marriage equality and advance so-called "religious freedom" measures. Rubio, at age 44, is supposed to represent the future of the party. Yet his positions on a range of issues, including LGBT concerns, smack of the 1950s, not a "new American century" (which, by the way, started 16 years ago).

It is simply unimaginable that an LGBT voter could support any of these candidates. The Log Cabin Republicans should sit out this election and hope for a Democratic landslide so the GOP can finally get serious about retooling for a new era. Maybe then Log Cabin will carry more meaningful influence with party leaders and convince them to renounce homophobia in the platform and to oppose laws that dissuade or prevent African Americans from voting. After Mitt Romney's 2012 thumping, RNC leader Reince Priebus announced plans for an "autopsy" to right the ship and appeal to a broader base of voters. The report concluded that, "among the steps Republicans take in the Hispanic community and beyond, must be to embrace and champion comprehensive immigration reform."

On gay voters, the report noted, "Already, there is a generational difference within the conservative movement about issues involving the treatment and the rights of gays — and for many younger voters, these issues are a gateway into whether the Party is a place they want to be."

So what happened? Instead of immigration reform, we got Trump promising to bully Mexico into building a nearly 2,000-mile border fence, a laughable goal embraced by legions of his deluded supporters. Instead of moderating on gay rights, we got Rubio and Cruz vowing to attack us in new, creative ways and even contending that the U.S. Supreme Court ruling on marriage is not "settled law." Trump, meanwhile, flip-flopped on previous pro-gay statements and pledged to reverse nationwide marriage equality, apparently unaware of how the three branches of government operate.

In short, the Republican Party is a nonstarter for any serious minded LGBT voter who cares at all about his or her basic rights under the law. Make no mistake: If any of the Republicans manages to get elected, the LGBT community will be back on defense, fending off attacks on marriage equality, transgender rights and more. The next president will likely get multiple Supreme Court picks, raising concerns about fresh lawsuits seeking to undermine marriage equality. In addition, we can be sure that a Republican president would undo many of the various pro-LGBT administrative changes enacted by President Obama.

Priebus and the GOP establishment have lost control of their party. It's been fun to watch, but the joke will be on us if Trump, Cruz or Rubio lands in the White House.

"That time I interviewed David Duke," Nov. 14, 2016

Trump's rise and early pronouncements reminded me of David Duke's attempts at recasting himself from KKK grand wizard to semi-plausible political candidate. It was a terrifying revelation that the country had indeed just elected a president who hesitated at distancing himself from Duke's endorsement. I interviewed Duke for the Daily Collegian while a student at Penn State; this piece recounts that episode and the comparisons decades later to the president-elect.

Donald Trump has elevated the voices and influence of some truly frightening figures. Steve Bannon, the noted anti-Semite from Breitbart, will be the top adviser to the next president. Ken Blackwell, a senior fellow at the hate group Family Research Council who believes being LGBT is a "lifestyle choice," was tapped as a senior adviser. And Reagan relic Ed Meese, who backed Indiana's "religious freedom" law, is aiding in the transition.

But all of them look downright sane and centrist compared to David Duke, who endorsed Trump and described election night as "one of the most exciting nights of my life." Duke tweeted, "Make no mistake about it, our people have played a HUGE role in electing Trump!"

His "people," of course, are the "deplorables"— racists, xenophobes, homophobes, anti-Semites, misogynists — that Hillary Clinton warned the country about. Trump was slow to distance himself from the KKK when it endorsed him early on. Duke is a former grand wizard of the Klan who nearly won a U.S. Senate seat from Louisiana in 1990. I interviewed Duke for Penn State's Daily Collegian shortly after that loss, in which he captured 60 percent of the white vote in the state and nearly 45 percent overall.

Watching Trump's rallies this year, I was reminded of that interview with Duke in the late fall of 1990. He boasted to me of his own rallies, filled with rural white supporters angry over the perceived rise of "Black militancy," as he described it. Most of Duke's office staff was comprised of college students and Duke told me his message played tremendously well on campuses.

"I've got standing-room-only crowds and standing ovations at almost every university," Duke said. "Overall the campuses have been very supportive of my candidacy both in and outside of Louisiana."

He ominously added, "I think I've begun a new civil rights movement across the country."

Those words haunted me as Trump's popularity grew and as videos of his own rallies emerged. Supporters chanted racist and anti-Semitic slogans; some demeaned women and hurled homophobic epithets at anti-Trump protesters. There were outbreaks of violence at multiple stops that Trump himself encouraged and seemed to enjoy.

Could Duke have been onto something back in 1990? Has the country really not progressed since then?

The election of Barack Obama gave us hope that Duke's America was a thing of the past. Now Obama's eight years feel like a mirage.

To be sure, Trump found support from voters who were turned off by his racist rants but who have legitimate concerns about the future of the country. The alarming rate at which health care premiums are increasing under Obamacare; the failure to engage in Syria that led to a crippling refugee crisis across Europe; the flight of U.S. companies and factories to countries with cheap labor; a new digital economy that has left many rural workers behind.

But it's hard to talk foreign policy and economics when the other side views you as second class. Thousands are protesting in the streets today not because Trump wants to defeat ISIS or bring back manufacturing jobs. They're marching because they've been personally attacked and demonized. Immigrants, Mexicans, African Americans, LGBT people and so many others are understandably worried about what's to come. House Speaker Paul Ryan says there won't be a deportation force targeting immigrants, yet that's exactly what Trump promised during the campaign. Trump himself now says marriage equality is "settled law," yet vows to appoint Supreme Court justices who would overturn it.

In this difficult time, when the country remains divided and friends and family members are turning on each other as disagreements over politics turn into friendship-ending attacks fueled by hyperbolic social media posts, we must try to remember there is much good in America. I witnessed it in Orlando this summer in the immediate aftermath of the Pulse massacre. Thousands turned out to donate blood, raise money for victims' families, attend vigils and embrace strangers in mourning. We stood together — gay, straight, young, old, Christian, Muslim, white, Black, Democrat, Republican — in downtown Orlando, vowing to respond to the hatred with love.

Those memories feel at odds with the results of Election Night, when voters embraced a very different vision for our future.

"Time for a new LGBT march on Washington," Dec. 6, 2016

Following the election of Donald Trump, I wrote this piece calling for a new march on Washington. A year later, on June 11, 2017, the march was held, spearheaded by a New York activist who'd started a Facebook page encouraging the demonstration against the new administration. I marched in the Blade's contingent; we carried signs reading "Alt Press, Not Alt Facts," and "The First Amendment, Our Last Defense." Tens of thousands marched from the White House to the National Mall near the U.S. Capitol in the Equality March for Unity and Pride. It was a rare and welcome time when I could ethically put my journalism hat down to engage in a little old school street activism.

Since the unthinkable happened last month and U.S. voters elected a racist demagogue as president, I have been inundated with emails and personal requests for reassurance. After all, we've seen worse — George W. Bush, AIDS, etc., right?

Indeed, we have seen worse, though the impact of a President Trump on our community is so far unclear. He has appointed a cadre of wealthy, anti-LGBT ideologues — some with no government experience — to senior advisory positions and Cabinet-level posts. Some were anti-marriage activists; at least one is a hero of the KKK. It's hard to fathom that this is our 2017 America, but here we are. After eight years of progress — from the economic recovery to unprecedented advances on LGBT rights under our first African-American president — we're about to take monumental steps backward. The excuses offered by Hillary Clinton's campaign manager Robby Mook and others about Russian interference and James Comey's recklessness ignore the reality that her campaign lacked a coherent message and that the candidate was deeply flawed from the beginning. In a change year, the Democrats put forward the ultimate insider politician, someone who voted for the disastrous Iraq war before apologizing for it; who supported TPP before opposing it; who cosponsored a bill to criminalize flag burning; who was woefully late to the marriage equality fight; and who even praised Ronald Reagan's record on AIDS.

Despite Clinton's flaws and her campaign's apparent indifference to Rust Belt states critical to her Electoral College strategy, there was only one responsible choice on Election Day. About 2.5 million more voters made that choice than supported Donald Trump, but lopsided margins in California couldn't offset Clinton's lack of appeal across the South and Midwest. And so, here we are.

Trump's gay defenders — and there are a handful — have said not to worry, that Trump reached out to gays during his convention and that he won't undermine LGBT rights as president. But most of us are more concerned about a disengaged President Trump empowering anti-LGBT figures like Vice President-elect Mike Pence, whose anti-LGBT views are well known, and Reince Priebus, whose party platform was labeled "the most anti-LGBT platform in the party's 162-year history," by the Log Cabin Republicans. There's also Trump's disturbing pledge to appoint justices in the mold of Antonin Scalia to the U.S. Supreme Court.

What's coming won't be pretty. But this isn't 2000 or 2004, when George W. Bush cynically used anti-gay animus to motivate conservative voters. The Obama era has produced great advances toward equality that will prove difficult to undo. From opinion polls that show growing acceptance of our relationships to court victories like Macy v. Holder and Obergefell v. Hodges, the LGBT community is on much surer footing than eight years ago. Our advocates (and journalists) will need to readjust to playing defense again and fight to preserve those victories. Those strategies should include a new march on Washington for LGBT equality.

Many younger voters came of age during the Obama era and are unaware of our community's history as a despised and discriminated against minority. Maybe that's why many of us of a certain age didn't slip into a post-election depression — we've been here before. We've marched on Washington and protested government indifference to the pandemic in front of the White House, decades before we were ever welcome inside. A new march would serve to educate and galvanize a younger generation in the way previous marches in 1979, 1987, 1993, 2000 and 2009 inspired many of us. We should send a message to Trump and his supporters that LGBT Americans are NOT returning to the closet and will not abide a rollback of our hard-fought advances. It's a new era but we've been here before. We know how to fight from outside the White House gates.

"Say No to Normalizing Trump," Jan. 16, 2017

This prescient piece predicted Trump's eventual attacks on the transgender community and called for acts of civil disobedience in response.

Don't listen to those who seek to normalize Donald Trump and downplay the setbacks to come.

Don't worry, they say, marriage is settled law. Yes, but Roe v. Wade is more established than Obergefell yet it's at the top of the GOP target list.

Don't worry, they say, the country's come a long way on gay rights and it's too late to turn back the clock. That may — or may not — be true for privileged gays like Peter Thiel, but make no mistake that the trans community, among others, will suffer under President Trump.

Don't worry, they say, the marquee issues of the LGBT movement are finished — marriage, "Don't Ask, Don't Tell" repeal, a federal hate crimes law. Yes, but what about the less visible issues like LGBT youth homelessness, HIV infection rates, violence targeting trans people of color, not to mention all the myriad ways in which a hostile Trump administration could undo executive orders, guidance to federal agencies and other such changes. Make no mistake that the negative repercussions of this election on LGBT progress are already underway. A Justice Department led by racist Sen. Jeff Sessions won't continue the Obama administration's guidance on trans students' use of bathroom facilities. An Interior Department led by Rep. Ryan Zinke isn't going to designate any more LGBT sites as historically significant, even though the National Park Service last year unveiled a Theme Study recommending more than 100 such sites.

And the climate for LGBT federal workers has already changed; a chill has descended across the government, sending many back into the closet. For a recent story, the Blade reached out to more than a dozen LGBT federal workers for their thoughts on the incoming

Trump administration. We even offered them anonymity. No one would speak — even off the record or on background.

I remember walking into OPM shortly after President Obama took office where I was meeting with several gay and lesbian employees. The atmosphere was cheerful. It was as if a cloud had lifted. After eight hostile years under George W. Bush in which gay whistleblowers were targeted for retaliation and LGBT federal workers mostly remained closeted, Obama's victory was liberating.

Over the course of Obama's eight years, I had the privilege of a front-row seat to the change he fostered: the signing of "Don't Ask, Don't Tell" repeal; White House Pride receptions; and numerous invitations to speak to various federal agencies about LGBT rights and the Blade's work, including to the SBA, the Census Bureau and, most memorably, to the Pentagon's Defense Media Activity staff at Fort Meade. I couldn't have imagined when I began working at the Blade in 2002 that soon I'd be an invited speaker at a U.S. military installation celebrating Pride month. But those days are over and, sadly, many federal workers will be afraid to openly celebrate Pride. Already, some have told the Blade they won't attend this weekend's Women's March for fear of being spotted by their new bosses.

This is not a joke. It really will be as bad as you fear. This is a time to again embrace protest and civil disobedience as thousands will do this weekend. A president who would attack civil rights legend Rep. John Lewis during MLK Weekend respects no one and will eventually come for the gays, too. That's why it's more important than ever to come out, stay out and stand up. After years of complaints that our Pride celebrations are nothing more than shallow corporate-sponsored street parties, we have an opportunity to reinvent the annual rituals into something more meaningful, bold and powerful. Capital Pride organizers should seize this opportunity to embrace a provocative new vision for the 2017 event. With the U.S. Capitol as Capital Pride's backdrop, we have a unique responsibility to send an unwavering message to the country that we will not sit idly by as LGBT rights are undermined and reversed.

Kudos to the handful of journalists, including Ben Smith at Buzzfeed, who are challenging Trump and his cronies. Kudos to Rep. Lewis and the other Democrats boycotting the inauguration (as Hillary Clinton should have done). Kudos to the women who will march this weekend. We must all in our own way say no to normalizing Trump.

"First Fag Hag Ivanka's role as gay defender," Feb. 7, 2017

Incredible and implausible as it may seem, there were LGBTQ advocates in 2017 who pinned their hopes on Ivanka Trump to protect the community from Donald's inevitable assaults. Fast forward to 2022 and Ivanka was conspicuously absent from her father's 2024 campaign announcement. Maybe they were right about her all along.

We can thank Ivanka Trump and her husband Jared Kushner for thwarting an anti-LGBT executive order that would have enabled widespread discrimination against the community, the New York Times reported last week.

According to the report, "Mr. Kushner, a lifelong Democrat, and Ms. Trump, an independent, travel in liberal social circles and have long supported L.G.B.T. rights. Neither had seen the order before details were leaked. They expressed their dissatisfaction to Mr. Trump's other advisers, and then weighed in directly with the president, who opposes same-sex marriage but has spoken out against discrimination."

So should we all rush out and buy some of Ivanka's tacky jewelry on QVC in thanks? Should we feel grateful that the only thing standing between LGBT Americans and legalized discrimination sanctioned by the president himself is his privileged liberal daughter and her urbane husband?

And what happens when Steve Bannon pushes Kushner out the door, which seems increasingly likely as the days pass? Who will stick up for the poor gays then, Melania and Milo?

It's still hard to believe that we've gone from fierce advocate President Obama to First Fag Hag Ivanka in a few short weeks. Obama spoke movingly about the LGBT progress seen under his watch in his final press conference when he called on the Blade's Chris Johnson for one of his last questions as president. (The significance of that moment was widely underreported; it marked the first time a sitting president called on an LGBT media outlet in a press conference. It may seem like a small thing, but it was the result of untold hours of hard, thankless work by Johnson and others before him who toiled in obscurity in the briefing room waiting for a break.)

In his trademark modest delivery, Obama said: "The primary heroes in this stage of our — our growth as a Democracy and a society are all the individual activists and sons and daughters and couples who courageously said, this is who I am and I'm proud of it.

"And, that opened people's minds and opened their hearts. And, eventually, laws caught up. But, I don't think any of that would have happened without the activism, in some cases loud and noisy, but in some cases just quiet and very personal."

We've gone from Obama's poignancy to Ivanka's whispered pleas for mercy, a fraught trajectory for sure. LGBT rights shouldn't hinge on the private pleadings of the president's daughter. Trump pledged to support the LGBTQ community and he should honor it by rejecting so-called "religious freedom" orders, not because Ivanka and Jared have some gay friends who might not invite them to brunch but because it's the right thing to do.

There are reportedly hundreds of draft executive orders circulating among Trump's incompetent advisers. This is no way to run a White House. It's only a matter of time before Bannon and Mike Pence get their way and reward their bigoted base with an overt attack on LGBT equality.

"Impeach the SOB," Sept. 26, 2017

Proof that I was among the earliest to call for Trump's impeachment. The issue here was his attacks on free speech that I correctly labeled a threat to American democracy. But Trump's attacks on the NFL struck me as another front in his plan to divide the American people, separating us from longstanding traditions that once brought us together. There aren't many traditions left that unite Americans — we're pretty much down to the Super Bowl and Christmas. If a pandemic can't bring us together, then absolutely nothing will. In 2017, Trump took on one of those last two unifying traditions by demonizing the NFL leadership for not punishing Black athletes who kneeled during the National Anthem. He worked overtime to divide us and came precariously close to kneecapping the NFL and destroying yet another American tradition that has long brought people together, no matter their race, income, gender or other characteristic. It's one of the reasons I love football — you can go to a game and sit next to someone with whom you have absolutely nothing in common except your love for a particular team. By halftime, you're laughing, buying each other beers and taking selfies. You'll never see this person again, but for a couple of hours, they seemed like your best friend thanks to a shared love of a football team.

Our national nightmare continues, this time with the president of the United States using the power of the bully pulpit to condemn freedom of speech. If you are not chilled by this display, then you're not paying attention.

At a rally last Friday in Alabama, Trump said, "Wouldn't you love to see one of these NFL owners, when somebody disrespects our flag, to say, 'Get that son of a bitch off the field right now. Out. He's fired. He's fired!'" He reiterated that message in a series of unhinged weekend Tweets.

Note to Trump and his white supremacist base of supporters: You do not get to dictate the when and where of someone else's protest against injustice. Watching coverage of this weekend's NFL protests, Trump supporters denounced the players for taking action on the field and polluting the Sunday football ritual with politics. They misunderstand the point of protest. It's not about choosing a convenient time and place for expression; it's about disrupting norms and getting people to pay attention and think about something they might not otherwise think about. Imagine if the ACT UP protesters of the 1980s and '90s had tiptoed around all the straight people who hated them and quietly picketed on the discreet sidelines. No! They closed roads, disrupted church services and deployed shocking images of the suffering to awaken the world to the horrors of AIDS and government indifference to an epidemic that was killing unpopular people.

You don't get to tell oppressed people when and where to protest their oppression.

Of course, the NFL is a private entity and its owners can enact whatever rules of conduct they like. They could ban protests of the "Star-Spangled Banner" and fire players who refuse to stand, as Trump suggests. But they haven't done that. Instead, owners and coaches finally joined players on the field to send a message that Trump's insults and efforts to undermine free speech won't be tolerated.

It's one thing to oppose on-field protests. It's quite another to oppose the right of American citizens to take a knee if that's their chosen form of protest speech. I abhor the KKK, but would defend their right to freely associate and to speak their hate. The answer to speech you don't like is more speech.

Make no mistake that Trump's outburst is consistent with his pattern (plan?) of dividing Americans along racial lines. It's also meant to distract us from the latest effort to repeal the ACA, the signature legislative achievement of the country's first Black president whose legitimacy was challenged by Trump's racist birther attacks. And while Trump spent his weekend fighting with athletes on Twitter, brown people (fellow Americans) in Puerto Rico were coping with the complete devastation of the island after Hurricane Maria.

Coddling and excusing white supremacists in Charlottesville while calling for the termination of Black football players from the NFL is just the latest in a long string of racist attacks from Trump. The ultimate irony is that while he tries to divide us, the NFL sent a powerful message of solidarity. Even Tom Brady and Robert Kraft — Trump buddies — spoke out against him this weekend. The best outcome of this would be for Americans to unite against Trump's message of division and embrace again the principles that made America great in the first place. The absolute freedom of the press and of expression are key among those principles.

Sadly, some members of the LGBT community haven't gotten the message about Trump's racism, homophobia and anti-trans attacks. The Log Cabin Republicans this week are holding a fundraiser at Trump International Hotel in D.C., an inappropriate attempt at currying favor with the administration by lining Trump's pockets. Imagine their outcry if President Obama had owned a hotel in D.C. and the Human Rights Campaign held its fundraisers there. It's a disappointing decision from the group, which rightly declined to endorse Trump during the campaign. Log Cabin should rediscover its integrity and move the event. We should not tolerate an American president who is so hostile to the basic tenets of our Constitution, a document he swore to defend.

"10 WAYS TRUMP IS ATTACKING LGBT RIGHTS," JULY 31, 2018

As Trump kept the country distracted via Twitter attacks on everyone from Meryl Streep to Colin Kaepernick, I tried to remind folks of what he was really up to, namely rolling back LGBTQ progress while the mainstream media talked about the bullshit.

Keeping track of the endless Trump scandals is a Sisyphean task: As soon as you fully dissect one anti-Democratic transgression, the rock rolls back down the hill as our faux president torches another American norm.

Attacking the free press, embracing murderous dictators, retaliating in the pettiest of ways against critics, enforcing an overtly racist ideology, demonizing longtime allies and late night tweets ridiculing everyone from Oprah and Meryl to Trudeau and Merkel. The list goes on.

Sadly, too many of us are taking the bait and wasting time and resources playing along with social media posts of our own responding to Trump and his enablers. Mainstream cable news outlets have devoted endless hours of pearl-clutching commentary to all the tweets. Instead, we should remain focused and resist being distracted by the sideshows. They are a smokescreen intended to hide what's really going on, which is a systematic dismantling of the U.S. government. And it's happening across agencies, from the State Department to the Department of the Interior. As Trump tweets, his sycophants roll back environmental regulations, abandon treaties, gut healthcare. And make no mistake that Obama-era LGBT protections are in the crosshairs. The Blade chronicles these attacks on a near daily basis so it's hard to keep up. Here's a primer on what's been going on while you were vacationing this summer, in no particular order.

#10 Abandoning LGBT people in need around the world. The State Department used to advocate on behalf of LGBT rights in hostile countries. Now we have Trump kowtowing to Vladimir Putin behind closed doors. Do you think he raised the issue of Chechnya's anti-gay crackdown in that meeting? Meanwhile, U.S. Rep. David Cicilline (D-R.I.) recently told the Blade that there is no policy in place that addresses the needs of LGBT immigrant children the Trump administration has separated from their parents. Where the United States once strived to set the example for equality, we now inspire autocrats in other countries to crack down on their press and suppress the rights of minorities. Our example matters. The bully pulpit is real. And it's being used to embolden dictators and to green-light attacks on free speech and assembly.

#9 Undermining LGBT adoption rights. A House committee just last week approved an amendment that would allow taxpayer-funded adoption agencies to deny placement to LGBT families over religious objections. The measure would empower the secretary of health and human services to withhold 15 percent of federal government funds from states and localities if they penalize adoption agencies for acting on their religious beliefs in child placement decisions, as the Blade reported.

#8 Pushing federal workers back into the closet. As we reported, in a letter dated June 28 to Defense Secretary James Mattis, eight House Democrats expressed concern about lack of formal recognition of Pride this year, saying the Pentagon is "backing away from supporting and celebrating" LGBT service members and Defense Department employees. That issue crops up across the government. Where federal workers were proudly out and happy to talk to us about their Pride plans during the Obama years, now they are largely afraid to talk on the record. Trump and his anti-LGBT cronies like Attorney General Jeff Sessions have cast a shadow of fear across the government. The Justice Department, meanwhile, hosted a Pride event for its LGBT attorneys and law enforcement officials — but for the first time in 11 years, the ceremony wasn't held in the building's Great Hall. It was closed to media and attendees were too afraid to talk about it afterwards. The Small Business Administration removed LGBT references from its website, even though the agency won a prestigious award from Harvard University for its groundbreaking outreach to LGBT entrepreneurs during the Obama years. When the SBA reached out to me to assist in putting together its Pride celebration, I declined citing the removal, which was later reversed after much protest, including from the NGLCC. And for the second year, Trump declined to issue a proclamation recognizing June as Pride month.

#7 Stacking government panels with anti-LGBT zealots. Senate Majority Leader Mitch McConnell named Tony Perkins, president of the notoriously anti-LGBT Family Research Council, to a two-year term on the U.S. Commission on International Religious Freedom. Perkins, whose organization was long ago labeled a hate group by the Southern Poverty Law Center, presided over a three-day "religious freedom" conference the State Department held last week in D.C. The event brought together some of the most bigoted homophobes of the far right, granting them the prestige and legitimacy of being endorsed by the U.S. government.

#6 Banning the Pride flag. A Republican lawmaker in the U.S. House has introduced legislation aimed at barring U.S. embassies from flying the Pride flag. Rep. Jeff Duncan (R-S.C.) introduced the measure last week, which seeks to "prohibit the flying of any flag other than the United States flag over United States diplomatic and consular posts, and for other purposes." The State Department didn't respond to the Blade's inquiries on the matter. Will our openly gay ambassador to Germany, Ric Grenell, have anything to say about this effort? Although it's not a Trump initiative, make no mistake that the anti-LGBT forces of the far right and their supporters are now unleashed thanks to Trump and the base tone he has set for the country.

#5 Undoing bias protections for trans people. The Trump administration has asserted that transgender people aren't covered under Title VII of the Civil Rights Act of 1964, which bars sex discrimination in the workplace. In addition, Sessions has rescinded Obama-era guidance requiring schools to allow transgender kids to use the restroom consistent with their gender identity.

#4 Attacks on trans health. The Trump administration plans to roll back an Obamacare rule barring health care providers from denying treatment to transgender people, including gender reassignment surgery.

#3 Advocating for "religious liberty." This is a common theme now, as the far right often pivots from overtly anti-LGBT statements, which don't play well with independent voters, to their favorite code term for anti-LGBT bias, "religious liberty." The White House in June hailed as a win for religious freedom the U.S. Supreme Court ruling in favor of a Colorado baker who refused to serve a wedding cake to a same-sex couple.

#2 Trans military ban. A federal appeals court recently reaffirmed an injunction barring the Trump administration from enforcing its cruel and discriminatory transgender military ban. That's good news, but the move sets up a potential showdown at the Supreme Court. So far, the Trump administration is mum on its next steps.

#1 Anti-LGBT judicial appointments. Last November, New York Times reporter Linda Greenhouse wrote a column about the "conservative plan to weaponize the federal courts." She cited a 37-page plan written by Northwestern University law professor Steven G. Calabresi, founder and board chair of the conservative Federalist Society, in which he declared their intention: "undoing the judicial legacy of President Barack Obama."

To that end, we have Neil Gorsuch and now Brett Kavanaugh likely headed to the Supreme Court. But while the mainstream media are focused on Kavanaugh, there are scores of lower-level judicial appointees moving toward confirmation, many of whom have disturbing anti-LGBT records. Mark Norris, for example, was nominated by

Trump for a seat on the U.S. District Court for the Northern District of Tennessee. Norris served for 17 years as a member of the Tennessee Senate, where he advanced anti-LGBT legislation as Senate majority leader. A lawyer who defended Prop 8 in court is nominated for a seat on the U.S. District Court for the District of Utah. And so on.

These attacks, as reported by the Blade, have occurred in just the last few months. They will only increase as the midterms approach and Trump needs more red meat to feed his brainless base of bigots and rednecks. This motley crew was aptly described by Hillary Clinton as "deplorables." They disdain education, ignore hypocrisy and racism and even basic facts, in defense of a bloated con man who will stop at nothing to line his pockets and those of his equally corrupt family and friends. Congressional Republicans in their blind allegiance to Trump have lost the moral authority to criticize any Democrat for any behavior for a generation. They have cast their lot with a wannabe demagogue and are in bed with the murderous Putin, whom they admire for his zero-tolerance of dissent and diversity.

There is one way out of this mess: Everyone offended by it must vote in November and again in 2020. Sadly, a new poll suggests that only 28 percent of millennial-aged voters plan to vote this year. You can march every weekend in protest and launch a million petitions on change.org, but if you don't vote then the deplorable one-third of Americans who still support Trump will win again.

"Go suck Hillary Clinton's c***,"Aug. 8, 2018

My Trump top 10 list elicited some colorful commentary from the MAGA crowd. They were spurred on by Trump's nonstop attacks on the media and free press, despite the Capital Gazette shooting in Annapolis, Md., in 2018 that killed five journalists, one of whom I had worked with at the Baltimore Sun. Trump's calls to violence led to surges in hate crimes during his presidency, the Jan. 6 insurrection

and, more recently, the attack on Nancy Pelosi's husband. Trump is evil, incorrigible and without conscience.

Much is being made in the mainstream media right now about the threats being directed at journalists thanks to President Trump's incessant and reckless attacks on the media.

In the aftermath of the Annapolis shooting, Trump has doubled down on labeling the media as the "enemy of the people." When his mindless supporters begin to physically attack reporters — and they will — then Trump will have blood on his hands again.

Not to be left out, the Blade has come in for some, er, colorful attacks from the pro-Trump zombies. Below are some actual, unedited quotes that came to me after publishing last week's op-ed titled, "10 ways Trump is attacking LGBT rights."

"You sir are a socialist piece of shit that needs to go suck on Hillary Clinton's cock!"

"Why don't you let people think for them self's!"

"You are a maggot on society!"

"Thank you for your lies and bullshit propaganda that you pose on the American public!"

"Unfortunately for you not all Trump supporters are idiotic rednecks that have their hands full of meat! Whatever that might mean!"

"I don't understand why you waste your time with your lies and why you wouldn't want to try to manipulate people into voting for a murderous tyrant such as Hillary Clinton!"

"People like you I do nothing but spreading hatred And causing riots and disrupting Businesses!"

"You're probably scared of guns to just like most of you pansy liberals and you want to just arm American public so criminals can take over?"

"Do you want ever take away guns from American citizens and when you try to that's when you will have your Civil War against liberals."

"Are you trying to insinuate Some sort of American Civil War is a good idea? Because it seems to me that's exactly what you and your ill-informed friends and colleagues you're looking for!"

"It's pretty funny that you're calling Trump supporters such as myself simple minded idiots whatever terminology like to use at the same time knowing that if you we are trying to reach are the least informed so good luck with that!"

"I think you should take your socialist ideas and propaganda and move to a country that shares your socialistic ideas and see how good that works out for you! It sickens me that people like you exist on this planet let alone live in my country and badmouth our commander-in-chief!"

"I'm not really sure where you come up with this crap that you're trying to ensue on people but I applaud you for having the time to think up all of these lies that you were telling Young manipulable millennials."

"I also don't understand why you think spending taxpayers money on parties for gay people is justified. If they want to have parties and they should fundraiser."

"And your article you also wrote that we should all be upset the transgender people should all be allowed to have sex changes for free at the taxpayers expense!"

"The proof is in the numbers! And they are twice as high as your little lover boy Obama's!"

"The Karmic Deliciousness of Falwell's Downfall," Sept. 1, 2020

This is another essay that falls into the category of outliving our oppressors. And further proof that those who doth protest too much are usually doing the worst and most hypocritical shit. I remember the relief many of us felt when Jerry Falwell Jr.'s father died. He was

a ubiquitous presence in the '80s, along with fellow evildoers Jimmy Swaggart, Strom Thurmond and others who rose to prominence on the backs of the LGBTQ community. My heart sank when I later learned Falwell had an equally hostile son who would assume the mantle of chief anti-gay propagandist. Turns out the son likes to don a Speedo and watch his wife have sex with the hot pool boy. You really can't make this stuff up.

Jerry Falwell Jr.'s downfall just may be the only good thing to come of 2020 so far.

Handsome pool boy Giancarlo Granda outlined the salacious details of his years-long affair with the Falwells in a stunning ABC News interview last week, in which he hinted that Falwell masturbated while watching Granda have sex with his wife, Becki.

Falwell, who served as president of Liberty University since 2007, resigned after pressure from the school's board. This week, the board said it has hired a "leading forensic firm" to investigate Falwell's tenure at the school, Politico reported. Just a reminder: Liberty University is among the most hostile to queer students. The school's honor code reads: "Sexual relations outside of a biblically ordained marriage between a natural-born man and a natural-born woman are not permissible at Liberty University." Falwell's interim replacement as president, Jerry Prevo, is an outspoken homophobe who has fought against LGBTQ rights in Alaska for decades.

As the Blade reported in 2013: "An Alaska church's decision to no longer sponsor local Boy Scouts of America troops over its opposition to the inclusion of gay scouts has sparked controversy. ... The Anchorage Baptist Temple's decision has left Boy Scout Troop 1316 and Cub Scout Pack 316 without a place to meet. Rev. Jerry Prevo, who is the congregation's chief pastor, referenced the Bible as he defended his decision to the newspaper. 'No homosexual will enter the Kingdom of God.'"

Liberty's hostility to its LGBTQ students was codified by its founder, the evil Rev. Jerry Falwell Sr., one of the leading homophobes of the '80s whose cruel and constant attacks on gays undoubtedly led to the suicides of many young gay men demonized during the height of the AIDS epidemic and sent to conversion therapy. "AIDS is not just God's punishment for homosexuals, it is God's punishment for the society that tolerates homosexuals," Falwell Sr. famously said. He's also the one who labeled Ellen DeGeneres as "Ellen Degenerate" after she came out. His hate wasn't limited to gays. Falwell Sr. was also a racist who questioned the landmark ruling in Brown v. Board of Education: "The facilities should be separate. When God has drawn a line of distinction, we should not attempt to cross that line," he said.

Fast-forward to 2020 and that man's son is now out of a job and disgraced after a sex scandal that not only continues to worsen and expand, but that is tinged with gay undertones.

Granda describes Falwell Jr. as a "predator" who was drunk and "giggling" wearing a Speedo at their first sexual encounter. "It's his thing" to watch, Granda says Becki told him. The evangelical couple also visited a swingers club, Miami Velvet, according to Granda.

Granda later went into business with Falwell's son, jointly owning a Miami youth hostel with him that is described as "gay friendly."

"After the affair, the Falwells invested $1.8 million in a property deal to help Granda open a 'gay-friendly youth hostel' in Miami Beach, which Politico described as 'a cesspool of vice,'" Vanity Fair wrote.

So, Rev. Falwell's son, the head of Liberty University, where drinking alcohol is verboten, is drunk on a bed in a Speedo watching a hot young guy have sex with his wife. He later loans Granda money to invest in a hostel that caters to gay guests and is known as a "cesspool."

It's almost too good to be true. And proof that sometimes you really do outlive your oppressors and get a ringside seat to their delicious, karmic downfall.

Let's celebrate now that one more hypocrite who uses religion to attack LGBTQ people while engaging in the same behaviors he publicly deplores is exposed and, yes, canceled. Maybe 2020 is turning a corner.

"The Sad, Closeted Hypocrisy of Lindsey Graham," Oct. 16, 2020

This was yet another attempt at outing a closeted enemy of the community. It's inconceivable to me that South Carolina voters — not known for their progressive ways — have been duped by Sen. Lindsey Graham for so long. Yet, shortly after this piece was published, Graham was reelected yet again. On a trip to Charleston a few years ago, our gay tour guide talked about the "open secret" that is Graham's sexual orientation. A few years back, I put Graham's face on the cover of the Blade's annual "Most Eligible LGBT Singles" issue, drawing some media attention and a link on Drudge. Despite those efforts, Graham has never come out and the mainstream media have mostly given him a pass.

Sen. Lindsay Graham returned to the national spotlight this week, overseeing the confirmation hearings for Amy Coney Barrett. The irony of this appears largely lost on the mainstream media.

Graham, for years and years rumored to be gay, is rushing the confirmation of a Supreme Court justice who will likely rule on challenges to the Obergefell marriage decision that will undoubtedly curtail its scope, if not overturn it entirely, as Justices Alito and Thomas revealed last week as their goal.

The confirmed bachelor's efforts to keep his sexual orientation a secret suffered a blow this summer, when male escorts and porn stars created a stir with the "Lady Graham" hashtag and revelations about "ladybugs" (Google it if you have an iron stomach). Porn star Sean Harding went public on Twitter, alleging Graham has hired multiple D.C.-based escorts over the years who signed nondisclosure agreements, which have enabled this farce to persist for so long.

Closeted figures like Graham have done so much damage over the years, from Donald Trump's idol and mentor Roy Cohn, to Sen. Larry Craig of Idaho, passing laws and judgment against members of their own community while cowering in the shadows. It's remarkable that in 2016 Graham ran for president and is now running for reelection to the Senate while largely avoiding questions about his sexual orientation from the media. His disdain for the LGBTQ community is established in a string of votes against our interests, from voting against the Employment Non-Discrimination Act to cosponsoring the Defense of Marriage Act, to shoving a hostile Supreme Court justice down our throats two weeks before a presidential election after vowing he would never do such a thing.

Graham was asked about marriage during a recent debate with Jaime Harrison, his well-funded Democratic opponent in the South Carolina Senate race.

"My partner and I have been married for five years and we've been together for 22. What will the candidates do to ensure our rights are protected — the rights of the gay people, married in the state of South Carolina," asked Louis Yuhasz during the debate.

"The law of the land by the Supreme Court is that same-sex marriage is now legal," Graham replied. "I accept that ruling. We're a conservative state, there are a lot of religious people around this state that believe in traditional marriage. They're not bigots, they're not neanderthals for believing in that but this man, under our law, has the right to his relationship. I'll honor the law of the land. ... I've tried to be tolerant. I've tried to understand that people have different life experiences. I do; I'm not a woman, I'm not a person of color. I listen, but I can tell you right now that when it comes to South Carolina, I think I've been an effective voice for who we are and to the gentleman, the law of the land is that same-sex marriage is legal and we will honor that."

Of course, that's a far cry from actually endorsing marriage equality, as the "law of the land" will likely change given the new 6-3 conservative majority on the high court.

It appears unlikely that Harrison will unseat Graham, but if enough South Carolinians recognize the harmful hypocrisy that Graham embodies, maybe, just maybe, we'll see much needed change on Nov. 3.

Patti LuPone said it best when she tweeted earlier this year: "Lindsey Graham you are a disgrace. On a personal note, why don't you just bite the bullet and come out. You might just come to your senses."

"Happy to see Limbaugh dead," Feb. 18, 2021

I tried to resist weighing in on the death of Rush Limbaugh, but after enduring fawning tributes from the mainstream media, I caved. Yes, that headline is harsh, and I was predictably accused of celebrating someone's death. I am not celebrating Limbaugh's death, but I refuse to participate in a celebration of his life.

One of the more colorful responses I received to this piece ended with this: "You are pathetic, and your article is trash, and you should resign immediately. I'm sure the LGBT movement would be much better without you, trying to build bridges with 50 million people, instead of saying that you are 'happy to see Limbaugh dead.' You are a threat to society and human decency, a sociopath that needs to be investigated for writings against humanity. Thank goodness the circulation of the Blade is so small, to protect society from you and the blatherings of a demented, mentally ill, and soulless creature." Luckily I have a thick skin.

Rush Limbaugh was a terrible human. He was a racist, sexist, homophobic, drug-abusing adulterer who mocked gay men dying of AIDS.

The revisionist history that occurs when disgusting people like Limbaugh (and Jerry Falwell, Strom Thurmond and Antonin Scalia before him) die is galling. Let's tell the truth about these hypocritical bigots in death as many of us did in life.

Limbaugh referred to feminists as "feminazis" and once called Chelsea Clinton the "White House dog." He was forced to resign as an ESPN football commentator after making racist comments about Philadelphia Eagles quarterback Donovan McNabb. Florida officials investigated Limbaugh over allegations that he paid a former maid to buy prescription drugs for him over a prolonged period of time. He changed wives like other people change bedsheets.

He referred to AIDS as "the Rock Hudson disease" and featured a segment on his radio show called the "AIDS Update," which was introduced with the song "I'll Never Love This Way Again" by Dionne Warwick, as recalled by veteran journalist Karen Ocamb. Limbaugh compared marriage equality to pedophilia, once saying, "They want us to all think that pedophilia is just another sexual orientation." He mocked the death of Freddie Mercury.

Limbaugh last February said, "America's still not ready to elect a gay guy kissing his husband on the debate stage as president" in reference to Pete Buttigieg kissing his husband, Chasten. And even more recently, he praised the insurrectionists who stormed and desecrated the Capitol on Jan. 6, seeking to execute Nancy Pelosi and Mike Pence.

For all this reprehensible behavior, President Trump presented Limbaugh with the Presidential Medal of Freedom.

Mainstream media outlets now reporting on Limbaugh's death must not gloss over the reality of who he was in life: A bully and a bigot who celebrated the agonizing deaths of gay men to AIDS and who used his considerable platform to spout racist, sexist views and dangerous, un-American conspiracy theories.

Good riddance to Limbaugh and his ilk. They are a stain on our country and should be rebuked in life and death.

"Gay, Catholic and confused," Nov. 26, 2004

I was raised Catholic and believe there's a lot of good to be found in the church, despite all the problematic and anti-LGBTQ messaging from the Vatican. Even Pope Francis, who has tried moderating that messaging, has been inconsistent in his efforts at inclusion. Exposing children to church (or synagogues or mosques) and to religious teachings is a good idea, imparting basic values of loving thy neighbor and the like. We could use a lot more of that these days. Although my brother and I would do anything to get out of attending Sunday mass, including faking sick, I do have fond memories of our little Catholic church in Ellicott City, Md. Today, I find an occasional Catholic mass a comforting, quiet place for reflection and meditation, even though I left the church decades ago over its anti-LGBTQ rhetoric. The rituals and pageantry of it all are a mesmerizing throwback to a more formal time in our world of sweat pants and sloth — the choirs, incense, flowing robes, and stained glass. In this essay, I wrote about my sister's 2004 wedding at a Catholic church in Baltimore and its surprisingly gay-friendly outreach efforts. The Catholic Church remains filled with closeted gay priests and other officials. I've known several gay priests who found it easier to enter the priesthood than to reckon with their sexuality and come out as gay. What a sad, tortured way to live — lying to yourself and loved ones (and God) about something so fundamental. In 2022, the church seems to have learned nothing from its child sex abuse scandal, still preferring stubborn denial to an honest dialogue about realities on the ground.

The Catholic Church is mired in an identity crisis. Pope John Paul II, sounding more and more like an out-of-touch curmudgeon clinging to bygone days of 1950s-style morality, again this week intoned against tampering with the "irreplaceable" institution of marriage. Meanwhile, as Catholic bishops met last week in Washington, D.C., there were signs that not all bishops are towing the Vatican line against gay relationships. As gay protesters descended upon the Conference of Catholic Bishops, at least two bishops — including auxiliary Bishop Thomas Gumbleton of Detroit — greeted demonstrators, while others merely glanced away and walked by quietly. Word of the pope's staunch opposition to gay rights initiatives, and same-sex marriage in particular, is clearly not trickling down to all of the church's local pastors.

Just three months ago, my sister was married in a Catholic church in Baltimore. Fearing Old Testament-style tirades against gays and warnings to my sister that she obey her husband, I visited the church for a Sunday morning mass prior to the wedding day. My fears about the church couldn't have been more off base. Upon arriving at the church, I was greeted enthusiastically by a rather effeminate priest. Granted, it's a stereotype, but I've run into enough closeted priests at Central Station and the Hippo to know that all these guys aren't exactly adhering to their celibacy vows. I read a copy of the church bulletin while waiting for mass to begin and was surprised to see an ad publicizing a meeting of the church's gay and lesbian ministry. It was then that I started noticing all the gay and lesbian faces in the half-empty pews.

This beautiful, historic church with 100-year-old stained glass windows, mosaic tile floors, marble-covered walls and sturdy mahogany pews offers just one mass each Sunday. And the church was half empty. "White flight" has depleted this church of its congregants and it seems the only worshippers left are a few hardy old-timers along with pioneering gay men and lesbians who are buying up and restoring properties in the old neighborhood. To their credit, officials at this church, which I won't name so as to spare its priests certain ex-communication, are openly welcoming gay worshipers. During my visit just before Fat Tuesday this year, the priest and deacon even wore Mardi Gras beads during the service. The priest urged everyone to "party hearty, because after Tuesday, it's all over!" Was this a Catholic mass or a circuit party?

A few weeks later, my sister received a letter from the parish explaining that the church welcomes everyone, including gays. The letter added that the local parish does not agree with the Vatican's denouncement of gay relationships and gay rights initiatives. Mixed messages indeed. As the wedding approached, I met the priest who would marry my sister. He had been alerted that the bride's brother is gay, has a partner, and would be serving as a groomsman. After being introduced to me at the rehearsal, the burly priest with a booming voice wrapped me up in a warm embrace, assuring me that this is the most gay-friendly church in Baltimore. Since the Catholic Church is not a democracy, it is unclear how this struggling little inner-city church can get away with its gay outreach, other than by flying below the radar. Surely, no bishop or other official in the church hierarchy saw that letter or knew of this church's status as "gay friendly."

The problems of repression in the church go beyond the failure of church leaders to cope responsibly with the sex abuse scandal. That same culture of fear, silence and denial that enabled pedophile priests to shift around from parish to parish is restricting the ability of local pastors, priests and deacons to deal honestly and fairly with the question of how to welcome gay worshipers. Individual priests know who their gay parishioners are — they are active in their churches, donate time and money and, in some instances, even operate outreach programs to other gays in the community. But the Vatican, and this narrow-minded, misguided pope in particular, are preventing the full acceptance and open, honest participation in the life of the church by gay Catholics.

If only more Catholic officials would acknowledge publicly what they privately know to be true: that gay and lesbian parishioners are already playing vital roles in their churches and deserve to be recognized instead of demonized. The church has seen what happens when its leaders keep quiet and choose secrecy over honesty. If they have learned anything from the sex abuse scandal, it should be the need for more openness and honesty in church life. It's time for all those pro-gay priests who whisper words of quiet support for their gay parishioners to stand up for the full, proper inclusion of gays in church life. As Christmas approaches, there could be no better gift for gay Catholics.

"When Scientologists attack," May 18, 2007

It's a frustrating truth that in 20 years of Blade news stories and editorials, a short blog post about the film "Hairspray" in 2007 generated the most attention and traffic of anything I've written.

The movie was a take on the 1988 John Waters film, which I consider a classic. I've been a Waters fan since the mid-'80s and so it was surprising and jarring to be publicly at odds with him during this episode. My blog post encouraged gay fans to boycott the new film because its star, John Travolta, was Scientology's No. 2 spokesperson and his cult was known to engage in reparative therapy, the debunked practice of changing one's sexual orientation. The fact that Travolta has long been rumored to be gay provided further fodder for the boycott. That short post didn't even appear in the print edition of the Blade; it was a few hundred words crafted in a huff. Shortly after, a writer at MSNBC picked it up with the headline, "Gays boycotting Hairspray." Then all hell broke loose as the post went viral before we called it that. My voicemail and email filled up with indignant messages about my bias against Scientology. It grew into an international phenomenon that dogged stars of the film as they traveled the world promoting it. Travolta himself was asked about my criticisms; Waters denounced me in the New York Daily News. Then I was contacted by Fox News and asked to appear on hit show "The O'Reilly Factor," which I gladly accepted. That interview lives on thanks to YouTube. But what viewers don't see is what happens behind the scenes at Fox, before the cameras are on. O'Reilly couldn't have been friendlier — said he knew the Blade, chatted me up about our work in the LGBTQ community. When we went live, he switched gears from Mr. Nice Guy to his over-the-top angry man schtick. He compared Scientologists' work "curing" gay people to their work reforming drug abusers, which I shut down with an indignant, "So you're comparing gays to drug addicts?" That only angered him more. "Don't be a wise guy, Mr. Naff," he snapped back. Although I more than held my own, I did commit the sin of referring to Scientology as a "cult" on national television, which made matters significantly worse.

The next morning, I arrived at work to a slew of voicemails that included death threats. One Scientologist was going to bash my head with a baseball bat. Amid the various threats came a message from the president of the D.C. Scientology church inviting me to meet with her. I was intrigued but nervous given the vitriol and threats directed at me by these supposedly religious and kind followers. I called her back and said I'd accept her offer but only if I could bring my publisher with me, afraid of being abducted or locked in the basement sauna.

She agreed and my publisher and I arrived to the L. Ron Hubbard House, also known as the Original Founding Church of Scientology, in Dupont Circle, the heart of D.C.'s gayborhood, because, where else would a bunch of closet cases set up shop for their cult?

The president of the D.C. "church" was a pleasant, soft-spoken, middle-aged woman who greeted me at the door of the stunning Spanish Colonial Revival mansion, and offered a tour. We began in an immaculate first-floor formal office complete with oversized mahogany furniture and grand windows overlooking bustling 16th Street. "Wow, whose office is this," I asked. "This is Mr. Hubbard's office," she replied, "every church maintains an office for Mr. Hubbard." She was, of course, referring to Scientology founder L. Ron Hubbard, who died in 1986.

And in that moment, I realized there would be no reasoning with these people, so I grinned politely and moved on. Next we moved to the basement, where I spied the rumored giant 20-man sauna. The rumors were true — the "church" really did operate saunas, part of a so-called purification program to treat drug addiction that was championed by actress Kirstie Alley. The program was also used to remove "poisons" from new church members.

As the Boston Herald reported, "according to health experts, the Scientology detox program is untested and possibly health-threatening. The method requires vigorous exercise, five hours of saunas, megadoses of up to 5,000 mg of niacin, and doses of cooking oil. This regimen is repeated daily for two or three weeks. Every Scientologist, including young children, must go through this detox procedure as an 'introductory service — a first step in the church's high-priced teachings, according to church documents and ex-members."

It gets more bizarre.

After leaving the basement — and imagining wild orgies with Tom Cruise and John Travolta unfolding in the huge sauna — we moved to the third-floor attic space, which was carved up into tiny rooms large enough for two people facing each other across a small desk. On the desks were a small device known as the "e-meter" that resembled a soup can with wires sticking out. I'd heard of these contraptions, so when the president asked if I wanted to try it out, I jumped at the chance. She explained that the devices measured "brain mass" and instructed me to hold onto the tin can, then start thinking about a sad or traumatic event in my personal life. My aunt had recently passed away, so I thought about that and the meter started moving wildly, supposedly recording my brain's reaction to the traumatic memory of my aunt's death. Then I returned the tin can to the desk and she told me to pick it up again and repeat the process, recalling the same sad memory. This time, the meter moved but not quite as wildly. This, she exclaimed, was proof that it worked — by forcing me to think about a traumatic memory over and over, my brain would be less and less impacted by it.

Umm, OK, but can we get out of the attic now?

After the tour, we moved to the president's office back on the first floor. When she opened the door, everything I'd ever written or said about Scientology had been printed out and the pages arranged on a massive conference table. Suddenly the sweet, nonthreatening lady morphed into a stern and vaguely threatening figure, confronting me about all the nasty things I'd said about her beloved church. The "cult" line from O'Reilly particularly bothered her. I explained that I wasn't on a campaign to destroy Scientology, but that the church's use of reparative therapy was dangerous and debunked. We agreed to a truce and I left.

But the weird shit didn't stop there. A few days later, I was at my desk when the phone rang with an ominous invitation. Someone purporting to be from the hacker group known as Anonymous wanted to meet for coffee. She was in the building and asked if I could slip away to the coffeeshop downstairs in our lobby at the National Press Building. Nervously, I agreed, and asked how I would know her; she said she knows what I look like and would find me. So I headed downstairs and after a few minutes, a demure, shifty woman approached. We sat down and she began regaling me with stories of her efforts to infiltrate and protest Scientology. She claimed that after attending anti-Scientology protests at the D.C. church in disguise, that she was followed home on the Metro. She expressed paranoid fears about phones being tapped, hence the cloak-and-dagger nature of our in-person meeting. Anonymous was pleased with my criticism of Scientology and with my appearance on O'Reilly's show to denounce the church as a cult. She wanted to know my plan, my next line of attack, and how she could assist. I assured her that I am not an activist and that the Scientology thing was a fluke — I had other issues to write about and needed to get back to the Blade's bread-and-butter politics coverage. Scientology was not a new beat at the Blade and we'd likely not be writing much else in the near future. We parted and I never heard from her again.

But this chapter wasn't over yet. The film's premiere finally arrived in July 2007. I lived in Baltimore and commuted to the Blade offices via train, often with my good friend Maureen who also worked in D.C. One night in July, we were commuting back to Baltimore on the MARC train when we noticed spotlights in the sky. Just one block from Baltimore's Penn Station sits the historic Charles Theatre, which I've been patronizing since high school. As we walked off the train and looked up Charles Street, we could see cars lined up in front of the old movie theater and then realized: The "Hairspray" premiere was being held right here in Baltimore and we'd stumbled onto it. I couldn't resist a closer look after all the media attention my boycott call had received. So we walked into the adjacent tapas restaurant and noticed a large table set up for dinner. The restaurant and movie theater were connected and the cast was walking the red carpet into the theater, then through a door and into the restaurant for dinner. Maureen and I took a small table next to the large table that was soon filled with stars of the movie, including Zac Efron, James Marsden, Amanda Bynes and the director, Adam Shankman. Travolta was a no-show. We said hello to some of the stars and Marsden and Efron proved friendly, shaking our hands as we welcomed them to Charm City. They had no idea who I was. A bold gesture was in order, so I called our waitress over and asked her to deliver a shot to Shankman with a note I'd written: "Best of luck on the film, Kevin Naff." She obliged. I watched nervously as Shankman read the note. He sprang to his feet and eyed me, then approached. A former dancer, Shankman is short. He tried to intimidate me by standing over me, but, at 6 feet 3 inches, I stood up and towered over him. He seemed annoyed and suggested my boycott calls would cost the film box office. I told him that my boycott call and media interviews had generated more publicity than anything his marketing team could have dreamed up and that he ought to be thanking me. Needing to bring down the temperature, I pivoted, remembering that Shankman had danced in Janet Jackson's video for "Escapade." "Hey, didn't you dance for Janet?" I asked. "I'm her biggest fan." He melted and we had a disarming chat about our favorite icon. Then Shankman downed his shot, shook my hand and returned to his table. All seemed to be forgiven. In the end, "Hairspray" took in more than $200 million at the box office, so I guess my boycott call wasn't very effective. And I never did get a thank you note from Shankman — or Travolta.

Years later, Waters and I reconciled over a glass of Chardonnay at a Baltimore Museum of Art exhibit opening. He explained that he'd gotten to know Travolta and there wasn't a homophobic bone in his body. We posed for a selfie and agreed to let bygones remain just that.

The cult of Scientology is back in the news this week, after a video of a BBC reporter shouting down a church spokesperson hit YouTube.

The BBC's John Sweeney claims he was followed and harassed while working on a documentary about Scientology. The spokesperson in question is the son of actress Anne Archer.

"I have been shouted at, spied on, had my hotel invaded at midnight, denounced as a 'bigot' by Scientologists, brain-washed — that is how it felt to me — in a mock-up of a Nazi-style torture chamber and chased round the streets of Los Angeles by sinister strangers," Sweeney said.

On Monday, CNN's Anderson Cooper interviewed another Scientology spokesperson who denied that the church attacks its critics. It's a false claim, as the church has a record of suing media outlets and others who dare criticize it, including CNN's parent company Time Warner.

Last year, Rolling Stone magazine published a lengthy expose on Scientology by Janet Reitman. In it, she notes that science fiction writer L. Ron Hubbard, who created Scientology, drafted a policy called "Fair Game," which maintained that all who opposed Scientology could be 'tricked, sued or lied to and destroyed."

I watched Cooper's interview with interest, after my own run-in with the Scientologists a few weeks ago. I wrote a blog post about the new "Hairspray" film being released in July that stars prominent Scientologist John Travolta and urged gays to boycott the movie. The tongue-in-cheek nature of the post was lost on Scientologists.

As a devoted Waters and Divine fan since the mid-'80s, I find the new film a lame waste of time. The original is cinematic perfection, an engaging blend of Waters-esque gross-out humor and a socially conscious message told through music, dance and teen angst. It wasn't self-aware, pretentious or sanctimonious.

And Travolta has no business reprising an iconic gay role, given his cult's stance on gay issues. It's well known that Scientology has claimed to "cure" homosexuality via reparative therapy. Travolta's role in the film is even more galling given all the gay rumors that have followed him for years.

Following that blog post, I received angry emails from purported gay Scientologists, claiming that the church is welcoming and supportive. One gay Scientologist even contacted the president of the Blade's parent company in New York, telling him that my post was "... an all-out slander of a perfectly upstanding religion. ...You should be ashamed that [Naff] works for your publication." Others wrote that Scientology has never tried to "cure" gay members.

More false claims. Michael Pattinson, a gay former Scientologist, sued the church in 1998, claiming that it lied to him about its ability to "cure" him of his homosexuality.

"Scientology considers being gay as an 'aberration' that needs to be erased," he wrote in an essay that has been widely circulated online. "However, they don't erase it and are in actual practice anti-gay (as I and others got sent to 'ethics' correction for such behavior)."

According to Wikipedia's entry on Scientology, "The lawsuit also argued that the Church of Scientology had often told Pattinson that actor John Travolta was proof that Scientology can transform a homosexual into a happy heterosexual. Travolta's lawyer asserted that his client was not gay, and is happily married to a woman."

As Reitman reported, a Scientologist's harmful or negative acts are called "overts." She wrote, "Another overt is homosexuality, which Hubbard believed was a form of sexual 'deviance' best treated by therapy, or institutionalization. ... Scientology as an institution takes no formal position on issues like gay marriage, but homosexuality, sexual promiscuity or any other form of 'perversion' ranks low on Scientology's 'tone scale,' a register of human behavior Hubbard described in his 1951 book "Science of Survival: Prediction of Human Behavior."

In that book, Hubbard wrote of homosexuals, "Such people should be taken from the society as rapidly as possible ... for here is the level of the contagion of immorality and the destruction of ethics. No social order will survive which does not remove these people from its midst."

And in case there was any doubt about just how bizarre these fools are, consider this description that Reitman offered of church beliefs:

"They assert that 75 million years ago, an evil galactic warlord named Xenu controlled seventy-six planets in this corner of the galaxy, each of which was severely overpopulated. To solve this problem, Xenu rounded up 13.5 trillion beings and then flew them to Earth, where they were dumped into volcanoes around the globe and vaporized with bombs. This scattered their radioactive souls, or thetans, until they were caught in electronic traps set up around the atmosphere and 'implanted' with a number of false ideas — including the concepts of God, Christ and organized religion."

There's no law against being bizarre or crazy, so why should gays care about Scientology and this latest row? Because the so-called church has helped advance the false notion that homosexuality can be cured. Whether it's coming from Scientologists or the group Parents & Friends of Ex-Gays and Gays, it's a reckless claim long ago debunked by every credible medical association in the world. And the "ex-gays" are not a dim bunch of 1950s holdovers quietly praying for salvation. They are active in chapters around the country, filing lawsuits to force their backward, unscientific views into high schools.

PFOX filed a lawsuit this month against a Northern Virginia school board for refusing to distribute its fliers to high school students there. And in progressive Montgomery County, Md., school officials have endured a lengthy, litigious ordeal just because they wanted to tackle a few benign facts about homosexuality in health classes.

Those who espouse therapy as a means for "curing" homosexuality conveniently ignore the implications of their own logic. If you can be cured of being gay, then it follows that after a few weeks of comparable therapy, that straights can be cured of heterosexuality.

Whether it's the Church of Scientology, PFOX or Love in Action espousing the false notion that sexual orientation is changeable, it's important for the rest of us to denounce and counter their false claims so that another generation of gay kids doesn't grow up on a diet of destructive lies about the true nature of human sexuality.

"Israel as 'gay heaven'? It's complicated," Nov. 10, 2013

This was published in the Blade and in the Times of Israel following a trip I took to Israel and Ramallah as part of an LGBTQ delegation sponsored by Project Interchange. It was an eye-opening, life-changing experience to see so much history and conflict up close.

When a delegation of nine LGBT leaders from the United States arrived last week in Israel for an intensive seminar, we knew the gay residents of progressive Tel Aviv enjoyed broad acceptance and myriad legal protections. But imagine our surprise when TV personality and commentator Gal Uchovsky announced that we had arrived in "gay heaven."

Israel is "the best LGBT country in the world," he told us, adding that the nation's LGBT residents face no serious problems that he could identify. A gay child growing up in rural Israel is better off than a similar kid in the rural United States, he observed. Homelessness is rare here and Israeli parents embrace their gay kids because, well, better to be gay than dead.

Uchovsky is a proud cheerleader for his country, which is endearing, though his privileged worldview has perhaps shielded him from some unpleasant, inconvenient realities. Life for LGBT Israelis is, indeed, more complicated than Uchovsky's rosy assessment and, thus, our trip's catchphrase was cemented: "It's complicated."

The stellar seminar, sponsored by Project Interchange, a program of the American Jewish Committee, brought me well out of my comfort zone and right into Ramallah and to the edge of the Gaza Strip. The focus of the visit — LGBT issues — was often overshadowed by the frustrating stalemate of the Palestinian-Israeli conflict. Why can't the two sides come to an agreement on a two-state solution? It's complicated. And, as we learned, it's far more complicated than American mainstream media seem to grasp.

And so from the West Bank to Jerusalem to Tel Aviv to the Negev, the nine of us trekked to learn all we could from a diverse range of perspectives, including from Palestinians and Israeli experts critical of the country's record on LGBT rights.

We toured Tel Aviv's bustling, posh community center, touted as the only such center in the world that is municipally owned. As we made our way up the stairs to meet with Uzi Even in the community center, we could hear the giggles of young children and stepped over a pile of neatly arranged kids sneakers in a hallway. Another sign of the times.

The government's funding of such centers and related LGBT causes is a mixed bag. In the United States, small LGBT nonprofits and HIV service providers jockey for limited public grants, often leading to turf wars. But most such U.S. groups aren't beholden to the government or muzzled by fears of government retaliation. It's not clear that the same is true in Israel. It's a dilemma: accept public money to advance your important work and mute your criticisms of the government or reject public funds and risk financial shortfalls that will curb programming. As one speaker put it, "I'd rather our public money went to gay causes than to building another bomb."

The highlight of that visit for me was hearing from Uzi Even, the first openly gay member of the Knesset and a pioneering elder statesman of the Israeli LGBT rights movement who has helped rid the military of discriminatory policies and liberalize adoption laws.

In a true sign of the times, his latest cause involves sorting out Israel's divorce laws as they relate to same-sex couples.

My advice to Israeli LGBT advocates: Take time now to celebrate and honor the contributions of Even and others like him. Record his personal history and share it with young people. It wasn't so long ago in Israel when gay sex acts were illegal. Such lightning-speed progress doesn't happen by accident and brave pioneers like Even deserve our gratitude.

Several speakers emphasized the role that a 2009 shooting played in advancing gay acceptance. On Aug. 1, 2009, a gunman burst into the LGBT community center in Tel Aviv and opened fire, killing two and injuring at least 15 others. It's hard to quantify how significant a role that tragedy played in changing Israeli attitudes toward gays, but our speakers agreed it was a turning point.

It's a stark contrast to what we see in the United States, where violent hate crimes continue to plague our community, from trans women routinely killed in our inner cities to the recent murder of a gay man in the heart of New York's gay village. Americans are so inured to violence that these crimes barely register in the mainstream media, let alone lead to a widespread change in attitudes.

After a couple of days in progressive Tel Aviv, we made our way to Jerusalem. In addition to the usual religious sites, a group of us visited the Jerusalem Open House, an LGBT community center engaged in broad grassroots work in the face of complicated problems like funding, space constraints, religious critics who have sometimes turned violent and the ever-present challenge of building relations with Arab residents of the city.

Celebrating gay Pride in Jerusalem has been complicated, too. They don't agree on much, but anti-gay animus was something that united the world's major religions as conservative Jewish and Arab leaders denounced plans for Pride parades in the holy city in recent years. In 2005, marchers were attacked by an ultra-orthodox Jewish man who stabbed three participants. The following year, Jerusalem was selected to host WorldPride, which led to more unrest and violent protests. Some lawmakers in the Knesset attempted to ban gay Pride parades in Jerusalem, but those efforts fizzled. Our hosts in Jerusalem insist that relations are improving and that Pride is safer than in the recent past. Here, another stark contrast to the way we celebrate in the United States, with our corporate-sponsored pride villages, beer gardens and all-night parties.

From Jerusalem, we took a day trip and toured Efrat, a small city in the Gush Etzion settlement bloc with its mayor, Oded Ravivi. The issue of settlements commands a lot of attention in U.S. media coverage of Israel and so I was curious and excited to see one up close. Efrat has eschewed the barbed wire fences that snake through so much of the Israeli landscape and officials have worked to cultivate economic ties with surrounding Palestinian villages. But we learned that such efforts only go so far. When the mayor approached a Palestinian schoolmaster about sending teachers to Efrat to teach Arabic to Israeli kids, he declined, fearing he would be "slaughtered" for collaborating with the Jews.

In one awkward moment, a member of our group asked Mayor Ravivi how he would react if one of his children came out to him as gay. He seemed startled by the question and suggested it couldn't happen in his family. Cue the eye rolling among some of us. Such reactions are common among many who proclaim they don't discriminate but haven't devoted much thought to the underlying issues.

After absorbing the complicated problems and history of Jerusalem, some of us needed a release and our gracious hosts at Open House took us to the one gay bar in Jerusalem, called Video, where we had a few drinks and danced till the wee hours alongside a diverse crowd of revelers. Music, indeed, makes the people come together.

The concept of "pinkwashing" emerged as a hot topic throughout the week. Some critics claim the country's embrace of LGBT rights is merely a propaganda effort to claim the mantle of modernity and establish a stark contrast to homophobic regimes in the West Bank, Gaza and elsewhere in the Middle East. These critics claim the government's support for gay rights doesn't threaten or undermine the structure of Israel and amounts to a "fig leaf," and an attempt at distracting attention from the difficult problems of finding peace with the Palestinians.

I'm not convinced. Politics is about the art of the possible, not the ideal and certainly not the perfect. Sometimes we have to accept imperfect solutions or motives in the interest of securing protections for people in need. What's most striking about Israel's LGBT record isn't what it has achieved legislatively or through court rulings, but the fact that all this progress is happening in the heart of the Middle East. Our group trip featuring nine outspoken American LGBT advocates is simply not possible anywhere else in the region.

Even compared to the progress we've seen recently in the United States, Israel stands out because it is such a young country enacting these reforms. Americans are notoriously forward thinking and, as a result, we tend to forget our history. It was less than 10 years ago when President George W. Bush called for a federal constitutional amendment banning same-sex marriage and scores of states enacted their own constitutional bans. The architect of this shameful attack on LGBT rights was Ken Mehlman, a closeted gay man and modern-day Roy Cohn who has since come out as gay and now raises money for marriage equality campaigns. The change afoot is new and fast but fragile. Would America be seeing such dramatic change now if Mitt Romney had won last year's election?

Meanwhile, Israel opened its military to out gays and lesbians and transgender service members — something still barred by the U.S. military. There is relationship recognition, if not full marriage equality. The government directly funds and supports the LGBT movement, for better or worse. And it doesn't hide that support, but promotes it.

Still, some see nefarious motives.

Upon returning home from this trip, I received a letter criticizing the visit from a group called New York City Queers Against Israeli Apartheid. It read, in part:

"The delegation met with some unspecified 'Palestinian officials in Ramallah,' which strikes us as nothing but a token gesture. Worse, 'pinkwashing' — the attempt to use Israel's supposedly decent record on gay rights to whitewash Israeli occupation and apartheid — has been front and center in international LGBT organizing over the past several years, particularly in the US. Any delegation of LGBT 'leaders' to Israel that doesn't address it is clearly intended to contribute to pinkwashing."

Our group was sensitive to pinkwashing from the outset and several of us requested meetings with gay Palestinians and their representatives. Project Interchange worked hard to provide a balanced view of the issues and invited two Palestinian LGBT groups — alQaws and Aswat — to meet with us. Officials at the Tel Aviv and Jerusalem LGBT centers were also asked if they could assist in persuading those groups to meet our delegation or knew of other Palestinian LGBT representatives who would be willing to meet us. Sadly, the groups refused to meet with us. Change is simply not possible without dialogue and I deeply regret this lost opportunity the Palestinians had to engage with an open-minded group of visitors seeking nothing more than understanding and education.

(I invited NYCQAIP to respond to this story and they accepted. I look forward to publishing their reaction and thoughts on pinkwashing in the coming days.)

We met with Abu Zayyad, a scholar and Fatah and PLO adviser. It seemed somewhat silly to ask him about the state of LGBT affairs given all the day-to-day challenges facing Palestinians in the West

Bank. But he insisted that there is a level of gay acceptance, even if such views differ widely among family members, noting there are no laws in Ramallah related to gay issues and that there are at least two nongovernmental organizations that espouse gay rights. He spent most of his lecture discussing the state of life for Palestinians and much of what he said was not encouraging. He lamented the lack of mobility for Palestinians, who don't have passports, making international travel difficult at best. Locally, the checkpoints that Ramallah residents must navigate just to visit nearby Jerusalem create daily headaches. Zayyad, who said he spent three months in prison for participating in an anti-Israel protest, fears that a two-state solution will be impossible five years from now, when an estimated one million Israelis could be living in West Bank settlements.

"It will explode again," he warned.

It's often been said that Israel is a land of contradictions and that assessment came into sharp focus last week. Israel celebrates its status as the only Democracy in the Middle East, while its non-Jewish residents live under a flag adorned with religious iconography. In a nation so steeped in history, Israel is just 65 years old and is surprisingly lacking in many traditions. Located in the heart of the Middle East, where homosexuality can be punished by jail time or even death as in Iran, Israel has emerged as one of the world's most pro-LGBT nations. A country that is more than 60 percent desert has perfected drip irrigation and desalinated water from the Mediterranean to solve a decades-old water crisis. And in a nation with such ancient religious influences, a large chunk of the population — estimated by one speaker as high as 50 percent — identifies as secular or atheist.

It's impossible to summarize our weeklong adventure in a couple thousand words. A sincere and heartfelt thank-you to the team at Project Interchange, all of our speakers and to the people of Israel for all your hospitality. We were serenaded by Ivri Lider; walked the Stations of the Cross; toured Yad Vashem, the Western Wall tunnels, the Mahaneh Yehuda Market and indulged in far too much of Israel's impressive cuisine. We visited Sderot, Mitzpe Ramon and slathered ourselves in mud before floating in the Dead Sea.

It was in that moment — nine of us standing half naked, covered in mud — that I perceived a lasting bond forming among us. Despite our differing views on policy back home and occasional misunderstandings, we'd been through something emotional, powerful and unique together. An experience impossible to explain or summarize here, because, well, it's complicated.

"Learning from tragedy," Feb. 16, 2007

This was one of the saddest stories we've covered at the Blade — the suicides of a young lesbian couple in progressive Montgomery County, Md., amid a debate over LGBTQ inclusion in school curricula spearheaded by right-wing forces. I spoke to one of the teens' parents and we all assumed they'd run away, caught up in teenage love and emotions and would return safely. They wound up taking their own lives. Their tragic story drives home the real-world impact of anti-LGBTQ propaganda. It also highlights the degree to which I've tried to cooperate with law enforcement over the years. We've written our fair share of stories critical of the police, but sometimes their work and ours come together in beneficial ways. Initially, the Montgomery County police wanted us to hold off publishing a story, afraid that a perceived outing would exacerbate the situation. In other cases, we've worked with police to publicize missing persons as the police understand our readers might have unique insights into these cases or know that someone is closeted.

Journalists are taught not to get emotionally involved in the stories they cover. After all, it's just a job and there will always be another tragedy to cover next week.

I've always observed that rule, remaining professional and stoic while covering murders, house fires or plane crashes. Twice in my career, however, emotions got the best of me.

The first time came in 1991 while working as an intern for WUSA-TV in Washington. The assignment editor sent a reporter, TV crew and me to cover the stabbing death of a Korean teen who was surprised by burglars while opening his family's shop for business early in the morning. We were among the first on the scene, beating most of the police responders and saw the teen's parents reacting to the sight of their son who still lay in a pool of blood just inside the front door.

Later, the reporter sent me to the family's home and told me to knock on the door and request a photo of the victim. It seemed intrusive and disrespectful but I knew that Channel 7 was right behind us and would certainly have the photo for its broadcast.

I'll never forget what the reporter told me: "This is the hardest thing you'll ever have to do as a journalist." So I walked nervously to the front door and knocked gently. The boy's father answered and I expressed my condolences, requested the photo and returned to the station.

Back at my desk, the assignment editor — an impossibly busy person responsible for monitoring scores of police scanners and phone lines — left his post and rushed to my side. I was pale, my eyes glazed over: He knew what I'd seen and asked if I was OK. It was a rare moment of human compassion inside the pressure cooker of broadcast news.

That was 16 years ago. The second time my emotions got the best of me at work was last week upon hearing that Rachel Crites and Rachel Smith, two missing Montgomery County teens, had turned up dead in an apparent double suicide.

The Blade received a call from a family friend shortly after the two disappeared, seeking to publicize the disappearances in the local gay community. Montgomery County police have said they were unable to confirm the teens' sexual orientation, but speculation ran rampant that they were a couple.

Crites' father released a diary entry written by his daughter that read, "wherever I end up laying, whether buried or cremated, I want to stay with my true love, buried next to her. This is my choice, I'm sorry."

A few hours after a Blade reporter began making inquiries, the Montgomery County police called and asked that I kill the story because they feared the consequences if the teens perceived themselves as having been outed in the media. I resisted at first, arguing that one of our readers might know something about their whereabouts.

But then one of the parents called and pleaded with me not to publish the story. I deferred to the parents' wishes, as other local media outlets did. They were grateful and one parent even offered to cooperate with the Blade on a follow-up story. Of course, we assumed the teens would be found alive. Things changed a few days later when Crites, 18, and Smith, 16, were found in a remote, wooded area in a car, dead of apparent carbon monoxide poisoning.

Many of us at the Blade — and I suspect in the D.C. gay community — were pulling for the teens, regardless of their sexual orientation. Many of us know the feelings of isolation and despair that drive so many young people to take their own lives. Gay teens are especially susceptible to those pressures.

Montgomery County is one of the wealthiest, most progressive counties in the country. Its public schools have a sterling reputation. And yet, even there, these two teens saw no way out of their presumed depression and feelings of isolation. It's a heartbreaking story.

As the teens were laid to rest last week, there was a sad confluence of events in Montgomery County.

The group Citizens for a Responsible Curriculum, which has been fighting the inclusion of gay topics in the county's health education curriculum, filed an appeal to the state board of education in an effort to block a revised lesson plan approved last month. The curriculum, titled "Respect for Differences in Human Sexuality," explains concepts like sexual identity using nonjudgmental language. Eighth graders are taught how to define human sexuality and gender identity, while 10th graders examine topics like coming out.

The conservative group, along with Parents & Friends of Ex-Gays & Gays, wants its damaging and debunked views on reparative therapy included in classroom instruction, even though such notions have been derided by every reputable medical organization in the world. PFOX even has the nerve to claim discrimination, whining that the schools don't teach their views.

The timing of the challenge to the new curriculum couldn't be more insensitive or ironic, given the deaths of Crites and Smith.

Regardless of their sexual orientation, the teens' suicides have drawn renewed attention to the plight of at-risk youth. But the people behind Citizens for a Responsible Curriculum and PFOX are ignoring those cries for help and this opportunity to reach out to troubled young people.

They have contributed in no small way to a culture that says homosexuality is wrong, can be "cured" and should be overcome. It's a reckless and dangerous message that is being distributed in Montgomery County's schools. As the Blade reported two weeks ago, students at two county schools received fliers last month about quashing same-sex attractions. The PFOX handouts were given to students in accordance with a 2004 court ruling that required the district to treat its flier distribution system as a public forum.

We don't know if "the Rachels" were romantically involved or if they were ever exposed to PFOX's message. But there's no doubt that other teens in Montgomery County who are in the process of sorting out their sexual identity are subjected to the "ex-gay" myth in their schools.

These anti-gay crusaders have no shame. County officials should denounce their efforts and fight the curriculum appeal to its defeat. Let us hope something positive can come from this horrific tragedy and that other young people feeling alone and confused will find understanding and compassion from adults in their community instead of hateful and reckless propaganda.

"A Tale of Two Stories," Dec. 28, 2007

When a producer from a major TV network pulled me aside at a journalism conference with a tip, I was naturally intrigued. He claimed that his network was refusing to cover the story of three Black teens

> murdered in New Jersey because of a rumor they were gay and headed to a Black Pride event. He also alleged the police were covering up the anti-gay angle to the brutal killings. The Blade jumped on it and uncovered disturbing evidence that indeed the killings were likely motivated by anti-LGBTQ animus. I naively waited for the national outcry and mainstream media attention. It never came. The case haunted me and I felt we'd failed these three kids. The comparisons to Matthew Shepard were obvious and, yet, despite the deaths of three young people, the TV cameras never came for the New Jersey victims. As I wrote then, "Maybe if they were white the world would know more about their story." It took years to catch and prosecute the six killers, most of whom received lengthy prison sentences exceeding 200 years. Their names aren't worth repeating here. The victims were Iofemi Hightower and Dashon Harvey, both 20, and Terrance Aeriel, 18. Terrance's sister, Natasha Aeriel, 19, was shot in the head but survived.

It was certainly a busy and memorable year in gay news. From ongoing fallout over the 2006 resignation of gay Rep. Mark Foley to the excitement surrounding the Democratic takeover of Congress to the Sen. Larry Craig scandal to the divisive ENDA debate and collapse of hate crimes legislation, there was no shortage of material to fill these pages.

It's impossible to predict what will resonate with readers or what kinds of gay news will be picked up by mainstream outlets. Two stories the Blade covered in 2007 that were received very differently illustrate the "lightning-in-a-bottle" phenomenon and just how frustrating it can be to work in media these days.

Back in May, I wrote a short blog item for the Blade's website urging gays to boycott the new "Hairspray" film because the lead role — originated by the inimitable Divine — was being played by John Travolta, the nation's second-most-prominent Scientologist. In the interest of avoiding another round of death threats, let's just say Scientology has a "complicated" history when it comes to its treatment of gays.

There was no reaction to that initial blog post. Six weeks later, MSNBC gossip scribe Jeanette Walls stumbled upon it and led her column with it. The headline claimed that "gays" were boycotting the film. The ensuing media craze included coverage in the Los Angeles Times, New York Times, an appearance on "O'Reilly Factor," endless blog posts and international stories as the movie opened abroad.

I don't think any story we've ever covered has generated that amount of attention. In fact, it continues to make headlines. The film's producer, John Waters, one of my favorite filmmakers, resurrected the "controversy" just last week in an interview with Canada's Ottawa Express newspaper.

"There was one gay activist [Washington Blade editor Kevin Naff], and it got him national attention," Waters said. "He was at the Baltimore premiere and was too cowardly to even come over and say anything to me. I thought it was ridiculous. If John Travolta is a Scientologist, I don't care what he does. Are we going to police the religions of our cast? If [Travolta] was really homophobic, he would've had a heart attack working [on Hairspray] since there were so many gay people working on this film. Really, I want to thank [Naff] because I couldn't think of a way to make Hairspray controversial."

A few quick replies. First, I'm not an activist. Second, I never sought national attention. Most of the news stories were written by reporters who never bothered to call me. Third, I did not attend the premiere. I was at a nearby restaurant where I bought a drink for the film's director, Adam Shankman. I never saw Waters that night and am certainly not afraid of him. And fourth, I have never suggested Travolta is homophobic. That's Waters' way of dodging the issue of Scientology's record on gays.

In sharp contrast to the hysteria of the "Hairspray" saga, the story of three teens shot and killed execution-style in Newark, N.J., was met with irresponsible silence by the national media.

It didn't start out that way. The killings were a natural topic for national TV shows — "if it bleeds, it leads" — and all the networks reported on the tragedy of four college-aged kids shot on a playground (one survived). It evolved into one of those "sign of the times" stories the sanctimonious cable network anchors love to milk for ratings.

But shortly after the national media's attention moved on to other pressing issues like Britney Spears' weight or Paris Hilton's jail sentence, the Blade began investigating the Newark killings as a possible anti-gay hate crime. A mainstream reporter tipped us off, claiming his employer — a major TV network — balked at covering the gay angle and alleging a police cover-up.

After several weeks spent interviewing those close to the case, we published a front-page story asserting that one or more of the victims was gay and that they were targeted because of their sexual orientation. The police claim the motive for the grisly murders — the full details of which we have declined to publish — was robbery. But multiple sources told the Blade's Lou Chibbaro Jr. that the teens' wallets, jewelry and cell phones were found at the crime scene. The robbery motive is dubious at best.

Then came the revelation that one of the suspects went to high school with one of the victims. It doesn't take brilliant detective work to imagine a scenario in which the suspect spots a former classmate he perceived to be gay and instigates a confrontation. The victims were also reportedly headed to a Black Pride event in New York the next day.

After enduring the absurd and over-the-top attention generated by "Hairspray," I naively assumed the national TV networks would see the Blade story and jump at pursuing this new and disturbing twist.

Instead, they ignored it. Except for a handful of bloggers, no one wanted to touch the story, which was complicated by issues of sexual orientation and race. The New York Times only recently addressed the issue in a fleeting reference. Otherwise, mainstream outlets abdicated their journalistic responsibilities to a few bloggers who pursued it as far as they could. But the real power of bloggers lies in their ability to call attention to issues being ignored by the masses and the media. In this case, the media were actively boycotting the story and so no amount of blogger finger-wagging would move them.

The contrast between the Newark killings and the "Hairspray" boycott illustrates the media's obsession with celebrity and its fear of dealing honestly with issues of race and sexual orientation.

Hounding Don Imus out of a job is easy and politically correct, as is dutifully following Al Sharpton and Jesse Jackson around Jena, La. But holding elected officials and the police accountable for their investigations into the deaths of three young kids proved too uncomfortable.

It's my biggest disappointment and frustration of 2007. Three kids are dead and another barely survived the tragic events of that night. It's Matthew Shepard times three. Maybe if they were white the world would know more about their story. They deserve better.

"An Epiphany in Rosedale," April 27, 2011

Transgender inclusion in the gay rights movement was never a given the way it is today and arriving at that place of "LGB" and "T" together in one acronym took decades of work by committed transgender activists who too often fought in the shadows of the better-funded and slightly more accepted gays and lesbians. My own commitment to trans equality is rooted not just in my beliefs about social justice, but also in my relationships with actual trans people. One of my Blade colleagues, Danielle King, became a friend and confidant and I admired her courage in living an unapologetic life of authenticity. I remember walking with Danielle into our new offices in the National Press Building in D.C. That building — and its esteemed National Press Club — were long a bastion of straight, white, cis, male journalists. Indeed, walking through the lobby, you pass a series of plaques commemorating various well-known journalists, nearly all of them white and male. So when the Blade moved its offices there, it felt momentous. An LGBTQ publication taking up residence in this shrine to straight, white maledom. And even more empowering, a Black transgender woman walking those halls and past those plaques each day felt like we had achieved something akin to walking on the Moon. Moreover Danielle was no junior staffer; she ran our classified division and was responsible for a large percentage of the Blade's revenue (long before Craigslist and other sites decimated print classifieds).

And so when the story of a Baltimore County transgender woman being beaten nearly to death in a McDonald's broke, I knew I had to cover it. I drove to the neighborhood where a rally was planned and couldn't believe my eyes: It seemed the entire working class community had turned out to support and rally around one of its own, who just happened to be transgender. A sign of hope and progress, for sure.

Earlier this week, I attended the rally for Chrissy Lee Polis in a Rosedale, Md., McDonald's parking lot along with about 300 others and was immediately struck by the upbeat vibe.

Polis, a transgender woman, was beaten inside the restaurant last week after attempting to use the women's restroom; the incident captured national headlines after an employee recorded the beating rather than coming to Polis' aid and posted the video to YouTube.

Polis' mother described the rally as a "wonderful night." Mary Washington, a lesbian member of the Maryland House of Delegates, said it was an "LGBT moment." Indeed, something about that night felt transformative; it was as if the fight for transgender visibility and acceptance was coming together in Rosedale, of all places. We weren't in the Castro or Dupont or Chelsea. We were standing in working class Baltimore County surrounded by locals who wanted to show the world that their neighborhood supports Chrissy and won't tolerate violence against one of their own. They weren't going to let that YouTube video forever define their community.

It's unfortunate that members of the Maryland Senate who killed a transgender rights bill just a week before the attack couldn't be bothered to show up. If they had, I'm confident they could never cast a vote against trans equality again. Let's hope this tragedy brings momentum to finally add gender identity to the state's nondiscrimination laws.

"One life ended and one forever changed," May 22, 2014

This feature story I wrote for the Blade took months to organize and began with letters back and forth to Brian Meegan, a gay, HIV-positive inmate in Delaware serving 15 years for killing a fellow gay man in Rehoboth Beach, Del. Meegan was a bartender who got drunk on his shift, then drove home and struck and killed one of his gay patrons from the bar. I'm including this piece because it touches on several issues important to the community, including the treatment of HIV-positive inmates and the widespread problem of alcoholism and the threat posed by drinking and driving.

REHOBOTH BEACH, DEL. — Before Brian Meegan left for work on June 30, 2012, he updated his Facebook status, "Working [a] double today, ready for Super July Fourth Week."

The double shift bartending at the L Bar was long, extending from afternoon happy hour to past close at 1 a.m. and there was a promotion that day. Representatives from a vodka company were on hand promoting new flavors and cocktails and Meegan joined in, downing shots throughout his shift.

Even though he had two previous arrests for driving under the influence, Meegan left work early in the morning and climbed into his 2003 Jeep Wrangler. He turned left onto Rehoboth Avenue, headed for Route 1 when he hit what he thought was a bicycle from a nearby bike shop. For a moment, he couldn't see anything through the windshield but kept driving, finally pulling over in a CVS parking lot nearby. He got out and noticed a bike stuck in the wheel well and tried to pull it out when he was spotted by police.

Meegan had struck a fellow gay man and one of the L Bar's patrons that night, Russell Henman, 44. The impact sent Henman onto the hood and windshield of the car. He was carried 400 feet before the Jeep struck a curb, sending Henman onto the road. He died at the scene.

Meegan's blood-alcohol level was nearly three times the legal limit; he was charged with first-degree vehicular homicide and driving under the influence, pleaded guilty and sentenced to 15 years with a chance to reduce the sentence to eight-and-a-half years by completing a drug and alcohol rehabilitation program in prison.

Nearly two years after that tragic night, Meegan is serving his time at the Sussex Correctional Institution in Georgetown, Del., and is one of the only openly gay men at the facility. He granted the Washington Blade his first interview to discuss the events of that night and what he hopes to do with his life during and after prison.

There are conflicting versions of exactly what happened at the L Bar that night and lingering concerns about the problem of drunk driving in Rehoboth and the safety of busy Route 1. Some of Henman's friends remain angry that Meegan was allowed to drink alcohol while working; others are frustrated with Delaware officials for not making safety improvements to Route 1 in the wake of the crash.

Meegan touched on a wide array of topics during about two hours of interviews, conducted in prison with Meegan wearing a white Department of Correction jumpsuit and handcuffed to the cinderblock wall of a private office. He'd had no visitors in prison, until this interview.

"I wouldn't want to be anyplace else," Meegan said, "because I killed someone. It was one of the Ten Commandments I thought I could never commit."

He continued, "This is someone I never knew, someone who had never done anything to me or anyone I know and I never met and I have no animosity for. There's no way to ever take it back, to make it better; there's nothing you could ever do. I remember watching TV afterwards and something was funny and I was laughing and I just felt horrible because that's something he could never do again."

Asked if he had anything to say to Henman's family and friends, Meegan replied, "I really hope this article doesn't hurt them. I don't want to hurt them more than I already have. There is nothing to say. I hate the fact that it doesn't change how people drink and drive. It doesn't stop us. ... To his family I should just be dead. I want to hide and for them to never remember who I am. I don't think anyone wants to hear from me."

To the gay community in Rehoboth, Meegan offers a piece of advice: "Get a designated driver and stick to it. The first thing to go is your judgment. If my story stops one person from drinking and driving, then it's worth telling."

Meegan said he didn't know Henman and doesn't remember seeing him in the bar that night. He also said he has no idea how much he drank that day, but that it was a lot.

"It was not unusual for bartenders to drink," he said.

But John Meng, the L Bar's co-owner, denied that Meegan was drinking during his shift.

"Brian was not drunk," Meng told the Blade in an interview last year. "We have video of him at work. I don't understand what the State Police said. He was not drinking while on his shift."

Meegan disputes Meng's assertions and said definitively, "I was drinking."

Some of Henman's friends questioned why Meegan was allowed to drink on the job, but there's nothing in Delaware law that prohibits bartenders from consuming alcohol while working.

"There's nothing that says they can't," said Robert Kracyla, deputy director of Delaware Alcohol & Tobacco Enforcement. He noted that legislation would not be required to make it illegal for bartenders to drink on the job. Such a rule could be enacted by the Alcoholic Beverage Control Commission.

Kracyla said there was no fine or penalty assessed against the L Bar for what happened the night Henman was killed.

"We conducted a full investigation," Kracyla said. "We were not able to move forward with enough to issue a violation on our end. We did a parallel investigation to the police but there was not enough forensic evidence."

Delaware is not a dram shop state. Such laws allow for the criminal prosecution of a bar owner or anyone who provides alcohol to someone who causes injury or death as a result. Meegan was not interviewed as part of the investigation as he invoked his Miranda rights against self-incrimination, according to Kracyla.

One issue that remains unclear is whether the company promoting its vodka that night violated a rule about giving away alcohol for free. Meegan said representatives of the company gave him the vodka he consumed. Meegan identified the company as Absolut, but the Blade could not confirm that account.

"According to Alcohol Beverage Control rules you can't give away alcohol, so if that was going on that would be a violation," Kracyla said.

The L Bar, which catered to a gay clientele, has since closed and been replaced by a dance club that appeals to a mixed crowd. Meng and his business partner retain ownership of the building, though they are not operating the new club, called Dive.

"Meegan had a DUI and came back to work unsupervised and was allowed to drink, that's one thing I'm angry about," said Barbara Kessler, 56, a close friend of Henman's. "From a business point of view, the bar should have done something to intervene."

Kessler and her husband, Steve, 59, live part-time in Rehoboth. They met Henman at a popular area Mexican restaurant, Dos Locos, listening to live music, and quickly became close friends, with Henman regularly staying at their home.

"He was the biggest-hearted guy in the world," she said. "He loved his family and was utterly devoted to his mother."

Henman had two brothers who have families of their own and he lived with his mother in Snow Hill, Md. "He used to always say, 'I'm going to take care of my mom,'" Kessler added. Henman had always dreamed of owning a place in Rehoboth and just eight weeks before he died had purchased a trailer there, she said.

"He was loving life, this was going to be his summer, he had his own place to call home," Kessler said. "It was so unfair it was snatched from him."

Asked about Meegan's sentence, Kessler said, "I feel bad for his situation but he killed my best friend. I don't know what to think of that. I miss Russ every day. I feel for Brian's family having a son who went to the dark side. I've forgiven him, it doesn't bring Russ back to hate him."

Her husband Steve echoed other friends who said they hope Meegan will find help while in prison.

"It's a confounding thing that people can have so many DUIs and remain on the road," he said. "To drag him and then drive away, we were distraught over that. I don't know what's fair but nothing brings Russ back. I hope he uses prison to turn his life around."

Barbara Kessler said Henman's mother has decided against pursuing a civil lawsuit against the L Bar. "She said 'we're not the type of people that sue, nothing can be gained from it,'" Kessler recalled.

Meegan moved to Rehoboth in May 2012 from Fort Lauderdale. He had never been to Rehoboth before but said he met some people from the area in Florida who encouraged him to visit. He was arrested six weeks before Henman was killed on a DUI charge in Rehoboth after he said he backed into another car in the L Bar parking lot.

"The other guy wanted a police report," Meegan said. "He called the cops and they did sobriety tests and I got arrested for a DUI."

In 2005, Meegan was arrested in New York on a DUI charge. He said he drove 20-30 miles out of his way on the Southern State Parkway in Long Island, headed in the opposite direction of his intended destination.

"That's one of those moments when, as a drinker, you delude yourself," he said. "You should say, 'I'm an alcoholic' and instead you say 'Wow, I'm a really great driver.' It scared me then, but it didn't last."

He was sentenced to attend driving classes but received no jail time.

Meegan, 39, grew up in Garden City, N.Y., a small town of 22,000 mostly white residents about 20 miles from Manhattan. A 2007 estimate put the median income for a family there at more than $160,000. It's a wealthy enclave and a privileged place to grow up.

"One thing about rich white suburban kids is that we drink," Meegan said. "Drinking was fun especially if you feel awkward."

After high school, Meegan pursued a degree in marine sciences at the University of Miami but dropped out in 1994 after just one year. He said he wanted to come out to his father but feared being cut off financially as a result. His mother discovered he's gay in high school, but Meegan said they kept it from his father. He dropped out and became independent so his father wouldn't have financial control over his life.

"My Dad didn't want me to go through the struggles associated with being gay," Meegan said. "He was afraid of me getting HIV and he still doesn't know I'm positive."

The pressure of fitting in and feeling "awkward" is something Meegan said he experienced again later in life when he came out as gay.

"Going into the gay community is like going through adolescence again," he said. "So you feel like a 13-year-old awkward kid again and now you're legally able to drink and it helps."

Looking back, Meegan now says that dropping out of school was one of the biggest mistakes he made. After leaving school and coming out to his father he spent some time in Miami working as a bartender, then moved to New York City. That period began a spiral of destructive behavior, including drug abuse, prostitution and stripping that spun out of control. There were years spent following the gay party scene — Miami, Fort Lauderdale and Aspen in the winters and Fire Island and Provincetown in the summers.

He also found work as a model, which ironically led to more problems with his self-esteem.

"I was not a cool kid," he said. "Suddenly to be a bartender and model and to be sought after by people was hard for me. I'm a geek who's fat with braces and bifocals and now people want to pay me $7,000 to stand in front of a camera."

He turned to alcohol and drugs to cope, a strategy familiar to many in the LGBT community, which suffers disproportionately high rates of alcoholism and drug addiction, according to the Centers for Disease Control and Prevention.

"When you start doing the bartending and acting and modeling, they are scenes that are very big on drinking and drugs so it just becomes part of a normal life, you don't think of it as this seedy lifestyle," Meegan said. "You're not going to the back alley to get these things."

In 2001, just after the terrorist attacks of Sept. 11, Meegan returned to the city from Fire Island to check on an ex-boyfriend who lived near the towers. His friend was OK but on that same day, Meegan said he received an email from a former client of his prostitution services informing him that he was HIV positive and urging Meegan to get tested. A few weeks later he did and learned he, too, was positive.

"At the time, HIV was more of a death sentence," he recalled. "I obliterated my feelings [with alcohol] so I don't remember that time very well."

Crystal meth soon became his drug of choice.

"I drank for confidence and comfort, then I met meth," he said. "I was thin, felt sexy, had energy to do everything I wanted. I could clean, cook, do laundry, have sex, spend time at the beach and work because I barely slept."

In 2007, he said he started to gain weight and to sleep on meth and that's when he knew he was doing too much and quit on Aug. 4, 2007, cold turkey. His weight ballooned to 250 pounds and he continued to drink.

"My ex dumped me for weighing 250 pounds but he was supportive of me quitting drugs," he said.

Meegan's peripatetic existence eventually led him to Rehoboth, another gay-popular resort town.

Henman loved Rehoboth, according to friends, and he saved money for five years to purchase his first place in 2012.

"As Rusty got more enamored with Rehoboth he wanted to see if he could swing a place on his own," said Brian Gray, 46, a close friend and part-time Rehoboth resident. "He bought a camper and was renting space and was talking about buying a permanent mobile home."

Friends describe him as fun loving, someone who appreciated an over-the-top gesture and who enjoyed entertaining, spending weekends with friends and especially karaoke.

"He lived a simple life but would give you the shirt off his back," Gray said. "He loved Rehoboth, karaoke, Rigby's, he loved Purple Parrot, anywhere with karaoke. He loved music and he liked to sing."

Henman worked for about 25 years as a loan officer at PNC Bank and was single when he died. He adored his dog Maddy.

"He always did things by the book," said Bryan Hecksher, another close friend. "His heart was as big as he was. He loved to cook and to do crafts. I used to joke with him that 'I'm not that gay,'" he said laughing. "I really miss his Facebook posts on what he made for dinner. I used to look forward to those every night and would comment on them."

In a small town like Rehoboth, everyone crosses paths with everyone else eventually. Hecksher knew Meegan from the L Bar and even picked him up from the police station after his first Rehoboth DUI arrest in May 2012.

"I made him promise not to do it again," Hecksher said. "People cared for Brian too. I don't hate Brian Meegan but I don't understand his actions. You can call a cab or call a friend — he could have called me. He had plenty of choices."

Gray, meanwhile, was with Henman on the night he died and even offered him a ride home just minutes before he was killed. Earlier in the evening, he was at Henman's home for a cookout and the two decided to go to the L Bar. When the bar closed at 1 a.m., they walked to 7-Eleven, ordered a pizza and sat in a nearby park talking and eating. Gray recalled that Henman talked about his family and his young niece in particular. After about an hour in the park, Gray said they walked back to the L Bar, where Henman had left his bike. Gray said Henman turned on his bike's safety blinkers and invited him to breakfast in the morning.

"I offered to drive him and put his bike in my car and he said no," Gray said. "He rode into town most evenings and felt safe doing that. He avoided Route 1."

Gray insists neither he nor Henman was intoxicated. Other friends said Henman wasn't a big drinker. Meegan, on the other hand, appeared drunk, Gray said. He said he and Henman observed other customers in the L Bar buying shots for Meegan.

"His eyes were bloodshot," Gray said. "He seemed under the influence of something. You never see that happen at the Blue Moon — you don't see bartenders drinking. All of the bartenders were doing shots that night."

Gray said he followed Henman for a short distance, then drove home. It was only minutes later that Meegan pulled out of the parking lot.

"I texted him the next morning about breakfast and there was no response," Gray said.

Meegan said he remembers very little about what happened.

"I thought I hit the curb, I couldn't see out the windshield," he said. "The police were adamant that I must have known but I didn't. I remember the police being very upset that I wasn't more upset. I had one cop tell me, 'I've had people arrested for shoplifting and they're crying,' but I was in shock."

Despite his lengthy sentence, Meegan said he doesn't regret pleading guilty. The prosecutor sought six years in prison, but in February 2013, Judge Richard Stokes sentenced him to 15 years, reduced to 8.5 years upon completion of the "Key" program, a drug and alcohol treatment program. "The judge decided to make an example of me," Meegan said.

Today, Meegan's days are spent reading, writing and serving food in the prison cafeteria. Early on, he described fits of crying at night. Now he survives by isolating himself from other inmates and writing. As an openly gay man, he knows there are constant risks to his personal safety. He said he endures frequent anti-gay slurs from inmates. "Sometimes the corrections officers chime in, too."

"I'm upfront about being gay," he said. "When someone new starts talking to me, I tell them right away because just for talking to me, people are going to hate you."

Even the lone minister at Sussex Correctional preaches against homosexuality, he said. "The only minister who comes in every Sunday is against it and I have people saying things like 'God bless you, fucking faggot,'" he said. Meegan has stopped attending services but has maintained contact with his former Episcopalian minister from New York, who did not respond to a Blade inquiry.

Despite the abuse, Meegan seems to have found a purpose in coming out behind prison walls — a purpose inspired by Rusty Henman. Meegan said Henman's mother talked at the trial about her son's advocacy work for LGBT and other charitable causes.

"I think my sentence here is to make it easier for the next generation," he said. "I know some people in here who are in their 20s and have long sentences and are gay and they hide it. They won't talk to me because it would implicate them. They're worse to me than other inmates. If I can make people understand that being gay isn't this horrible thing ... maybe that could help."

He added that he prays for Henman's mother every night and has even talked to Rusty in prison.

Although he's out as gay, Meegan said the inmates do not know he's HIV positive. He lies to them about the daily medication he takes when they ask, "What's the Skittles you're getting?" He's been positive for 13 years and his health is good, he said. He attends weekly Alcoholics Anonymous meetings.

Henman's friends seem satisfied with the sentence and hopeful that Meegan will turn his life around after prison.

"I hope he uses this time to change his core behavior," said Hecksher. "I think the sentence was fair and will give him time to reflect."

Gray echoed that sentiment.

"People make mistakes in life," Gray said. "Hopefully he'll have an opportunity to take care of the alcohol problem he has. He's being punished and hopefully when he gets out he'll be a changed person."

Barbara Kessler urged forgiveness. "I think he's hurting also," she said. "You have to find forgiveness in your heart, otherwise it'll eat you up."

Another thing they agree on: Sussex County needs to improve pedestrian safety on Route 1, especially the spot where the highway intersects with the main road leading into downtown Rehoboth and the service road where Henman died.

"What's tragic is that two years later, we're still working on ideas for improving safety on Route 1," Hecksher said. "Something should be done."

Gray said there are plenty of ideas for improving safety, including construction of a jersey wall at the accident site to better insulate the service road from Route 1. In addition, he noted the lack of crosswalks in the area and said a seasonal shuttle should be expanded to year-round service.

"Absolutely nothing has been done to improve safety on Route 1," he said. "How many people have to die for Sussex County to wake up and do something?"

The other fear they share is of drunk drivers, especially in summer, which arrives unofficially this week with Memorial Day celebrations.

"In Rehoboth, I worry all the time about drinking and driving," Hecksher said.

In prison, Meegan has settled into a new routine and he worries that as life goes on, he will forget the details of what he did that put him there.

"We have a very easy time of disassociating," Meegan said. "Something I thought I would never stop thinking about every single day, in here, there are days when you forget completely now, which feels horrible the next day when I remember it. How could I do that and now it's becoming a distant memory, which feels horrible."

The memory remains fresh for the friends and loved ones left behind.

"One life ended and one is forever changed," said Hecksher. "One careless move left a huge void in the whole community."

"Why I Marched in Baltimore," April 30, 2015

The death of Freddie Gray was another in a seemingly endless list of Black men and women who have died in police custody. The Blade covers these stories for a couple of reasons. First, they're important and the LGBTQ population intersects with every other population. So, violence committed against Black Americans is violence committed against LGBTQ Americans. Second, the LGBTQ community knows a thing or two about police violence. Think Stonewall. The very first issue of the Blade in October 1969, just four months after the Stonewall Rebellion, featured a story about police in Dupont Circle writing down the license plate numbers of cars that spend too much time in the area known as popular with gays. It is a testament to our progress — following a lot of hard work by dedicated leaders like Brett Parson — that today, the D.C. Metropolitan Police force is recognized as a leader in community outreach and affirming policies in policing. From those early days in the 1950s and '60s of police harassment and raids on our bars, to the fearful '80s when police and fire departments would avoid the homes of AIDS patients, our road to a better relationship with the police is long and fraught. From those dark days to now, when the Blade routinely collaborates with local police jurisdictions to help solve anti-LGBTQ hate crimes or find missing persons, we have seen dramatic change. But this piece reminds us that the work is far from finished.

As a journalist, I'm not supposed to protest or become involved in activism, but the events of this week in Baltimore are too personal and wrenching to watch from the sidelines.

I grew up in Columbia, Md., one of the early James Rouse "pioneers" who never saw race as an issue. In Columbia, we had Black friends and neighbors and teachers; I took my Black best friend to prom and no one thought twice about it.

Columbia occupies an enviable location between Washington and Baltimore, and, growing up, I cultivated a deep appreciation and love for both cities. My early memories of Baltimore involve Orioles games at Memorial Stadium and trips to downtown before Harborplace was built. Before they tore down Memorial Stadium, I was among the first in line to purchase and salvage two of the stadium seats — one for me and another that I restored for my brother. Our shared love of baseball was born in that stadium.

Years later, after college and a stint in New York City, I moved to Baltimore and fell in love all over again. The authenticity of Baltimore is hard to match and residents have a collective feeling of being in this together. Sure, I've been robbed and my car has been broken into. But such is life in urban America anywhere. My partner and I bought a house. I worked for the Baltimore Sun. And tutored inner city kids in reading. And served on the board of Live Baltimore, a nonprofit that advocates for homeownership in the city. I've led seminars in D.C., urging Washingtonians to move north and buy in Baltimore — it's cheaper! I was always a Baltimore booster — cheering the Ravens and Orioles and cringing when "The Wire" became a phenomenon. On a trip to Honduras a few years ago, a local we met recoiled in horror when I told her we were from Baltimore. "It's SO dangerous there," she exclaimed. That sentiment has been echoed countless times by gays in D.C., as I've worked at the Blade since 2002. I've always ignored all the judgments and snobbish remarks and the turned-up noses because I know that Baltimore is something special and I don't care about the stigma.

And then this week happened. It began with Facebook posts from friends working downtown. Law firms and accounting firms were closing at 3 p.m. Downtown traffic was snarled early, as the suburbanites were desperately fleeing the chaos that hadn't even begun yet. What did they know that the rest of us didn't?

Then the protests, or at least the TV images of what looked like protests, began. We'd later learn that innocent school kids were prevented from going home — their buses boarded and emptied by police, their Metro stops closed down. They were stranded, confused and afraid. And they finally snapped and lashed out. As the violence erupted, I watched Mondawmin Mall — where I do my Target shopping — looted and vandalized and wondered along with CNN's Wolf Blitzer, "Where are the police?" Then it got worse — fires, police cars trashed, journalists assaulted. The mayor and police commissioner were MIA for hours. The newly elected governor made belated excuses about waiting to hear from Stephanie Rawlings-Blake. His phone doesn't dial out? And Rawlings-Blake, who clearly underestimated the need for help on Monday, then overreacted and has kept in place an infantilizing curfew that only hurts local small businesses and their many employees. Her City Hall office has become a military encampment — barricades, machine-gun toting troops, military vehicles. If she feels she needs all of that to be mayor then perhaps she's in the wrong job.

On Monday, we needed help and security. But after the energy of Monday subsided and the dust settled, it became immediately clear that the young people were trying to show us something. They are in pain and feel abandoned. They are attempting to learn in schools with inadequate heat and air conditioning and outdated textbooks. They have no after-school options — no jobs, no playgrounds, no community centers. It's time the grownups woke up.

On Thursday, I sat in City Café, a restaurant in Mount Vernon that I've frequented for 20 years and listened as the couple next to me talked ignorantly about the events of the week. The staff fretted about lost wages thanks to the curfew. The TV above the bar was tuned to CNN and there were scenes of protesters making their way up Charles Street, directly toward us. The couple next to me panicked, paid up and fled; I paid up and headed out to join the marchers.

An older Black man spotted me on the curb and motioned for me to join him, which I gladly did. The marches are entirely peaceful; the marchers mostly Black, but multi-racial, young and old. We chanted, "All night all day, we will fight for Freddie Gray." And my personal favorite, "We love Baltimore, we want peace!" A tear ran down my cheek as I wondered if all my years of pulling for Baltimore, of trying to contribute and do the right thing, had really mattered at all.

CNN's cameras panned the crowd and three helicopters hovered overhead, no doubt anxiously waiting for us to start smashing windows so they'd have a better story and bigger ratings.

My feelings remain conflicted. I disagree with violence as a means to any end. My brother is a cop. My brother-in-law is in the National Guard and was deployed to downtown Baltimore. They've been put in an untenable position thanks to years of shitty government policies that have decimated America's middle class and shipped our jobs overseas. Of course there are bad apples in the police force, but they are rare and the depictions of them as killers are just as wrong and dangerous as the depictions of Black youth as "thugs," an offensive, racially charged term used by even President Obama and the Baltimore mayor. Demonizing the police erodes public trust in the most fundamental pillars of our society. It must stop. We should prosecute the bad apples without indicting the legions of good cops who risk their lives to keep us safe.

I'm heartbroken by what's happening to my city. People don't break their own spines — no one is buying that. The police and state's attorney need to expedite their investigations and make the results public.

It's time for the National Guard to go home. It's time for the Orioles to play ball — at home. I read the Tweet from John Angelos, son of O's owner Peter Angelos. It was nice. What would be nicer is for the O's to play the Tampa series in Baltimore and for the Angelos family to donate all the proceeds to the neediest schools in the city.

The kids had their say and now the adults must step up. Each of us who lives here must find a way to contribute to the solution. We can be mentors or tutors; we can donate money or time. Call the school nearest to you and find out what they need. If you own a business, reach out to underserved communities the next time you're hiring. If you give money, look around your own city before cutting checks to out-of-town charities. On Election Day, SHOW UP! How many city officials are elected by a tiny minority of voters? You'd be surprised.

And if you're white and watching the events of this week unfold from the comfort of home on CNN, get off your ass and join the marches. Meet your neighbors and show them solidarity. You never know when you might need someone to march for you.

"A TRIBUTE TO GAY BARS," JUNE 14, 2016

I was lying in bed on Sunday, June 12, 2016, about to get up and head out for a long day working the Blade's booth at the annual Capital Pride festival, the most important day of celebration for the LGBTQ community of the year. My phone was blowing up with texts that I was struggling to ignore, desperate for a few extra minutes of sleep. Finally, I picked it up. "You need to check CNN!" came one message. I turned on the TV and saw the first images of Orlando's Pulse nightclub after the massacre that killed 49 mostly LGBTQ people. At first, CNN reported the body count as a dozen. Then 20. When it hit 30, I knew we were watching one of the most significant events in our movement's history unfold before our eyes. And on Pride weekend. We scrambled to respond; one Blade reporter, Michael K. Lavers, headed for the airport and flew immediately to Orlando. The rest of our reporting team worked the story. Our marketing director agonized over our booth at the festival — was it appropriate to celebrate and decorate a booth on this horrific day? We pivoted and printed signs expressing solidarity with our Orlando brothers and sisters. That night, with the death toll at 49, the worst mass shooting in U.S. history at that point, I booked a flight to Orlando on Monday morning. I wrote these next two pieces in response to the violent

violation of our sacred space that occurred in Orlando. With the November 2022 mass shooting at Club Q in Colorado Springs that killed five LGBTQ people, these essays take on renewed relevance. In December 2022, the Department of Homeland Security issued a terror threat bulletin warning that domestic extremists were ecstatic over the Club Q shooting and likely planning copycat attacks. In response, gay bars across the country were forced to boost security.

The world watched in horror this week as the proudly resilient LGBT community here coped with unthinkable tragedy.

Sadly, our community has a lot of experience with such things.

From the AIDS crisis in which we fought an indifferent government and hostile neighbors. To an untold number of previous attacks on our bars and clubs, including the 1973 firebombing of the UpStairs Lounge in New Orleans that killed 32 gay men. To enduring the playground taunts and everyday slurs that go along with being "different" in this country.

We were horrified, too, about what happened at Pulse, though not as shocked as our straight counterparts. They will never know what it's like to walk through life with a permanent target on your back. To pause before each touch; to hesitate before exchanging a hug or kiss with a partner or spouse. To calculate before coming out at work. To endure the judgmental stares when checking in at a hotel or booking a restaurant reservation on Valentine's Day. To walk around the block, scanning the scene before mustering the nerve to walk into a gay bar. To be insulted, mocked, beaten up just for loving someone of the same sex. We've all been there.

So much has been written in recent years about this "post-gay" world in which we supposedly live. A world in which there's no need for LGBT-identified spaces like bars, clubs, coffee shops, bookstores and, yes, newspapers, because we're "integrated" and "accepted" now.

What happened in Orlando is a heartbreaking reminder that there's no such thing as "post-gay," and that our spaces are sacred. Where outsiders see only a bar or club, we see a community center or the place where we formed our closest friendships or met our significant others. Our bars and clubs have played a heroic role in supporting the community, serving as gathering places in times of triumph and tragedy and helping to raise countless dollars to fund our causes, to fight HIV, to aid our own. When the government turned its back, the first dollars raised to fight AIDS came from the bar and club scene.

The attack in Orlando was an attack on all of us because there's a Pulse in every city in this country. A place where we can let our guard down, be ourselves, embrace our friends and kiss our partners openly. We need those places because regardless of whether you live in Dupont Circle or rural Alabama, there is a risk in engaging in public displays of affection if you're LGBT.

A look at the public response to the Orlando massacre reveals just how much work lies ahead. The Florida governor has tried to erase LGBT identity from the attack. We can't even get validation in death in some quarters. The lieutenant governor of Texas tweeted homophobic Bible verses on the morning of the attack yet somehow still has a job. Last week, before the attack, Rep. Rick Allen (R-Ga.) read a Bible verse on the U.S. House floor that calls for the death of gay people. Shortly after, the House voted overwhelmingly to reject a spending bill that included discrimination protections for LGBT workers.

Even those Republicans who have issued milquetoast statements offering "thoughts and prayers" are left to reconcile those sentiments with their own voting records hostile to LGBT causes. The presumptive GOP nominee for president, whose name I can't bear to include in a tribute to Orlando, claims to care about what happened, yet has pledged to nominate Supreme Court justices committed to overturning the marriage equality ruling.

Hillary Clinton is right — this isn't the time for politics. As we struggle with how to respond to the massacre and to those who would demonize and discriminate against us and cast us back into the closet, we should resist the urge to lash out and respond simply with love.

It's been humbling to be here in Orlando this week, watching members of our community cope with such grace, dignity and determination. They didn't shut down the community center in fear, instead they opened the doors wide to all while working tirelessly to raise money for the victims, collect donations of water and supplies for blood centers overwhelmed by volunteers, negotiate deals with airlines to fly loved ones to town for unexpected funerals and more.

One of the remarkable people I've met here this week, Pastor Brei, said it best:

"Have faith and believe that evil and hate can be eradicated one person at a time. How do you treat someone? How do you embrace someone who treats you wrong? We all bleed, laugh, hope and have great victories and major defeats. And so, you know me, even if you don't know my name — I'm you."

"Will we ever be truly equal?," June 24, 2016

It starts at an early age. Usually in elementary or middle school with kids saying, "That's so gay" in a derogatory manner, uncorrected by parents and teachers.

From there it escalates. To the playground, bus stops and school hallways where LGBT students first encounter overt and violent displays of homophobia and transphobia.

In preparation for college, I've had students ask me if they should self-identify as LGBT on resumes and college applications, whether to list membership in Gay Straight Alliances and other LGBT-specific organizations. Already, the calculating begins.

The process starts anew while hunting for that first job. Yes, even in 2016 — in industries as diverse as finance and construction. Do you come out during the interview process or stay closeted and quiet until you're in the door and getting rid of you would be something of an HR problem?

All that bigotry stoked and affirmed by legions of politicians — mostly Republicans — who have cynically used social issues for decades to court former rural, southern Democrats to the GOP cause on promises of attacking minorities. Abortion restrictions for women. Voter ID laws for African Americans. Immigration restrictions for Hispanics. Marriage bans, bathroom bills and "religious freedom" laws for LGBT people. The Republican establishment may yet live to regret that strategy, which led to short-term success, but that ultimately deposited Donald Trump at their doorstep. After all those bigoted, empty promises to mostly poor white Americans, the GOP failed to stop marriage equality. Or the success of a two-term Black president. Or end abortion or thwart immigration. They failed and those voters finally figured out they were being exploited by a Republican Party that didn't really care much about those issues. Instead of returning America to a 1950s straight/white/Christian utopia for those voters, the GOP exported their jobs overseas and gutted the middle class while enriching their Wall Street masters. So now they're pissed off and prefer the chaos of a Trump administration to four more years of Bush-Romney-McCain status quo.

What does this have to do with Orlando, which will haunt our movement and our nightmares for years to come? Orlando didn't occur in a vacuum. It didn't spring forth from the mind of a crazy, disconnected lone gunman. It took years to nurture that kind of hate. Years of our society tolerating anti-gay name calling and bullying. Years of political attacks on our right to work free of discrimination. Attacks on our right to marry. Or to serve in the military. Decades of messaging from political and religious leaders that we are less than. Second class. Other.

After the Obergefell ruling just one year ago, we got carried away and naively believed we'd won. That everyone loves the gays now.

Every straight couple now has a fun gay couple next door that they barbeque with on the weekends, right? We're finally accepted and equal, right?

Processing Orlando is a struggle. We all know intellectually that the proper response is love — to love those who hate us. To endure the taunts and insults and bullets with a patient smile, knowing we're on the right side of history and that our time will inevitably come.

But the devil on my other shoulder isn't so sure. Will they ever really accept us? Will we ever be truly equal? Are we forever relegated to second-class status? Remember that the Obergefell ruling was decided by a single straight, white guy — Anthony Kennedy — in a 5-4 decision that could just as easily have gone the other way. We thought the courts were catching up to popular opinion, but maybe we got it backward. Maybe the courts are leading the charge and the people aren't ready for the sight of two men kissing after all.

So after years of political and religious messaging that LGBT people don't matter, and fears that "the gays" (as Florida Gov. Rick Scott refers to us) were getting ahead of themselves after Obergefell, the backlash arrives. In the form of "religious freedom" bills. And states defying the Obama administration directive on trans bathroom access. And a gunman targeting one of our sacred spaces for an unprecedented massacre.

I still hope that love will conquer hate. But it's going to take a lot longer than we thought.

"Return to high school," March 30, 2007

I've never met anyone who had an easy time in high school. They are awkward, challenging years for many reasons. But for LGBTQ kids, it's magnified. For me, middle school and the first year of high school were hell. I was the target of a group of neighborhood bullies and involved in many fistfights during those years. They threw rocks at me after getting off the bus. I used to sometimes carry a pocketknife in middle school in case things got too out of control. There were days I pretended to be sick just to avoid the terrifying walk to middle school, never knowing when and where the bullies would emerge hurling their slurs and threats. I was once suspended from school for fighting one of the bullies in gym class; he shoved me, I shoved back, he punched me in the forehead. When my mom found out, she marched into the principal's office and successfully demanded I be reinstated since I was the victim of the unprovoked attack. Ironically, when I look back on those years, I am grateful. In the immortal words of Christina Aguilera, "Thanks for making me a fighter!" In those days, you didn't cry to mom or even to the principal. You didn't call the police; there were no anti-bullying laws. You stood up to the bullies, fought back and if they insulted you, then you insulted them, their mother and their shoes. It wasn't easy and I cried myself to sleep plenty of nights, exhausted and intimidated, but I never gave up. And those formative years led me to a career in social justice, unafraid of standing up to authority. Those experiences made me strong, so I thank the bullies of Skyward Court in Columbia, Md. — you know who you are.

Several recent events have highlighted the plight of gay and lesbian youth in a society that is coping with rapidly changing perceptions of homosexuality.

Just 19 years ago, when I was a high school senior living in Howard County, Md., there were no gay-straight alliances. With very few exceptions, students didn't dare come out as gay. The notion of same-sex marriage seemed a fantasy.

Today, there are GSAs operating throughout the Howard County school system, gay couples are legally marrying in Massachusetts and gay rights issues figure prominently in our national politics and presidential campaigns.

I recently returned to Howard County to speak to the Parents, Family & Friends of Lesbians & Gays chapter there. It was a surreal night, returning to my childhood neighborhood where I long ago grappled with my sexual orientation and fended off bullies as a kid. If someone had told me 20 years ago that I'd be back to deliver a speech on gay rights, I wouldn't have believed it. There was an element of triumph to the evening, but my nerves were fried just the same.

What would I say to a high school student now attending my alma mater? Would they view me as old and irrelevant? Or a loser for spending those early years in the closet?

I met a group of county students, several of whom serve as president of their GSAs. It's difficult to convey how much has changed in 20 years without sounding like a geezer, but I wanted them to understand that the gay rights movement is progressing at a uniquely fast pace and that they shouldn't take for granted the freedoms they have that my generation did not.

The students were not what you might expect. They weren't angry, confrontational, withdrawn or forlorn. During my remarks, they sat quietly while poring over copies of the Blade I'd brought with me. Afterwards, they approached me, clearly surprised by what they'd read, which included the usual tales of anti-gay discrimination and violence that are routinely reported in these pages.

"Wow, there's a lot to be mad about," one student said.

It was refreshing to meet a young person surprised to learn that gays and lesbians can be legally fired from their jobs in most U.S. states. It just doesn't occur to young people that such discrimination would exist — and that it could be legal. Recent polls of this generation confirm that attitudes on homosexuality, and even toward same-sex marriage, are softening dramatically.

After a long Q&A session with the students and their parents (and grandparents), I turned the tables and asked the family members what inspired them to become activists. Many parents eventually accept their gay children (to varying degrees), but it's quite a leap to activism for many.

One father replied that his high school-aged daughter came out as a lesbian. He was OK with it, but was later shocked to learn that his daughter's close friend also came out and that her parents responded by packing her bags and depositing them on the front lawn. It was then he knew he wanted to get involved in PFLAG.

All parents of gay children should attend a PFLAG meeting like this one. It was moving, empowering and a reminder of the struggle that so often accompanies the coming out process.

Unfortunately, GSAs aren't nearly as prevalent in D.C. public schools as they are in neighboring suburban counties. In fact, there is just one GSA currently operating in the city's public school system, though a second is planned at Anacostia Senior High School, where a courageous young lesbian is blazing a trail.

Danielle Staley was elected senior class present at Anacostia Senior High last year — as an out lesbian. Unfortunately, she was recently arrested after being involved in a fight at the school, which she says was instigated by a former girlfriend.

The school's principal Ronald Duplessis, reinstated Staley, 18, after suspending her and threatening to expel her following two fights on March 16. It was the right decision, especially considering Staley's impressive accomplishments. She is a member of the school's varsity volleyball and softball teams and last week was awarded a college scholarship by the Greater Washington Urban League.

Woodrow Wilson High School, in the upper Northwest section of Ward 3, is the only city school that has a GSA, even though the Gay, Lesbian & Straight Education Network says there are more than 3,000 GSAs operating across the country.

It's about time D.C. schools caught up to the rest of the country in establishing these important groups for students. Staley and others working to establish a chapter at Anacostia High deserve much credit and praise for their efforts.

Staley and the students I met in Howard County are the lucky ones. For too many gay and lesbian young people, coming out to their parents leads to eviction from the family home. And as the Blade reported earlier this month, resources for homeless gay youth are scarce.

The National Gay & Lesbian Task Force recently released a study in conjunction with the National Coalition for the Homeless on the plight of gay youth.

Of the 1.6 million homeless youth in the United States, the study estimates that 20-24 percent are gay or transgender, which would mean that more than 500,000 gay youth are homeless.

That's a shocking and unacceptable statistic in a country of gross excess like this one. There are only a handful of shelters across the country specifically for gay youth and federal funding for the problem is on the decline.

"This report underscores what many of us have known for a long time," said Matt Foreman, director of the Task Force. "The national response to this epidemic has been nothing short of disgraceful."

Perhaps in another generation gay youth won't require any federal funding for homeless shelters. In the meantime, it's important to keep up the work for visibility and equality under the law and to recognize the brave efforts of gay teens who are making strides that most of us never dreamed possible.

"Reflections on 40," Oct. 7, 2010

Freaking out about turning 40 feels melodramatic after now passing 50. But I wrote this 40th birthday essay in the immediate aftermath of Tyler Clementi's heartbreaking suicide triggered by bullying and

humiliation by a college roommate who recorded video of Clementi kissing another man in his dorm room. The tragedy received national media attention and put cyberbullying in the spotlight. Tyler's parents founded the Tyler Clementi Foundation, which continues to combat bullying. Tyler's roommate, Dharun Ravi, who set up the video camera and invited friends to watch a private encounter between Tyler and another man, was convicted on 15 counts, including invasion of privacy. He served just 20 days in prison and was not deported. Years later, after a change in New Jersey law, most of those convictions were overturned and Ravi pleaded guilty to a single charge of attempted invasion of privacy, a third-degree felony, and was sentenced to time served. It was just another in a long line of bias-related crimes targeting the LGBTQ community the Blade has covered over the years that led to minimal consequences for defendants. The tales of miscarriages of justice for LGBTQ crime victims would fill an encyclopedia. Prosecutors remain reluctant to invoke hate crimes laws because they fear they won't be able to prove bias-related charges.

I celebrated 40 at home with friends and asked party guests to bring donations for an LGBTQ-affirming homeless shelter in Baltimore in lieu of gifts. We raised $1,500 for the church-run shelter. When I arrived unannounced to drop off the money, the director hugged me and cried. It didn't seem like much money, but our inner city shelters that welcome homeless queer youth are few and strapped.

The milestone that all gay men dread is upon me. I turn 40 on Monday, National Coming Out Day.

It's overwhelming to think about the progress we've made in those 40 years, which have taken us from the dark days of the Stonewall raid to legalized same-sex marriage.

But just when I was ready to pop the Champagne and celebrate 40, a series of teenage suicides reminded us of the distance we've yet to travel. And the events of recent weeks took many of us right back to that childhood playground or bus stop or lunchroom where we were terrorized for being different.

I was one of those kids mercilessly bullied in middle and early high school. I remember vividly the fear, the tears, the suicidal — and sometimes homicidal — thoughts. There were days I snuck a pocketknife into my jacket, just in case things got so bad that I needed a weapon to fend off the bullies. The walk home from school was particularly terrifying — I walked alone and my tormentors would often follow, hurling rocks and anti-gay slurs. Sometimes the fear was so intense that I would feign sick just to avoid a day of the torture.

There was the day I finally snapped, in seventh grade, while being taunted by a kid in gym class. The insults and threats became too much and all the anger rushed out of me; I went after him, throwing punches, kicking and yelling until the teacher pulled me off of him and sent us both to the principal's office. He landed a few blows, including a punch to the face that left me with a huge welt, but I defended myself. And it felt good.

All those memories came flooding back last week as a rash of reports emerged about young kids killing themselves after suffering anti-gay bullying.

Seth Walsh, of Tehachapi, Calif., hanged himself last month in his backyard after enduring anti-gay abuse and bullying. At just 13, Seth was already out to his supportive mother.

Asher Brown, also just 13, from the Houston area, shot himself last month after coming out. He had reported being bullied at his middle school.

Billy Lucas, 15, from Greensburg, Ind., hanged himself on Sept. 9.

Tyler Clementi, the Rutgers freshman who jumped from the George Washington Bridge to his death, was targeted by a roommate who set up a camera in their dorm room and broadcast video of a sexual encounter between Clementi and another man online.

Seth and Asher were out to family members. Asher lives in the Houston area, where the mayor is openly lesbian. Despite the support they found and the visibility of LGBT role models, they ended their lives.

I can't help but take these suicides personally. What's been the point of all these years spent informing and educating readers on these pages if kids are still killing themselves? What progress have we made if young LGBT people would rather end their lives than face that long walk to school? I'm sure I speak for many LGBT activists, politicians, journalists, donors and others connected to the movement when I say that the reason we're engaged in this work is to ensure the next generation won't know the pain of the closet. We focus so much on our legislative battles that we sometimes forget about the battles still happening on the playground.

The public response from our community has been uplifting, from Ellen DeGeneres' moving remarks on her talk show, to the Dan Savage-led "It Gets Better" video campaign. In Greensburg, Ind., where Billy Lucas lived, an organization called "Angels and Doves" put up a billboard to draw attention to the problem of bullying. I didn't have such public role models or expressions of support 30 years ago and many of us suffered in pained silence, incapable of envisioning a day when it would "get better."

But it does. Forty years ago, there were no openly gay kids in my high school. Today, there are thousands of gay-straight alliances operating in high schools — and even middle schools — around the country. We can legally marry in a handful of states; there are out gay politicians at all levels of government and more LGBT representation in media than ever before. As for those bullies, I long ago forgave and even learned to thank them. They forced me to cultivate an inner strength that has served me well ever since.

I don't wish that experience on anyone, but for gay kids reading this, it really does get better. Find someone — a close friend, family member, teacher or guidance counselor — to confide in. If you can't trust anyone, contact the Trevor Project, 866-488-7386 or trevorproject.org, or your local LGBT community center. There's only one way out of the pain and isolation and that's coming out of the closet. If it's not safe to do that, then you must find just one person to talk to. It will begin a slow, gradual process of opening up and coming out that will ease the burden one conversation at a time until one day you discover for yourself that it will not only get better, but that life will get great, filled with love and friendship and family.

And then one day you'll turn 40 and those years of pain and isolation will be long gone and you can cope with other problems. Like wrinkles, hair loss and joint pain.

"Wake Up! Listen to Black Student Protesters," Nov. 18, 2015

This was one of many columns on race I wrote over the years. It references a pivotal ordeal I endured at Penn State while serving as opinions editor of the Daily Collegian in 1992. I published a column by a Black staffer that expressed provocative views on race, including that white people are "devils." We went viral before the term existed. Oprah, Phil, and Geraldo called. The story appeared in just about every newspaper in America. I received death threats from the Klan and offers of police protection. It was insane and followed me for years afterward, costing me a job opportunity at a Pennsylvania newspaper. As difficult as it was to hear myself being attacked on the news ("drug abuser," "crazy"), I learned at a young age the power of the press and how it feels when the world is against you. How hard it can be to fight back. I learned the importance of being fair to sources and accurate in reporting. Mistakes (or intentional sensationalizing) can destroy reputations and lives.

The issue of race relations on college campuses reemerged last week following highly publicized incidents at Yale and the University of Missouri that triggered protests at schools across the country. Much of the reaction and commentary included patronizing remarks that minimized and trivialized the plight of African-American and other minority students navigating life on majority-white campuses.

At Missouri, students protested a string of racist incidents that were largely ignored by administrators, leading to the resignation of University of Missouri System President Tim Wolfe and Columbia campus Chancellor R. Bowen Loftin. They stepped down only after the football team threatened a boycott, jeopardizing lucrative sports revenue for the school. The athletes' brave act of defiance should be a template for students elsewhere looking for creative and effective ways to fight back against apathetic administrators.

Meanwhile, at Yale, a Black undergraduate student claimed that she was barred from a fraternity's "white girls only" party. Sigma Alpha Epsilon denied the report. In another incident, a faculty member was accused of racial insensitivity after defending students' right to wear potentially offensive Halloween costumes. The seemingly isolated incidents at Yale and Mizzou have proven anything but, with solidarity protests being staged across the country.

Leading Republican presidential candidate Donald Trump predictably sided with the status quo. "I think the two people that resigned are weak, ineffective people," he told Fox News. Ben Carson assailed the "politically correct police" for the resignations.

Numerous publications and commentators have weighed in, belittling the students and ignoring the larger issues. This isn't about Halloween costumes or the coddling of spoiled elites who miss their helicopter parents. It's about the disparate treatment of minority students everywhere who face real obstacles to obtaining their education and degrees that are mostly unknown to their white counterparts.

The recent incidents call to mind my own eye-opening experience with race issues as a student at Penn State University in 1992, where I served as editorial page editor for the Daily Collegian student newspaper.

Back then, Penn State saw protests led by Black students decrying low minority enrollment and inadequate efforts by the university to retain minority students. There were sit-ins and street demonstrations. One of my regular columnists, a Black student, penned a column titled, "African Americans should not trust devilish white people." It contained some harsh language and warnings to fellow Black students to bear arms to defend themselves. "White people are irredeemable racists, who have never loved or cared about Black people," he wrote.

The column wasn't the most profound or original take on race, but it certainly reflected the genuine fear and isolation that many Black students felt on campus. One Black friend told me that when traveling to campus from home, he gassed up his car in New York City and didn't stop again until he pulled into his dorm four and a half hours later, ever fearful of having to make an unexpected stop in rural Pennsylvania along the way to State College.

The university was overwhelmingly white, with just 3.1 percent Black enrollment. Many students were from small towns with zero Black population. I had a roommate who had never met a Black person before arriving on campus. When he saw a photo of me with my Black prom date from high school, he said, "You took a Black girl to prom?! What did your parents say?"

Such was the atmosphere for minority students. And so when I edited the column, I knew it would get a lot of attention on campus but I was young and naïve and had no idea the maelstrom that it would trigger. On the day it was published, I received an early morning phone call at my apartment from the newspaper office. "Kevin, you need to get down here. There are protesters picketing the office."

When I arrived, there were two white students pacing in front of my office carrying signs bearing crosshairs that read, "White Man, Shoot Here." It was startling but hardly a mass protest. I dismissed it as minor and went about my day. Later, I got a call from an Associated

Press reporter in Harrisburg who'd heard about the protest. I explained that it was a brief demonstration by just two people. He wrote a story that moved across the AP state wire that night while I was still in the office. Our news editor flagged it for me. It read that our offices were besieged by a "wave of protests" following publication of the column. I was disappointed by the irresponsible sensationalism of the AP writer but it was only the state wire. Not a huge deal. Later that night, the story moved across the national AP wire and appeared in every major newspaper in the country the next morning. All hell broke loose.

The office phones rang incessantly. Penn State administrators denounced us in the media as a "hate publication." Student organizations yanked their advertising. Oprah, Donahue, Sally Jesse and Geraldo called seeking interviews with the author and me. The story was covered by the New York Times, Washington Post, CNN and every media critic and major news outlet. Death threats began arriving to our offices. The author's life was threatened in a flier distributed across campus with a rifle's crosshairs superimposed across his photo. I received a death threat at my apartment from the Ku Klux Klan, which operated in a nearby town. The police visited my office offering protection. Alumni canceled donations to the university and administrators searched for ways to retaliate against the newspaper, which is an independent corporation unaffiliated with Penn State. Professors denounced our actions openly in classes. Collegian staffers were harassed on the streets.

Despite all the fear mongering in the media about us instigating a "race war at Penn State," the only violence we saw came in the form of death threats against newspaper staff. It's surreal to turn on the radio or TV and hear your name being trashed by commentators. I was labeled a "drug addict," "racist," "crazy" and worse. I lost a job offer because of the uproar.

All this because I'd defended a Black staff member who'd written a column from a place of fear and isolation. Yes, he wrote some inflammatory things. But on a college campus, students deserve a wide berth when exploring complicated and emotional issues for the first time on their own. As former Yale University President Benno Schmidt once said, "A university ought to be the last place where people are inhibited by fear of punishment from expressing ignorance or even hate, so long as others are left free to answer."

It was a life-changing experience and I wish every practicing journalist could walk for a day in the shoes of someone being castigated by the national media. It taught me the importance of fairness. Words matter and they can hurt when applied recklessly.

Fast-forward nearly a quarter century, and to my dismay students are still grappling with the same issues of racism and low minority enrollment and retention. Indeed, the list of grievances from University of Missouri students is strikingly similar to a list compiled by students in the 1960s. As the Huffington Post reported last week, "The 1969 list expressed concern about the 'nonchalant attitude on the part of the university,' saying it made it 'a haven for comprehensive institutionalized racist and political repression.' Those feelings were echoed by many protesters this week."

Instead of dismissing these students' concerns, we should listen and help. The condescending response from Trump, the Wall Street Journal editorial board and others ignores the genuine fears of students who face threats of violence and racist epithets — one of which was scrawled in human excrement at Missouri.

Often it's the covert manifestations of racism that sting most, like the indifferent response of administrators and media critics. Or the persistent problems with retaining minority students and faculty at major universities that are instead focused on building multi-billion dollar endowments while neglecting needs of current students.

There are no easy solutions to these entrenched problems, but we've seen the result of propagating the status quo, from Ferguson to Baltimore and beyond. At the very least, we can listen to these students respectfully and engage with them. Football players don't boycott games and students don't initiate hunger strikes for kicks or attention. The problems are real. As Spike Lee implored us in his 1988 film "School Daze," "Wake up!"

"Dear millennials: Please vote," Oct. 9, 2018

The numbers in this piece speak for themselves. Apathy among the American electorate is our greatest enemy and it's especially acute in younger generations. There's a popular meme making the rounds in the wake of the 2022 midterms that if only 50 percent of Americans vote, then Republicans win; if 60 percent vote, then Democrats win; if 65 percent vote, then Democrats win in a landslide; and if 70 percent vote, then the GOP ceases to exist. There's something to that logic. Indeed, when more people vote, fewer wannabe authoritarians get elected. Also, I warned again in this piece that Roe and Obergefell were on the line and urged young people to vote.

If every person inviting me to a protest or to sign a Change.org petition had bothered to vote in 2016, we wouldn't need all these protests and petitions.

The good news from 2016 voting patterns is that the much-maligned millennials voted for Hillary Clinton over Donald Trump by a 55-37 percent margin with 8 percent citing "other/no answer."

The bad news is that barely 50 percent of millennials showed up, more than eight points below the overall turnout of 58 percent, according to the Pew Research Center. Millennials continue to have the lowest voter turnout of any group. Millennials (defined as between the ages of 18-35) comprise a whopping 31 percent of the electorate — the same as the Baby Boomers. But nearly 70 percent of

Boomers voted in 2016, a rate identical to their 2012 turnout. Nearly 63 percent of Gen X voters showed up in 2016.

What's even more ominous as we look to next month's critical mid-term elections is that only 28 percent of millennials say they are "absolutely certain" to vote, according to a summer poll from the Public Religion Research Institute. Another poll from the AP showed that 32 percent of young voters would "certainly vote." By comparison, 74 percent of seniors plan to vote next month.

As Dave Wasserman of the Cook Political Report put it, "Right now the 'blue wave' is being powered by suburban professional women, but to fully capitalize on 2018, Democrats need to energize young voters and voters of color."

One problem for Democrats is that while millennials are more likely to identify as liberals, they are less likely to identify as Democrats, revealing a declining trust in the national political parties.

This is an alarming trend because, like it or not, we are a two-party system. This isn't Europe where fragile coalition governments are frequently formed to secure enough votes for a leader. The time for fanciful voting in the United States comes during the primaries. Sure, feel the Bern; hell, vote for Princess Leia or Kermit the Frog if you want to. But in the general election, it's time to get serious and choose one of the viable major party options. Much was made in 2016 of the millennials' need to be "inspired" by their political leaders. Let's hope they have learned the cynical lesson that our choices are sometimes less inspirational and more practical. But for about 70,000 votes spread across three Midwestern states, 2,000 immigrant children wouldn't be living in cages right now and Brett Kavanaugh would be but an obscure, beer-swilling judge that you never heard of.

The stakes couldn't be higher next month. If the Democrats can't flip the House, then Trump gets another two years of unchecked power. If they can miraculously flip the Senate, then his efforts to take over the judiciary and stock courts with right-wing ideologues can be stopped. A Democratic House can bottle up Trump's legislative agenda, launch full investigations into Russian meddling (and myriad other scandals) and even impeach Trump and Kavanaugh. With the Mueller report expected possibly in the first quarter of 2019, the balance of power in Congress becomes even more important.

Elections have consequences — and Kavanaugh's appointment to the Supreme Court will be the most grave. During his confirmation process, Kavanaugh was grilled by Democratic senators on gay rights issues. He declined to answer specific questions and ominously cited the Masterpiece Cakeshop decision, which happens to be the one ruling that went against gay interests. Kavanaugh's time as staff secretary in the Bush White House is even more troubling, as he refused to answer questions about the push for a Federal Marriage Amendment banning marriage equality. The Trump administration refused to make public Kavanaugh's correspondence from that time. We can safely assume that he argued in favor of such a ban. Kavanaugh has spoken in favor of "religious liberty," which we know to be code for anti-LGBT discrimination.

With Roe and Obergefell in the crosshairs of the right-wing evangelicals who call the shots in this administration, the mid-terms are the only way to stop the country's march backwards.

"WITH FRIENDS LIKE THESE," FEB. 13, 2004

This essay serves as an important reminder that the politicos and organizations we now take for granted as "progressive" and reliable LGBTQ rights supporters were not always so reliable. In 2004, the Washington Post's editorial board backed civil unions instead of full marriage rights for gay couples. And John Kerry endorsed a Massachusetts constitutional ban on same-sex marriage while opposing the same ban at the federal level. Sounds crazy right? Yet, it's true.

So many of our presumed "allies" in the early 2000s were only supportive in private or when it was convenient to solicit votes or, more commonly, financial contributions from wealthy gay donors. When the cameras were rolling, it was a very different story.

Perhaps it was inevitable that the heady days of gay rights victories in the summer of 2003 would give way to the sobering reality of the campaign season in 2004. Last year, Massachusetts Sen. John Kerry, the presumptive Democratic presidential nominee following this week's primary victories in Virginia and Tennessee, proudly announced his support for a range of gay rights issues — from support for the Employment Non-Discrimination Act to opposition of a federal marriage amendment.

This year, with the primary season just about over, it's time to tweak the message for the broader masses and head back to the political center. In an interview this week on National Public Radio, Kerry expressed support for a constitutional amendment banning gay marriage.

His campaign staff quickly reassured a Blade reporter the next day that Kerry was talking about an amendment to the Massachusetts state Constitution and that he maintains his opposition to the federal amendment. Of course the national radio audience that heard Kerry didn't learn of that distinction, because the question was not specifically addressed to the Massachusetts state Constitution and neither was Kerry's answer. It was the second time in recent weeks Kerry has fudged the gay marriage issue. Asked by ABC News after the State of the Union address to respond to President Bush's opposition to gay marriage and his call for a constitutional amendment, Kerry said his position was the same as the president's, never clarifying for the national television audience that he was referring to Bush's position on marriage, not a constitutional amendment.

And how is it that Kerry can oppose an amendment to the U.S. Constitution banning gay marriage, while supporting a similar constitutional amendment for Massachusetts? The same principles that Kerry uses to oppose the federal amendment apply to the Massachusetts version: Writing discrimination into the constitution — any constitution — is wrong.

Kerry's pronouncement this week directly contradicts the stance against a gay marriage amendment he took two years ago when a similar campaign was launched to amend the Massachusetts Constitution. In a letter dated July 15, 2002 and signed by Kerry, the Massachusetts congressional delegation wrote, "The proposal to add to that document — essentially a charter of liberty and democracy — a provision as harsh both in its intent and its effect on our gay, lesbian, bisexual and transgendered constituents is in conflict with the generous spirit that motivated its adoption, and that should continue to govern us today."

Kerry deserves credit for his pro-gay voting record in the Senate and for continuing to express (at least via his spokesperson to the limited readership of the gay press) his opposition to the federal marriage amendment. But with this week's apparent flip-flop on the Massachusetts question, gay rights advocates — and gay voters — will need to keep a closer eye on Kerry's morphing positions on our issues. Kudos to Patrick Guerriero, executive director of the gay GOP group Log Cabin Republicans, for criticizing President Bush's patently discriminatory support of the FMA. Guerriero told the Blade that LCR has "reached a certain breaking point," and that "whatever remnants of blind loyalty that had remained, the ground rules have shifted. This has been the most significant gut check the organization has had in its history." If LCR withholds its endorsement of Bush — and it should — it would demonstrate real political courage and a welcome sign that the organization is not a rubber stamp for the GOP.

Gay Democrats must show the same courage in standing up to their candidates and demanding fair treatment, not just during the early primary season when it's easy to court dollars and votes by supporting gay rights causes, but when it really counts. Gay Democrats should resist the urge to vote blindly for any candidate. Now is the time to hold candidates accountable for their positions. Remember, candidate Bill Clinton promised gays the world, while President Clinton delivered "Don't Ask, Don't Tell" and the federal Defense of Marriage Act.

Unfortunately, Kerry isn't the only gay rights ally waffling on support of gay marriage. The influential editorial board of the Washington Post this week wrote in support of civil unions as an acceptable substitute for full marriage equality for gays. I guess the board is suffering from collective amnesia. On July 5, 2003, the Post wrote in an editorial that the U.S. Supreme Court's landmark sodomy ruling "inevitably raises the far more contentious issue of whether such recognition should be extended to gay couples. We think it should, not because the Constitution requires it, but because it is the right thing to do." This week, the Post pronounces itself "skeptical that American society will come to formally recognize gay relationships as a result of judicial fiats, and we felt that the 4 to 3 majority on the Massachusetts court had stretched to find a right to gay marriage in that commonwealth's 224-year-old constitution."

According to the editorial, the Post board continues to support full-fledged gay marriage. But rather than praise the courage of the court, the editorial board laments the judges' decision, "refusing to allow the people of Massachusetts to choose civil unions as an alternative." Gay rights advocates and our fair-weather friends need to acknowledge that civil unions are a cowardly cop-out and an unacceptable compromise. As the fair-minded and enlightened justices of the Massachusetts Supreme Judicial Court put it, the "history of our nation has demonstrated that separate is seldom, if ever, equal."

"Democrats' gay problem," Jan. 18, 2008 and "Dems' love for us is on the down-low," Feb. 8, 2008

Another doozy, this time involving the Democratic National Committee and its then-Chair Howard Dean. When Dean fired the DNC's head of gay outreach after his partner criticized the party in a public statement (obvious retaliation), the terminated staffer, Donald Hitchcock, filed a lawsuit. That suit triggered the release of an avalanche of embarrassing DNC staff emails as detailed here. In one, DNC Deputy Finance Chair Julie Tagen wrote that she uses the Blade for "the bottom of the birdcage." How original! And DNC Communications Director Karen Finney plots revenge against the Blade for our critical coverage, suggesting they hand an exclusive interview to the Advocate to get back at us. (The Advocate was the DNC's preferred outlet since it submits quotes for approval, something the Blade would never do.) It all came to an ugly head weeks later when two attorneys arrived at the Blade offices for a meeting with me and our publisher, Lynne Brown. They said they represented Dean's chief of staff, Leah Daughtry, but DNC officials later bragged about the lawyers' performance, strongly suggesting that the DNC was behind the visit and the threats against us. The two yelled at us, red-faced, threatening to sue the Blade and us personally over our criticism of the DNC and its handling of the Hitchcock lawsuit and our criticism of Daughtry, whom we learned was a member of a conservative Pentecostal church whose members speak in tongues.

The two dropped the "f bomb" several times during their abusive, unhinged tirade. I've never appreciated Lynne more than in that moment when she calmly informed them that their threats don't scare us and our coverage would continue. She then showed them the exit. I later wrote about the incident, of course, triggering some blogger demands for DNC resignations. Under pressure from gay bloggers to say something in defense of the nation's oldest LGBTQ newspaper being threatened by the DNC, the National Lesbian & Gay Journalists Association drafted an op-ed expressing support. The problem was the version they sent to me included all the tracked changes, enabling me to read the original text of the document before it was edited into a watered-down, milquetoast defense of press freedoms. It illustrated how much the LGBTQ movement was co-opted by the DNC, which paid lip service to our issues and delivered next to nothing in return for our votes and, more importantly, donations.

In fact, during the flap over the Hitchcock lawsuit, I received a lunch invitation from Andrew Tobias, the then-DNC treasurer, who happened to be gay. Over lunch, Tobias informed me that the party had detected a noticeable drop in financial contributions from gay donors and the DNC blamed the Blade and me — specifically the tough op-eds I'd written, which are included below. It was an ah-ha moment that verified for me the Democratic Party cared only about the money it received from its loyal, rich gay donors and not so much about the votes of our small niche community.

I met Dean once privately in his office before things got so ugly. He was pleasant and seemed genuinely interested in LGBTQ issues. I thought it was the beginning of a new relationship between the Blade and DNC but, as you can see, things soured quickly. Dean, in a deposition in the Hitchcock lawsuit, referred to the Blade as "the Fox News of gay journalism." I responded by calling him the "Gomer Pyle of politicians." That one still makes me laugh.

Last week brought another example of the consequences of gay rights advocates aligning themselves too closely with one political party.

Emails written by senior staff members of the Democratic National Committee were leaked to the Queerty blog that exposed what they really think of the gay media, notably the Blade.

In the emails, the staff debates whether to give lesbian columnist Deb Price access to Howard Dean for an interview. They decide it would be too risky and expose the DNC to too many "hits."

In another exchange, they complain about the Blade's coverage of the DNC. Spokesperson Damien LaVera writes it is "outrageous" that the Blade didn't adequately cover the DNC's gay delegate training program. To get back at the Blade for this slight, DNC communications director Karen Finney suggests handing an exclusive story to the Advocate or another Blade competitor. Deputy finance director Julie Tagen then adds that she uses the Blade and other gay newspapers for "the bottom of the birdcage."

The reality is that the Blade has covered the DNC and its delegate training program. In addition to two news stories on the subject in the past year, I personally extended an invitation to the DNC to draft an op-ed on its program, which I later published.

The "birdcage" email was leaked from a batch of documents subpoenaed in a lawsuit filed by former DNC gay outreach director Donald Hitchcock. In the lawsuit, Hitchcock says he was the target of discrimination, retaliation and defamation during and after his tenure as director of the Gay & Lesbian Leadership Council. Hitchcock was fired in May 2006, just days after his domestic partner, Paul Yandura, a longtime party activist, criticized DNC Chair Howard Dean in an open letter to gay Democrats.

"For many months, a number of us have made appeals to Howard Dean and party officials to care about and defend the dignity of gay and lesbian families and friends, in the same way they defend the dignity of other key constituencies," Yandura said in his letter.

"All progressives need to be asking how much has the DNC budgeted to counter the anti-gay ballot initiatives in the states," he said.

"We also need to know why the DNC and our Democratic leaders continue to allow the Republicans to use our families and friends as pawns to win elections."

But the line that certainly doomed Hitchcock was: "My advice is don't give any more money to the Dems."

Less than a week later, Hitchcock was gone. Don't mess with the Democrats' lock on gay money.

In a less-than-convincing statement released after Hitchcock's dismissal, Finney said, "It was not retaliation. It was decided we needed a change. We decided to hire a proven leader."

Yandura, of course, saw it differently.

"This is retaliation, plain and simple," he said. "This shows what they think about domestic partners."

It probably shows what the DNC thinks of gay money, more than what it thinks of domestic partners. In any case, we now know what DNC officials think of the gay media. LaVera in particular, is perturbed that the Blade publishes statements from anonymous sources. The party's treatment of Hitchcock and this email exchange demonstrate why we allow certain trusted sources to speak anonymously: whistleblowers at the DNC clearly are justified in fearing for their jobs if they dare to criticize Dean or the party.

As for Tagen, who penned the very clever and original "birdcage" line, I won't go so far as to demand her resignation, as at least one gay activist did.

"If a DNC staffer disparaged Black, Latino, or Jewish media the way Deputy Finance Director Julie Tagen did LGBT media, that person would already be out of a job," wrote Lee Bolin, a former member of the National Stonewall Democrats executive committee.

My skin is a tad thicker; I'm not losing sleep over Tagen's assessment of the Blade. Her remark, however, was unfortunate in that it cavalierly dismisses the hard work of a dedicated group of journalists working for a newspaper that is hardly hostile to the Democratic Party.

We strive to cover the news in a fair way, but certainly Democratic voices are more than fairly represented in our pages.

Unfortunately for the DNC, this flap over the gay media is just the beginning of the embarrassment. Not only are DNC employees' emails being made public, but there are the gleeful New York Post headlines to endure ("Gays sticking it to Dems"). It's unfathomable that the DNC hasn't settled this lawsuit.

And it serves as a reminder of what happens when one party knows it can count on the support of a constituency group, no matter what. We have seen this problem manifest before. When Maryland Gov. Martin O'Malley, a Democrat who once publicly supported gay marriage, changed his position and invoked the Catholic sacraments following that state's high court ruling upholding a gay ban, our national advocacy groups were silent. It's a safe bet that if O'Malley were a Republican, the indignant press releases would have been flying and rallies would have been scheduled for Annapolis.

When Democrats like John Kerry and 2004 running mate John Edwards announce support for anti-gay state marriage amendments and gays line up dutifully behind them anyway, we teach the party that there are no repercussions for betraying us.

This doesn't mean gay voters should pull the lever for any of the Republicans now in the running. Rather, gay voters, donors and campaign staffers need to learn the art of the barter system: you give something, you get something. No one knows that concept better than the evangelical Christians. When they stay home in November and a Democrat wins the White House, you better believe the GOP will take them more seriously in 2012. It's time for gays to demand more for their contributions to the Democratic Party.

"DEMS' LOVE FOR US IS ON THE DOWN-LOW"

The lawsuit filed by a gay man alleging the Democratic National Committee discriminated against him is yielding more insights into how the party interacts with gay media outlets and the sometimes tortured positions it takes on gay issues.

In one telling email, Gretchen Cook, a writer for the Advocate, sends a note to Damien LaVera, a DNC spokesperson, regarding a story she's writing about the party's outreach to religious voters.

"As promised, I'm sending the quotes I'd like to use (though probably will get edited down in the final draft but it's the gist of what I'd use from that conversation.)" Cook wrote. "I can't imagine you'd have any problem with me using them but please let me know soonest."

And what if LaVera did have a problem? Would the Advocate capitulate and allow a source to edit its story? It's a disturbing revelation that calls into question the independence and toughness of the magazine's reporting. Is this sharing of notes and submitting of stories for approval by sources common practice at the Advocate?

Another series of emails shows how skittish DNC officials are when it comes to publicly expressing gay-friendly positions. When Peter Pace, President Bush's former chair of the Joint Chiefs, described homosexuality as "immoral" in an interview with the Chicago Tribune, many Democrats fumbled what should have been a no-brainer response.

Democratic presidential candidates Hillary Rodham Clinton and Barack Obama initially tried to sidestep the issue, but both later realized they had offended gays and sought to clarify their positions.

Newsday reported at the time that Obama did not directly answer when asked if same-sex relationships were immoral. He issued a statement a day later that, "I do not agree with General Pace that homosexuality is immoral. Attempts to divide people like this have consumed too much of our politics over the past six years."

Clinton, meanwhile, told ABC News that it's for "others to conclude" whether homosexuality is immoral. But, like Obama, she released a follow-up statement after being criticized. Clinton said that she'd heard from gay friends who said her answer sounded evasive.

"I should have echoed my colleague Senator John Warner's statement forcefully stating that homosexuality is not immoral because that is what I believe," her statement said.

It turns out Clinton and Obama weren't the only ones struggling with how to respond to Pace's remarks. LaVera penned a brief statement that rightly described Pace's comments as "anti-gay" but fell far short of taking a strong stand. He wrote, in part, "Chairman Pace's comments are not constructive."

The weak and carefully constructed statement was then circulated among DNC higher-ups for review and comment. LaVera emailed Karen Finney, DNC's director of communications: "Brian [Bond] is concerned that we might take hits if we don't comment on it — not so much on the merits of the 'don't ask, don't tell' but on Pace's language about immorality, etc. Personally, I'm concerned that we'll create too many problems if [DNC Chair Howard] Dean condemns the sitting Chairman of the Joint Chiefs during a time of war. I think it's better to do a statement from a DNC spokesperson saying Pace's rhetoric isn't constructive."

What ensues is a laughable series of emails among senior DNC staff struggling to craft the lamest possible response. Leah Daughtry, Dean's chief of staff, writes, "What are the pros and cons of issuing a statement?"

Well, Leah, the pros would be publicly defending a constituency from whom you happily and shamelessly collect lots of money and votes. Oh, and there's that quaint notion of doing the right thing, too. The cons? Daughtry's fellow Pentecostal worshippers who also speak in tongues might be offended that the Democratic Party stood up for those sinful gays who are going to hell.

In the protracted email exchange obtained by the Blade, LaVera and Daughtry advocate for sending a statement only to reporters working for gay press and keeping any mention of it off the DNC website. They also oppose sending the statement to mainstream news wires. That way, the DNC can have it both ways — placating the gays with a toothless statement while ensuring that any faintly pro-gay statements don't gain traction or visibility in mainstream media. The DNC leadership wouldn't want to go out on a limb and actually stand up for the dignity of gay service members who had just been called "immoral," because that might offend one of those religious voters that Dean and Daughtry are so desperate to please.

Daughtry's behind-the-scenes role in this and other gay-related debacles is becoming more troubling. She is Dean's chief of staff, yet helped insulate him from the Pace controversy so he didn't have to issue a public statement. She's the head of this summer's Democratic National Convention, but has undermined efforts at establishing quotas for gay delegates, even though every other conceivable minority group benefits from such mandatory goals. She leads party outreach to "values voters," but is on the record opposing same-sex marriage — something that many gay voters value.

If the DNC employed a gay staffer who sought to undermine the influence of Black members within the party, there's no question that person would be fired faster than Donald Hitchcock, who was canned shortly after his partner dared to criticize the party. The double standard that allows Daughtry to get away with her anti-gay behavior is a slap in the face to gay DNC donors. Gay supporters of the Democratic Party deserve better from Daughtry, Dean and the rest of the senior staff there.

"DO THE WRONG THING," MARCH 14, 2008

This captured my frustration with politicians on both sides of the aisle who either attacked our community overtly (Republicans) or made private promises of support that they later abandoned or denied (Democrats). It reflects how much things have changed in the years since then that most Democrats are now on board with most pro-LGBTQ legislation and some Republicans are coming along, now that more than 70 percent of American voters support marriage equality. In September 2022, Sens. Tammy Baldwin (D) and Susan Collins (R) even cowrote a Washington Post op-ed in support of marriage equality, a development unthinkable even 15 years ago. It's important to remember that this level of support can evaporate and we must always keep the pressure on both parties. Just look at Sen. Kyrsten Sinema who touted her bisexuality to win the support (and money) of LGBTQ groups and donors during her campaign, then turned her back and refused to ditch the filibuster to pass the Equality Act and voter protection measures. In response, Emily's List announced in 2022 it would not endorse her reelection, though, predictably, LGBTQ groups did not follow suit.

But the DNC's duplicity in 2008 was about to change as an inspirational new figure broke into the national consciousness and, thankfully, he was not a creature of the party system.

The fall of New York Gov. Eliot Spitzer (D), who once pledged to bring "passion" back to Albany, was greeted with slack-jawed expressions of shock by cable news commentators. But, really, what's so shocking? From Sen. David Vitter (R-La.) to Sen. Larry Craig (R-Idaho) to former Gov. Jim McGreevey (D-N.J.) to former President Bill Clinton (D), we've seen it all before — men so blinded by power that they forget laws apply to them, too.

Even if you believe, as I do, that prostitution is a victimless crime that shouldn't be prosecuted, the hypocrisy and arrogance of Spitzer's behavior still required that he resign. Spitzer sold himself as a squeaky-clean reformer. Whether or not you agree with state and federal laws against prostitution, they exist. And a tough-talking, sanctimonious former attorney general could not plead ignorance and ask for a pass.

Politicians were behaving badly elsewhere this week. In Oklahoma, the Victory Fund exposed state Rep. Sally Kern (R) as a homophobe, after it posted to YouTube audio of anti-gay remarks she made. In the speech, Kern described homosexuality as, "the biggest threat our nation has, even more so than terrorism or Islam." She likened homosexuality to a cancer that will "destroy this nation."

Kern's remarks are especially disturbing given the shooting death of California teen Lawrence King last month in an apparent anti-gay hate crime. Politicians who ridicule and demonize gays contribute to a culture that still says it's OK to discriminate against gays. Sadly, that mindset all too often leads to acts of physical violence perpetrated against us.

Meanwhile, Maryland's politicians continue to betray their gay constituents. After the state's high court, in a 4-3 ruling, upheld a state law limiting marriage to heterosexual couples, gay residents looked to their elected officials to right a judicial wrong. And once again, they are being let down.

While gay couples in committed, long-term relationships are still viewed as strangers under the law and remain desperately in need of a legislative remedy, lawmakers have turned their attention to more pressing matters, like banning cell phone use while driving and upholding a ban on online wine sales. This is not the behavior of courageous political leaders; it is the hallmark of cowards so separate to hold onto power that they fear creating a ripple on the pond.

And this is in Maryland, a decidedly "blue" state where Democrats control both houses in the Assembly and the governor's mansion. It's become apparent that a full marriage rights bill is doomed and the state's lawmakers aren't even embracing the cop-out of civil unions. That's not surprising, considering the powerful Senate President Thomas V. "Mike" Miller, a Democrat, opposes civil unions.

Unfortunately, you won't hear a peep of criticism from national gay rights groups, because the perpetrators of these wrongs in Maryland are Democrats.

And what happens when a gay person dares to criticize a Democrat for failing to keep promises and honor commitments? I got a taste of the Democratic wrath last month, after criticizing DNC Chair Howard Dean and his chief of staff, Leah Daughtry, in an editorial.

In the piece, I wrote that the DNC's response to anti-gay remarks made by Gen. Peter Pace, President Bush's former chair of the Joint Chiefs, was insufficient and weak.

In response, Daughtry sent two lawyers to the Blade's offices to berate me and our publisher, Lynne Brown. The meeting was beyond contentious and featured lots of red-faced cursing and threatening of lawsuits. They claimed to represent Daughtry and not the DNC. But DNC officials have gloated behind the scenes that since the confrontation in the Blade's office, the paper has stopped writing about a gay man's lawsuit against the party, his former employer. Donald Hitchcock accuses the DNC of firing him after his partner, Paul Yandura, publicly urged gay donors to think twice before giving money to the Democratic Party.

Of course, to suggest that the Blade would abandon a story because a couple of angry lawyers made a scene in the lobby constitutes wishful thinking. One thing every journalist learns early on is that when people start yelling and making threats, that means you're onto something.

One source told the Blade this week that in Dean's deposition in the case, he denounced the Blade as "the Fox News of gay journalism."

This is what happens to gay people who challenge Democrats to be better on our issues. Dean and others at the DNC have derided the Blade as a right-wing birdcage liner. Both criticisms are absurd; no fair-minded person could reasonably consider the Blade a conservative publication and judging by the innumerable references to the Blade in the Hitchcock case depositions, DNC officials spend an inordinate amount of time worrying about what we write. They may line their birdcages with our pages, but not until they've read them cover to cover.

If the Blade is the Fox News of gay journalism, then Howard Dean is the Gomer Pyle of politicians — a national laughingstock whose amateurish stewardship of the party puts the prospect of a Democratic victory in November in doubt when it ought to be a slam-dunk.

From bigots in Oklahoma and cowards in Maryland to hypocrites in New York and petty hacks in D.C., this nation's politicians prove again and again just how out of touch they are with the people they are supposed to represent.

"Democratic disappointments," Aug. 22, 2008

The 2008 campaign was the gift that kept on giving, with Hillary Clinton and Barack Obama fighting it out until June. But once the fight ended, one side should have endorsed the other and moved on; Hillary's campaign didn't quite go that route, as outlined here. For sure, the 2008 Democratic National Convention was historic — the first Black presidential nominee from a major party and a record number of out gay delegates along with platform language calling for repeal of "Don't Ask, Don't Tell." Yet, somehow the Democrats always manage to get in their own way. I take a backseat to no one when it comes to holding the Democrats accountable. After all, they took all the gay money and votes, so the expectations were always higher than for the GOP. Despite all that homogenous support, the Democrats gave us Bill Clinton, who signed the Defense of Marriage Act and "Don't Ask, Don't Tell"; John Kerry, who endorsed an anti-gay marriage amendment in Massachusetts in 2004; and John Edwards, who referred to gays as "those people." Those people? As in the people writing him checks? For some reason, that expression has always stuck in my craw. "Those people" has been used to describe Black people, LGBTQ people, basically anyone deemed "other" by the mainstream. It's such a dismissive, bigoted expression and it really set me off when Edwards reportedly used it during the 2004 campaign. What an ass.

But back to 2008. It's unthinkable today that a Democratic presidential nominee would describe marriage as the union of a man and woman because "God's in the mix," as Obama did in 2008, even though same-sex couples were marrying legally in a few states then. It's a reminder that even the most progressive Democrats weren't always so and needed our pushback and criticism along the way. That's an important reminder for today's youth, that even our allies need to be held accountable and criticized. It would take Obama four more years to announce his public support for marriage equality.

Some gay bloggers described me as having "un-endorsed" Hillary after this piece was published. Not so. I was merely calling attention to the obvious: She lost and by dragging her feet in wholeheartedly endorsing Obama, Hillary was quietly sabotaging him.

As the Democrats convene in Denver this weekend for the kickoff of their convention, it's sobering to consider how the party continues to disappoint some of its most loyal supporters and jeopardize its chances of retaking the White House.

Let's start with John Edwards, who went from the "moral candidate" and vocal critic of Bill Clinton's sexcapades to the latest hypocrite-in-chief to fall from grace.

Edwards managed to attract support from an impressive list of gay activists and donors, including David Mixner (someone I admire) early in primary process. I never understood the attraction, beyond Edwards' obvious physical qualities. He's an unremarkable, unaccomplished one-term senator who, according to Bob Shrum, was uncomfortable around gays, whom he once referred to as "those people."

It takes an ego the size of Mount Rushmore to campaign for president while trying to conceal an extra-marital affair (and possible love child). What if he'd won the nomination? Edwards' actions risked wrecking the Democratic Party on the eve of its convention.

Bill Clinton's "I did not have sexual relations with that woman" speech looks quaint in comparison.

Then Sunday brought the spectacle of pastor Rick Warren hosting Sens. Barack Obama and John McCain for a presidential "forum," which was held in a church. The attacks on same-sex marriage were inevitable. Some liberal pundits suggested that gays got off easy, as Warren didn't dwell on marriage and abortion in his questioning. But those pundits are wrong.

When Warren asked Obama to define marriage, he answered, "I believe that marriage is the union between a man and a woman. Now for me as a Christian ... it's also a sacred union. God's in the mix."

Obama's answer is incorrect and offensive on multiple fronts. First his definition ignores the law in Massachusetts, California and New York, where same-sex couples are marrying legally or having their marriages recognized by the state. Second, God is not "in the mix." Civil marriages confer state-sponsored rights and privileges and God has absolutely nothing to do with it. And third, I don't care if Obama — or any other politician for that matter — is a Christian, an atheist or a Muslim. Obama is supposed to be above "identity politics," until it comes to religion and pandering to evangelical voters.

Meanwhile, Bill and Hillary Clinton continue their sour grapes tour in the wake of her primary loss to Obama. Their selfish actions serve to jeopardize the party's chances in November and some have speculated that the Clintons would relish a McCain victory because it would give Hillary the chance to run an "I-told-you-so" campaign in 2012. But gay Americans can't afford four more years of a Republican White House with Supreme Court appointments looming and all gay voters should be offended by the Clintons' behavior.

I endorsed Hillary early on in the primary season and have regretted it for some time. That sense of regret was magnified as plans for the Democratic convention emerged.

First, Obama agreed to give both Hillary and Bill prime-time speaking slots. She earned that honor; he did not. Then his camp agreed to allow her name to be put in nomination at the convention, supposedly so "all the voices can be heard."

This ridiculous pandering to the losing side must stop. Obama won and Hillary's supporters need to simply get over it and move on. Her behavior since June is not that of a gracious politician. It's the behavior of an obsessed egomaniac who refuses to bow to voters' wishes. What is to be gained from placing her name in nomination? It will create a circus environment in which her die-hard supporters can whoop it up on national TV and wave anti-Obama placards. So much for unity.

(On the positive side, maybe some actual, bona fide news will come out of the convention, instead of the usual carefully choreographed pablum.)

Initially, Hillary's supporters said they would accept the outcome only if all states were allowed to vote. After the final votes were cast, they changed their tune and said that Hillary needed a few days to plot her next move; they would get on board with Obama after a short mourning period. Then Hillary gave her belated concession speech and again the terms of reconciliation changed: Obama must choose her as his running mate. When that idea became increasingly unworkable, the Hillary worshippers decided to turn Obama's convention into their own, inserting language into the platform all but blaming sexist media outlets for her defeat and extracting the two prime-time speaking slots for Hill and Bill. But still that wasn't enough and now Hillary's name will be placed in nomination.

No doubt there will be more terms to come now that her followers have been trained that they can whine and stomp their feet and Obama's camp will mollify them. Maybe if he bent over and kissed her ass on live TV the Hillaryphiles would be happy. Then again, recent history suggests otherwise.

The Clinton era has passed and it's past time for Obama to get tough — not on McCain, but first on Hillary. The winner gets to plan a convention, choose a running mate and articulate party positions, not the loser. Hillary should go back to work in the Senate. If she can't find anything to keep herself busy besides undermining Obama, here's a suggestion: Take over for Sen. Edward Kennedy and introduce and fight for ENDA in the Senate.

In their defense, the Democrats have come a long way from 2004, when Sens. John Kerry and Edwards backed state constitutional amendments banning gay marriage. Hillary and Obama oppose them and both called for federal recognition of same-sex couples' rights. It's a dramatic and welcome change; time will tell if either will more than pay lip service to gay rights issues and instead introduce federal legislation aimed at banning anti-gay job discrimination and repealing "Don't Ask, Don't Tell" and the Defense of Marriage Act.

For all their words of support, the Democrats have disappointed gay constituents repeatedly over the years. Bill Clinton proved that politicians can betray gay voters and they'll line up to vote for you anyway. It's a lesson too many Democrats have taken to heart.

Let's hope the 2008 convention —— which includes a record number of openly gay delegates and platform language calling for repeal of "Don't Ask, Don't Tell" — brings the change that Obama claims to represent.

"Alas, Poor Activism, We Knew Her Well," June 26, 2009

Another takedown of two-faced Democrats who took our money and votes and delivered lip service for too many years. And this piece references an issue that remains a problem for the LGBTQ movement today: the lack of an identifiable national leader to respond to issues of the day in the national media. I never understood the reluctance of various Human Rights Campaign leaders to take up that mantle.

Today, the closest we have is probably GLAAD's Sarah Kate Ellis, who has done a tremendous job of turning around the media watchdog group and making it relevant again.

Also referenced in this piece is John Berry, former ambassador to Australia and former head of OPM. I met Berry several times and toured OPM with him shortly after President Obama took office. I was struck by how many gays and lesbians worked there and they were visibly relieved and elated that George W. Bush was gone and they could finally be out at work under a president who appointed an out gay man to head the federal government workforce — the largest employer in the United States.

Forty years after the rebellion at Stonewall, the business of activism is in a sorry state.

Four decades after a group of gay bar patrons humiliated the New York police department by repelling their regular raids with physical force (from kick lines to bottle throwing), a group of wealthy and connected LGBT donors was preparing to sip cocktails with Vice President Joe Biden at the posh Mandarin Oriental Hotel in Washington last night and enjoy the 10,000-square-foot spa at a Democratic National Committee fundraiser.

When the Obama administration's Justice Department defended the indefensible Defense of Marriage Act in a legal brief that would have made George W. Bush proud, there were flickers of Stonewall-era activism. Maybe, just maybe, lady activism would make her triumphant return.

Some prominent donors, like David Mixner and Bruce Bastian, announced plans to boycott last night's DNC event. Servicemembers Legal Defense Network said it would protest at the hotel, even though two of its board members planned to attend. Officials from the Human Rights Campaign and National Gay & Lesbian Task Force declined to attend.

But activism, that poor faded dame, didn't stand a chance. Other donors shrugged off calls to boycott the DNC, which has vacuumed up untold millions from the LGBT community over the years and delivered precious little in exchange. Like moths to the flame, lured by the magnet of proximity to power, the gay donors planned to open their checkbooks once more in the futile hope of being accepted by a party that prefers its gays rich, supplicant and invisible. And did I mention rich?

Several of those who planned to attend the DNC fundraiser are friends and surely mean well. But during the past week I have heard more than one of them say they would protest the event by only making the minimum contribution of $1,000. That'll teach 'em! No one who was present at the Inn 40 years ago would recognize such behavior as activism.

In the decades since Stonewall, we've redefined activism and watered it down to its current, unrecognizable state. Of course we need to pursue change from within — there should be out gays working in the highest levels of government. OPM's John Berry, for example, is already making tremendous progress at leveling that playing field for LGBT federal workers.

But as last fall's spontaneous street protests against Proposition 8 demonstrated, not everyone can afford $1,000 fundraisers and those voices should be heard too. When longtime activists Cleve Jones, Robin Tyler and David Mixner recently called for a national march on Washington to demand gay rights, they were immediately attacked and derided by some who labeled them naïve for suggesting such a radical thing. Maybe a national march thrown together in a few months isn't the most sensible way of bringing activism out of her long slumber, but those calling for such a protest surely don't deserve to be ridiculed and dismissed. If they want to march, then so be it. It probably won't win us any legislative victories, but that approach can't be any worse than the checkbook activism of recent years.

The New York Times this week published an opinion piece that attracted much attention within gay activist circles. It was titled, "Why the Gay Rights Movement Has No National Leader."

"Gay people have no national standard-bearer, no go-to sound-byte machine for the media," wrote Jeremy Peters. "So when President Obama last week extended benefits to same-sex partners of federal employees, there was no alpha gay leader to respond with the movement's official voice, though some activists criticized the president for not going far enough."

Peters posits several explanations for the lack of national leadership on LGBT issues, from the AIDS epidemic decimating a generation of leaders, to the focus on local activism in a push for nondiscrimination laws that didn't require a national spokesperson leading the call for change.

There's another reason for this lack of visibility: the reluctance of gay activists to criticize politicians who aren't Republicans. It's a frustrating pattern that has played itself out innumerable times, as Democrats betray their gay constituency and are rewarded with more money and votes. You can't be the national face of activism if everyone perceives you as a tool of one political party. When Democrats throw us under the bus, they should be held accountable. Instead, activists look the other way.

There was John Kerry's support for state constitutional amendments banning same-sex marriage, Bill Clinton's signing DOMA and "Don't Ask, Don't Tell," and countless other examples from Marion Barry's recent flip-flop on marriage to Maryland Gov. Martin O'Malley invoking the "sacraments" to justify our exclusion from marriage rights to Virginia gubernatorial candidate Creigh Deeds' vote for the draconian Marshall-Newman Amendment.

There will never be a recognizable face of national leadership on LGBT issues (beyond Melissa Etheridge and Ellen DeGeneres) as long as the party in power is immune to criticism.

The best way to commemorate the historic events at Stonewall — which served as a catalyst for the creation of this newspaper — is to renew that spirit of activism at this critical time.

Those efforts should be directed at Congress, where spineless Democrats are not moving nearly aggressively enough on legislation. First we were told that a hate crimes vote in the Senate could happen last week, then Sen. Harry Reid said it would happen before the August recess. We'll see. Rep. Barney Frank has introduced a trans-inclusive ENDA, but acknowledged that more Democrats in the House doesn't necessarily mean more support for the bill.

All of us — LGBT activists, donors, voters and ordinary citizens — must hold the Democrats accountable now. They have everything they've said they need to advance gay rights legislation: solid majorities in both houses, a supportive president and a Republican Party in total disarray. If the Democrats can't move on these bills now, then when? There may never be a better time. The time to act is now.

With the energy of a younger generation becoming more engaged and the watchful eyes of bloggers and LGBT media keeping everyone honest, maybe lady activism will finally reemerge and we'll see more of those gay donors stand up and demand more than cocktails and canapes in exchange for all their cash.

"Not so fast, Mikulski fans," March 2, 2015

When it comes to LGBTQ issues, the Democratic Party can mark time like this: Before Barack Obama and After Barack Obama. BBO, the Democrats paid mostly lip service to LGBTQ issues, caring mostly about wealthy gay donors who cut regular, generous checks to the party without demanding much in return. One of my roles BBO was to call out those two-faced Democrats, since almost no one in the LGBTQ movement would dare. That was left to the LGBTQ media and a handful of bloggers. It's a thankless job as you get attacked from the left and the right, even if some of those advocates privately thanked me for saying out loud what they wouldn't (or couldn't). One of those slippery Democrats was Maryland Sen. Barbara Mikulski, who faced decades of rumors about her sexual orientation and efforts to out her after she voted for the Defense of Marriage Act. I confronted Mikulski at a Baltimore event in 2004 but she refused to answer the question of whether she's a lesbian. As of 2022, she has remained silent.

As usual, when a prominent Democratic politician or public figure makes headlines, LGBT advocacy groups develop a case of amnesia about that person's record.

Today's example: Sen. Barbara Mikulski, the iconic Maryland Democrat who has indisputably blazed a trail for women in the U.S. Congress.

But her record on LGBT issues is far from heroic, though you wouldn't know it from the barrage of press releases today hailing her supposedly long record of support.

"Sen. Mikulski's work has improved virtually every facet of life for LGBT Americans," HRC trumpeted. "... the LGBT community will miss working with her."

For a more complete, rounded view of her legacy, consider that she voted for the Defense of Marriage Act. She spent her entire life hiding in the closet and refusing to answer questions about her sexual orientation, even as she was casting horribly anti-gay votes. And the tales from her staffers about the abusive environment she cultivated in the office would make Anna Wintour blush.

The rumors about Mikulski's sexual orientation go back to the 1980s, when Linda Chavez described her as a "San Francisco-style Democrat" while running against her for the Senate. Mikulski's relationship with congressional aide Teresa Mary Brennan — the two briefly lived together — also raised eyebrows. After her vote for DOMA, Mikulski was ambushed in New York while on a book tour by LGBT activists who rightly demanded to know how she, as a closeted lesbian, could support DOMA and come to the heart of the city's LGBT community to plug a book. She refused to answer their questions about her sexual orientation. She was similarly targeted by activists in other cities and always ran for cover, refusing to engage.

In 2004, as Congress prepared to vote on the Federal Marriage Amendment, which would have barred same-sex marriage, Mikulski's position was unclear. It was a stressful time and bloggers and LGBT media outlets, including the Blade, were working to out hypocrites on Capitol Hill.

I confronted Mikulski at a Baltimore event in 2004 and asked her directly about her intent with regard to the FMA vote and whether or not she's gay. Per usual, she ducked the questions and scurried to a waiting car.

The FMA failed and Mikulski ultimately did the right thing and voted against another marriage ban effort in 2006. She finally came around on LGBT issues and cosponsored the Hate Crimes Prevention Act, ENDA and a repeal of DOMA.

All of that is good and appreciated but truly supportive and courageous politicians stand up before it's safe and popular, as some of her colleagues did in opposing DOMA in 1996.

The mindless praise of politicians like Mikulski by HRC and others ignores history and does a disservice to LGBT people. Now that she's freed from having to run another campaign for reelection, perhaps Mikulski will sit down and finally answer all the questions about her long career and not just the self-serving ones. No one disputes Mikulski's great achievements, especially the work she's done on behalf of her Baltimore constituents and her role as the "Dean of the Senate Women." But there's more to the story and so far it's not being told.

"Undeserved Praise for George H.W. Bush," Dec. 3, 2018

One of my jobs at the Blade is to guard against revisionist history — a phenomenon that occurs each time a horrible homophobe dies. The death of President George H.W. Bush was no exception to that rule, when mainstream media and everyday Americans ignore horrendous records hostile to equality and mindlessly praise someone simply because they died. The media must learn to do better.

There's nothing more galling than revisionist history and last weekend's reactions to the death of former President George H.W. Bush brought an onslaught of it to many social media feeds and, more predictably, to mainstream media.

I was stunned to see my own feeds filled with tributes to the 41st president — some written by gay men. And on World AIDS Day, no less.

Even the Advocate — once a leading critic of the Reagan-Bush administrations — joined this chorus of glossing over Bush's anti-LGBTQ record. In an Advocate story posted on World AIDS Day about Bush's death, the word "AIDS" appears just once in a reference to Reagan. The headline describes Bush as "no enemy of LGBTQ people."

In Neal Broverman's Advocate story, Bush is credited with signing the Hate Crimes Statistics Act. But he fails to mention that the measure was a far cry from passing a real hate crimes bill that Democrats and LGBTQ allies wanted in 1990 but was impossible to achieve given Bush was in the White House. Broverman also cites the 1990 removal of a ban on "sexual deviation" from the Immigration and Nationality Act that Bush presided over. But this glosses over the reality that removal of that language was part of a much larger immigration measure. Bush was no LGBTQ advocate. Quite the opposite.

He referred to gay men as "those people," assailed ACT UP for its efforts at fighting AIDS, described same-sex parents as "not normal" and vocally supported the military's ban on gay service members. He gave voice to the far-right evangelicals who now dominate the GOP and appointed Clarence Thomas to the Supreme Court. But worse than all of that, Bush was one half of the Reagan-Bush administration that was criminally negligent in responding to the emerging AIDS crisis of the early 1980s.

Bush is being lauded for his "civility" this week in breathless tributes from the mainstream media that mercilessly mocked him as president. In death, Bush has morphed into a saint because he was "civil" compared to the current White House occupant. The bar is low.

Bush's patrician approach to the job was woefully out of step for the dire times in which he served as president. From a crippling recession to the horrors of the AIDS plague, America needed a bold fighter, not a polite placeholder president. He hated ACT UP because its members represented the direct opposite of Bush's approach — they were loud, rightly angry and demanded accountability from the government that was ignoring them and the plight of tens of thousands of mostly gay men dying. Fuck civility when we're losing an entire generation of American gay men. Bush and his predecessor Reagan turned a willfully blind eye to the epidemic because they and their evangelical base of supporters didn't care about the lives of gay men, people of color and drug users, three groups disproportionately impacted by AIDS.

Bush refused to tackle AIDS honestly, repeatedly calling for "behavioral" changes rather than addressing education and prevention efforts directly and urgently to the communities most directly affected. He was so bad, even the Log Cabin Republicans wouldn't support him.

Fast forward 28 years and all of that easily Google-able, damning information is somehow forgotten or ignored as the country embarks on a weeklong, saccharine embrace of a failed president who time and again chose callous political expediency over doing the right thing.

And 28 years later, even some gay men are joining the Bush white-washing effort. We can express sympathy for Bush's grieving family without ignoring the unforgivable damage his "service" did to the LGBTQ community.

Nostalgia for the Bush era is misplaced. Those who died at the hands of an uncaring government presided over by Bush and Reagan deserved better on World AIDS Day.

"The Treachery of Gay Republicans," Aug. 26, 2019

I've had my ups and downs with the Log Cabin Republicans over 20 years, but after the group's craven endorsement of Trump in 2019, it's been all down. Gone are the thoughtful Log Cabin leaders of years past and now the organization — what's left of it — is dominated by cynical toadies happy to sell out their own community to curry favor with a racist, transphobic administration. History shall not be kind to their betrayals. Shame.

What to make of the Log Cabin Republicans' endorsement of Donald Trump's reelection bid?

The surprise move came in a Washington Post op-ed from Log Cabin chair Robert Kabel and vice chair Jill Homan earlier this month.

It came despite Trump's well-documented racism and his myriad attacks on the LGBTQ community.

It came despite Log Cabin's own precedent in how it awards endorsements. Traditionally, a candidate had to meet with Log Cabin to win its support, as George W. Bush did in 2000 and Mitt Romney did in 2012. But Trump didn't meet with Log Cabin. It's a safe bet Trump has no idea who Kabel and Homan are or what Log Cabin does. The group has also traditionally withheld its endorsement until after the convention. We don't even know who Trump's Democratic opponent will be and just this weekend he picked up a second Republican primary challenger. Yet, Log Cabin rushed its endorsement more than a year before the election. The op-ed was not signed by Log Cabin executive director Jerri Ann Henry, fueling rumors that she has been sidelined by the board.

In their op-ed, Kabel and Homan praised Peter Thiel's speech at the 2016 GOP convention in which he said from the podium, "I am proud to be gay. I am proud to be a Republican. But most of all, I am proud to be an American." It was a nice moment, but talk is cheap. Kabel and Homan conveniently ignore the fact that the Republican platform that year contained the most anti-LGBTQ language in history, including support for "ex-gay" conversion therapy. It was so bad that Log Cabin declined to endorse Trump that year.

They praise Trump for his efforts to end HIV/AIDS in 10 years; to push for decriminalization of homosexuality around the world; and his economic record, which they contend has helped create new LGBTQ-founded small businesses.

Let's take a closer look. First, on HIV/AIDS, it's a commendable goal but amid the hoopla around "ending HIV," Trump's administration has initiated attacks on LGBTQ patients, with HHS proposing a rule that would allow insurers and providers to discriminate against trans patients. HHS has also sought to roll back ACA protections and enable providers and insurers to deny care and coverage to LGBTQ people based on religious or moral beliefs. As for decriminalization, sure, another worthy goal. But, gee, the bar is awfully low if he wins an endorsement for merely asserting that gays shouldn't be locked up. Finally, on small business, Kabel and Homan again conveniently ignore that the SBA, which won a prestigious award from Harvard University for its creative and inclusive outreach to LGBTQ entrepreneurs under President Obama, deleted LGBTQ-related content from its website after Trump's inauguration and only restored the information after an outcry.

The real problem with the endorsement is that it gives cover to a president, a vice president and an administration that continue to attack LGBTQ Americans. Just last week, the Blade's intrepid Chris Johnson asked Trump a question about his efforts to roll back LGBTQ protections. Trump ignored the substance of the question and instead pivoted to brag about his Log Cabin endorsement. He predictably had trouble recalling the name of the group that had endorsed him. And Trump's language during the exchange was telling as he deliberately avoided using the word "gay" or the "LGBTQ" acronym. Instead, he said he's "done very well with that community."

Then, just three days after the exchange with Johnson at the White House, Trump's Justice Department submitted a voluntary 34-page brief to the Supreme Court arguing that the Civil Rights Act of 1964 doesn't apply to cases of anti-gay discrimination. As the Blade reported, with only 21 states having laws barring sexual orientation discrimination, the 2020 high court ruling on the extent of protections under federal law will have a broad impact on gay, lesbian and bisexual workers.

There's simply no legitimate rationale for an LGBTQ organization — even a Republican one — to endorse Trump. It is the ultimate in white privilege that Kabel and Homan can ignore children in cages, immigrant deaths in U.S. custody, racist Tweets, the trans military ban and so many other attacks and affronts and back Trump in 2020. Rewarding Trump's cruel record with praise will only inspire more attacks. What a heartless stunt from a soulless and increasingly irrelevant organization.

"Ellen's extreme wealth has twisted her brain," Oct. 9, 2019

In this pop culture example of revisionist history, we find Ellen DeGeneres hanging with George W. Bush, as a photo of their bonhomie triggered a firestorm of disgust.

The sight of Ellen DeGeneres (one of the most significant LGBT figures in pop culture history) getting chummy with former President George W. Bush (a homophobic war criminal) at a football game last weekend represents the height of selective memory and revisionist history.

As if yucking it up with the man who cynically won reelection in 2004 on the backs of our relationships wasn't unseemly enough, DeGeneres went on to justify the encounter in an awkward commentary on her show.

"I'm friends with George Bush ... we're all different and I think we've forgotten that's OK that we're all different."

She has a point, of course, inasmuch as we should resist Donald Trump's efforts to permanently divide us from one another based on exaggerated partisan views. But she misses the larger point that we must not blithely ignore or excuse away the horrible behaviors and abuses of our oppressors without some semblance of apology or remorse.

As a reminder, Bush aggressively pushed for the Federal Marriage Amendment, which would have permanently ensconced anti-LGBT discrimination in the law, barring recognition of our relationships at a time when such recognition was growing. He used the State of the Union Address to plug his heartless plan, demonizing us in front of a global audience. Imagine the impact of his words on a closeted kid, sitting in front of the TV listening to the president of the United States attacking same-sex relationships in the State of the Union. Reprehensible.

As if that wasn't bad enough, the man tasked with advancing the plan — and pushing for similar amendments in 11 swing states — was closet case Ken Mehlman, our modern-day Roy Cohn, who ran the RNC and the Bush-Cheney reelection campaign.

That's to say nothing of Bush's Iraq war that was justified and launched based on lies and false information that killed hundreds of thousands of people. Or his reckless economic policies that nearly triggered the next Great Depression.

Sure, people make mistakes. In light of the latest Republican nightmare occupying the Oval Office, some even look back fondly on the Bush years. But we must not forget the assaults on the LGBT community spearheaded by Bush.

Maybe if Bush went on Ellen's show and explained himself, apologized to the LGBT community and vowed to earn our forgiveness, we could accommodate him. But he hasn't done that. The Blade has since reached out to Bush's office seeking an interview to find out whether he still supports the FMA and has regrets about his handling of LGBT issues. He likely won't respond to us, but he would to Ellen. She should use her platform to conduct that interview so Bush can finally explain his actions and begin to atone for them, as Mehlman has commendably done.

So far there's no indication such an interview is in the works. Ellen's extreme wealth has twisted her brain such that she sees nothing wrong with socializing with the man who sought to ensure she could never marry her wife. She is the poster child of privilege.

Everyone deserves a shot at forgiveness and redemption, but only if they ask for and earn it. Bush, so far, has not.

"Gay Republicans a disgrace to an otherwise united community," Aug. 21, 2020

The Log Cabin Republicans command a disproportionate amount of attention considering their small size and limited influence. But I have always worked well with its leaders and believe in its mission. We must work for change from within — whatever the institution or organization. And so the Blade's pages have long been open to Log Cabin members. I even once retained a Log Cabin board member to pen a biweekly column, to the consternation of many progressive Blade readers. She didn't last long; too many personal attacks from the gay left drove her to resign in tears.

But something changed at Log Cabin between 2016, when it declined to endorse Donald Trump, and 2020, when Log Cabin delivered an early and enthusiastic endorsement, months before the Democratic nominee was even known. Where Log Cabin once took principled stands (like refusing to endorse George W. Bush) and extracted concessions (like personal meetings) in exchange for endorsements, this new Trumpy Log Cabin held meetings in the Trump International Hotel. Imagine their outcry if the Obamas had owned a fancy D.C. hotel and the Human Rights Campaign held its fundraisers there. This was simply not the Log Cabin I'd known for so many years. On an LGBT ambassadors trip to Israel in 2013, I hit it off with then-Log Cabin president Gregory Angelo, memorably bonding on a visit to Jerusalem's sole gay bar on Halloween night and dancing to "Thriller" until the wee hours. Seven years later, Angelo's politics and behavior were unrecognizable to me as he left Log Cabin and took a position in the Trump administration. He can be seen grinning and clapping wildly in several videos of Trump sendoffs at the White House. It was the same with Ric Grenell, tapped by Trump first as German ambassador and later as acting Director of National Intelligence. That last role vexes LGBTQ movement leaders, as technically a Republican became the first openly gay Cabinet-level official. (Pete Buttigieg would later become the first Senate-confirmed Cabinet official.) Grenell, like Angelo, drank that Trump Kool-Aid, debasing himself and undermining his reputation. Grenell was a reasonable guy. We'd had lunch years ago and he offered advice about putting the Blade's unique political coverage behind a paid firewall. And so it was with real disappointment that I wrote this next piece about the descent of gay Republicans into Trump cult worship.

How to explain the unlikely, perverse phenomenon of a gay Republican in 2020?

Delusion? Denial? Blinded by privilege? Daddy issues rendering them subservient to Master Trump?

Whatever the underlying issue, it's truly sad to watch the once respected Log Cabin Republicans sink into further irrelevance. From Rich Tafel and Patrick Guerriero to R. Clarke Cooper and Patrick Sammon, Log Cabin has been led over the years by smart, committed advocates working to change the Republican Party from within. Whatever your views on the GOP, it's important to fight from the inside, whether it's inside political parties, organized religions or sports leagues, to bring about change.

But 2020 is no ordinary year and Donald Trump is no ordinary president. Anyone who defends Trump's indefensible behavior is lying to themselves. There's no excusing racism, sexism and transphobia. There's no looking the other way when Trump allows his buddy, the murderous Vladimir Putin, to put bounties on the heads of American soldiers. And there's no justification for snatching screaming toddlers from their mothers' arms and locking them in cages.

Trump is running a criminal enterprise out of the people's house; Steve Bannon is just the latest senior Trump official to be charged with felonies. What the hell more do people need to see to conclude that Trump is unfit for office, incapable and incompetent, and likely to leave Washington in handcuffs?

Despite the overwhelming and undeniable evidence, these hypocritical gay Republicans continue to carry water for their criminal master. The latest is Ric Grenell, the former acting Director of National Intelligence (key word: acting), who released an unintentionally hilarious video touting Trump as the "most pro-gay president in American history."

In the Log Cabin-produced clip, Grenell refers to "gays and lesbians" throughout, notably eschewing the more common "LGBTQ." That's because while Trump's attacks on gays and lesbians may be more subtle, his assault on the transgender community is overt and aggressive. From banning transgender service members from the military, to enacting an HHS rule that ends nondiscrimination protections for trans patients, Trump has used the transgender community as a punching bag to score cheap points with his bigoted base.

In the video, Grenell criticizes Joe Biden for not congratulating him on his acting appointment. Maybe that's because the short, temporary, non-Senate-confirmed appointment was roundly criticized by experts in the intelligence community due to Grenell's stunning lack of experience. "This is a job requiring leadership, management, substance and secrecy," John Sipher, a former CIA officer, told the New York Times. "He doesn't have the kind of background and experience we would expect for such a critical position." That's quite the diplomatic understatement.

Grenell touts his experience as ambassador to Germany, another short-tenured post that led to widespread criticism about his inexperience and ham-handed efforts to interfere in internal German politics.

He references Trump's purported effort to decriminalize homosexuality around the world, but that effort seems to exist in word, not in deed.

Grenell further criticizes Biden for his past anti-gay positions. Yes, Biden, along with most other Democrats and Republicans, has evolved on LGBTQ issues over the decades (as have a majority of Americans), but we must allow allies to grow, change and ultimately fight with us.

By contrast, Trump's assault on LGBTQ equality is long and well documented. From picking the notoriously homophobic Mike Pence — who doth protest too much — as his vice president, to naming a slew of hostile, right-wing judges to the federal bench, to advocating for so-called "religious freedom" carveouts to enable anti-LGBTQ discrimination, Trump has undermined decades of work in just four short years.

Grenell isn't the only gay toadie still standing in Trump's corner. Robert Kabel, Log Cabin's board chair and a former Reagan administration official, this week announced the impending release of his new book. In the press release announcing it, Kabel "is proud to call the GOP the true party of equality — not the Democratic Party."

Again, these delusional sycophants cherry-pick empty Trump gestures to justify their support while ignoring a tidal wave of attacks on LGBTQ Americans. Has Kabel read his own party's platform?

The 2016 platform was recently readopted for 2020. As the Blade reported, "it calls for ending same-sex marriage either through judicial reconsideration or a constitutional amendment, offers veiled support for widely discredited conversion therapy and objects to enforcing civil rights laws to ensure transgender people can use the restroom consistent with their gender identity. Although the 2016 document doesn't explicitly mention conversion therapy, it includes this line: 'We support the right of parents to determine the proper medical treatment and therapy for their minor children.'"

Grenell, Kabel and the rest of Trump's twisted enablers aren't just on the wrong side of history, they're on the wrong side of the law. LGBTQ voters see through these last-gasp attempts by his enablers to hang onto power. From the botched COVID response that has claimed thousands of American lives, to the stoking of racial division and support for white supremacists, to retreating from the climate change fight and the rolling back of LGBTQ equality, Trump has shown the world he is unfit for the presidency. He knows that clinging to power by any means necessary is the only way he will avoid prison.

Instead of Grenell and Kabel, let's look to Pete Buttigieg for inspiration. As he put it in his convention speech Thursday night, "I believe in this country because America uniquely holds the promise of a place where everyone can belong. ... Joe Biden is right: This is a contest for the soul of the nation."

Indeed it is. Some of us will emerge with our dignity intact. Others like Grenell and Kabel will have to explain how they sided with a monster who worked to dismantle our government, destroy our democracy and harm members of our LGBTQ community.

"All the News Straight Enough to Print, Feb. 10, 2006"

I have a complicated relationship with the Washington Post. My very first published opinion piece appeared in the Post in 1981; I was a 10-year-old baseball fan upset about the MLB strike that year and wrote a letter to the editor. Years later, I wrote a long piece for the Post about my experiences in dot com land and the itinerant absurdities of internet startups of the late '90s. For sure there are dedicated, talented even brilliant journalists working there, like Marc Fisher.

But for years, from 1991-2008, the Post was led by executive editor Leonard Downie, whose problematic tenure the Blade and I critiqued extensively. Downie was known to "straight-wash" Post stories, removing references to a source's sexual orientation, even if they were publicly out. In one publicized spat between Downie and me, I criticized the paper's handling of the killing of a gay service member in Iraq. The Post's ombudsman agreed with my critique and the Columbia University School of Journalism investigated and produced a report on it all. More on that later. In this piece, I was responding to several Post stories in early 2006 that ignored a subject's sexual orientation.

Gay newspaper readers have become adept at reading between the lines. When someone is described as "flamboyant," "eccentric" or "a lifelong bachelor," we know what's being implied. Whether straight readers get it is another question. Readers of the Washington Post had better hone their gaydar skills, because in story after story, the news gathering behemoth either ignores questions of sexual orientation or employs endless winks and nods to convey what would be better spelled out.

Take the Post's lengthy profile of figure skater Johnny Weir, which ran as the lead sports story on Feb. 7. The writer, Amy Shipley, describes Weir as eccentric and notes that some have nicknamed the Olympic medal contender as "Johnny Weird." She devotes extensive attention to Weir's costume choices, and references his penchant for hair dye, sequins, glitter and even chinchilla scarves. The accompanying photo shows Weir, 21, on the ice sporting a costume with "one arm covered with fishnet and sequins, part of a silver-and-white cascade of glitter and sparkle designed to evoke his choice of music." Weir's father is quoted as saying, "My child's not weird."

But the article never addresses the 800-pound gorilla in the room. Readers are left to wonder whether the "eccentric" Weir is gay. A profile like this should answer those questions, not raise them. Of course, a news story reporting the outcome of one of Weir's competitions wouldn't include a reference to his sexual orientation, whatever it is. But in a lengthy personal profile, in which parents and colleagues are interviewed, the sexual orientation question is a glaring omission. Unfortunately, this kind of "straight-washing" isn't limited to the Post's sports section.

When Randi Miller won a recent competition to record the "doors closing" message for Metro, the Post published the obligatory profile story. The article contains no mention of family or significant other. It does mention that when Miller won, she celebrated with friends. My gaydar went off, a Blade reporter made a couple of calls and quickly confirmed that Miller is, in fact, an out lesbian. You can read a more complete profile of her on page 40 in this week's Blade. And the Post's straight-washing isn't confined to personality profiles. Regular Blade readers know that the D.C. City Council passed — and Mayor Anthony Williams signed — a sweeping new domestic partnership bill that makes the city one of the most progressive in terms of extending rights to gay couples. Only Massachusetts, California, Connecticut, Hawaii and New Jersey offer comparable or greater D.P. benefits. The Domestic Partnership Equality Act provides inheritance rights, child-support and alimony requirements, among other benefits and obligations, for opposite and same-sex domestic partners.

Williams signed the measure on Jan. 26 without fanfare in the privacy of his office. It's clear that Williams chose to avoid public attention to the D.P. bill because of a fear that conservatives in Congress will try to overturn it during the required 30-day legislative review period. So is the Post in cahoots with Williams to keep the lid on news of the new law? The largest newspaper in the region has largely failed to report on the matter. At a time when lawmakers in neighboring Maryland and Virginia are proposing constitutional amendments to ban gay marriage, D.C. is moving in a much more tolerant direction. But Post readers wouldn't know it.

Another story making Blade headlines recently is the apparent suicide of Sgt. Robert Schoonover of the D.C. Police Department's Fifth District. Schoonover was openly gay and cofounded the Gay Officer's Action League in the Washington area. Schoonover's death merited just a one-sentence mention in a Post story about another officer who committed suicide while on duty. Many newspapers have policies against reporting on suicides, so the initial failure to report Schoonover's death may appear insignificant. But a Blade report two weeks ago revealed credible allegations of homophobia, racism and sexism in the Fifth District that likely played a role in Schoonover's death. Again, Post readers wouldn't know about that. These kinds of failures at the Post are not a recent phenomenon. The paper was woefully negligent in reporting on the myriad scandals that plagued the city's HIV/AIDS Administration, which eventually resulted in a City Council investigation and the firing by Mayor Williams of the agency's director. Last year, the Post, along with other mainstream publications, was rightly criticized for ignoring the sexual orientation of several high-profile people in published obituaries, including Luther Vandross, Susan Sontag and Ismail Merchant.

It's time for mainstream media, including the Post, to grow up and take a more complete and honest approach to covering the news. If a reporter thinks that a medal-contending skater is gay, then ask him and report what he says. When a famous gay person like Ismail Merchant dies, interview his longtime partner for the obituary. And if an openly gay police officer commits suicide amid charges of institutional homophobia in his district, then investigate it. The very fact of an interview subject's sexual orientation should not be considered a private issue any more than a heterosexual person who is asked about having a spouse or children. When straight athletes, stars and other public figures are profiled in the media, they are always asked — and always answer — questions about their wives, girlfriends and children. It's a frustrating double standard that those same kinds of questions are considered off limits to "eccentric" personalities.

"JUST THE FACTS," FEB. 9, 2007

This piece touches on one of my longstanding frustrations — the lack of respect afforded to the queer press. It's like because we're alternative media, we're somehow illegitimate; we don't follow the same journalistic principles as mainstream outlets; we're inherently untrustworthy. Just another symptom of the homophobia we encounter while doing our jobs. If I had a dime for every time I had to reassure a source, advertiser or another mainstream reporter that I attended journalism school at Penn State and worked for mainstream outlets before joining the Blade, I could have retired young. Over the years, our staff has endured such disrespect that it's impossible to recount here. Those tales could fill an entire book of their own, from our White House reporters being forced to stand in the back of the room for decades, to endless institutions denying us press credentials because we represent the LGBTQ community.

During the fight over the Employment Non-Discrimination Act, I sat on a panel discussion with other experts on the issue. The morning of the panel, the Washington Post published an opinion piece endorsing ENDA; the author was on the panel with me. When he was introduced, the audience erupted in applause. When it died down, I asked, "I'm curious where you got your information for the op-ed because the Washington Post's newsroom hasn't written a single word about ENDA." He stammered, "Oh well, I used the Blade." Of course he did. And of course he never credited us in the piece. That happens a lot.

You have to develop a rhinoceros's skin to work in LGBTQ media. You'll never get the credit or respect you deserve. The homophobes will attack and insult you at every turn and even threaten your life. My colleagues are brave journalists and far tougher, I'd argue, than our straight counterparts.

Keeping tabs on mainstream media coverage of gay issues is becoming a full-time job as gay visibility increases and more outlets devote time and space to our plight.

Two recent examples illustrate ways in which old-school journalists and online upstarts still get our stories wrong.

A Blade reader emailed an interesting tidbit last week. It seems there's been a debate raging at Wikipedia about the biographical entry for openly closeted CNN anchor Anderson Cooper.

The Blade and numerous other publications have written for years about Cooper's sexual orientation. Cooper refused to discuss his private life, even though he's more than happy to sit for endless interviews and to be featured on magazine covers and in CNN's ubiquitous ad campaigns promoting his show.

He told New York magazine in 2005, "You know, I understand why people might be interested. But I just don't talk about my personal life. It's a decision I made a long time ago, before I ever even knew anyone would be interested in my personal life. The whole thing about being a reporter is that you're supposed to be an observer and to be able to adapt with any group you're in, and I don't want to do anything that threatens that."

Of course, this is completely disingenuous because Cooper was willing to talk to Oprah about his brother's suicide. It doesn't get much more personal than that. And to suggest that a reporter can't cover a story if his sources know his sexual orientation is patently absurd. Do straight reporters take off their wedding rings and deny being straight to cover the news? Does being African American or female impede the ability of women and Black people to work as reporters? Cooper's argument is illogical, evasive and raises more questions than it answers.

The new wrinkle is that an editor at Wikipedia last week deleted a reference on the site to an editorial I wrote in 2005 criticizing Cooper for his evasive answers in the New York magazine profile. The editor writes, "There is no evidence the Washington Blade is a significant, nontrivial, reliable source.

I'd argue there's no evidence that Wikipedia is a reliable source.

The Blade has a rich history in the D.C. community dating to 1969. The debate over citing the Blade in Cooper's bio, which is playing out in a Wikipedia discussion thread, notes that other mainstream media sources, including ABC News and U.S. News & World Report, have cited the Blade as a credible news source. I could go on, but I think most thoughtful readers know that the Blade is a credible journalistic enterprise with award-winning journalists on staff.

Moving on, a Wikipedia editor writes, "We have an obligation to make certain that WP is not seen as a vehicle that can be used to 'Out' people, or in any other way be used to damage or smear people."

Let's just ignore this blatantly homophobic comment. Suggesting that describing someone as gay constitutes a "smear" is a tired old insult.

The editor adds, "At no point do we have verification from Cooper or any other reliable source that he is in fact gay, only speculation. Speculation is not encyclopedic, nor does it have any room in WP."

The reality is that without speculation, we wouldn't know about the sexual orientation of many notable people. But times have changed and laws have changed. No one is going to charge Anderson Cooper with sodomy if he comes out. And the point of my original editorial wasn't so much to "out" anyone, it was to highlight how ridiculous and insulting it is for rich, famous, successful people to refuse to answer "the question." No straight person denies being straight.

Getting back to Wikipedia and its overzealous "editors," it's important to point out that anyone can edit an entry on the site. "On Wikipedia, and its sister projects, you are welcome to be bold and edit articles yourself, contributing knowledge as you see fit in a collaborative way. So, go ahead!"

I've always instructed reporters never to use Wikipedia. It's not a reliable source and its content is subject to manipulation from anyone. In this case, a CNN staffer? A Cooper fan? Cooper himself? Who knows?

It's just another reminder that as our sources of news and information evolve, it's important to consider the source and double check your facts. Wikipedia's bio of Anderson Cooper is now incomplete and straight-washed. What does that suggest about the reliability of the rest of its site?

Meanwhile, journalists at decidedly mainstream, established outlets continue to trip up when telling gay-related stories.

There was a telling error in the Washington Post late last month. In a Jan. 24 Style section story about gay-friendly B&Bs in Virginia, Post reporter Gary Lee writes, "Although no public facility can lawfully discriminate against guests based on sexual orientation, some warm more easily than others to two men (or women) checking in together."

Of course, as area gays and lesbians know all too well, public facilities in Virginia absolutely can — and do — discriminate based on sexual orientation.

The Virginia Human Rights Act states: "It is the policy of the Commonwealth to 1. Safeguard all individuals within the Commonwealth from unlawful discrimination because of race, color, religion, national origin, sex, pregnancy, childbirth or related medical conditions; age, marital status or disability; in places of public accommodation, including educational institutions and in real estate transactions; in employment; preserve the public safety, health and general welfare; and further the interests, rights and privileges of individuals within the Commonwealth; and 2. Protect citizens of the Commonwealth against unfounded charges of unlawful discrimination."

Notice that there is no mention of sexual orientation. Beyond that omission, Virginia has on its books some of the most anti-gay laws in the nation, including a same-sex marriage ban and the Marriage Affirmation Act, which bars gays from entering into contracts with each other for anything resembling marriage rights. It's not a place gay couples should flock to spend their money, but that's another quibble.

It's troubling, though not surprising, that the Post is unaware of these basic facts. So many straight people, many of whom are gay friendly, have no idea that legalized discrimination is a fact of life for gay people.

The Post's Lee and his editors probably just assumed that in the year 2007, the law would bar overt discrimination against gays. But, alas, Virginia is woefully behind the times.

The Post finally issued a correction this week after several messages left with the ombudsman. Its editors and reporters should familiarize themselves with local laws when covering gay issues and endeavor to do more aggressive reporting on the very real — and perfectly legal — discrimination faced by many of its readers.

"Washington Post's gay problem," April 4, 2008

The Post's reporters and editors have often disappointed on LGBTQ issues — from using Blade coverage without credit to relegating queer stories to the Style section (that's still mostly the case). When the Blade's former parent company filed for bankruptcy in 2009, the Post deemed it important enough for a front-page story with photos of staff carrying their boxes out of our offices. When the Blade came back and in 2019 celebrated its 50th anniversary with a gala, the Post didn't write a single word about the milestone. By way of comparison, the neighboring Baltimore Sun published a prominent feature story by David Zurawik, the nation's leading media critic.

This story chronicles some of those problems under former Post executive editor Len Downie, who was notoriously skittish about identifying anyone as gay. In another sign of progress, the Post now boasts many openly LGBTQ reporters and editors, including Jonathan Capehart and Dan Zak. Many of us advocated for the Post to repeal its arcane style policies on LGBTQ issues. The paper's openly LGBTQ staff have been crucial to pushing for change. Things have certainly changed there, but as media companies like the Post are taken over by billionaire owners, the risk of backsliding is ever present and readers should remain vigilant. It's the same thing at the New York Times, where not so long ago the paper wouldn't publish the commitment ceremonies or civil union announcements of same-sex couples. Young LGBTQ readers are accustomed to seeing themselves in mainstream media coverage, but it wasn't always that way and there's no guarantee it will stay that way.

The story of a gay Army major who died in Iraq has presented the Washington Post and other mainstream media outlets with an opportunity to revisit and update their stylebook policies regarding when to identify someone as gay.

As the Blade reported last week, Maj. Alan Rogers, by all accounts a hero for his brave acts while serving in Iraq, was killed in January and buried at Arlington National Cemetery. Rogers lived as openly gay a life as he could, given the military's discriminatory "Don't Ask, Don't Tell" policy. He had many gay friends in D.C., patronized gay businesses and even worked as treasurer for the D.C. chapter of American Veterans for Equal Rights, a group working to overturn the military's gay ban.

But the mainstream media accounts of his death omitted any reference to his sexual orientation. These were not benign omissions. The Washington Post, in particular, worked overtime to exorcise any mention of Rogers' sexual orientation. It did not even report his work for AVER. Several of Rogers' gay friends told the Blade that they were interviewed by a Post reporter at the funeral, but their memories were not included in the paper's coverage.

Even in death, the military succeeded in keeping Rogers in the closet — until his grieving friends began speaking out. It's one thing for the military to hide the truth of this hero's life, but it's quite another for the media to play along.

The Post ditched its responsibility to the truth, opting instead to enforce its 1950s-era views of sexual orientation that require gay subjects to remain in the closet.

The paper's ombudsman, Deborah Howell, agreed that the paper had erred.

"The Post was right to be cautious, but there was enough evidence — particularly of Rogers' feeling about 'Don't Ask, Don't Tell' — to warrant quoting his friends and adding that dimension to the story of his life," Howell wrote in a column Sunday. "The story would have been richer for it."

The story would have been accurate for it. Most disturbing about the Post's coverage is that it wasn't a Metro section reporter or even a junior editor who made the call to straight-wash Rogers' life. That decision was made by Executive Editor Len Downie himself, according to Howell.

The reporter's original story included accounts of Rogers' sexual orientation and the issue triggered a debate among editors who deemed it an "agonizing decision." But "the decision ultimately was made by Executive Editor Len Downie, who said that there was no proof that Rogers was gay and no clear indication that, if he was, he wanted the information made public."

And there we have it, at last, an explanation for the antiquated way the Post so often deals with the issue of sexual orientation in its coverage: the top editor doesn't get it.

It's incredible that reporting such a basic fact about someone led to an agonizing debate among editors, necessitating Downie's involvement. How frequently does Downie get in the weeds of stories appearing inside the Metro section? Doesn't the top editor of the Washington Post have more pressing issues to worry about?

Downie seeks "proof," yet he removed any mention of Rogers' gay friends from the story. He worries that Rogers may not have wanted this information made public, but Rogers worked for a gay rights group. Clearly, Rogers was not afraid of people knowing the truth about his life. There was concern that Rogers' few surviving family members — cousins — didn't want the Post to report on his being gay. But what gay people know is that many of our family members would prefer we stayed in the closet. That decision should not be left to disapproving relatives. For so many gay and lesbian people, friends become a chosen family. And in Rogers' case, they should have been trusted to speak on his behalf.

Downie's decision, and the Post's stylebook policy, help perpetuate the notion that being gay is something to hide. If Rogers had been straight, there would be no heated debate about making references to relationships or hobbies that implied he was heterosexual. At the very least, Downie could have left intact a reference to AVER, a basic and hardly controversial fact.

The Post's stylebook states, "A person's sexual orientation should not be mentioned unless relevant to the story ... Not everyone espousing gay rights causes is homosexual. When identifying an individual as gay or homosexual, be cautious about invading the privacy of someone who may not wish his or her sexual orientation known."

The policy is outdated and overly broad. Of course you don't mention sexual orientation when not relevant, but in an obituary? As the cliché goes, on your deathbed, no one wishes they'd spent more time on the job; they wish for more time with loved ones. Reporting the identities of those loved ones and their relationship to the deceased ought to be mandatory.

But the Post's problems go beyond the obit section. Another recent example of the wrong-headedness of the stylebook policy comes to mind. When Metro held auditions to find the new voice for its "doors closing" announcement, the Post interviewed and profiled the winner — a lesbian. Is it relevant to the story about Metro that its new public voice is gay? Not in a straightforward news account. But in a feature story about that person's life, it's essential. The Post ignored her sexual orientation and left readers with more questions about this woman than answers.

The same goes for the Rogers story. His friend Lara Ballard put it best: "Anyone who didn't know Alan was gay didn't know Alan very well."

The Post's gay problem manifests itself with unfortunate regularity — from the straight-washed obituaries of gay figures like Susan Sontag and Ismail Merchant to a recent travel article erroneously stating that anti-gay discrimination in public accommodations is illegal in Virginia.

The Rogers case represents a chance for the Post and other mainstream media outlets to thoughtfully reexamine how they view sexual orientation. It is not a private fact for straight people and it should not be considered a private fact for gay people. It's time to abolish that offensive and destructive double standard.

Maybe when the media grow up and deal in a mature, responsible and factual way with sexual orientation, the military will follow and finally end "Don't Ask, Don't Tell."

That's what Rogers worked for and it would be a fitting tribute to his life.

"Our mission continues," Nov. 20, 2009, D.C. Agenda

To say that fall 2009 was eventful for the Blade would be a monumental understatement. Shortly after President Obama signed the nation's first federal LGBTQ legislation into law, the Blade celebrated its 40th anniversary with a cocktail reception, VIP guest speakers and even a party crashing by the infamous Salahis — Tareq and Michaele of White House party-crashing fame. The then-couple arrived unexpectedly and donated a case of wine from their own vineyard to the party; Michaele — who was part of the cast of "Real Housewives of Washington DC" — even wore a stunning blue evening gown, the Blade's logo color. Before I knew what was happening, she grabbed the microphone and made a speech, congratulating the Blade on its milestone. It was all unplanned and odd, but added to the fun of the night. Maybe they were rehearsing their act, because just one month later, the couple entered a White House State Dinner uninvited, triggering a national scandal that led to subpoenas from the Committee on Homeland Security. The Salahis invoked their Fifth Amendment right against self-incrimination and declined to answer questions 32 times at the hearing. I was shocked to see the couple on the news after what had transpired at the Blade 40th soiree and recognized them immediately.

A week after the Blade party, Tareq called me at the office and asked if the Blade would sponsor his annual event, the America's Polo Cup, which a "Real Housewives of Washington DC" costar memorably described as a "goat rodeo." We declined. The "Housewives of DC" was mercifully not renewed and the Salahis endured a melodramatic break-up and divorce.

If only that were the end of the fall 2009 drama.

Just weeks after celebrating our 40th anniversary, I arrived at the Blade's offices in the National Press Building around 8:15 a.m. on Monday, Nov. 16, 2009. I was almost always the first person in the office, even though I had the longest commute (from Baltimore). The office was surrounded by glass walls and I could see two figures in our conference room, an unexpected sight that early. When I walked in, I recognized two senior executives from our parent company, Window Media. They were in town from Atlanta. This can't be good, I thought.

When I walked into the office, they informed me that the parent company had filed for Chapter 7 liquidation, we were closed effective immediately and had until the afternoon to clear out our personal property. Gobsmacked, I retreated to my office, closed the door and crumpled to the floor in tears. As editor, I felt responsible and couldn't imagine presiding over the demise of this important community institution, just weeks after our triumphant anniversary party. I immediately called my partner, Brian, and sobbed. In his usual calm-and-collected way, he reminded me that I'm the boss and not allowed to cry. He was right and I pulled myself together and started calling the staff, beginning with our publisher, Lynne Brown. Gradually, the staff trickled in to get the news that our paychecks for the preceding two weeks were voided. Later, we learned the company had stopped paying our health insurance premiums and some employees were stuck with unpaid medical bills. The staff began packing up and there were lots of hugs and tears. Of course, no one in D.C. can keep a secret and within an hour, my phone was lighting up with media calls. Inconveniently for me, many of those outlets had offices inside the Press Building and it didn't take long for a bank of TV cameras to arrive, their lenses aimed through the glass, capturing the staff packing and crying. In an effort to appease them and shoo them away, I decided to make a statement, but needed to pee first. The bathrooms were in the hallway behind the cameras. I approached the reporters, then promised I would return after peeing first. One outlet included that charming detail in its report of our bankruptcy.

I made a vague statement that we would be back and to stay tuned, but really had no idea nor much interest in what would happen next. The bankruptcy wasn't a total surprise; there had been speculation and reporting about our parent company's tens of millions of dollars in outstanding SBA loans. Lynne, our sales executive, Brian Pitts, and I even tried to buy the Blade from Window Media but were rebuffed. Months later, we were relieved because we ended up buying the Blade's assets for pennies on the dollar from the bankruptcy court.

Window Media had also stopped paying the web hosting company, which promptly deleted the Blade's online archives upon hearing of the bankruptcy. We worried about the 40-year print archive, which contained valuable and one-of-a-kind articles and photographs in a dozen metal filing cabinets. But now the archive belonged to the bankruptcy court and we were locked out at 3:30 p.m.

I made my way home in a zombie-like state. Not only was I out of a job, but this had become a major news story in D.C. and beyond. The Washington Post, which couldn't be bothered to even mention the Blade's 50th anniversary in 2019, played the bankruptcy story on the front page with a photo. Everyone loves a funeral! It was everywhere and I felt humiliated and totally demoralized.

My partner was out of town on business, so I was home alone. My close friend Greg Alexander showed up later with four bottles of wine. "I wasn't sure which to bring, so I brought them all," he announced. We drank them all and I passed out.

When I woke up, head throbbing, I checked email and to my great shock discovered more than 400 messages had come in overnight from all over the world. I had no idea the reach of the Blade and couldn't believe all the people near and far who wanted to help. There were financial contributions from as far away as France and Turkey. Local college kids said they had no money to donate but could deliver papers for a new venture. Real estate developers offered us free office space; writers, photographers, designers volunteered their services. It was an overwhelming outpouring of love and support that we couldn't ignore. I swallowed four Advil and hopped the train back to D.C. for a coffeeshop meeting of the staff that wanted to attempt a new venture.

I felt like shit and wanted to go back to bed but the rest of the team couldn't wait to get to work. "The Blade hasn't missed a week in 40 years and we can't start now," was the mantra. This was Tuesday morning and the Blade is distributed on Friday. We had no offices, no computers, no money, printer, distributor or even a name. There was no website, URL, legal entity, insurance, street boxes or anything needed to pull off launching a new publication. I figured we'd get organized, then re-launch something in a few weeks. But the undaunted team at the Blade wouldn't allow that — we would publish Friday, in three days.

Lynne, our publisher, stopped at a gay-owned restaurant for lunch that day and was recognized by another customer. He asked her if we were going to publish something and she said yes. He then asked what the first printing bill would cost and she replied, "about $2,000." This stranger pulled out a checkbook and gave her a check for the full amount. We were back in business.

Meanwhile, I felt oddly drawn to Lambda Rising, the iconic gay bookstore where I'd first discovered the Blade way back in high school. Its owner, Deacon Maccubbin, opened the store in 1974, and was a legend in the community and we were acquainted. I walked to the store and sat down in his office. I have no idea why I went there; I needed to unload on someone who understood the legacy of the Blade, I guess. He was kind and sympathetic as always and let me vent.

Over the next few days, I commuted to D.C. as usual but had nowhere to go, so I office-surfed as friends let me crash for a few hours in-between media interviews about the bankruptcy. One memorable interview came at WYPR, D.C.'s NPR station with Kojo Nnamdi, who hosted a popular talk show for many years. He had me as a guest for a full hour and we talked all things Blade. He took a call from a woman who said she was a D.C. public school teacher. "Kevin, if I had a million dollars, I would give it to you and your staff," she said. "My gay students bring the Blade to class and I see them reading it. It's such an important resource for them."

I could feel the tears welling up in my eyes, then heard Lynne's voice in my head, "There's no crying in newspapers!" So I meekly thanked her for the kind words and moved to the next caller.

While I kept the Blade in the media spotlight in hopes of finding an angel investor, the staff was busy writing stories, selling advertising, creating a website and logo and more. And four days after being kicked out of our offices and shut down, we published a modest, eight-page newsletter called the "DC Agenda." We distributed it ourselves. We were back. Two weeks later, we upgraded from newsletter format to newsprint again. Everyone was working for free while collecting unemployment but that wouldn't last long. Weeks later, our attorney secured the Blade's assets — the brand name and archive — from the bankruptcy court for a song. And in April 2010, my new business partners — Lynne Brown and Brian Pitts — and I re-launched the Washington Blade brand. Gradually, the full staff returned to payroll. This was the front-page essay I wrote on that fateful Friday, just three days after the bankruptcy.

Don't judge us too harshly — the edition of DC Agenda you're holding is a modest, early iteration of what we hope to achieve in the wake of Washington Blade's sudden closing this week.

The news that parent company Window Media was shuttering and liquidating its newspapers came as a shock to the staff, some of whom devoted their careers to the paper that became an institution. We were ushered out the doors of our officers with no severance, canceled paychecks and more questions than answers about why this was allowed to happen.

The former staff of the Washington Blade remains united and DC Agenda represents our effort at continuing the important mission and work of the Blade. It will grow and evolve to include a much larger and diverse group of voices. But the core of the Washington Blade's work remains unchanged. We will cover Congress, the White House, the LGBT rights movement, the D.C. marriage fight, local hate crimes and other political issues important to the LGBT residents of the city.

It's been a tough week for us, but we are buoyed by the outpouring of support from people all over the city and beyond. We welcome and need your help and will respond to each offer as soon as possible. Thank you to all who have pledged to stick with us, especially our advertisers. Please visit savetheblade.com for updated information on DC Agenda or to make a gift to support the new venture.

The strength of the Washington Blade did not lie in its brand name — it came from the spirit of those who worked passionately to serve and inform our community. Those people are still here. Our work continues.

"That time I entered the 'No Spin Zone,'" April 21, 2017

After years of dominating Fox News, karma finally caught up to Bill O'Reilly after he was accused of serial sexual harassment and he was fired. I couldn't resist acknowledging the moment and reliving my own experience in the "No Spin Zone."

About 10 years ago, I entered the "No Spin Zone," as a guest on Bill O'Reilly's now-canceled Fox News show. The topic was my criticism of the cult of Scientology, which I bashed for, among other things, its use of "reparative therapy" to "cure" gays.

When I arrived on set — and before the cameras were rolling — O'Reilly was friendly, chatty and full of questions about the Blade, how long I'd worked there, etc. We talked amiably for several minutes about various topics before he started the show.

Then it was my turn in the hot seat and suddenly O'Reilly's personality shifted from friendly and warm to the caricature so perfectly lampooned by Stephen Colbert — the ever-angry, red-faced defender of American values. When he likened gays to drug abusers, I called him out and he quickly replied, "Don't be a wise guy."

What most of his viewers don't realize is that O'Reilly's biggest talent isn't as a broadcaster or author, but as an actor.

Prior to launching his Fox show, he hosted "Inside Edition," an entertainment news show. Then he brilliantly created his angry everyman persona and turned it into a lucrative and mega-successful enterprise. Reports suggest he's leaving Fox with a $25 million golden parachute.

That huge sum probably isn't enough to soothe O'Reilly's outsized ego after his public fall precipitated by the brave former female coworkers who exposed his serial sexual harassment — a situation that even O'Reilly couldn't spin his way out of.

"Why do we need the LGBT media?" May 1, 2019

As we prepare to celebrate the 50th anniversary of the Stonewall Rebellion, panel discussions are breaking out all over the country about the LGBT movement, its history and future. One of the topics getting some attention is the role of the LGBT media in the movement.

The Los Angeles LGBT Center is hosting a panel discussion on May 8 titled "Breaking News, Breaking Barriers," a conversation with LGBT journalists about the coverage and representation of LGBT people in the media from the late 1960s through today. The Los Angeles Blade's tireless news editor/reporter Karen Ocamb will serve on the panel, along with LZ Granderson and Bettina Boxall of the LA Times and Luis Sandoval of Despierta America.

No doubt, they will be asked to address the question of why we need the LGBT media in 2019. It's a question I encountered countless times during the 2016 presidential campaign, when Hillary Clinton was assured victory and would cement all the progress toward equality of the Obama years. Clinton may have neglected the Rust Belt during her campaign, but she remembered her LGBT base and granted the Blade an interview late in the campaign.

We get the rather insulting question about why we need our own niche press a lot in social media comments, usually after identifying a source as LGBT. "Who cares if Pete Buttigieg is gay?!? Why does it matter?!?" Cable news pundits have wondered the same. The reason it matters is that it's never happened before at this level. And imagine the inspiration Buttigieg is providing to the confused, closeted kid in Indiana right now.

Insulting the LGBT media and questioning the need for our existence is a particular form of disrespect and homophobia. That disrespect has come from all sides. Prominent Washington Post opinion writers for years relied on the Blade's coverage to inform their commentary without citing us, a professional faux pas bordering on unethical. The Democratic National Committee's former director of communications, Karen Finney, once wrote in an email that she used the Blade to line her birdcage during a tumultuous period when the DNC was being sued by its former LGBT liaison and we were running critical stories. The birdcage line is a lame insult, but if she'd directed it at the African-American press or Jewish press, she would have been fired.

The need for our work is clearer now that we're back to a hostile administration in the White House. Mainstream reporters rarely ask questions in the White House and State Department briefing rooms about LGBT topics. As Barney Frank used to say, "If you're not at the table, you're probably on the menu." Underrepresented communities need to tell their stories through their own lens. Take a look at the New York Times or Washington Post straight-washed obituaries of prominent LGBT people over the last 30 years and compare them to obits in the LGBT press and you'll see that importance.

More recently, the Blade has focused on Latin America and immigration, embedding with LGBT migrants at the border since their plight is unique and largely ignored by mainstream outlets.

LGBT media outlets also speak the language of our community — and in a way that's not patronizing. Take the recent trolling in the New York Post of a supposedly closeted bisexual presidential candidate jealous of Buttigieg's surging poll numbers. We know they're talking about Sen. Cory Booker, even as the Post hides behind dated, cheeky innuendo in raising the longstanding but unconfirmed rumors.

LGBT media are also unafraid of writing about the sexual orientation of public officials when they are attacking their own or working for an administration undermining our equality. Most heterosexual, mainstream reporters and readers would be shocked to learn that President Trump has possibly appointed a gay Cabinet secretary in the EPA's Andrew Wheeler. That as-yet-unconfirmed rumor has swirled since his days as counsel for the notorious homophobe Sen. Jim Inhofe. We've never had an openly gay Cabinet secretary, so Wheeler has a chance to make history if it's true.

And he's not the only senior Trump official who may be hiding a gay secret (stay tuned). LGBT outlets were ahead of mainstream outlets on everyone from Sen. Larry Craig to Fox News' Shepard Smith.

As the Washington Blade prepares to celebrate its own 50th this year, all of us are working hard to fulfill that longstanding mission of telling LGBT stories and writing the first draft of our own history.

"Thank You for Trusting Us with Your Stories," Oct. 18, 2019

This was adapted from my speech delivered at the Blade's 50th anniversary gala on Friday, Oct. 18 at the Intercontinental Hotel. The event marked the end of a busy year commemorating the Blade's founding in October 1969, just a few months after the Stonewall Rebellion. I was passionate about the gala and determined to mark the occasion in a big way — fancy ballroom, VIPs in the audience, distinguished speakers. Mayor Muriel Bowser declared it "Washington Blade Day" in D.C. and Rep. David Cicilline, the senior openly gay member of the House, spoke. Philanthropist Ariadne Getty and her children flew in from L.A. to accept the Blade's Lifetime Achievement Award. Broadway star Frenchie Davis performed and killed it. (We initially signed a contract for "American Idol" loser Jeremiah Lloyd Harmon to perform, but he canceled the contract just weeks before the gala and bailed. Of all the egomaniacs and entitled divas I've encountered in this job, Harmon is among the worst.) Davis proved a superior choice and had the sold-out ballroom on its feet. My speech followed her performance, which wasn't ideal scheduling, but my remarks were well received — and I didn't cry.

It is impossible to sum up 50 years of what this newspaper has meant to the community in a few short minutes. The New York Times describes the Blade as the "newspaper of record" for the LGBTQ community. That's true. From Lou Chibbaro's unflinching coverage of hate crimes in the city to Chris Johnson's tireless work at the White House to Michael Lavers' investigative work in Latin America and the Caribbean to Joey DiGuglielmo's insightful and entertaining celebrity interviews to Michael Key's award-winning photos documenting it all, we keep busy as the nation's newspaper of record.

But as we know, our readers feel a real connection to the Blade. From my friend Kenji Mundy, who spoke of turning to the Blade for news on "Don't Ask, Don't Tell" when no one else was paying attention; to Isaiah Poole's account of meeting his future husband in the Blade personals, our readers are connected to us and we to them.

During my 17 years at the Blade, I have been privileged to have a front-row seat to some of the most historic moments in our movement — witnessing President Obama sign the repeal of "Don't Ask, Don't Tell," attending the first-ever White House Pride receptions and so many other unforgettable events. This job has had its exciting moments, like the time I introduced Antonin Scalia to Laverne Cox. But the stories that have stayed with me and affected me most are those of ordinary people who find themselves in extraordinary circumstances because of bigotry and discrimination. One such story we covered more than 15 years ago involved a young gay couple in Baltimore, long before the arrival of marriage equality. They were public school teachers. One partner, who was estranged from his conservative Christian family, was diagnosed with a terminal illness and died. Despite having a will and all legal protections available at the time, his parents later sued the surviving partner to move their son's body back to the family plot in Tennessee. They won in court and the surviving partner was faced with the prospect of digging up his partner's grave. The Blade covered the story. National legal groups got involved. He kept fighting and eventually won on appeal but only after losing everything he had, his life savings, his car, just to keep his dead partner in the ground.

It was a story of resilience. And that's a theme I have seen repeated in our coverage over the decades. The story of a resilient and loving community fighting to overcome ignorance and hate. We saw it during the height of the AIDS crisis and we saw it again on the ground in Orlando after the Pulse massacre. And we see it today as we stand up to the current administration's attacks on the transgender community.

In 2016, people used to ask me, "Why do we need gay press or gay bars? We have marriage and Hillary is going to win and cement everything." Well, no one says that anymore. As Barney Frank used to say, "If you're not at the table, then you're probably on the menu." I can assure you that the Blade is at the table, working every day to ensure our issues are addressed and our political leaders held accountable.

In the final press conference of his presidency, President Obama called on the Blade's Chris Johnson for the third-to-last question of his presidency. Chris asked him how LGBT issues would factor into his legacy. And President Obama gave a thoughtful answer in which he declined to take credit for all the LGBTQ progress under his administration. He said, "The primary heroes in this stage of our growth as a democracy and a society are all the individual activists and sons and daughters and couples who courageously said, 'This is who I am and I'm proud of it.'"

I'd like to echo that sentiment and thank all the people over 50 years who agreed to trust us with their stories. It's a responsibility we continue to take seriously. Without the courage of all those people over five decades who stepped up, came out and talked openly about their lives, all of our legislative victories would have been impossible. As we wrap this celebration of 50 years, we remain committed to our longstanding mission of telling LGBTQ stories through our lens and writing the first draft of our own history. Thank you for being here and congratulations to the Blade on its first 50 years.

"PETE'S WIN IS A HISTORIC FIRST AND DESERVES ITS MOMENT," FEB. 7, 2020

The mainstream media's penchant for erasing underrepresented communities is a constant source of frustration and the reason we have alternate, niche media. From straight-washing the obituaries of LGBTQ people, to dead-naming trans people, the list of affronts is long. Like this incident of almost entirely ignoring Pete Buttigieg's primary triumph.

The biggest downside of the Iowa debacle is that it cheated Pete Buttigieg — and the rest of LGBTQ America — out of our moment.

It was OUR moment. The moment that an openly gay candidate won a presidential nominating contest. That's never happened before and the significance of it was overshadowed by coverage of failed apps and delayed vote counts. Sure, the major networks mentioned it, but imagine the difference if, on caucus night, Buttigieg had been declared the winner in prime time.

It would have been a huge story and, more importantly, the fund-raising bump — estimated in the tens of millions — he could have expected from such a win would have boosted him further.

But the bumbling Democratic Party of Iowa trusted an untested app that failed and so all the countless hours of door knocking and the millions spent on campaigning and ancillary projects were undermined. The head of the party should be fired and the antiquated caucus circus must end. In fact, maybe Iowa should go last in 2024.

Back to Pete. Those of us who covered the 2004 George W. Bush reelection campaign have a vivid and painful memory of the cynical attacks Bush and Cheney launched that year. That campaign was run on the backs of gay and lesbian couples, demonized in attack ads and ballot initiatives in 11 swing states to ban same-sex marriage. The heartless campaign was run by a closeted gay man — Ken Mehlman — who later came out publicly and worked for redemption.

To think we've gone from those dark days to an openly gay (and married!) man winning Iowa in the span of just 16 years is pretty damn mind blowing.

Congratulations to Buttigieg and his team. Regardless of what happens next, no one can take this victory and its significance away from him — or us.

Is America ready for a gay president? Maybe, maybe not. But Buttigieg has changed the narrative around what's possible for openly LGBTQ public officials, in part by confounding Republican bigots with his military service and eloquent speeches about faith. LGBTQ Americans are not a monolith; we come in many surprising packages. Buttigieg may not be "gay enough" for some or "too gay" for others. But he just showed the rest of the country that if you stay positive, on message and focus on the issues that matter to everyday voters, you can overcome the doubters and the haters. What he's achieved this week is reminiscent of what Danica Roem did in Virginia two years ago, winning a state delegate seat from the most homophobic, transphobic bigot in the state by focusing on local issues important to constituents.

Imagine what's possible in the next 16 years. Imagine the young kids out there watching who will never live in a world where an openly gay presidential candidate is a first or an oddity.

There's no overstating the importance of this moment for LGBTQ America. Thank you, Mayor Pete.

"Blade's mission continues amid crisis," March 25, 2020

I thought I'd seen it all at the Blade — financial crises, a much-publicized bankruptcy — and then 2020 arrived. I'd watched the YouTube videos from Italy of young people stuck in their homes, warning Americans that this was our future. I didn't want to believe it. In early

February, my husband and I traveled to Mexico for a friend's birthday; later that month, we went to Manhattan for another birthday celebration, partying in crowded bars and nightclubs; in early March, I spent two days in an ICU at a local hospital visiting a friend who'd suffered a stroke. No one wore masks or seemed bothered by the storm about to hit us all. Then it happened. My husband and I were in Rehoboth Beach where we own a home, working out at our YMCA. But it didn't feel right. I stepped off the elliptical after just a few minutes, walked over to Brian and told him we should leave. Later that day, we went to lunch at our favorite Dewey Beach, Del., restaurant, the Starboard. Again, we fled after only minutes, uncomfortable by the crowded setting. The next day, Monday, the world shut down. We were out walking on the boardwalk when the police escorted us off the boards and said it was closed. Everything shuttered overnight and nothing would ever be the same. I was freaked out, not only because of the unthinkable tragedy unfolding, but because of what it could mean for the Blade. I couldn't bear another bankruptcy. Overnight, our advertising base collapsed; all arts and entertainment venues were closed, which represented a good chunk of our ads. Many of the places where you could pick up a printed Blade were now closed and who wanted to pick up a printed paper anyway given the risk of contagion? We immediately suspended payroll and everyone went on unemployment. But we'd been here before. If anyone could navigate this unimaginable crisis, it was our team at the Blade. The Payroll Protection Program offered a short-term lifeline and everyone returned to payroll into the summer, but that wouldn't last. Ultimately, we were forced to lay off several employees, some of whom had worked for me for more than 10 years. It was devastating. But we survived. Our community has gotten pretty good at that.

Despite the economic chaos and uncertainty unleashed by the coronavirus pandemic, the Blade staff continues to work hard bringing our readers the local, national and international news needed to navigate this crisis.

On Tuesday, the White House pool report for the world's press was written by the Blade's Chris Johnson, who spent the day shadowing

President Trump, even as Trump continues his reckless attacks on journalists.

Also this week, our own Lou Chibbaro Jr. is working hard to cover the virus's impact on D.C., just as he covered the AIDS epidemic in the 1980s. And Michael K. Lavers is interviewing LGBTQ activists around the world, including in hard-hit Spain, to assess the unique impacts on our community overseas.

Sure, we're all in this together, but the LGBTQ community suffers unique challenges. Our elders are more likely to live alone and suffer from isolation and depression; our youth are more likely to be homeless and thus susceptible to the disease; we are disproportionately entrepreneurial, putting many of our businesses in jeopardy; the HIV-positive among us are more susceptible to infection; LGBTQ and HIV-positive migrants face considerable risk. We're working to cover all of these stories and more impacting the LGBTQ community.

Small businesses, including the Blade, are particularly vulnerable right now, as the government ponders massive bailouts for undeserving cruise lines and airlines, while tossing crumbs at small businesses, the backbone of the U.S. economy. If you are in a position to donate to support our work, please visit bladefoundation.org.

Indeed, as Los Angeles Mayor Eric Garrcetti told the Los Angeles Blade's Karen Ocamb last week, "This community has been through tougher days than this and the most important thing is to not only be resilient but to be calm ... The overwhelming majority of people are going to not only make it through this but we will come back, but we can be leaders."

He's right. When the world turned its back during the height of the AIDS crisis, it was LGBTQ activists who led the way, fought for new drugs, held the government accountable, and shamed religious and political leaders into action.

We must take up that role again today, telling the truth about President Trump's irresponsible and dangerous approach to coronavirus. He uses the power of the bully pulpit to spout misinformation that proved fatal to one man who ingested chloroquine based on Trump's ill-informed recommendation. Worse, Trump ignored warnings in his security briefings about COVID-19 for weeks in January and February, costing us precious time that has led to the deaths of more than 600 Americans as of mid-week. The final toll will be far higher and likely more than the death toll of our deadliest war, the Civil War, which claimed roughly 750,000 American lives.

He talks about being a "war-time president," yet refuses to invoke the Defense Production Act to procure desperately needed personal protective equipment for hospital staff and first responders. His failure to supply adequate tests for the virus is an inexcusable dereliction of duty. We are seeing the full scope of what it means to elect a reality TV show host with no government experience to run the country. We can only hope the latest polls showing Joe Biden with a landslide-scale lead hold up.

In the meantime, stay safe and off the streets and practice social distancing. The Blade will publish in print as long as is feasible as well as online. Stay informed via our social media posts on Facebook, Twitter and Instagram. Sign up for our email newsletters at washingtonblade.com/subscribe. Advertise if you can (email my colleague Brian Pitts at bpitts@washblade.com).

Most importantly, don't panic. We've survived a pandemic before and will persevere again.

"Thank You to the Reporters Who Brave the Briefing Room," April 27, 2020, and "Trump's Attack Dogs Turn on Blade Reporter," May 19, 2020

These two essays shed light on how reporters were treated by the Trump administration, namely with disdain and hostility. The effort

to kick CNN's reporter out of the front row and swap her with the Blade's reporter in the back row backfired mightily as we successfully raised thousands of dollars from sympathetic donors in the wake of the stunt.

Real journalists do not aspire to become the news; in fact they recoil at the prospect. You don't go to J-school to learn PR.

But sometimes circumstances conspire against you, as was the case last Friday when Washington Blade White House reporter Chris Johnson was told to swap chairs with CNN's Kaitlan Collins at the daily COVID briefing.

He rightly refused the order from a White House official, who later threatened him with Secret Service enforcement of the order. (The Secret Service later denied its agents were involved.)

The seating assignments in the briefing room are determined by the White House Correspondents Association, not the White House. The reason for that oversight, which dates to 1914, is to ensure that an administration can't retaliate against reporters who ask tough questions, as current Correspondents Association president Jonathan Karl of ABC News explained this weekend.

Johnson, who has never enjoyed front-row access in the briefings, courageously refused the order and remained in his assigned seat in the back, to the consternation of Trump's staff. As CNN's Jim Acosta noted that night, "it took almost an act of civil disobedience to foil their plans."

And what was the plan? Surely, to punish and embarrass CNN and Collins due to her tough questioning of the president amid his embarrassingly incompetent response to the coronavirus outbreak. This is what the president is doing amid a pandemic that will likely kill upwards of 60,000 Americans by week's end? Plotting petty revenge against reporters he doesn't like and who don't toe the Trump line?

After the seat swap plan failed, Trump pouted, cut the briefing short, and refused to take questions.

Kudos to Johnson and Collins for standing their ground and staying focused on doing their jobs. It's important to note that neither of them has granted interviews, despite scores of requests to talk about the incident. Their actions speak for themselves. The reporters in that room will need to continue looking out for each other as this administration continues its dangerous attacks on journalists.

Trump's actions speak volumes, too. As the coronavirus continues to infect and kill Americans everywhere, he has encouraged violence against local governments in blue states like Minnesota and Virginia, urging his followers to "liberate" them. And they listened, as protesters swarmed multiple state capitals last week, many of them armed with semiautomatic rifles, demanding to be liberated. Multiple outlets reported this weekend about the so-called "boogaloo" movement of right-wing militias hoping to instigate a civil war over quarantine restrictions, which they view as an ominous sign of an unchecked government terrorizing its people. One "boogaloo boy" was even arrested after he live-streamed his efforts to find and assassinate a police officer.

Just as we saw during the "pizzagate" fiasco, when Trump talks, his followers listen. When the president uses the bully pulpit to pitch inane ideas about drinking bleach to cure COVID, gullible Americans flood health departments and hospitals with calls asking if they should ingest Clorox.

With new polls showing the president trailing Joe Biden in a string of critical battleground states, Trump is feeling the walls closing in on his presidency. Unfortunately, as the nation continues to bury its dead and the economy hits Depression-level unemployment, our president is consumed with self-preservation and self-aggrandizement. It's all about Trump, even as we near 60,000 deaths.

It's never been more important to have smart, seasoned journalists in the White House, holding our political and health officials accountable. Thank you to the reporters, like Johnson and Collins, for braving the briefing room to keep us informed. We can add them to the long list of patriotic Americans doing their best to help the rest of us in these unprecedented times: doctors, nurses, transit workers, janitors, police and firefighters, grocery store staff, truck drivers, pharmacists and other everyday people risking their health to keep us safe and fed. Thank you.

"Trump's attack dogs turn on Blade reporter"

Washington Blade political reporter Chris Johnson last week challenged White House Press Secretary Kayleigh McEnany, over her opposition to marriage equality and the administration's preparedness for the upcoming Supreme Court decision on whether Title VII applies to sexual orientation and gender identity.

They were legitimate questions, especially given the gravity of the upcoming high court ruling, which could bar employment discrimination against LGBTQ workers in all 50 states.

And McEnany's record of opposition to LGBTQ rights is long and well documented. She's now a senior adviser to the president of the United States, unlikely as that may seem, so her views are relevant as the government prepares for the ramifications of a potentially sweeping ruling on job protections for LGBTQ workers.

McEnany followed the lead of her three immediate predecessors in the job, avoiding the question and acting exasperated in the process.

After the briefing, Trump's toadies in the right-wing twitterverse and blogosphere jumped into action, attacking Johnson with personal insults and anti-gay slurs. The instantaneous attacks came by the hundreds.

Johnson was called "Chrissy" and "light in the loafers" and labeled a "gaystapo clown." Of course, the ever-charming and predictable "faggot" slur was deployed.

This was no coincidence. Trump has an army of mindless sycophants ready to defend him from any hint of challenge or criticism. From the big guns like Fox News and Rush Limbaugh to the bloggers at Breitbart and RedState and many more lesser-known figures, Trump deploys them to trash, threaten and intimidate anyone in the media deemed critical of his administration.

Make no mistake: We have a White House that openly threatens reporters, disdains the First Amendment and emboldens its supporters to insult and intimidate journalists at outlets large and small.

Fortunately, Johnson is a pro and we have a pretty thick skin in the LGBTQ media. But we're at a dangerous crossroads, folks. Trump and his cronies are determined to dismantle our government and with it, democracy itself. Americans everywhere and from both parties need to speak out and vote in November if we are to reclaim the country from this madness.

Kudos to Johnson and the other members of the White House press corps, who are working at personal risk to merely ask questions of this corrupt administration.

"SURVIVING A YEAR LIKE NO OTHER," DEC. 30, 2020

I'm including this reflection on 2020 because it succinctly describes the unprecedented year of lockdowns, business closures, and protests that jeopardized every small business, including the Blade. I'm immensely proud of our team for innovating and surviving.

How to make sense of the year that was 2020? As one prominent editor put it, we're covering the 1918 pandemic, the Great Depression, the 1960s Civil Rights Movement and a presidential election all at once.

And as journalists, we didn't always have the luxury of doing our jobs virtually. Blade reporters and photographers were hit with rubber bullets and pepper spray during White House protests over racial injustice. Our work critical of the inept, corrupt Trump administration was often met with derision, crude insults and even threats. Our intrepid White House reporter, Chris Johnson, refused to switch seats with CNN's Kaitlan Collins under reported Secret Service threats, as Trump wanted to punish CNN by moving its reporter to the back of the room. Johnson held firm and refused to move, winning praise from his CNN colleagues.

Meanwhile, we fought for the release of one of our own from ICE detention, Yariel Valdés González, a gay Blade contributor from Cuba who was imprisoned and held in inhumane conditions after legally applying for asylum. The Blade's tireless Michael K. Lavers documented every step of Yariel's case until he was finally freed in March.

When the Trump administration unlawfully ignored a Blade FOIA request, we joined the Reporters Committee for Freedom of the Press and filed a lawsuit. The Blade filed a FOIA request for emails within the Department of Labor related to the Trump administration's proposed rule change allowing a religious exemption in employment nondiscrimination requirements for federal contractors. After a year of ignoring the request, we took action to force the release of emails that will shed light on the motivation behind the proposal and whether it was to enable anti-LGBTQ discrimination in the name of religious freedom. As of mid-December, the administration was forced to release more than 100 pages of heavily redacted emails. The case continues to unfold as we seek answers to these important questions.

And the Blade itself was not immune from the devastating impact of COVID restrictions and shutdowns, though we toughed it out and never missed a week of publishing our now 51-year-old print edition in addition to regular digital updates. As our annual Pride events and Best Of party were canceled, our events team, led by marketing director Stephen Rutgers, pivoted and produced a series of successful, informative virtual events. When the Blade sales team was faced with the unprecedented closure of city businesses, they worked overtime to find new sources of advertising and revenue. Our sister paper, the Los Angeles Blade, soldiered on as well, led by publisher Troy Masters, also never missing a week of publishing amid nearly a year of lockdowns.

None of this would be possible without the support of our advertisers, sponsors and donors. Thank you for recognizing the importance of an independent, free press and supporting the work of the Blade. As we begin to clean up from the wreckage of the Trump administration, it will be critical to have the voice of the LGBTQ community inside the White House asking questions and holding the new administration accountable for the many promises it made during the campaign.

If you're able and so inclined, please consider a donation to the Blade Foundation to ensure the queer community's place at the table remains secure. Go to bladefoundation.org to donate.

Again, our sincere thanks to all of our readers, advertisers and supporters for helping us to navigate this painful year. And remember: until the vaccines arrive, wear a mask and practice social distancing. Those of us with personal experience with this disease know how highly contagious and painful it can be. No holiday celebration or New Year's party is worth contracting COVID. Stay safe and we look forward to celebrating the end of this nightmare in person sometime soon in 2021.

EPILOGUE

After reading through 20 years of opinion pieces and occasional rants I wrote for the Washington Blade, I hope it's clear how we won LGBTQ equality. It was not about a single activist or event or even president. It wasn't just about lawsuits and legislation. Or even AIDS. It was really about a vast community of diverse people over the course of decades coming out of the closet, sharing their lives and refusing to accept second-class status. President Obama acknowledged as much in his final press conference, when he answered the Blade's question about how LGBTQ rights would factor into his legacy. He replied that the credit for all the progress lies with the individual Americans who bravely came out over the decades. He was right. The lawsuits and legislation were important, but impossible without the visibility that preceded them.

All that visibility and the frustration over so much injustice came to a head over the last 20 years, culminating in the election of a supportive president and mostly supportive Congress and the appointment of a Supreme Court that was ready to do the right thing.

It wasn't about filing lawsuits willy-nilly and hoping for the best. It was about filing the right lawsuits at the right time in the right districts — for marriage equality and overturning DOMA and for privacy rights and workplace discrimination protections. And assembling the best lawyers from our own legal advocacy groups like National Center for Lesbian Rights and Lambda Legal.

It wasn't about torching the system and blaming hostile politicians for our woes. It was about creating an organization from scratch — the Victory Fund — that worked to elect openly LGBTQ candidates to positions all across the country, eventually landing us an out candidate for president and Cabinet secretary; a groundbreaking lesbian senator; many out members of the House; gay, lesbian and bi governors (and soon, I predict, a transgender governor, perhaps in Delaware); and too many openly LGBTQ elected officials in every city in every state to mention.

It wasn't about playing by the rules and waiting patiently for progress to come. It was about bold and innovative protests, from dropping a giant condom over Jesse Helms' house to protest his ignorance over AIDS to chaining ourselves to the White House fence to protest the unjust "Don't Ask, Don't Tell."

It wasn't about always fighting from the outside. It was about getting in the door and working the system from the inside; forming our own effective lobbying groups like the Human Rights Campaign, Task Force, National Center for Transgender Equality and so many more.

It wasn't about just fighting in D.C. We had to organize in all 50 states and then extend a hand to our counterparts in other countries. Each state's equality organization played a key role in all this progress, pressing local lawmakers and holding them accountable; raising money locally and crafting the right messages to appeal to voters. The right message in urban D.C. didn't necessarily resonate in rural Alabama. It took strategy, compromise and patience.

It wasn't just about convincing stuffy old white politicians in D.C. that our rights were worthy of protection. It was also about engaging with Hollywood, with film and TV producers and celebrities, to ensure our stories were told and we were included in pop culture. And that we had a national organization, GLAAD, working with all the networks, film studios and streaming services to advance understanding and push always for greater inclusion.

It wasn't just about sticking to our comfortable arguments for legal protections. It was about getting out of our comfort zone and engaging religious leaders in a dialogue about who we are and why, if you believe in God, you have to believe he (or she) doesn't make mistakes.

It wasn't always about fitting in. When it was too intimidating to play in an organized sports league, we formed our own leagues, in everything from football to cornhole — to socialize, exercise and show the world we can excel in any arena just like our straight friends.

How did we win equality? We fought in every arena, from the courts and congresses, to the churches and synagogues, to the football arenas and tennis courts, to movie sets and music halls. We started out fighting the police — literally — and ended up partnering with them and training them. It took sustained visibility, not just from our national leaders, but from every individual who came out to their family, friends, neighbors and coworkers.

So now what? The second part of this book's title refers to the efforts of our enemies on the far right who are determined to roll back all of this extraordinary progress. They are hard at work and emboldened after the Supreme Court's ruling overturning Roe. If this activist court will overturn nearly 50 years of precedent on abortion, its far-right conservative majority will not hesitate to throw out the Lawrence, Griswold and Obergefell rulings that enshrined our privacy and marriage rights into law.

Of course, it's not just marriage in the crosshairs. Our enemies have discovered that attacks on the trans community resonate with some independent voters, specifically suburban parents, won over by assertions that parents should have control over school curricula, which books get stocked in school libraries, who's eligible to play youth sports and even who's allowed to use the bathroom. Glenn Youngkin cynically used the issue in his winning campaign for Virginia governor, as did Ron DeSantis in his landslide victory for reelection in Florida. Make no mistake that this is a preview of what will only get worse and nationalized in 2024. Trans kids are on the front line of the far-right's destructive attacks. The fights are already playing out, with one Virginia Beach state lawmaker introducing a bill to ban trans athletes from school sports teams in late 2022; meanwhile, in neighboring D.C., Sen. Mike Lee introduced an amendment to the Respect for Marriage Act that would prohibit D.C. from enforcing laws protecting same-sex couples from discrimination. It will take a massive educational campaign and a wave of trans coming-out stories to fight back. Just as America came around to marriage equality (at least 70 percent now approve, including 55 percent of Republicans) after they got to know same-sex couples, they will have to become acquainted with trans people to expand understanding and acceptance.

Many of these fights will fall to younger generations. It's my hope that this book can help by serving as a template, illustrating how my generation chose to fight. Sadly, the end of that fight is not in sight now that the badly discredited Supreme Court has shown its intent. By lying to Congress under oath, Trump's three picks brushed off questions about Roe being settled law. The three of them are young and will likely sit on the court for 20 or more years. That's a long time to wait for justice, but it's the reality of our system. With the added votes of Samuel Alito and Clarence Thomas — who have both publicly called for revisiting Obergefell — they have the majority necessary to do whatever they choose.

So there will be setbacks, as we've seen in Florida's "Don't Say Gay" law and in the anti-trans legislation that has been introduced around the country, like Alabama's law criminalizing medical care for trans youth. Obergefell could fall. Attorney Mary Bonauto, who argued the Obergefell case before the Supreme Court, told Bloomberg in 2022, "We're in fight mode."

In those discouraging moments, remember all the setbacks we overcame in the last 20 years, starting with the Lawrence decision that overturned sodomy laws. Before that, the court had ruled in 1986 that the 14th Amendment did not prevent the states from barring private sex between gay couples. It was a disastrous ruling that criminalized our community and it stood for 17 long years before being overturned in Lawrence. There will be more setbacks but we will persevere and overcome.

If there's one overarching, simple lesson I've taken from the last 20 years at the Blade, it's that our movement and our community are rooted in love. And love wins. Always. It's that simple. Stay true to that mantra and we will prevail over our enemies. When they killed us at Pulse, we showed up the next day and got to work; we didn't cry and hide. We rallied, mourned, protested, fought for gun reform and forced the governor to see us. When voters approved Prop 8 in California banning our nuptials, we didn't give up; we fought and eventually love won and the state's couples were marrying. It's the same today, as the legal team at GLAD prepares for the assault on Obergefell and works to combat anti-trans laws.

Twenty years ago as I started my job at the Blade, George W. Bush was president and he wanted to ban our marriages via constitutional amendment. Consensual, private sex was illegal for gays. The military banned openly LGBT service members. The federal hate crimes law didn't include us. There were few out celebrities, politicians or media figures.

Twenty years later, we have President Biden, who has described trans rights as "the civil rights issue of our time." Marriage is legal in all 50 states. Sodomy laws are gone. The military welcomes gay, bi, lesbian and trans service members. The hate crimes law has been updated and is now inclusive of sexual orientation and gender identity. And you can't swing a dead cat without hitting an LGBTQ or nonbinary actor, anchor, pop star or politician. An out gay man nearly won the Iowa caucuses in 2020.

I hope that after reading this astounding history of the last 20 years that some young folks are inspired to continue the fight, as I was back in 2002. As Sylvia Rivera put it, "I'm not missing a minute of this. It's the revolution!"

Our progress is undeniable. But it's not immune to erosion. And so we fight on, always with the knowledge that love wins.

ACKNOWLEDGMENTS

This book is 20 years in the making. It was not easy to write, even though much of it was written years ago. Revisiting traumatic events — the Blade's bankruptcy, painful election losses, my car accident — is never fun. There were times I walked away from the project for months.

The idea for this book originated five years ago as an outline for a magazine article that I pitched to Vanity Fair on the 15th anniversary of my time at the Blade. An editor there liked it, but ultimately told me, "This is fascinating, but what you have here is an outline for a book, not a magazine story." Convinced that I lacked the stick-to-it-iveness to write a book, I turned the outline into an hour-long speech that I delivered to a half dozen university audiences then forgot about it. Until the pandemic struck. Bored at home, I figured if this wasn't the time to write a book, then I truly would never do it. So I began the two-year process of digging into old stories and essays, then slowly began to update them with new insights and previously untold, behind-the-scenes anecdotes.

As this book represents nearly half of my life, there are quite a few people to thank. It's really the culmination of a half-century of living, so here goes.

Thanks first and foremost to my parents, Raymond and Victoria Naff, who always raised their three kids to be active participants in our democracy. I have memories of my mom taking me as a young kid to her polling station on Election Day and waiting for what seemed like hours as she stood in a long, snaking line to cast her vote. Our house was always stocked with newspapers, the Washington Post, Baltimore Sun, Columbia Flier and others. There always seemed to be a political news show on the television, even if I groaned when "Agronsky & Company" came on. When the pope came to D.C., we stood for hours to wave. When Russia threatened nuclear war or blew up a commercial jetliner, off we went to protest at the embassy. It was a childhood filled with lessons about the importance of citizenship and the reason I grew up obsessed with newspapers. Later in life, Mom and Dad accepted me fully when I came out and they've embraced my husband as a son. They're the best and I'm one of the lucky ones. Thanks also to my siblings, Keith and Holly, for a lifetime of memories. We've remained close over the decades and I can't imagine life without them. They've also been heavily influenced by my parents' insistence on being good citizens — Keith works in law enforcement and Holly is a social worker. Journalist, cop, social worker: not professions known for making the most money, but each is uniquely critical to society and we wouldn't have gone into those fields without the strong foundation built by our parents who emphasized the importance of civic responsibility and social justice. My parents changed and saved countless lives by raising their kids with such values.

Thanks to my husband Brian Buebel for 20 years of support as I took on the editor's job at the Blade. The early years were tough with late deadline nights that usually became all-nighters. When the bankruptcy happened, Brian never doubted we'd successfully re-launch the paper. He is a much-needed voice of calm and reason in my chaotic and stressed life. In 2023 we celebrate 25 years since our first date and just marked eight years of legal marriage. I can't imagine a more kind, loving and supportive partner with whom to navigate life. And we have so much fun. I love you.

This book really started with one audience in mind: our 11 nieces and nephews. I figured that one day, they might want to know what exactly Uncle Kevin did for a living. Now they can find out in these pages and I'm assured of at least 11 book sales. Without kids of our own, we've tried to stay closely involved in the lives of these 11 amazing young people. We couldn't love them more if they were our own. I'm not much for doling out advice, but I will offer just one piece to them: Always dream big because in our country, anything is possible. It may take longer than you expect, but in the end, you'll get there. So thanks to the kids for all the good times, laughter, love and inspiration: Chase, Caitlyn, Isabelle, Bolton, Zachary, Spencer, Maya, Dhara, Peyton, Alex and Meredith. Your uncles couldn't be prouder of you.

To my extended family, thank you: my brothers-in-law Bill Bickel, Ethan Bean and Michael Buebel; sisters-in-law Crystal Naff, Cynthia Freeman, Maria LaVia and Stacey Bean. Thanks to the best in-laws a guy could ask for, Maxine and Alan Rosenfeld, who welcomed me into the family from day one all those years ago. We've celebrated so many Thanksgivings together that I've lost count. Love you all.

I write about the theme of friendship and why friend groups are so important in the LGBTQ community. So many of us don't have the support of family, that we create our own families of choice. I'm lucky to have both. And the friend group is large. Thank you to Jack Wargo (and his wife Kelly) for more than 50 years of friendship. Not many people can claim to have a friend for that long, but we sure can, thanks to our moms introducing us at age 2. We survived living together for four years in college when everyone warned us against it. We've shared enough laughs and memories to fill another book. And your daughter Abby even worked as a Blade intern (one of the best). Thanks also to our cohorts, Mark Pasierb, Walt Gorba and Jim Wozniak for so many good times. To the Baltimore group: Have we really been together for more than 20 years? Thanks to Greg Alexander for so many years of close friendship. When things go south, you're always my first call. Thank you for listening. To Paul Williams, I can't believe you stuck around after that first limo ride, but glad you did. To Maureen Mooney, we've come a long way since NYC. And baked a shitload of Christmas cookies! To Lewis Atkin, glad you met Maureen on the ottoman; what a journey and what a ton of laughs. To Joy Beasley and Shayna Iglesias, you always know how to cheer a guy up — expensive red wine! I love you. To Peter and Cat Smith, life sure has changed since the straight strangers and their babies moved in next door. I am grateful for nearly 20 years of friendship, beach memories and, of course, our many epic Christmas Eves spent together. A special shout-out to Karen Aylor Chenoweth, friend and personal trainer, who taught me not just about weights and Pilates, but about positivity and gratitude.

When we bought a second home in Rehoboth Beach, it was supposed to be an every-other-weekend getaway but eventually became home. I'm so grateful for the new friends we've made — you make life a lot of fun. (Maybe too much fun, that's partly why it took so long to finish this book.) To John Bator, I know you won't cry reading this, so I'll just say I can't imagine a nicer guy to call bestie. To John and Brian Sparrow, we have shared a lot and I treasure our friendship more than you know. (And Sparrow deserves a special shout-out: Thank you for telling me that my various crazy stories were worthy of a book; I needed the encouragement — and nagging.) To the rest of the Rehoboth crew — Laura Mason, Chris Schapp and Mike Dillon, Tony Scavone and George Aldredge, Kevin Stansbury, Joe Pinto and Tom Phillips, Ann Crehan and Loren Sanders: thanks for all the beach trips, pool time, football games and assorted age-inappropriate fun. Love our life together. To Will Freshwater, thanks for the advice and martinis and for pushing me when I needed it. Thanks to Brooke and Mike Warner for all the home-cooked meals and decades of friendship and to Bryan Stark for helping to introduce me to the big gay world. And to my cousin Linda Mizejewski for her inspiration as the first published author in the family. And to Patrick Quattlebaum and Katie Dunaway for years of laughs and dancing — can't wait for your big move to the beach. To Neil Roland, I'm forever grateful to Barclay's in Manchester and will treasure memories of our late-night chats by the fire in Yorkshire and seeing you 30 years later at Ottolenghi. Happy I get to return the favor after you thanked me in your book.

To Paul D'Angelo, I'll never forget the night we met more than 30 years ago in 1989. We stayed up all night talking and talking and I knew I'd met a kindred spirit and soulmate. To my high school crew, some of whom I'm still in touch with: I wouldn't have survived those formative years without your friendship. Much love to: John Pelletier, Isabelle Yerger, Caryn Radlove, Chris Geisler, Pat Vargas, Eric Steinberg, Todd Duncan, Jenny Gallahorn Stavely, Dina Passman, Tara Gibbons, Joanne Miles, Jennifer Stanbro, Andrea McGovern, Sue Lamb, Julie Runyan, Jeff Favorite. To my dear Norre Holmes, you are missed. I look at your photo every day.

I was so fortunate to explore my early love of journalism at Hammond High School in Columbia, Md., where I edited the plucky Bear Press under the direction and mentorship of Sherry Conklin. Your love of words and passion for journalism stayed with me for a lifetime and I owe you so much. There's nothing more important than good teachers and I was blessed to have several. In addition to Ms. Conklin, I was inspired by Karen Dunlop, my French teacher of four years who instilled in us a passion to learn, read, travel, eat and explore. Those lessons have taken me all over the world, from Paris to Tel Aviv and Hong Kong to Athens. I can't say enough about those two smart, tough women who made such an impression on so many. We should celebrate (and pay) our teachers.

To my colleagues at Penn State's Daily Collegian, I found so much inspiration in your dedication to journalism, especially Lisa Loeffler, who walked with me to BOE meetings each Sunday morning past all the churchgoers while nursing our hangovers. Also thanks to my Baltimore Sun colleagues and friends for an educational, if occasionally turbulent, ride: Sara Barnard, Ross Settles, Larry Kessner, Tim Windsor, Dawn Tritaik, Jean Halle.

My gratitude to all the pioneers I wrote about, some of whom I was privileged to meet, including: Frank Kameny, Barbara Gittings, David Mixner, Urvashi Vaid and Kate Clinton, Jim Obergefell, Edith Windsor, Walter Naegle. Thanks also to the hard-working advocates I covered (and sometimes clashed with), including: Elizabeth Birch, Hilary Rosen, Joe Solmonese, Chuck Wolfe, Neil Giuliano, Sarah Kate Ellis, Rick Rosendall, Denis Dison, Cathy Renna, Justin Nelson, Chance Mitchell, Jonathan Lovitz, Mara Keisling, Rea Carey, Earl Fowlkes, Jr., John Klenert, Claire Lucas, Donald Hitchcock, Paul Yandura, Joe Kapp, Carlos Gutierrez, Chris Wood, Dana Beyer and too many more to mention.

This book wouldn't exist without the hard work of everyone at the Washington Blade. To all those who came before I arrived in December 2002, thank you for establishing a record of excellence and for paving the way. You are pioneers. Thanks to those who hired me back in 2002, Chris Crain and William Waybourn. To the team I've worked with for more than 20 years, you're the best and I am privileged to have worked with so many pros: Dame Brian Moylan, my partner in crime; Greg Marzullo, who did it all with style; Rhonda Smith, who kept us all in line; Lou Chibbaro Jr., whose professionalism and longevity are astounding; Chris Johnson, who broke barriers in the White House; Michael K. Lavers, who shines a light on injustice wherever he finds it (and even got kicked out of Cuba for doing so); Peter Rosenstein, who disproves the old maxim that if you want a friend in D.C., get a dog; Michael Key, who surprises us each week with his endless skill set; Phil Rockstroh, who keeps all the dysfunctional trains running on time; Joey DiGuglielmo, my right arm from our first meeting through 14 years of copy and deadlines and some damn good work (no one does a celebrity interview better, just ask Melissa Etheridge). To the next generation of Bladees, my gratitude

Made in United States
North Haven, CT
22 March 2023